IS ANYBODY LISTENING?

A True Story About the POW/MIAs

In The Vietnam War

by

Barbara Birchim

(With Sue Clark)

authorHOUSE™

1663 LIBERTY DRIVE, SUITE 200
BLOOMINGTON, INDIANA 47403
(800) 839-8640
WWW.AUTHORHOUSE.COM

First published by AuthorHouse 05/23/05

ISBN: 1-4208-3748-6 (sc)
ISBN: 1-4208-3747-8 (dj)

Library of Congress Control Number: 2005901853

Printed in the United States of America
Bloomington, Indiana

This book is printed on acid-free paper.

Cover Art by Brandon Baker
Cover Design by Leslie Brinskele
Graphics Coordinator: Adrian Silva (http://www.wintutors.com)

"Greater love hath no man than this: that a man lay down his life for his friends."

Jesus of Nazareth
John 15:13

Dedication

I dedicate this book to all those families who, like me, have been trying to find out what happened to their loved one whom the military had labeled a Vietnam War MIA so many years ago.

And to all those families who continue to wait for answers about missing loved ones, know that you are not alone in your quest.

To my family and friends who have stood by my side as I agonized over this POW/MIA issue, I can't thank you enough.

To my writer, whose labor of love has gotten this plethora of information into book form, I wish that I could think of the words to tell you thank you. You have helped me to heal, and hopefully this book will help others on their quest.

To my God, I know there were many times when I doubted Your presence and wondered why You were allowing this to happen. Your lessons are hard, but I'm now able to hear and trust Your message without the numerous questions attached.

To all of you, I dedicate my book.

Table of Contents

Acknowledgements

Without the help of the following family, friends and acquaintances, this book would not have made it to the publisher. A big thank you goes to Meg Cochran, Bob Jack, Patty and Earl Hopper, and Jerry Estenson for being my proofreaders excellante.

Former Senator Bob Smith, the Honorable Randy Cunningham, Red McDaniel, Sara Gist-Bernasconi, Michael Benge, Jo Anne Shirley, Marney Martin and Robert Frank reviewed my book, and offered many helpful and honest comments.

My heart felt appreciation goes to Lt. Tim Cotchay, U.S. Coast Guard, who unknowingly gave me the perfect title for this book.

My two computer gurus, Sidne George and Kim Castle, saved the day more times than I care to admit. A special thanks also goes to my transcriber Tonya Parks-Johnson.

To my son who could have given up on me as a result of my continual push for the truth, you are a gem for perservering.

Without Leslie Brinskele's artistic design of the cover, we wouldn't have captured the essence of my story.

My thanks would not be complete without mentioning my granddaughter, Katie, who was the inspiration and catalyst for my writing this book.

Foreword

Duty at the Presidio in San Francisco was supposed to be the ideal assignment for an officer about to leave the Army. In November 1968 the United States Army changed that and gave me an assignment I was not trained to perform or emotionally prepared to handle.

The Post Commander informed me that one of my former lieutenants was missing in action. And since we both were Special Forces Officers, he wanted me to notify his wife to explain what happened.

It is worthwhile to note that at the very core of the military officer's belief system is the imperative to perform their duty. I agreed with the Colonel that I was duty bound to notify the family and to provide whatever assistance I could.

Since my assignment prior to the Presidio was Vietnam, I had seen the immediate effect of war on the men on the line. Neither that experience, nor my previous military training, prepared me to deal with the effects of war on families.

It was this assignment that brought me to Mrs. Birchim's door. I was there to deliver the news no military wife wants to hear. Of all the assignments the Army had given me in the previous five years, looking Barbara in the eye, and informing her of Jim being lost in action, stands as the toughest.

In the sixties, the Army had different roles for individuals to play in dealing with MIA and KIA families. The notification officer delivered the news and provided immediate support. After the initial contact, the family was assigned to officers trained in survivor assistance. Since the notification officer might provide inaccurate advice, he was encouraged to let the professionals work with the family on benefits and other survivor issues. Much to my regret, this policy, plus my leaving the military, caused me to not make the effort to stay in touch with the Birchim family.

This changed in 1998, at my first Special Forces Convention, when I saw Mrs. Birchim, one of the participants in the POW/MIA memorial service. After the ceremony was over, I approached her and introduced myself. After we worked through the incredible emotions our chance meeting generated, Barbara took the time to fill me in on her long search for her husband and the truth about what happened to him.

As a gift to all, she has taken the time to tell her story.

For the civilian reader, Mrs. Birchim provides the human prespective about the price we ask our military personnel and families to pay for our freedom. She also provides the readers with a glimpse into the life of a soldier's wife who had her worst fear become reality. This is done by her candidly sharing her struggle to find truth while navigating through an unresponsive bureaucracy. All this is done while she raised two small children, dealt with the loss of her husband, and held on to her sense of self.

For all readers, her story provides a hopeful message of the strength within us, the power of truth, the need for absolute candor from our government representatives dealing with the POW/MIA families, and the lesson on how we all can gain prespective and wisdom if we live life to its fullest.

For me, reading the book helped me work at disassembling a wall I built to compartmentalize my life. In 1969, I walked away from a life as a soldier and did not look back. In 1998, I decided to reflect on that life and went to my first Special Forces gathering. It was after that convention, and meeting with Mrs. Birchim, that I started to face issues around survivor's guilt and a sense of never having done enough for her and her family.

Since our chance meeting, she has graciously let me make some deposits against debts of duty and honor I owe her family.

While I am sure Mrs. Birchim does not realize it, she exemplifies many of the qualities that made Capt. Jim Birchim a Special Forces soldier: ability to work in a hostile territory, honesty, candor, willingness to face her greatest fears, and most important a "no quit" attitude.

Barbara, may the rest of your life be full of peace.

Jerry D. Estenson
Associate Professor, Business Administration
Former Captain, United States Army Special Forces
Recon Team Leader – Det. B-52 (Project Delta)
5th Special Forces Vietnam

Preface

As an only child of World War II era parents, I lived a sheltered life, growing up in the same neighborhood, attending the same Catholic school.

It wasn't until I went to college and fell in love for the first time that things started to change. At nineteen, I married my sweetheart, James Birchim, who had just entered the United States Army.

At that point, I began a journey that had no road maps. All of a sudden, I became a member of an elite minority, not one of my choosing.

After Jim completed Officer's Candidate School (OCS), jump school, chemical school and Special Forces training, we were assigned to the Presidio of San Francisco. Six months later, in 1968, Jim was sent to Vietnam. Four months after he arrived in Vietnam, he was declared MIA.

I had never heard the acronym MIA (Missing In Action) until a knock at my front door brought two military men with news that my husband of two years was MIA.

With one baby in diapers and another on the way, my mind raced through all kinds of possibilities, but the one that seemed most plausible was that this was a mistake. In a few days, he would be found. Life would be normal again.

Of course, as time passed, it became evident to me that I was wrong. Jim was not coming back.

The next thirty-two years would become a journey that no one could ever prepare for. I discovered I had inner strengths I didn't know I possessed. Through the workings of the military and the U.S. government, I was led through a whole range of emotions--sadness, anger, frustration, and hopelessness.

I found that as sophisticated as the government was, they showed a complete unwillingness and ineptitude to truly find the answers to my puzzle. What happened to Jim Birchim?

As the years went by, I learned, on my own, how to travel to and through Vietnam at a time when the U.S. had no relations with them and had advised U.S. citizens not to travel there. It took me years of networking before I was able to take several trips to Southeast Asia in search of answers.

In my mind, I was sure that if I could show our government why there was a strong possibility that Jim was alive, they would stand by me and push the Vietnamese government for answers.

I was mistaken.

My obsession for answers was a hideous journey filled with broken expectations. Yet, it opened doors to both a beautiful, fascinating world, and one filled with deceptions and lies.

After a while, the dreams I had as a child, of being a nurse and working in Third World countries, became a reality. This led me to discover that you can attain almost anything you set your mind to, for this journey of mine took me to places in the world that most people would never consider visiting.

My quest for the truth surrounding Jim's case introduced me to various cultures with incredible health-care needs. When answers about Jim were slow in coming, I filled my time with collecting useable discarded medicines and supplies through my contacts in the U.S., and then I funneled them to the poorest of these people.

I learned some valuable lessons about the world and myself. I found that I could not rest until I had the answers to what happened to MIA James Birchim. Somewhere, somehow, someone had the information I was seeking.

Introduction

For 15 years, the turmoil of Vietnam had been put to bed. Now, ironically, it was in my bed, in my deepest sleep. Jim and Vietnam were revisiting me.

But where was this coming from?

Night after night, Jim would stand at the foot of my bed and plead for me to come help him, now, before it was too late.

Vietnam had been a dead issue as far as the press was concerned, and nothing had come to me in the mail from the Army in years. So, what was triggering these nightmares?

I soon realized that this would be the start of a roller coaster adventure of intrigue that would take me from the jungles of Vietnam's tri-border region where Vietnam, Laos and Cambodia meet, to the halls of government buildings in Washington D.C. I would be tested and challenged beyond my wildest expectations.

I was to embark on an education for which there are no textbooks or classes--only long hours, endless dead ends, and many lost hopes.

Could I hold on to my sanity? Would truth prevail? Would I have the answer to what happened to Jim?

The road that lay ahead was truly full of landmines and obstacles. My faith in God, truth, and mankind would be tested to the max.

PART I

Our Destiny

"All the wrong people remember Vietnam.
I think all the people who remember it should forget it,
and all the people who forgot it should remember it."
                                        Michael Herr

Chapter One

Two Warriors

My husband Jim was missing as of November 15, 1968, after he had been in Vietnam only four months. But, that's not when our story began.

I met Jim in the Washateria when we were both attending Santa Rosa Junior College, in Santa Rosa, California. I was carrying my dirty clothes in, and he was just sitting there on top of one of the washing machines, having a great time talking to another guy. And they were both "excuse me" good looking. By my first impression, Jim was quite a crazy guy.

Then, I got embarrassed when it dawned on me that I was going to have to wash my undies in the machine right in front of the two guys. All I could think of was don't drop anything, Barbara, please. Well, things progressed from there, needless to say.

Jim had come from Bishop on the eastern side of the Sierra Mountains, where his family lived.

I had graduated from Presentation High School in San Francisco, thinking that I was going to nursing school at St. Joseph's Hospital in the City. However, one of my classes wouldn't count toward my science credits.

I didn't find out about the missing credit until June 20, and it was too late for me to enroll because summer school started on June 10. I was so bummed. My mom remembered that one of her sorority sisters who lived across from Santa Rosa Junior College had a small apartment off her garage that she rented to students. My mom called her and to our surprise, Winnie had not rented it yet. I moved in and enrolled in the college.

The year was 1965. The draft was in full force and unless male students kept a full load, they were no longer eligible for deferment.

Unfortunately, during Jim's winter quarter, he had to drop one of his classes, which put him in jeopardy of being drafted. He decided to enlist in the Army so that he could choose his military schooling rather than be drafted and leave it to chance.

We were married in August 1966 after Jim volunteered to go into the Army and completed his basic training. Jim was in Officer Candidate School (OCS) from August '66 to February '67 at Ft. Benning, Georgia. Afterwards, he attended jump school, then chemical school in Anniston, Alabama, and Special Forces school at Ft. Bragg, North Carolina. He volunteered for each of these steps in his training--all were his first choices--the direction he wanted to follow in his military career.

He kept filling up his dance card with more schooling, so we were home free. He didn't have to go to Vietnam. By then, he had only nine months left on his three-year tour.

We were at Ft. Bragg in the fall of 1967 when a whole family dynamics thing fell into play. His younger brother was in line to be drafted, and he did not plan to go through OCS. That meant Jim's brother would be in the infantry and would be sent straight to Vietnam after completing his basic training. Because of this, Jim felt the necessity, as the eldest brother, to be the one to go to war, not his younger brother.

Jim had been studying to be an entomologist in college. He had already helped publish books with a doctor and was looking forward to returning to California to start collecting insects again and to do further research work, so he asked for a change in duty station. I told him this would be an automatic red flag for a tour of duty in Vietnam. He said, "No, that won't happen."

When he made the phone call to me, it was December, and I had come to San Francisco to visit my parents for Christmas. Three days later, Jim called back and said, "I got the assignment at the Presidio in San Francisco. Don't even come home. I'll pack and call the movers because my assignment starts on the first of January."

At that time, Special Forces recruited young men, so it was my understanding that this branch of the Army was an advisory group. Jim had a unique background, both in his knowledge of chemistry and in his previous experience in wilderness survival. That is one of the reasons I think Special Forces were so interested in him.

The idea behind Special Forces was to help the indigenous become better at defending their property, to understand the techniques of war, and to be trained so they could fight. They were also supposed to go behind the lines in Vietnam to see what was going on and relay that information to Washington D.C. That was nice in theory, but it didn't turn out that way. Ask any Green Beret from the Vietnam War if he was just an advisor and never saw combat.

Our assignment at the Presidio was short-lived. In February, Jim got orders to report in July to Travis Air Force Base. His destination was Vietnam.

While Jim was performing Gas Chamber exercises at the Presidio, I was giving birth to our daughter, Kimberly, at Letterman General Hospital on base.

During these few short months, the news of casualties in Vietnam hit the media in a big way. But what brought home the loss of life even more was Jim's weekly ritual of x-ing off those guys killed who had been in his OCS class. He would take the yearbook, put a date over the face, and write KIA.

I still have that yearbook. It is very depressing to look at it because I can remember some of those guys.

In July, with Kim in the bassinet in the back of our new VW camper, Jim and I drove to Travis Air Force Base to say our final goodbye. Little did I know that this would not only be the last time I would have a face-to-face with Jim, but also it would be the start of a whole new journey.

* * *

Jim and I couldn't live on base at the Presidio because we were too junior. Since the Presidio was an ideal place to process out at the time of retirement, it was top heavy with high-ranking people. Plus, it was Sixth Army Headquarters. So, we lived across the Golden Gate Bridge in Marin County.

After Jim left, I kept the apartment through Chritmas of '68 because I was pregnant again. I was used to going back and forth between our apartment and my parents' home by the beach in San Francisco. Sometimes I'd spend a night or two with them. I had baby stuff in both places.

One Day, in November, I happened to be in the City, hunting for a couch that would pull out into a bed so when Jim came home and we had guests, there would be a place for them to sleep.

Mom and I had been shopping all day and didn't arrive back to her home until about five o'clock.

It's so funny what one remembers. I was in the bathroom when the doorbell rang. My mom went to the door. I can remember her turning around, as I was coming out of the bathroom, and saying, "There are some men to see you."

When I first looked at the men, my immediate thought was this is what I've been expecting. I remember being very business-like as I invited them into the house. "I know why you're here. Come in," I said.

After they stepped through the door, I asked Mom if she would take care of Kim, who was seven months old at the time, and needed to have her dinner.

Captain Jerry Estenson, who had been Jim's commanding officer at the Presidio, said, "I've got some bad news."

I said, "You're here to tell me he's dead, right?"

"No," he said, "I'm here to tell you that he's actually been classified as Missing-In-Action."

That puzzled me because I'd never heard of Missing-In- Action. Questions ran through my head. Did that mean Jim was on leave? Had he forgotten to tell me that he'd gone to Hawaii for a week? What was this Missing-In-Action stuff?

Captain Estenson went right from "Missing-In-Action" to reading an official TWX to me--a telegram that gave very little information about what happened. He offered his assistance as a liaison between the government and me if I had questions.

As we sat in my parents' living room, Captain Estenson explained all of the men involved in the incident had been interviewed as soon as they came off the helicopter. He told me that in 30 days a review panel would look over the information collected in the field. The panel members would determine whether to change Jim's status to Killed in Action/Body Not Recovered (KIA/BNR) or to keep him on the MIA list based on that information.

The original information surrounding Jim's status would then be funneled back to Washington D.C. Someone would be in communication with the Special Forces headquarters in Kontum during that next year in case they discovered any additional information. Washington D.C. (whoever they were) would then review the case and decide whether to continue Jim's status as MIA.

I was too numb to cry. I was too numb to do anything but thank the gentlemen and show them to the door. I knew in my heart that this had to be a mistake. Jim would be calling soon to say he was all right. I needed to get to our apartment to wait for his call.

The lives of my seven-month-old daughter, my unborn son, and mine had just changed--forever.

* * *

A month later, after the review board convened, Capt. Estenson and I sat down to go over the report of the incidents involving Jim's missing in action.

Jim had been part of a team sent in to a hostile area to help another team that was in trouble.

Of course, our U.S. troops were not supposed to be in Laos and Cambodia, so the report did not give us the location. At that time, reports would only say South Vietnam or North Vietnam. Usually it was South Vietnam where our ground troops were, unless a flyer was lost over North Vietnam.

I was told that Jim had been inserted into this place and that he was not to engage the enemy, only to find the other team that was in trouble and to get them out.

As soon as he got on the ground, his team was overrun. They played escape and evasion for three days, trying to pull back far enough so they could be extracted. During those three days, all of them were wounded in some way.

I was told that Jim's foot was broken or he had shrapnel lodged in it, but his team members did not take his boot off. Because they were afraid he wouldn't be able to hobble, they left the bootstrap tied. I later found out that he might have had shrapnel in his back, too.

After three days, Jim realized they couldn't do any more--they had to get out. So, he called in the heavy artillery on to his position to pound the Vietcong. And he called for an airlift evac to get them out.

The helicopters came, but they couldn't land. There was no clearing. The first helicopter lowered ropes, called McGuire rigs, through small openings in the trees, and took out the first four members of the team.

Gunfire was still erupting from enemy positions when the second helicopter came in. The remaining team was in jeopardy of being overtaken. When the McGuire rigs were dropped for the last four men, one of the ropes got caught in the trees. Jim got the two Vietnamese members of his team on two of the ropes, and then he and the other American hung on the remaining rope.

The helicopter took off--fast. Instead of going straight up in order to pull the men up and out of the trees, it took off at a slant and dragged them through the dense bamboo and the triple canopy.

Since Jim could not get clipped on to the rope, like the others, he and the other American turned topsy-turvy from the dragging/lifting motion of the helicopter. The other man's hands and feet were down, and his belly was the only part of him touching the rope. Jim ended up on the other man's back.

Of course, all of these guys were in full field gear along with their guns. The other American was supposed to have the radio. He didn't. He left it behind, which was a serious breach of military regulations. Lots of equipment hung off those wounded men.

I was told that Jim made it through the trees. However, after about 30-45 minutes of flying time, the other American blacked out and did not come to until he found himself at the Kontum airport.

Jim was not on the rig.

It seems that the two men who were hanging from the other two ropes did not see a thing. They had no idea what happened to Jim.

So began the journey I would take to discover the truth about what really happened to my husband.

Jim was declared missing in action on November 15, 1968.

* * *

6

THE INTERIM

Learning to be an MIA wife was not easy. The sense of isolation, deep sorrow, constant worry, frustration and disbelief were always present. There were no books, guidelines or instructions to show me the way to navigate this new course. The burnout rate of my Survivors Assistance Officers at the Presidio was horrendous. I was always assigned to the new incoming SAO. I was forever having to start at square one. The only permanent fixture in that office was a civilian secretary who became a friend.

The government didn't want family members to make waves by going to the press. We were told that everything was being done to find our loved ones. To my knowledge, I was the only Army MIA wife whose husband's case file was being handled at the Presidio, San Francisco. This meant that no one there knew how to handle me, much less what to do with me!

These were unchartered waters for all of us. At that time I had no idea what kind of mission Jim was involved in, so when my questions weren't answered logically, I was in a state of turmoil. I learned I couldn't show any emotion or I'd lose my credibility--a hard lesson, but I perfected it within the first year.

And then there were the people who called Jim a "baby killer" and were glad he was MIA. The bottom line was I didn't fit in with active duty people or civilians. I was an oddity with two infants.

No one knew what to say to me, so they didn't include me in their lives. While my husband was somewhere on the battlefield, I was learning how to do battle with the very entity that sent him to war.

* * *

THE BRIDGE

A couple of weeks after Jim's status had been changed to KIA/BNR, around late May 1971, I was invited to a Navy hosted luncheon along with other POW/MIA wives.

After Admiral Zumwalt gave his speech, the program allowed for questions from the audience. I raised my hand.

"Admiral Zumwalt, do you know if there is a new policy in regard to changing MIAs to KIA/BNR without any additional information since the serviceman's last review?"

There was silence in the room.

The Admiral said, "No, that's not our policy." Then he went on and on about the government's policy and the Pentagon, and the way things were done, and on and on.

I said, "I beg your pardon, but I've just been visited by my Army Survivors Assistance Officer, and there is no new information. I've gone through many review processes, and I was assured my husband, Jim, would be carried as MIA unless new information was received. And yet, without warning, the review board met and declared Jim dead."

I didn't tell the Admiral this, but the message the Army personnel delivered to me that day was that Jim had just been declared KIA/BNR and all paid allowances were severed. They had no other information. Just "hello and goodbye."

The huge ballroom where we met was full of military people, as well as POW/MIA wives. I'm sure that Admiral Zumwalt wanted to squelch any more questioning of this kind, so he sent his Aide-de-Camp, or whatever the gentleman was called, to get my name and address. He'd get to the bottom of that for me, by George.

I never heard from the Admiral or his Aide-de-Camp.

What made me so irate at this point was that there was no policy that said someone like Jim had to be declared dead after 12 months and his family cut off from benefits. I had documents and letters signed by majors, colonels, and generals saying just the opposite. Why did they decide to change their story about Jim's situation? Change was the key word here. What had changed?

The only conclusion I could come to was that someone was saying, "Let's make this case look like it needs to be closed. Let's make it look as if the wife is some kind of flaming idiot who we want to shut up. We'll get her off our books. We'll wipe her husband off. Case closed!"

This happened, by coincidence I thought, just a couple weeks after I went to the Presidio in San Francisco to ask them to check again on Jim's status. I was thinking of buying a house, and I needed to know how secure that portion of my income would be.

Thank God I didn't put my name on a mortgage.

* * *

From 1971-1988, the government knew where I was, but I'd received no information from them regarding Jim's case. For this reason, I assumed Jim didn't survive the November 1968 incident.

Although I watched the Homecoming of the POWs in 1973 on TV with great hope that maybe Jim would walk off the plane, he was not among them.

All my feelings from those early years of waiting flooded back in waves of unending sadness that day. As a result, the release of some of our POWs at Homecoming, plus the passage of time, at last made me a believer in the government's so-called truth that Jim was really not coming home. Although my questions were never answered, it was time for me to stop hoping I would see him again.

* * *

In February 1988, I began to have nightmares--a series of them--almost every night for three months. Jim always stood at the foot of my bed in his Green Beret uniform and screamed that I had to come, now, or it would be too late.

I couldn't understand what that meant. I hadn't really thought much about Jim since the early 70s. Why was I having these kinds of dreams. I mean--I was shocked at this whole scene, at first. The dreams were so real, and Jim's pleadings for help were more than I could rationalize.

Several weeks after those nightmares first began, I got a document from the government, the first time in years. The document was called a Dog Tag Sighting. I called Washington D.C. to find out what that was about.

Then I realized that this was sort of an anniversary--20 years since Jim disappeared in the Vietnam War. My son, David, was getting ready to go to college, and he wanted to join the ROTC. Because of that, I thought maybe the whole military thing with David had triggered my nightmares about Jim. Maybe it was a prediction of what would happen to David.

So, I invited David to go to a National League of Families meeting with me since I wanted him to see what they were about. That way, David and I could ask questions about the dog tag sighting document I had received.

I hadn't attended a National League meeting for years, but I felt it was time to go again. So, David went with me and saw all the craziness that was going on in regard to the POW/MIA situation in our country.

He still decided to join the ROTC and as it turned out, he graduated highest in Military Science at the University of Florida. He was also chosen to be the school's delegate to a military convention in Virginia.

At the same time that David was going to college, he joined the National Guard because he wanted to be a really good officer, and he thought that was one way to learn more than the ROTC could offer.

After graduation, the ROTC decided not to commission David. Their reason? They were beginning to downsize the military. Yet, his National Guard unit got a call to be on alert during the Persian Gulf War. Even though I didn't want David to have to go to war, I still thought it strange that the men below him got active duty commissions, but not David, who was so high in his class.

That was suspicious enough, but when he was told to come back every six months to check on his status, I began to believe that something was screwy . . . really screwy. After two years of this, he was told, "Well, we're going to make you Retired Reserve. We'll give you an ID card and you won't have to do any drills. You don't even have to do the two weeks training once a year. In addition, you're not responsible for paying back your college education."

That was nuts!

At this point, David began to think that maybe his last name had something to do with this. He remembered what happened when he went in for his ROTC interview. When David called me that night, his voice shook.

"Mother, I went to this room and military men sitting at the table knew all about Dad!"

I said, "Well, David, what did you expect?"

"But they knew everything about Dad!"

"Uh-huh."

For years I felt that David blamed me for not receiving his commission. By then, I had gone to Vietnam several times, making waves, and pushing myself into places and into situations when I thought it might help me learn more about what happened to Jim.

I still wonder sometimes if David harbors resentment toward me because of lingering doubts about not receiving his commission. I know in my heart that "they," whoever "they" are, didn't want another Birchim name anywhere--in any file, including fingerprints.

There was one other odd thing that occurred at the same time as my nightmares--another awakening for me after so many years away from the whole POW/MIA situation. When David and I were preparing for our trip to Washington D.C., for the National League of Families meeting, we received what they call COIN Assist. Congress had given permission for two primary next-of-kin family members to travel via military flights to Washington D.C. for briefings once a year. This meant that David and I had to go to Coronado, California, to catch our flight.

On the day of our departure, walking toward me on the tarmac at seven o'clock in the morning was a social worker client of mine. At that time, I was an administrator for a new home health company.

"Barbara, what are you doing here?"

Come to find out, Roni had a brother who was MIA, something she had never mentioned to me before. She was having nightmares at the same time as mine. She said Michael, her brother, would yell at her, "You have to come . . . now!"

Roni said, "I just don't know what that's all about, so I decided maybe I should go to The League meeting to see if I could find some answers."

That was really bizarre . . . really, really bizarre.

In hindsight, I guess I could say if a person goes with her gut feeling, she would make her life a lot easier. But, most of us are always trying to make logical sense out of everything. I must say, that has been my downfall throughout all these years of my trying to find out what happened to Jim.

To me, there is no logic.

I could sit in front of any military man, no matter what the rank, spit out all of the details I've learned in logical order, only to have that military person say, "Oh yeah, but that was a mix up." Or, "Well, you know, it was war time. We just didn't get all of the paperwork."

Now, after 25 years or more, I always preface my questions to military personnel with, "And don't tell me it's a clerical error." I can't tell you how many times I've been told, "Our Xerox machine was down." Or, "You know, we queried that, and I guess we just never got an answer to it." That kind of comment would always come after I'd been beating on their doors for nine or so months for a certain file or record or bit of information.

Stupid, stupid, stupid!

One time, in 1996, when I went back East to a National League annual meeting, I took the opportunity to review the charts in Jim's file. I found myself in a little room designated for the Army. I opened Jim's file, a huge, thick thing, and there on top were two fax sheets, not attached at the top like all the other pieces of paper. There was no cover letter, yet a time and a recent date were stamped at the top of the pages. The pages had been sanitized, all names blacked out. One document stated something about, ". . . source suspected Mr. (sanitized) was a former KGB official. . . ."

"So, where did this come from," I asked the Army clerk who got the file for me.

"You know, I don't know about that," he said.

What I had to do was write that question so I could submit it to Army Casualty who would then find the answer for me. That's the way we family members have to get our questions answered.

When I finally did hear from the staff, the answer had gone all the way up the food chain, finally stopping with an individual in the Defense Intelligence Agency (DIA). The response was written on July 4, 1997, but I did not receive it until January 8, 1998.

Lt. Cdr. Steven H. Dohl wrote, "A complete review of Captain Birchim's file failed to reveal any trace of the document or anyting in his case to which it might be related. DPMO analysts have studied the rest of the original, unsantized report and can find no connection to Captain Birchim whatsoever. It is a military intelligence report that does not relate to any specific missing

American. We have no idea as to who gave (Mrs. Birchim) this document or why."

So, basically the letter said I had made up the faxes, and I was the one who inserted them in Jim's file. I must have had a clandestine meeting with some spook who slipped the faxes to me in a dark alley.

If I didn't put the faxes in the file, then who did?

As an aside, it's interesting to note that the Army makes sure that the Casualty office staff is in constant change so that not one of the military personnel gets to know the POW/MIA families or their case too well. That's a ploy of theirs, as far as I'm concerned.

The Air Force doesn't do that. They've had one man in their Casualty Department for the last 30 years. He has become pivotal in the Air Force's relationship with their POW/MIA families. This man, who is now a civilian, knows all the families and all of the POW/MIA files. That's got to be great!

Later, I went to a local family POW/MIA update meeting in San Diego, and who should come but Lt. Cdr. Dohl from the Defense Prisoner of War/ Missing Personnel Office (DPMO) who wrote the letter. The wall was lined with military from the Department of Defense (DOD), DIA, and all the branches. In the center of the room stood a cluster of people. It was like the families (those on the covered wagons) were surrounded by the military (the Indians).

There was a break in the conference at which time I walked up to a Lt. Col. Salak, my Army Casualty Officer, and said "Do you know who this is. . . this signature?"

"Oh, yeah," she said. "He's right over there."

Good. So, I walked over to him and said, "Excuse me, is your name so-and-so?"

He said, "Yes."

"Well," I said. "I just want to say that I take serious offense to this letter (which I held up to his face), because in fact what you are calling me is some kind of liar."

As I got more excited, my voice got louder. Pretty soon, all those military men who'd been standing along the walls in the room were standing around me.

"You know, I'm giving you kudos for this one. You've come up with an answer you haven't tried on me before. Very clever!" I said.

I think he was somewhat taken back.

"Let's see. So you're saying I typed the messages on one of the government typewriters and then found a fax machine to send it to Casualty. Then, under the cover of night, I stole into your building, passed security and all of the alarms, got up to your office, found the fax machine with the incoming fax I'd sent, found the right file cabinet with Jim's file in it, and then surreptitiously slipped the faxes in it. And of course, exited the secure building unnoticed! Is that what you're trying to tell me I did?"

"Well. . .well, no. It must have been misfiled."

Misfiled? Yeah, right! "This is really absurd," I said.

"What do you mean?" was all he could say. Then, after a pause, he said, "I didn't sign that. I don't even remember having ever seen that letter."

"Excuse me," I said, turning the letter around so he could see it. "Is this not your signature?"

"Yes."

"Well, you know, what rolls down hill? You should know what you sign so you can take responsibility for it."

All of a sudden, it was like little bells were going off in his head. "Oh, yeah. I kind of remember that. Yeah, I know what this is about."

In short, he told me that those fax sheets should have never gone to Army Casualty. And secondly, they should never have been put in Jim's file.

Then, in front of all those military men, in a booming voice, I said, "Let me get this straight. Let me get this really clear in my mind 'cause I'm not sure I've got it. A fax is sent to nowhereville and just happens to land in that particular Army office, and the Army takes it off their fax machine, looks at it, and decides that it should go in some inbox on some desk, even though it's not addressed to them. Am I right?"

He stammered, "Uh. . .uh. . ."

I said, "Okay, so now some guy's got it out of the inbox, he looks at it, reads this thing and then says to himself, 'We need to put this in the Birchim file.'" I paused. "Do you think I'm an absolute idiot?"

The poor guy who was about my age got all red in the face and started to sweat. I'm sure that not only he, but also all the rest of the military men standing around me thought, oh my God, what has she done?

No one spoke up with an answer.

"You can't tell me it was misfiled. Look, if people want to get papers off their desk, they put them in the trash. They don't put them in some random file. Don't you think it is somewhat odd that the fax would end up in MY HUSBAND'S FILE?"

I told the Lt. Cdr. I wasn't buying his explanation, and he'd better go back to Washington D.C. and try again.

After that, I ran into the same Lt. Cdr. several times over the next few years. He just smiled. I couldn't let it go at that, so each time I said, "Oh, hey, how's the filing going?"

I joke about it because I guess what I'm trying to do is let them know that their answers are bizarre and beyond the realm of possiblity. The odds of this document with a Russian connection, being put in Jim's file by mistake, are astronomical.

So, the real question was, could anyone be trying to tell me Jim was still alive and connected to Russia in some way?

I marvel at the issue that should have died in 1971, but continues to thrive and generate, like a fungus. Somehow, more documents keep coming, yet when I tried to get a copy of the After-Action Report on Jim, there was none. I was told it had gone bye-bye.

According to the government, all After-Action reports were destroyed in Vietnam. Awhile ago, I found another member of an MIA family who'd found out those documents were being stored at a repository near Andrews Air Force Base, in Suitland, Maryland. The kicker is they're still classified.

And in addition to that, when I was told the FBI, CIA and Casuality Office did not have copies of Jim's fingerprints, that they were somehow lost, I found them in his file when I went through it the next time.

In Chapter 21, "The Women Who Wait," in The Bamboo Cage, I found a story quite similar to mine. Not only had many documents in Navy Lt. Cdr. James Dooley's file been sanitized to the point of being meaningless, but also Dooley's fiance, Pam Hicks, found that lots of documents had been removed and placed in other missing men's files.

Does that sound familiar, I asked myself?

I'm not sure Jim's After-Action Report was singled out. Is his truly gone? When I talk to people about that report, people who think I don't know anything, they say, "Oh, I don't know what you're talking about." Or, "We never did reports like that."

But that didn't end this particular episode. The next time I looked in the file, when I was in Washington D.C., I found four copies of the fax, all filed in different places in Jim's three-inch thick file. It's like "they" were trying to drive me crazy. I suggested that if we ever went to war again, I'd come to work in their Casualty office because at least I'd know better what to do. I can't believe all of the mistakes that have been made in keeping Jim's file up-to-date.

I must say, though, that when Lt. Col. Salak saw how disheveled Jim's case file was, she took it upon herself to put it in order. This was a first.

But, I jump ahead of myself.

Chapter Two

The Set-up

"Vietnam was a war that asked everything
of a few and nothing of most in America."
Myra MacPherson

In 1985, a document from the Defense Intelligence Agency (DIA) was enclosed in 1Lt. James D. Birchim's file. It reported the death of Jim as "unaccounted for." But, Col. John R. Oberst, who wrote the report, could not make a positive statement about Jim's death because there was a "lack of substantive information[1]."

This statement was made four years after Jim's father received a letter from Rear Admiral Jerry O. Tuttle, USN, Vice Deputy Director for Intelligence and External Affairs. The letter stated that "Your son James is one of those Americans who are carried in a killed in action category inasmuch as his MIA status was changed by the U.S. Army on 10 May 1971. There is no category known as MIA-dead[2]."

Just two weeks before this letter was written, Jim's mother received a similar letter from Rear Admiral Tuttle saying, ". . . his status was changed by the U.S. Army from MIA to presumed dead on 10 May 1971[3]."

The difference between "killed in action" and "presumed dead" became all-important to Jim's folks and me. Presumed dead meant that there was a chance that Jim was alive and perhaps a POW somewhere in Southeast Asia. Killed in action meant to us that the Army had proof of some kind that Jim was not a POW. And maybe they even had some eyewitnesses who could prove that, or they found his dog tag or his boot or something to identify him as having been killed.

This was not the case.

We were devastated!

One of the reports in Jim's Army file was "sanitized" but from what was not inked out, I was able to determine that a Vietnamese refugee had reported hearing about a U.S. Army Special Forces Captain named Birchim. The refugee was an interpreter to the U.S. Special Forces operation in Kontum Province.

This refugee said that the Captain was lost when he fell from a McGuire harness during extraction. He heard that Captain Birchim "had fallen from a high altitude and probably was killed instantly when he hit the ground."

15

Following is an excerpt from that DIA report and evaluation. It happens to match, word for word, the Refugee Report Interview, Knowledge of MIAs in Vietnam, and the Joint Task Force – Full Accounting (JTF-FA) Circumstance of Loss Report.

". . . the loss of First Lieutenant James Douglas Birchim, USA, 5th Special Forces, who was killed on 15 November 1968. 1Lt Birchim was the leader of a long-range reconnaissance patrol on a search mission in Laos, approximately 54 kilometers southeast of Attopeu City, when the group was ambushed. In evading the enemy, 1Lt Birchim suffered a broken ankle and fragmentation wounds. He requested that the patrol be extracted that evening. Difficult terrain prevented helicopters from landing, thus the patrol was to be picked up by McGuire extraction rigs. After four of the men were successfully extracted by the first helicopter, the second aircraft hovered to pick up the remaining four men with only three rigs. 1Lt Birchim insured that three men were accommodated and then hung onto the back of one of his men. Their rig was dragged through the trees, almost dislodging them. But 1Lt Birchim held on for what was estimated to have been between 30 and 45 minutes before falling from a height of about 2,500 feet. The exact location where 1Lt Birchim fell from the helicopter can only be estimated by the time from the known pick-up point, which would put the loss approximately 50 kilometers northwest of Kontum City in South Vietnam. 1Lt Birchim remains unaccounted for."

Now I ask you, how can a refugee report the times, altitude and map coordinates of an incident? The background/comments on the Refugee Report and Evaluation say, "The fact that the refugee provided names, approximate dates, location, organization and circumstances of loss makes this correlation extremely probable."

Not to me!

Another DIA Evaluation of U.S. POW/MIA Information Provided by Vietnamese Refugee states ". . .the remains of an American advisor which were buried south of Dak To in southern Vietnam. (Sanitized) in April 1971 was a member of the (Sanitized) which was part of a larger force trying to break the siege at Firebase 5 in the tri-border area . . .The American remains were buried with the Vietnamese remains in a shallow, unmarked common grave about 800 meters (direction unknown) from Firebase 5. . .The American advisor was described as Caucasian, with a very thin face and wearing a mustache. . .Assuming that (sanitized) recollection of the date of the incident is correct there was only one loss in 1971 within a 55 kilometer radius of the area described, which involved an unaccounted for U.S. serviceman, and whose incident of loss bears any similarity to the information provided. . ."

I have been told numerous times that Jim was the only one lost and presumed dead in that area in 1968. Could the date of 1971 above be correct? Or was the refugee referring to Jim? And if not, what was this report doing in Jim's file?

* * *

From the beginning, I felt there was more to this story of what happened to Jim. I tried over and over again to get some sort of agreement between officials or witnesses or reports so that I could put to rest what was the truth. However, every story varied in some way.

Sp4 Frank L. Belletire was one of the three men hanging from the three rigs on that 2nd helicopter. He was the one Jim clung to as the helicopter rose out of the trees. Here is the official report. Belletire's name appears on the bottom. The report was notarized by a faint penciled-in name with the words Notary Public handwritten, not an official seal.

"First, let me say, in my opinion, Captain Birchim is KIA. Due to two things: (1) the fall, and/or (2) shock. According to the copter pilots, we were up 8,000 feet. We were lost, and in severe weather conditions. The trip back to Kontum took about 60 to 90 minutes. Captain Birchim had broken or severely sprained one of his ankles (he could put no weight on it during our escape). We were severely battered around on takeoff, hitting numerous trees. When he hit the ground and trees, he must have taken a severe beating. Also, before he fell, we were in a great deal of pain. The rig with two men in it is far from comfortable.

What happened the day of the 15 Nov 68 was something I'll never forget. Here is a short version.

We were looking for another recon team on the afternoon of 15 Nov 68, when we were ambushed by NVA (maybe a platoon or more). Finally, after spending several hours running and fighting, we came to a LZ. It was getting dark by this time. They dropped the rigs (4 of them), but we could only get to 3 of them. I got the two Vietnamese in their rigs, and Birchim and I got in the remaining one. Upon takeoff we were battered around bounding off of trees. Both of us became unseated hanging upside down with Birchim on top of me. The weather was miserable (cold and rain), and after about 15 minutes of this we started to struggle and move around trying to get more comfortable. The pain (hanging upside down and the belt of the rig cutting off blood) was indescribable. I started to blackout after about 30 to 45 minutes. All this time we were struggling and moving about. About this time I wanted out, I couldn't take the pain anymore. I told Birchim this. He told me to hang on a little while longer. We were still struggling and moving about. After about 45 minutes of this, Birchim fell. I blacked out when the rig twisted around my arm and neck. The next thing I remember is being at Kontum."

Years later, Lt. Col. Mack Brooks, head of Army Casualty at the time, and I agreed that Belletire's statement was most probably written for him and may not have even been signed by him.

Captain Van Thach Bich, of the ARVN, filed this written report about the incident.

". . . Sgt Ngo van Chien, Bang, Teo, Tok and Mlang, reported that when the team started to move to a dry stream the enemy opened fire. Lt Birchim, by using hand and arm signals, signaled to Sgt Chien that Interpreter Nam was hit in the chest and was dead. When they arrived at the dry stream bed they all saw that Lt Birchim's foot was hurt and blood on his back. During the second attack we lost Mland, Bang, Tok and Teo, who were later picked up by helicopter. Hlur, Phier and Mlon are still MHA. At this time there were only Lt Birchim, SP4 Belletire, Sgt Chien and Beng. Lt Birchim made contact with FAC and was told to go to an open area for helicopter pick-up. It was dark and raining and the LZ was very small so the helicopter could not land. The helicopter dropped two ropes, one in front and one in back. Sgt Chien and Beng used the front rope and Lt Birchim and Belletire used the back rope. When the helicopter started to take off from the ground Sgt Chien and Beng saw Lt Birchim and Belletire by the light of another helicopter. They all took off at the same time but because Beng was wounded and Lt Birchim and Belletire had fainted and it was dark no one could see Lt Birchim when he fell off."

The helicopter pilot's report says someone on the ground waved him off. Who was that? Did Jim decide to stay behind and try to hold off the attacking Viet Cong, single-handed? If this happened, then search teams would have a place to go to look for Jim. The pilot also said that all four lines were taut. That couldn't be, since one line was lost.

* * *

A lot of discrepancies were beginning to appear as I acquired more reports of Jim's last hours. This next one is a U.S. Personnel Biographical Data report that has questions to be filled out about particular personnel. The report is dated 20 Mar 67. I assume the person who wrote that meant '69. I have no idea who filled out this report, but this is what it says.

"5c. Had SUBJECT ever voiced strong opinions concerning the war, the Vietnamese, or of Communism in general? Yes. His comments were favorable to the position of the United States Government. On the day he departed for his mission he told SP4 Belletire that he wanted to make contact with the enemy and capture a POW.

5f. SUBJECT'S ability to get along and mix with other members of unit: Lt Birchim was an affable individual. He got along well with everyone.

5g. Commander's estimate of individual's physical and moral courage and opinion of individual's ability and will to survive the rigors of enemy interrogation, indoctrination, and imprisonment. It is the opinion of this man's immediate commander that his physical and moral courage were (sic) above and beyond that of most soldiers. The same applied for ability to withstand interrogation, indoctrination and imprisonment.

8. List name(s) of other American(s) wounded, missing or killed in same immediate area or battle . . . and if bodies of these dead were recovered.

There were no other Americans wounded, killed or missing in this action. SP4 Frank A Belletire, RA 16 904 710, is a survivor of the same operation.

10. Give a brief summary of events leading up to Individual's present status.

Individual was conducting an operation that was a search for two other American's of this unit that had become missing in action. While conducting this operation Lt Birchim's team came under several contacts with enemy forces. The fighting became so furious that Lt Birchim had to request that his team be extracted from the area. Helicopters, equipped with McGuire rigs were sent to extract the team. The helicopters could not land on the LZ due to the hostile fire, so they hovered over the LZ and dropped McGuire rigs to the team. Four members went out on the first helicopter. This left Lt Birchim, SP4 Belletire and 2 SCU members of the team on the ground. The second helicopter only had three rigs on it. Lt Birchim made Bellitire and the two SCU get into these rigs and he held onto Bellitire's back. Lt Birchim had suffered a broken ankle and frag wounds during the enemy encounters. The pain he was suffering because of his wounds and injuries are probably what caused him to fall from Belletire's back. Belletire had suffered injuries when he had been dragged through the trees during extraction and he passed out in the rig. Therefore he cannot say when or where Lt Birchim fell from the rig.

11. Other useful information. It is felt that the helicopter was at approximately 2500 feet when Lt Birchim fell, therefore, it is reasonably safe to assume that he is dead."

Now, let me go back and make some comments about this report. First, 5.c. - Since Belletire wasn't a regular member of the patrol, how could he have made a statement witnessed by the person filling out this form, prior to his going on the mission with Jim?

5.g. - Is there a clue there in the words "withstand interrogation, indoctrination and imprisonment?"

8. - Why did the writer of this report say there were no "other Americans wounded, missing or killed in the same immediate area or battle," I ask you? What about the two men on Jim's team who were killed? What about the other team members who were all wounded? What about the men Jim's team went in to rescue?

Another 1971 report in Jim's file is almost solid acronyms, but I was able to find one item that said, "Presumptive finding of death[4]." So it was presumed?

One letter, also dated in 1971, made me chuckle, if one can consider this a chuckling matter. It was written by J.S. Warren, Lt. Col., Infantry, Commanding. In the letter he said, "At ur (sic) request (Apr '71) I furnished you a detailed 'background' synopsis of the circumstances - - which in my opinion then - - led to the death of the Lieut." . . . "Department of the US Army called me on 11 May 71 requesting that I forward a second statement which would not point up a possible conflict of interest between the Lieut's wife and his parents.

MY COMMAND RECOMMENDED, RESPECTFULLY, THRU CHANNELS, IN 1968 THAT THE LIEUT BE DECLARED KIA. This recommendation - - I understand - - was favorably received by the Commander, 5th Special Forces Group, 1st Special Forces, APO SF 96240.

I shall NOT reiterate what I wrote to you this April.

Please ask yourselves WHY you did not act on the MIA board action concerning the Lieut in 1969[5]."

Major General S.H. Matheson, USA Commanding, sent me a letter on June 26, 1969. He is a distant relative of mine. In his letter, below, he wrote what he had been told happened to Jim, so it's not first hand, but interesting nevertheless.

"While attempting to evade to an LZ for extraction, the lieutenant broke his ankle. However, with the aid of an air strike, three team members were extracted in two McGuire rigs. Birchim and SP4 Belletire shared one rig. During the extraction, Birchim and Belletire were bounced and dragged through trees and both became unseated from the rig. Belletire wound up hanging upside-down with the lieutenant hanging onto his back. Due to darkness, rain, and the tactical situation the helicopter crew was unable either to see the men in the rigs or to land. Belletire and Birchim hung onto each other for some thirty to forty-five minutes before being overcome by fatigue and pain, at which time Birchim lost his grip and fell, and Belletire passed out but remained attached to the rig. Since it appears that Birchim probably fell from the rig at an altitude of 2000 feet, it is inconceivable that he could have survived."

* * *

Jim was promoted to the rank of Captain in 1969 and, in 1972, he was awarded the Distinguished Service Cross and the Purple Heart.

* * *

I continued to be confused by the variety of terms that seemed to run through all of the material I read. A DIA letter written in 1990 by Col. Joseph A. Schlatter, USA, Chief, Special Office for Prisoners of War and Missing in Action, states that they have sent me all the documents in Jim's file, as I had requested. The DIA provided enclosures 1 through 13, but they "prepared enclosures 1 through 5 for direct release to Mrs. Birchim. Enclosure 3 has been excised in order to provide the information to Mrs. Birchim. The information in this document was properly classified, remains classified, and is therefore excempt from release pursuant to Title 5 U.S.C. 552(b)(1) because the release would cause an unauthorized disclosure of intelligence sources and methods."

* * *

After all these years, there is still some information that they will not give me because it might disclose some intelligence information? I can't believe it! That sure sounds like there are secrets about what Jim was doing that would embarrass someone in the Army or contradict what the public has been told about Special Forces operations, or heaven knows what!

Once, I was escorted into an office at the DPMO with my Casualty officer, but I was not allowed to take notes. If I had to go to the bathroom, I was escorted. I could only look at the documents once. My purse was searched as I entered the building, and I was not allowed any type of recording device. Of course, the only documents they let me see were unclassified.

I was the only family member allowed to see these unclassified documents. If everything they allowed me to see was unclassified, then why couldn't other family members see them, why couldn't I have a copy of them, and why couldn't I make notes?

You should have seen me race to the car and write everything I could remember as fast as I could. It's a good thing I have a good memory and I'm inquisitive.

* * *

In March of 1992, Jim's sister, Jean Birchim, asked for any information the Army could give her regarding Jim that had previously been held from us because of its classified status. She based this request on the Freedom of Information Act (FOIA) that was now in effect.

After several paragraphs about the FOIA, this is what they sent Jean regarding her brother.

"Captain (CPT) James D. Birchim was assigned to Command and Control North, 5th Special Forces Group (Airborne), 1st Special Forces. On November 15, 1968, CPT Birchim, then a First Lieutenant, was the leader of a Long Range Reconnaissance Patrol on a search mission. During the mission the patrol was ambushed and CPT Birchim requested extraction. The helicopter could not land, due to the difficulty of the terrain, so the patrol was picked up by McGuire extraction rigs. The helicopter picked up four men with three rigs as one rig was entangled in the trees. CPT Birchim ensured that his men were secure and hung on the back of one of them. The rigs were dragged through the trees, almost dislodging the soldiers. CPT Birchim was able to hold on for thirty to forty-five minutes, before falling from an estimated 2500 feet. The remaining elements of the 5th Special Forces Group were notified, but none ever reported finding the remains. CPT Birchim is currently listed on the rolls of the department of Defense as MISSING IN ACTION, PRESUMPTIVE FINDING OF DEATH."

* * *

In 1998, I received an e-mail from Darrell D. Redman, someone who knew Jim in Vietnam. In the e-mail he said, "I was in FOB#2, or CCC as it later was known. Jim was killed in Nov of 68 on an extraction from a hot LZ after a recon mission. Whether he was shot or fell from the rope which they were using to extract them I cannot remember. We could not find him, even with an extensive effort."

An "extensive effort?" My God, this was never mentioned before in any of the reports I had received. Although Jim's mother and I remember talking with Sgt. Smith on the phone shortly after we were first notified about Jim's MIA status, this "extensive effort" statement appears no where else in any of the documents.

Sgt. Smith had said that three patrols had been sent out to search for Jim in the area of Ben Het and some of the team had been killed. We've never been able to find Sgt. Smith since then and there are no documents that mention Ben Het in Jim's file. Jim wrote me about Sgt. Smith so I know there was such a person.

Then, in December 1995, I received a letter from the Office of the Assistant Secretary of Defense (SOD). In this account, the letter said, "Special Forces units in the area searched for his remains without success, in part because the exact loss location was unknown."

That letter from the SOD's office was in response to a request I made for more information about the site where Jim disappeared. Lt. Col. Mack M. Brooks, U.S. Army, Chief POW/MIA Affairs, wrote me in 1994 with a response provided by the Joint Task Force-Full Accounting of the Department of the Army.

I had asked for more information about the site so that I might search the area myself. Among the papers he sent was an unclassified document that the files contain no additional information about the loss site. In referring to SP4 Belletire, the report said, "This individual indicated CPT Birchim fell from the helicopter after they had been traveling 30 to 40 minutes. According to a qualified UH-1 pilot, the maximum speed for a UH-1 towing personnel in a McQuire extraction rig, under the conditions of the REFNO 1322 incident is 80 to 85 knots. Based on this airspeed, the helicopter would have traveled 40 to 70 kilometers. The reported flight altitude of 2,000 to 2,500 feet and an analysis of the terrain and elevation in the area indicate the helicopter could have departed the area in either of two possible air mobility corridors. The first corridor extends from the extraction area on a northern heading to a point near the triborder area. From that point it proceeds on an east-northeast heading to highway QL14 and proceeds south to Kontum. The second corridor generally follows a straight line on a southeasterly heading from the extraction site to Kontum. Because the extraction pilot made no mention of this egress route in his statement, the flight path of the extraction helicopter is unknown. The record loss location is approximately 48 kilometers from the extraction site and is located along the northern air mobility corridor. Based on all available information, the REFNO 1322 record loss location is a reasonable estimate. Without additional information, there is no basis to change this location. . . Files contain no information concerning the areas searched after the incident. . ."

I have tried to locate the family of one man who was a member of the team Jim's group went in to rescue. His family is from Ohio. I thought I could see what information they might have about him and Jim, but the names seem to be unlisted in the phone books.

I asked a casualty officer if I could contact this man's family. He contacted the parents for me because they needed permission to give out the phone number, but the parents said they didn't want to speak with me.

* * *

23

It wasn't until 1995, while researching Jim's file in the National Archives, that I stumbled across some new information leading to the Ben Het location. The case-file following Jim's was that of William Copley. Why I looked at it, I'll never know. But, there was Jim's name mentioned as the team leader who had been sent in to find Copley, the man about whom I had been trying to find some information. It looks like Jim never made contact with Copley and I had never found Copley's name on anything in Jim's file, up to this point.

Guess where Copley, a member of Recon Team Vermont, was supposed to have been lost? Bingo! Ben Het! Does that mean they inserted Jim's Recon Team New Hampshire into the wrong site, miles from Ben Het? Or was he really in Ben Het like Copley's file would lead one to believe? Ben Het is almost on the Laos/Vietnam border, and is very close to Dak To, which was a Special Forces site.

This new report said:

". . .on 13 November, another recon team, RT New Hampshire, was inserted into the area of the ambush to conduct a search and rescue (SAR) in an effort to rescue/recover SSgt. Copley. 1st Lt. James D. Birchim, team leader, SP4 Frank L. Belletire, assistant team leader and 10 indigenous personnel; comprised RT New Hampshire. Over the next 2 days an extensive search in and around the ambush site was conducted. During the search no sign of the missing assistant team leader or his remains were found.

"On 15 November, RT New Hampshire was also ambushed by communist troops in the same general area as RT Vermont. At dusk, and after engaging in a running gun battle with NVA forces, emergency extraction helicopters recovered 8 of the 12-man SAR team, including 1st Lt. Birchim and SP4 Belletire who were extracted by use of McGuire rigs. Of the four indigenous team members not recovered, three were listed Missing in Action and the fourth was listed Killed in Action/Body Not Recovered. On return flight to base, the recon team members remained in the McGuire rigs dangling below the helicopter. During the flight, Jim Birchim fell from the McGuire rig that he and Frank Belletire shared and was also listed Missing in Action[6]."

William Copley was listed as MIA on November 16, one day after Jim.

Later, I found an unclassified document in Jim's file dated September 1969.

"Under prov MPA review of status of Cpt James D Birchim SSAN and Sgt William M Copley must be made one year after missing dates and decision made whether continue indiv as missing, change status to captured or is presumptive finding of death. Req this office be furn complete resume all info obtained other than that furn in board rept. Also include recom whether in your opinion status of indiv should be cont as missing changed from missing to cap or from missing to presumed dead. Justification and reasoning for your recom also req. Further req repts be forwarded to reach this ofc NLT 20 days prior review date."

Another interesting bit of information was the mention of a Sgt. Smith in connection with the name William Copley in the Ben Het area. Could it have been this Sgt. Smith who called both Jim's mother and me telling us that teams were being sent to search for Jim? Since I've never been able to find this man, I guess I'll never know.

If Jim was truly closer to Copley in the Ben Het area, then flying time between there and Kontum would have been reasonable. It also made more sense that if Jim's team had been sent in near the tri-border region, then the rescue team could have initiated a search for Jim right away. Sending the rescue team to the Attopeu area would have been a dangerous or impossible mission to find one missing Green Beret.

So many questions! So few answers!

In Jim's file is a letter I received from Lt. Col. John S. Warren on December 4, 1968. Among other things, he wrote, "Jim fell from a McGuire rig. A search was launched to locate and recover Jim soon after he became missing. This effort continues and will as long as there is a chance of recovery. Jim is well trained in the art of survival, evasion and defense and we are confident in his ability to survive the elements. All of us were deeply saddened to learn that he was missing and we offer our sincerest prayers and hopes for his safe recovery."

If I had known then that they did not have the exact location where Jim fell, I would have had my first clue that something was wrong. But I didn't. And so, when I read a document that was added much later to Jim's file, that said, "Classified area by UH1D aircraft. Indiv fell out of McGuire rig from aircraft while under hostile fire. Search in progress. Investigation in progress," I would have shouted, "How can you do that when you don't know where to go?"

After visiting Vietnam in 1992, I received a letter from Vietnam forwarded to me by Dinh, a Vietnamese woman living in the States. It was written by a Montagnard, an indigenous in the area, and translated by Leon Witt in Washington State, in response to my request for some information that I left with the Vietnamese during my trip to Kontum.

In the handwritten letter, he wrote, "Please tell Miss Barbara that all the names of soldiers that she gave me to ask for her husband, I think three are still alive. I have met only one. His name is Ksor Nut. He used to work with her husband. He told me that her husband jumped off from the plane in the area of Ben Het (the spot where Miss Barbara went, but the authority did not allow to go further). As soon as her husband jumped off the steps of the plane, VC shot from the ground. Then he fell down. The plane went up, left away from the scene. Later on the plane did try to come back at the scene but did not find any life. They believe that he was shot and died at the spot.

"I went there and asked people to locate the bones but not her husband ones. I have the name of the MIA but cannot tell you in the letter because I am afraid of the censure, then I'll get arrested. I know that 2 more Montagnard soldiers are still alive. I'll contact them. Any news I'll let you know. Please tell Miss Barbara that I don't forget her. I don't want to write her in English because of my security problem."

Wow! Yet another accounting of what happened to Jim. What am I to believe? The truth has to be somewhere within all of this.

* * *

Jim's status was changed on May 10, 1971. Yet, on May 8, 1974, I received a copy of the official circumstances regarding the helicopter report. Why did it take three years after Jim was declared KIA for the following to be reported by Maj. Gray, Chief, Site Development?

"During the evening of 15 November 1968, a US Army UH1D helicopter hovered at an altitude of 100 to 120 feet while extracting four members of a long range reconnaissance patrol by use of three McQuire rigs. This action resulted in two individuals being lifted on the same rig. The helicopter then departed the area and climbed to an altitude of approximately 2000 feet while en route to its destination, with the rigs in tow.

Based upon these circumstances, request you compute as precisely as possible, the distances the helicopter would have traveled at the end of:

a.   30 minutes @ 50 KIAS – 25 NM or 31 NM
b.   45 minutes @ 50 KIAS – 37 NM

Information is needed on a timely basis to resolve the circumstances of the site[7]."

I have written the figures as they were calculated by the Chief, CSI. I wonder who said the helicopter flew 30-40 minutes before Jim fell off? It wasn't Frank Belletire because I asked him how he came up with that fact in his initial testimony, and he said he didn't know. Since he was the only man with Jim, who did come up with that fact?

I should note here that to this day, I have not found one other serviceman who had his status changed prior to the end of the war without a body or additional information, except Jim.

* * *

Through the years of networking with any and every Green Beret I came across, one phrase was consistent--"I can't talk about this due to the secret oath we take."

What could be so damaging to our national security, at this date, that these men would refuse to discuss with me?

* * *

". . .The memories within us are in stories we just can't share. They are the price that we alone have paid. For we were there. We saw the faces. We watched them die. We knew the pain and felt the pride. Dear God, we know how hard we tried. We can't forget. We pray that the price we paid was enough. . . Hear and feel our prayer. Remember us and all those men you never met."

From "Vietnam Memorials"

* * *

One of the problems I had with the statement Army personnel gave me on that fateful day in 1968 was how could Jim have fallen off the McGuire rig? I needed to know more about the helicopter that came to rescue him and his men. And I needed to know about the rope that was to hold only one man but held two that time, according to the various reports.

"When others were in need, you didn't point to the guy.
You rolled up your sleeves and went to work."
President Ronald Reagan – 2/3/87

In the book, Spite House: The Last Secret of the War in Vietnam, I found a description of a mission that sounded much like the one Jim was on. The author wrote, "There was no clearing for the helicopter to land - - only a hole in the canopy of trees - - which meant they would, in the lingo of the men who performed this circus-like but highly dangerous maneuver, 'come out on strings.[8]

Unfortunate as it was, this method of extracting our men from the thick trees was more usual than not. Another method was called the spie rig and it had a number of variations. One was a helicopter with three rigs that could carry six men. "The men hooked their arms around each other's waists -- outside men with one arm extended" to help balance them. The Special Forces used the spie rig most of the time for dropping recon teams, as well as extracting them. A ladder preceded the use of a spie rig[9].

It was common for the enemy to fire at the dangling men instead of the helicopter.

The helicopters the South Vietnamese flew were H-34 Sikorskys. The Americans flew Hueys, which were much more vulnerable. They were not like the Sikorskys which were "known to take seventy-six holes in the fuselage and still fly[10]." The American helicopter pilots often dropped their nose and flew away with the men hanging at tree line, which we've all seen in Vietnam war movies.

"It was not a pretty sight to see a guy who had been dragged through a forest of mahogany trees on a rope, and that was not as bad as being dragged through bamboo. 'The guys who suffered that fate looked like raw meat on a butcher block.'"[11]

The Sikorsky was known as HH-3 Jolly Green Giant Search and Rescue helicopter. It used a bullet shaped jungle penetrator rescue sling on a cable that could slip down through the trees. Once the man was strapped in, a winch would be used to bring him up.[12]

The Huey was a Bell UH-1 single engine utility helicopter. A single Huey would usually carry four McGuire rigs, or "strings" as they were called by the troops. They were 100-foot ropes with a 6-foot loop at the end and padded with a canvas seat, sort of like a child's swing. The ropes hung two on each side and were faster than a winch because four men could be lifted off the ground at the same time. The pilot would rise vertically, then proceed horizontally along the treetops until it was safe to gain altitude.[13]

"During an extraction the Huey pilot had to hold his bird at a steady treetop hover" twenty-eight feet above the ground "while his crew chief, lying on the aircraft floor and peering down, directed him over the hole by intercom. After dropping the ropes the crew chief watched the recon men climb into the seats, then told the pilot when to lift up - - a dangerous few seconds, because the ropes could become snared in the trees or a sudden barrage of fire could threaten the aircraft. . . 'If you got in trouble with the strings, the crew members would have to cut them . . . It didn't matter if anyone was on the ends of the strings or not; if you had to cut the ropes in order to save the aircraft, you cut the ropes. That was understood by everyone.' . . . your weight soon shifted to the crotch, eventually cutting off blood flow to your legs. There you were, swaying below the Huey, 3000 feet above the jungle, the air rushing past at 90 knots."[14]

In the book, SOG, The Secret Wars of America's Commandos in Vietnam, the author writes about Jim.

"Though many recon men's lives were saved, several men were injured or killed when dragged through trees or when they fell from strings. An especially tough case was that of Lieutenant Jim Birchim, lost 15 November 1968.

Birchim and a young Special Forces NCO had been lifted out in darkness after a long day of running firefights against determined NVA pursuers. Both were wounded but managed to lash themselves together in the only McGuire rig they could find; they would hold onto each other. The Huey lifted safely away but had to fly through a heavy tropical storm so violent that at times the whole aircraft shuddered. It was pitch black.

"When the storm-shaken helicopter finally descended back in South Vietnam, a waiting party rushed to the mass of ice-laden clothes and gear in the McGuire rig but found only the unconscious, shivering young NCO, rope burns cut deep into his hands where even his superhuman grip had been insufficient to hold Lieutenant Birchim. 'He had terrific rope burns,' recalled his recon company commander, Captain Ed Lesesne. 'It was an impossible human task to do what he did but I'm sure he feels guilty as hell that he dropped him.' Jim Birchim's body was never found."[15]

Another problem I had in reconciling what happened to Jim was the discrepancy between the various reports as to how high the helicopter was flying when Jim fell and how far the helicopter flew after picking Jim and his men up, before arriving in Kontum, where they are reported to have landed.

I am not very good at physics, but I do remember that old question about which falls faster, a rock or a feather. The rock would accelerate longer and have a velocity greater than the feather. However, I have recently learned that another factor is the orientation at which a body falls. If a body falls with a larger surface area perpendicular to the direction of its motion, it will experience a greater force and a smaller velocity. If it has a smaller surface area, then it will experience a smaller force and a greater velocity.

This really didn't answer my concern about whether Jim could have survived a fall from 2500' if that was truly the height the helicopter was flying. But it did give me some hope that trees and underbrush may have cushioned his fall. Physics-wise, who is to say whether his body would have had a large enough surface area to have slowed his fall.

I remember reading in the '90s about a woman skydiver who fell from 10,000 feet into a mud puddle and only had bruises. And another time I read about a man who broke a leg, or a hip, when skydiving, and he fell about 3,000 feet. Then there's the British soldier I read about who survived a 4,600-foot fall when his parachute failed to open in 1998. He only broke his legs and pelvis.

As far as how many miles the helicopter flew, and whether a man could have hung on that long, not being snapped to the rope by his McGuire rig, I have no answers.

One report said that the helicopter flew at 5000'. Several stated the helicopter was at 2500' all the way. Yet, a report from the NCO whom Jim clung to stated it was 8000'.

The average height that the Huey would have flown was 3000'. Since there are a lot of different elevations along the flight path, if the pilot was flying at 2500', he would have flown right into a mountain at times.

Did the pilot really not report the exact height and distance he flew on that mission? Seems mighty strange to me. But then, as some people have said to me through the years, who knows what falls through the cracks during a war, unless you've been there . . . done that.

On January 25, 2001, I watched Joan Lunden on the TV show, "Behind Closed Doors."[16] She got to be one of five people (4 men and her) extracted by a helicopter from the ground on one rope. Now, the ropes are designed so that someone can hang on with another person (arms around each other) at various positions up the rope. It was interesting to see all five of them hanging together as the helicopter rose up and moved above the trees into the distance.

I just have two questions at this point. Who was the man on the ground waving the pilot off? Was it Jim? And what about the phone calls that Jim's parents and I received right after being notified that search teams had been sent to look for Jim? If they didn't really know where Jim dropped off, then how could they send in rescue teams? Or, did they know Jim never got on the rig? There are no documents in Jim's file referring to these questions.

* * *

> "Anyone who has looked into the glazed eyes of a soldier dying on the battlefield will think hard before starting a war."
>
> Otto Von Bismark

One of the groups of Vietnamese that was recruited early in the war were the Montagnards (Mo-ton-yards), a French term meaning "mountain people." The Montagnards, like the American Indians, lived in tribal groups. They wore sarongs and loincloths with special patterns like the Scottish people still do with their tartans.

These men have a darker skin than most Vietnamese, and have stockier builds, somewhat like the Polynesians to whom they are ethnically related, along with the Mon-Khmer and Sino-Tibetan ethnic groups. The Montagnard tribesmen lived in the Central Highlands in over a hundred different tribes that survived by hunting or slash-and-burn farming[17]. They were the largest minority group in Vietnam in the 1960s and are in no way like the Vietnamese.

The Special Forces teams organized and trained the Montagnards as mercenaries. "They fought not for money but because they were proud of their tribe and village and detested the enemy . . . (the) Vietnamese[18]." They had a strong desire to be left alone and, therefore, had a great hostility against the Vietnamese[19].

The Americans called them the Yards. The Vietnamese called them "moi," which means "savage." They did not feel allegiance to the Vietnamese or the U.S., but they "were loyal and ready to die for their recon teammates[20]" whether they were Americans or Yards.

The Montagnards lived simply with a great amount of superstitution. The Green Berets had to learn about the Montagnards customs, dialects, the type of tribal food they ate, and their ceremonies and rituals. This was important because the Montagnards would not associate with those who did not share their lifestyles and dangers. The CIA approved of the Special Forces soldiers learning the ways of the Montagnards for they were important if the soldiers were to attempt blocking the VC's encroachment into Vietnam's backcountry[21].

The Green Berets loved the Montagnards because they were fierce fighters and quick learners. Our military gave the Montagnards the same care as any other U.S. soldier. Later in the war, they had their own hospital in Pleiku. The Montagnards and the Green Berets hung around together, too, with the Green Berets acting as big brothers or fathers to them[22].

The Montagnards, or Mountain Scouts, joined MACVSOG (Military Assistance Command Vietnam Studies and Observation Group) and other Special Forces units. A mercenary army, of forty thousand known as Civilian Irregular Defense Forces (CIDF), was led by the Green Berets and funded by the CIA through the DOA[23]. Among other things, they were used to penetrate Laos.

When the Yards were used to penetrate both Laos and Cambodia, a "sanitized" Green Beret accompanied them. The U.S. was not supposed to be in either of those countries. In fact, the American public was repeatedly told that our forces were not, and had never been, in Laos or Cambodia.

It is unfortunate that today, many years after the Vietnam War is over, the Montagnards are still being murdered or imprisoned because of their association with the U.S. during the war. They are being beaten and arrested, their churches are being burned down, and their ancestral lands are being confiscated. Many are injected (killed) like the KGB once practiced, and their deaths are reported as natural causes. Some of the Montagnard leaders have

31

bounties on their heads for as much as $15,000, more than five times the average Cambodian's income[24].

Many Montagnards now live in North Carolina. Others have fled to northeastern Cambodia.

The Montagnards are on the verge of extinction. "Without the courage and help of Montagnards, many more Americans would be listed on the Vietnam Memorial Wall. On innumerable occasions, their heroic actions saved the lives of Americans, often at the cost of their own lives. The Montagnard people have remained a committed and loyal ally of the United States[25]."

Y-Jut Buonto, (friend of Greg Stock, Special Projects Officer for Save the Montagnard People, Inc.), wrote, "I will never forget the Americans who fought with us and who gave so much. They are in my thoughts, they are in my dreams, their names are in my conversations. I think of them every day[26]."

At the end of the Vietnam War there were 1,500,000 Montagnards living in Vietnam. Due to the atrocities by the Vietnamese, 50% of them have been eliminated in the years since then. Through the years, their Christian beliefs have been at the root of the Vietnamese policy of vile genocide[27].

I read an article in the San Diego Union-Tribune on June 4, 2002[28], about more than 900 Montagnards leaving Cambodia for "resettlement in the United States, the last stage of a yearlong quest for freedom." It seems they all have relatives in four different cities in North Carolina where they will live.

"Vietnam's hill tribe people, collectively known as Montagnards, claim they were stripped of their farmland, persecuted for their Christian faith and faced systematic discrimination by Vietnamese authorities." They fled to Cambodia in February 2001.

I'm glad I have a picture of some of the Montagnards who fought with Jim before he disappeared.

* * *

"They gave their lives so that others might come home."
Donald Rumsfeld
Secretary of Defense

* * *

FRANK BELLETIRE

In 1990, I went to see Frank Belletire, the man who Jim clung to on the McGuire Rig that fateful day. Even though I had read his report on what happened, and a half dozen other accounts, I still wanted to talk to him face-to-face.

I had written to Frank on April 12, 1969, asking him for more information about what happened to Jim. This is what I said.

Dear Frank:

Your letter of 6 March was greatly appreciated. I realize and sympathize with you at how difficult it must have been to write that letter, because I'm now having the same problem. Please, if you do find time to write again, don't be afraid of saying the "wrong" thing.

I'm going to ask a favor of you. Enclosed is one of the many letters I've received from Gen. Wickham. It was so poorly written that it's hard for me to pick out the real facts. Could you straighten out what they're trying to say in the last paragraph on the first page?

If you were only 50 miles from the airstrip and you held on for 30 minutes, this would put you way past the airfield. My SAO officer has informed me that helicopters travel about 120 mph.

I realize that you were in extreme pain and under such terrible conditions that things can get a little mixed up. And I also realize that you are trying your utmost to give an accurate account. I'm only asking you to please level with me. If you don't really remember what happened, but only think you do, please tell me.

The Army had told me that they might have to carry Jim as MIA until the "cessation of hostilities." That could be another 20 or so years, and since the Army doesn't volunteer information, I have to play detective. Any information as to terrain or possibilities of survival would be appreciated. Has the area in which Jim might have been dropped been re-entered?

I'm sorry to bother you with all these questions. I do hope that your wounds weren't extensive and that you're feeling better now.

Well, it's bedtime for Kim, our 1 year old, and David, 3 weeks, so guess I'd better get to it. These two really keep me busy, which is a good thing.

God be with you.

Sincerely,
Barbara

Frank was very nervous at that meeting in 1990. I flew to Chicago, where he lives, with as many papers as I could carry, so I could show them to him. Before I laid all of the documents out on the table, I asked if he could tell me what he remembered about what happened to Jim.

So many of the documents in Jim's Washington D.C. file didn't support many of the details. So, I asked Frank a lot of questions, to see if I could get some clarification of those confusing incident reports.

"Are these your initials?"

"No."

"Is this your signature?"

"No."

"Why did you initial this?"

"I didn't."

"How did you know that you were hanging upside down for 30 to 45 minutes? I'm sure you weren't looking at your watch up there."

"I don't know."

"According to the helicopter pilot's report, he couldn't see the guys as they hung underneath. So, he can't help me with how long you hung upside down, or how long Jim clung to that rope."

Frank had no comment.

"It says here that you were wounded," I told him as I was looking at one of the documents from Jim's file.

"No, not really."

Not really? I was looking at a man who had had a serious head wound at some time. "So, you weren't injured at the time of Jim's disappearance?"

"No," he said. "My injuries came within the next nine or ten months. I was out on patrol again and got this head wound."

That made sense to me. Somewhere in the first year's review documents, it states in the communication log, "Unable to get statement because man is in a coma." It seems that each person who wrote a report about the evac and the loss of Jim was questioned again.

I also reminded Frank that the gunner on the helicopter could see nothing, according to the information I had.

Frank told me he and Jim held on for a while, but then the rope began to cut through all the webbing and the heavy material of his clothes. The gear he carried began to cut into him, too. "I couldn't take the pain any longer," he said. "I literally pushed your husband off the rig."

I had a strange reaction, now that I think about it. Instead of being angry or crying or hitting him, I realized at that point that Frank was filled with guilt. I kept telling him that his reaction was normal, and I didn't blame him for anything. I told him it was a simple knee-jerk response to the awful situation he was in.

"I pushed your husband off me, trying to get comfortable. . .and he fell. That's when the rope got twisted around me and I blacked out."

The report I had stated that from the time Frank blacked out to the time the helicopter arrived at the airport in Kontum was another 30 minutes. And the two Vietnamese soldiers hanging from the other ropes didn't see anything during all that time? I don't think so. They said it was dusk and when they were lifted off through the jungle, it was raining.

Maybe there are others who would not question this, but not me. I asked myself then, and I still ask myself the question--there are three ropes hanging down from one evac helicopter with men clinging to them, and none of the men on those ropes can see each other?

I'm sorry! Three guys waving around in the air might even bump or brush against each other as they swing to and fro. I mean, doesn't that make sense?

Through the years I've confirmed, with various helicopter pilots who flew missions in '68 for Special Forces, that they couldn't fly that long--over an hour with guys hanging from the rigs. It would be impossible to keep the aircraft under control for that long a period of time with bodies dangling beneath it.

Beside that, they wouldn't have had enough fuel because, remember, they had to fly to the extraction site, first.

And, thirdly, nobody I interviewed said they had ever heard of men swinging on the ropes below a helicpoter for any longer than five to ten minutes. Besides, those men would have arrived at Kontum airport frozen to death if they'd been hanging in the rain for over an hour, no matter how slow the helicopter was flying or at what altitude.

During the years, up to my meeting with Frank, I had asked various helicopter pilots what would happen if 150 to 200 pounds dropped off a McGuire Rig? Would they notice the change? Would the helicopter bounce? Would it swing to one side?

The response was always, "No." So, it appears that there was no way that the helicopter pilot would have said, "Whoops, somebody must have fallen off," or "Gee, we must have lost somebody," when Jim fell from the rope.

How could anyone have gone back to look for Jim if they didn't know where he fell off?

Frank told me, that to his knowledge, Jim's team disbanded immediately. Frank was sent back to Danang. He said that assignment was his first and only one with the Special Forces. He was a radioman and I have been told, sometimes a Special Forces team would grab someone from outside the

Special Forces to fill a position like radioman, when necessary. Frank said he always wondered why they sent him straightaway back to Danang and why he was never accepted again in the Special Forces circle.

Before I left Chicago, I asked Frank, "Do you think it's possible that when you came off this mission and Jim was not there, that you were wounded somehow. . .maybe not as bad as the others? I mean, the papers do say you were wounded, but. . . ."

Frank appeared to be surprised.

"Maybe they came to you with a story, you know, and had you sign a paper to that effect? And in the flurry of activity, the story seemed okay? I mean, you come off a horrific mission, and so you just sign the papers without questioning them?"

"I don't know."

"I realize that some of the things in these documents aren't true because they couldn't say Jim's team was in Laos. And I'm assuming that they had to make flying times longer in order to make it look like Jim dropped off in Vietnam. Maybe Jim was on the rig and fell off in the bamboo, if he got on the rig at all. Is that possible?"

"Well, gosh, I don't know."

I said, "The other thing about this is I know that Special Forces men have this kind of close-knit family feeling and they don't leave their comrades behind. And so it would be very difficult for them to own up to leaving Jim behind unless he dropped off in some nebulous spot where they would not be able to find him. Then it would not be as much of a disgrace to lose him."

I was on a roll now, so I kept on telling Frank my theories. "No one has explained to me, through the years, why I got phone calls for a while saying Special Forces was sending men in to look for Jim.

"How could they do that if they don't know where Jim fell off the rig? Or, does it mean they knew he was on the ground all along? That being the case, they could send a rescue team in for him."

I believe there was a mission. I think Jim didn't come back. I think there was a helicopter and the guys got wounded. But, as for everything else I've been told or read in the documents, I don't know.

The only conclusion I could come to, after meeting with Frank, was that something strange had been going on. There were too many discrepancies. None of the stories agreed on the details. Jim just flipped off the rope somewhere, and no one knows where. Since, according to the records I received, they didn't have a specific or even an approximate location, then how could they send search parties to look for Jim or his body?

No wonder the review committee had no new information during the 30-day waiting period after Jim was declared MIA.

If any sense can be made of all this, Jim's team must have been picked up much closer to the Vietnamese border in Ben Het, or at least in the near vicinity. If so, the flying time between there and Kontum would have been reasonable.

It also made more sense that the team had been originally sent in near the border, on one side or the other. And if that was the truth, then men could have been sent right away to rescue Jim. Sending them to the Attopeu area, which was located much farther to the west of Ben Het, would have been a much more dangerous or impossible mission just to find one missing Green Beret who had been left on the ground.

Or, was Jim the one who waved the pilot off and was picked up by the enemy, later to be tracked by the U.S. "powers that be?"

Of course, the question at this point is why would Frank Belletire say he pushed Jim off the McGuire rig if he didn't? And why was Frank so filled with guilt? Why did the Special Forces team disband after returning to Kontum? Did those two Vietnamese hanging from the helicopter, and the pilot and gunner fill in the blanks on a report that had already been written for their signatures?

Made me more than wonder!

Chapter Three

The Acronyms Begin

"We now know, without question, that Americans, both military and non-military, were left behind following World War II, the Korean War, and the Vietnam War. Hundreds were abandoned in Vietnam and Laos, thousands in North Korea, and tens of thousands in areas overrun by the Soviets in World War II."[1]

In 1961, the Soviets put a pilot plan into operation where they would receive American POWs as specimens for their experiments. These POWs in Vietnam were sent to the Soviet Union through Czechoslovakia with the aid of the Vietnamese.

According to the U.S. government, no Americans became prisoners of war until August of 1964. "This is more word games by U.S. officials, because this official position on the first POW deliberately ignores the civilians, CIA agents, and military involved in so-called black programs in Southeast Asia who were lost."[2]

In the book, President Kennedy: Profiles in Power, by Richard Reeves, it is stated that military pilots were recruited as early as 1961. They were asked to sign a statement that "they would be wearing civilian clothes and that their 'government would disclaim any knowledge' of them if they were captured."[3]

In 1962, North Korea joined the North Vietnamese and the Czechs in involving American POWs in chemical agent experiments for both the Soviets and the East Germans.

One of the Czech high priority test programs was biological involving unique diseases that had no known cure. Another was a new strain of viruses that acted within twenty-four hours to disable groups of people. "As was the case following the Korean War, Czech doctors participated in the medical experiments using Vietnam War POWs in the Soviet Union. The most important experiments were those dealing with the development of mind-control and behavior-modification drugs, the testing of biological warfare organisms, and tests of the effects of nuclear radiation."[4]

No American POWs returned from the hospitals in the Soviet Union, East Germany or Czechoslovakia for apparent reasons.

Most of this information came from General Jan Sejna, the highest level communist (Czechoslovakian) official ever to defect to the West. The DIA gave Sejna a staff position and used his information and knowledge for fifteen years. They must have felt him to be trustworthy. However, the CIA and the State Department felt antagonistic toward him because the information he revealed was not in accordance with "conventional wisdom" and "brought into question many of the fundamental assumptions upon which U.S. policies, such as détente, have been based."[5]

"The Vietnamese were . . . more interested in extracting vengeance than in conducting scientific tests." After the Warsaw Pact was signed in 1963, the Vietnamese decided that they would carry on some of their own medical experiments and would not export U.S. POWs to the Soviet Union. They did, though, cooperate with the Soviets in a plan to persuade captured officers to defect and to assist in analyses of U.S. military capabilities, technology and war plans.[6]

As soon as that happened, North Vietnam negotiated with the Laotians to have them participate in experiments with American POWs as medical human guinea pigs and "for testing the effectiveness of 'interrogation' drugs."

The Chinese also got into the act. They started a program as early as the Korean War by using American POWs that the North Koreans gave them.

The Soviets also used American POWs for testing new narcotic drugs. This resulted in their development of drugs that "produced better and longer-lasting highs, drugs that were cheaper and easier to produce, and drugs that were more rapidly addictive."[7]

A CIA Saigon Station cable, as reported in the Chinh Luan newspaper on March 20, 1971, stated, ". . .the exploitation of American POWs were removed from North Vietnamese treaty and that POWs were removed from North Vietnam and sent to China and Russia for further exploitation." State Department cables also provided this information that was released by Senator John Kerry on May 26, 1992. Two men, Jerry Mooney and Barry Toll, told the Senate Select Committee on POW/MIA Affairs that they had seen much classified material about American POWs being shipped to the Soviet Union.[8]

Jerry Mooney had worked for the National Security Agency (NSA) and Barry Toll worked as a special security officer in the Commander-in-Chief Atlantic Command (CINCLANT) emergency-actions section. He reported that he had seen CIA reports about Americans being shipped out of Southeast Asia.

"In all these cases, there has been clear negligence in tracking down the information, assessing its implications, correlating it with other data, and making the full record available to the public."[9]

In the final report of the Senate Select Committee, these words appear. "Something very real happened to each of those brave men, and our country will not be at peace with itself until we are morally certain we have done all we could to find out what."[10] Perhaps the U.S. Senators should reread those words, for nine years later we still have not found out what really happened.

No one has an accurate count of how many American men ended up as Soviet guinea pigs. It is said that the number from the Korean War was around 1,000 and from the Vietnam War there were close to 500. The number who died in Soviet prison camps from those two wars is anyone's guess. "Russia isn't telling and the U.S. government isn't asking."[11]

It seems that our American Senators and high-level government officials know that this whole POW/MIA true accounting situation is a farce. "None of them can be said to have a burning desire to learn what happened, or to rescue any Americans who may still be alive and held captive or are afraid to come home. Their main interest seems to be papering over the POW/MIA problem. Other reasons are all too obvious: the lure of business profits to be made; the need to avoid revealing the duplicity of high-level U.S. officials going back forty years; and the desire of the 'establishment' to hide the evils and crimes of socialist regimes."[12]

In a letter to the Editor, Washington Times, March 19, 1994, Roger Hall, former Marine and independent archival researcher, stated that the National Security Agency (NSA) had kept information about POW/MIAs from the public even though it had been declassified in 1993. This was done to deceive the people so they would not know what wrongs had been done.

Roger Hall wrote, "We don't want classified information on what the NSA is doing now. We want the POW information that has already been declassified and supposedly released to the public. The NSA is exerting control over information on abandoned U.S. military men whom it could have saved. Because of NSA's arrogance, it failed in its responsibility, and now its interference with documents compounds the original wrong. . . There is much more that the president, Congress and the Public are being deceived about. This wrong must be corrected; our elected government should not be defied by government employees. The President has declassified these documents; the public has a right to know."[13]

Long before the Vietnam War, American prisoners were missing from previous wars. For example, over 78,000 were missing from World War II, 8,100 from the Korean War, and in fact, reports show that the Soviets held American POWs from World War I. These figures were taken from the POW/MIA Accounting booklet I received at The League meeting, dated 6/7/01. So, this POW/MIA situation is not new to the United States government.

Yet, the fact that government officials deny that there are any POWs in Southeast Asia when report after report, year after year, indicates there are, makes the situation unimaginable and unacceptable.

In 1991, unconfirmed reports indicated that secretly returned American POWs were being held on Guam, Hawaii and a few places in the U.S. "There have been too many sightings, too many reports from military, Russian, Laotian and Vietnamese officials to write off all American POWs as dead. But that has been the official policy of the United States government from Presidents Jimmy Carter, Ronald Reagan and George Bush. Even Presidents Harry Truman and Dwight D. Eisenhower had to grapple with the Soviet imprisonment of thousands of American POWs once held by the Germans."[14]

When a privately financed contingency paid for and freed ten American POWs in Southeast Asia in 1991, according to unconfirmed reports, the U.S. government did not sanction the action. "But if the U.S. government is involved in a major cover-up on the POW issues, as claimed by several military officials, what would be the government's reason for not wanting POWs released?"[15]

John M.G. Brown wrote an article in The Sunday Oregonian, Portland, Oregon, December 2, 1990, in which he said that the United States had neglected its POW/MIAs through many wars, starting with 1918-1919.

His article runs through information on each war since then. Under Vietnam, he wrote that the long established U.S. policy remained in effect and classified. He talked about Robert Garwood, the POW who officials say was the last to leave Vietnam, and the hundreds of American POWs we left behind.

He mentions a list of "Americans with special training who were carried in a category known as 'MB' or 'Moscow-bound.'"

One paragraph reads: "The Vietnamese were known by U.S. intelligence analysts of the time such as Jerry Mooney (then of Air Force intelligence and the National Security Agency) to assemble pre-selected U.S. prisoners from South and North Vietnam at a special POW camp near Vinh, where they would be interrogated by the 'friends' (Soviet intelligence officers)."

The author says that many American prisoners were moved to a special prison near Sam Neua, Laos. Soviet intelligence officers conducted their final evaluation as to which men would be the most useful to them. Those Americans were flown to the Soviet Union.

As the article says, "This was merely a continuation of the decades long history of 'wink-and-nod diplomacy[16].'"

OPERATION HOMECOMING – and its results

In February/March 1973, Operation Homecoming was put into affect. The idea was to bring home every last one of the POWs and MIAs from Southeast Asia. On May 19 of that year, President Nixon said that all of our men had returned home in Operation Homecoming, and all of the POWs had returned. By making that statement to those families of the men who did not return, he inferred that they were going to be left behind. It was logical. How could they be returned if everyone was home? Before Operation Homecoming, Nixon told the world that we would leave no one behind in Southeast Asia.

Those who were returned in Operation Homecoming were flown to Clark Air Base in the Philippines where they were debriefed. No doubt, that was the most extensive intelligence debriefing of any during the Vietnam War.

The disturbing result of the process was that those debriefing documents have never been made available to the public. It seems they will be classified forever. Even when the Senate Select Committee on POW/MIA Affairs asked for them, the Pentagon said no.[17]

Jerry Mooney figured that only 5% of the men on his list of 400-500 known prisoners had been returned. According to Ann Hart, an MIA wife, it was obvious that our government was telling us, "We are so anxious to get out that we just took what we could get and left." Jerry Mooney had labeled those men on his list of prisoners with "MB" (Moscow Bound) when he knew they had special knowledge that Vietnam wanted. Those men, of course, were not on any prisoner list that Vietnam or Laos furnished the U.S., either right after the Paris Peace Talks or any time later.

Since the United States waged a secret war in Laos, our government could not admit that they had sent our military there. Therefore, there were a lot of statements made by various government and military officials that there could be no POWs or MIAs in Laos.

However, in the 1986 TV series, "We Can Keep You Forever," BBC/ Lionheart Television, Roger Shields, ex-Chairman of the MIA/POW Task Group, Department of Defense, said, "We never received an official list of men who had been captured in Laos. We knew several had been captured in Laos so we carried several (9) as prisoners but mostly they were in the MIA category simply because we had no intelligence as to what happened to them."

Now we find this out!

In response, the narrator commented that the CIA kept records of prisons where Americans were held captive in Laos. He said, "The CIA ran the war." And the POW/MIAs, too, it seems.

In fact, 600 men were lost in the secret war in Laos. Only 9 came back. The North Vietnamese had never moved them from Laos to Vietnam. The rest just disappeared. The official word was, "No American prisoner held in Laos was released from Laos." That soon changed to, "We had not knowingly left anyone behind."

Part III of "We Can Keep You Forever" featured Anne Holland's story about her husband who did not come back from Laos. His name was not on the POW/MIA list, either. She was finally told about his fate by certain authorities who insisted that she keep the information secret. No one, even her children, was to know that their father had been in Laos. Later, when she contacted the American Embassy in Laos to see what information they might have about her husband, she was told they had no record of his being missing in Laos, or anywhere in Southeast Asia. Yet, later the Ambassador signed her husband's death certificate because somehow her husband had been re-designated as a civilian.

In Part IV, Major Mark Smith, U.S. Army Special Forces (ret.), said, "You're talking (about) people who have no feeling whatsoever for the individual soldier in the field. Their answer to all this is to build a black wall in Washington and put all their names on it to pacify you and I."

Sgt. Mel McIntire, Special Forces, whose commander was Mark Smith, told of having evidence of live prisoners in Laos. His evidence had been ignored again and again.

While Ronald Reagan was president, he spoke to MIA families. From one speech, repeated in Part VI, he stated the following as an example of what he had tried to do during his eight years in office.

> "I said to all the nation, most especially to all of you, that
> we write no last chapters, we close no books, we put away
> no final memories until your questions are answered."

Too bad that many of those in our government who worked for President Reagan did not feel the same way that he did. Too bad that some people with authority marched to their own political drum instead of to what was the most important thing, morally and ethically, for our country at the end of that horrible war in Vietnam, Laos and Cambodia.

A part of the videotape featured a 1986 conference held at the University of Colorado, where Scott Barnes (his story is quite astonishing) provided additional information about his witnessing American POWs in Laos. He spent years trying to get someone in our government to believe him and act on it. Both parts of this taped conference are full of almost unbelievable information about the deplorable POW/MIA state of affairs up to 1986. As I watched, I couldn't help but say to myself, "Nothing has changed!"

When Lt. George Coker, POW from 1966 to 1973, returned home to Linden, N.J., he spoke from the steps of their city hall.

> "There was just one thing. . . that enabled myself and my buddies to stay alive those many years. Faith. Faith in my family, my God and my country."[18]

As far as I'm concerned, that's the way each and every one of our servicemen felt on their way to that war. Did those who became a POW or an MIA continue to feel that way when their country did not come after them? I wonder!

Bob White of Denver, Colorado, was the last man to be released from a Vietnam prison.[19] He was held in a 4 ½-foot bamboo cage in camps along the Mekong Delta from November 15, 1969, until his release at the end of April 1973. "There's no reason to believe that there aren't any prisoners still over there. . .They easily could have held me."

Daniel Ellsberg, a former Vietnam Marine, nuclear strategist and peace activist, was prosecuted for espionage for distributing the Pentagon Papers (secret history of the Vietnam War). He is known to have said in 1974 that the American public was lied to, month by month, by each of the five administrations--Truman, Eisenhower, Kennedy, Johnson and Nixon. "It's no tribute to us (Americans) that it was so easy to fool (us) the public."[20]

I have a copy of a Ron Reagan Show video from September 1991. Among those on the show's panel of speakers was former Congressman Bill Hendon, Chairman of the POW Publicity Fund, Capt. Red McDaniel, USN (ret.), former Vietnam POW and Col. Mike Peck, USA (ret.), former Defense Intelligence Agency Chief for POW/MIAs and highly decorated career officer.

Hendon stated that he was a firm believer that the DOD was not leveling with the public. "'I said, Mr. President, they're lying to you, just like this rug is lying here on the Oval Office (floor).' They're not leveling with the President. . . they're not leveling with the people."

He further told the viewing audience to just go to the Vietnam Memorial in Washington D.C. and look at all the names etched on that black wall. He had available to him ". . . report after report out of the Pentagon showing names of men alive in prison and in the most desperate of circumstances in Vietnam and Laos, and you look up there at that magnificent memorial (the Wall) and there're their names there. It says to the American people, they're gone, they're dead. And you look at these intelligence reports and it says they're alive and hurting."

Col. Peck had resigned from his position with the DOD because he didn't think enough was being done to find the POWs and MIAs. And his hands were tied to do anything about it. Once he resigned, he became very unpopular. He said on the show, it was a ". . . travesty (to believe) that national leaders addressed the POW/MIA issue as a national priority, and that any soldier left in Vietnam, even inadvertently, was in fact abandoned years ago."

Ron Reagan quoted a statistic on his show--that 80% of the enlisted men (at that time) believed that MIAs had been left behind in Southeast Asia.

Red McDaniel spoke up to say, "I went to Vietnam prepared to be killed or captured. I did not go prepared to be abandoned by my country. The thing that kept me alive in Vietnam for six years was the absolute belief that someday my country would come to get me."[21]

A year prior to this TV show, Red McDaniel was quoted in The San Diego Union, November 7, 1990. "Had I known in 1967 what I know now about my government, I could not have hung on (in captivity) for 2,110 days." He went on to say, "My advice to the boys in the Middle East is: Don't get captured."[22]

* * *

I found the following bumper sticker and T-shirt sayings in the San Jose Mercury News March 8, 1992 Perspective:

POWS NEVER HAVE A NICE DAY
ONLY HANOI KNOWS
RELEASE OUR POW/MIAS
AMERICAN POW/MIAS ARE ALIVE IN VIETNAM

* * *

"THE MIA MYSTERY: One Man's Journey"[23]

Vietnam veteran, Peter Gilboy, in an article he wrote for the August 25, 1991, Sunday edition of The San Diego Union, tells the story of his disappointment in trying to find a POW named Walter T. Robinson.

Almost a year before, he received an unexpected letter from POW Robinson who wrote, "I just want to leave this hell."

Along with the letter is an imprint of a dog tag and some crushed bones. This was not the first time Peter Gilboy had received information about MIAs or POWs. He had worked on " 'Egress Recap,' a code name for President Nixon's secret program to locate and rescue captured Americans."

Also in the package was information about Robert Penn, Jack W. Reynolds, Marian Dominiak, Edward Chase and Dennis U. Clark.

Peter began his investigation by trying to find the relatives of those men. He went from Vietnam Veterans of San Diego, to Senator Ted Kennedy's office, to Bo Gritz (retired, much decorated Green Beret), to Col. Cliff Stanley at the Pentagon's POW/MIA office.

He wrote, "I am beginning to get a taste for the helplessness the MIA families must feel as they pursue the fragments of their hopes. Everybody warns me against everybody else, and suggests that I speak only with someone on their side. The cast of characters is getting longer, and they are all questionable. Whom to trust? I'm not sure." He even wondered if he could trust the media.

"When you're holding in your hand what is supposed to be human bones with an American's name attached to them, you feel the entire MIA dilemma - - the intrigue, the families' heartbreak and despair."

After talking with Gritz, Peter decided that Gritz was unreliable and not the right person to turn over the information he had.

The person he spoke with at the Pentagon's POW/MIA office said he couldn't deal with anonymous leads. Peter told him he didn't trust that office, either. Then, he spoke with Bob Destatte, the Defense Intelligence Agency contact in the same office.

Destatte told him the information was no doubt bogus. Of the 5,031 reports of sightings their office had received, only 4% were real MIA names. The bag of crushed bones Peter got was either an animal or an Asian, Destatte said. As for the dog tags and other artifacts, soldiers "often left behind some personal effects, perhaps giving dog tags or other items to Vietnamese girlfriends."

He sent the contents of the bag to Destatte so the Central Identification Laboratory in Hawaii could test the bones. He thought the matter was closed.

However, he began to see photographs of reported MIAs who the families recognized, but the government said the photographs were frauds.

Again I quote Peter's article. "Sadly, recent history has taught me to be skeptical and suspicious of my own government. Vietnam, even more than Watergate, marked a turning point in many Americans' relationships to their government. Everyone who lived through it remembers the special circumstances of the war itself.

"It is the only war our country has fought which came to an end because Americans demanded that the government account for its activities or stop them. We felt cheated - - both those who served and those who waited. It was an era of listening to body counts every night on the evening news, and never knowing if our government was giving us the straight scoop.

"And when it ended, lies and deception continued to surface.

"Given this history, skepticism is healthy. But today it is commonplace to automatically assume that the government is untrustworthy. Because I now automatically assume a government cover-up, I must be cautious in another direction. I must question myself, to discover if these are well-founded suspicions or whether they are just fashionable suspicions.

"If this is difficult for me how much more difficult is it for the many MIA families?

"One item in my case is still unresolved for me. Since I was satisfied that all my information was false, I did not follow up with Destatte to learn the status of the bones."

Peter ended his article by saying that when he tried to find out what happened with Walter T. Robinson's letter and the crushed bones, he was given the run-around by Destatte's office, and an Air Force sergeant who was responsible for sending the bones to the Central Identification Laboratory in Hawaii. He was told that the Robinson file had been checked out to Destatte who was not available.

Peter couldn't help but continue to think about the letter that started him on his investigation, and the sentence that said, "I just want to leave this hell."

1996 DEPARTMENT OF DEFENSE AUTHORIZATION BILL

The DOD Authorization Bill for 1996 was signed into law with an "unheralded and virtually unnoticed" Section 569, Determinations of Whereabouts and Status of Missing Persons.

After a twelve-year battle, the DOD could no longer declare the death of a missing American serviceman simply because the individual hadn't been heard from for one year. From 1996 on, the DOD was supposed to explain to the family of an MIA why it is believed that the MIA is dead.

Following are some of the changes made in that bill:

1 – A Missing Person cannot be declared dead simply because one year has passed without any new information about that person.

2 – Constitutional rights denied by the old law are now guaranteed (i.e.: full hearings, legal representation, subpoena, and appeal).

3 – All information pertaining to each individual Missing Person, that is held by any agency of the U.S. Government, must be in or noted in the Missing Person's casualty file.

4 – Classified information, held elsewhere, must be noted in the file, as must the date it was last reviewed for downgrading.

5 – DOD must organize an office to control all Boards of Inquiry for Missing Persons. No longer is it left to the local commander's whim.

6 – All missing persons must have legal representation at all Boards of Inquiry.

7 – All Boards of Inquiry must have a member who is qualified in the same field as the Missing Person.

8 – Boards of Inquiry for persons missing while in a travel status, must have a member qualified in the type of transit in use at the time of the incident.

9 – All members of a Missing Persons immediate family will be invited to all Boards of Inquiry, except the original held in a forward area.

10 – Service personnel can designate someone other than a member of the immediate family, who will also be allowed to attend the hearings.

11 – Civilians who become missing while under military orders shall have their absence explained in the same manner as service personnel.

12 – In this change there is a "grandfathers clause" that will include service personnel missing in the Cold War, Korea, and Vietnam.

Command Sergeant Major, John R. Holland, USA (ret.), President of Americans for Freedom, Always! INC. (AFFA), initiated the fight to get the above changes put into law. Senator Bob Dole, Senator Strom Thurmond, and Congressmen Bob Dornan, John Rowland, Austin Murphy and Ben Gilman were among those who led that effort.

Once considered a "pipe dream," the American Legion, The National Vietnam Veterans Coalition, Veterans of the Vietnam War, VIETNOW, The National Alliance of Families, Rolling Thunder, and many small POW/MIA organizations and individuals supported the "long and tedious fight."[24]

I congratulate them for their hard work and thank them, on behalf of all POW/MIA families, for making it possible for better communications between the government and the families. I'm particularly thankful for items number 9 and 10. The only problem is that it is all so late in coming.

1976 HOUSE COMMITTEE ON POW/MIA

From a copy of a letter I received from Jay Veith on July 27, 1999, I learned that the 1976 House Committee on POW/MIAs was authorized to release all of their files to the public. The files consisted of 35 boxes, 11 of them containing classified material. It took three years to get the House to vote to release the boxes.[25]

What happened to the 1993 declassified information authorization that was supposed to take place?

MAJOR MARK A. SMITH, USA, RETIRED

I wish I had room to include the entire message I read in the Task Force Omega newsletter, "Keeping the Promise," June/July 1999, from Major Mark Smith. Task Force Omega of Southern California's purpose is to create public awareness for the return of our POWs and MIAs.

Major Smith was the first POW released to come home during Operation Homecoming 1973. He filed a suit, Smith v The President during the 80s, hoping to force the administration to accept the fact that Americans were still being held in Southeast Asia. The Supreme Court turned down the suit, saying it was a political issue.

In the seven-page commentary on the POW/MIA situation, Major Smith wrote, "Everything I have said above is documented fact. Are they there? YES! Does our government, including John McCain, know these things? YES! This is where I stand. I do not care what ex-POW comes to his defense. There is no excuse for the callous, arrogant attitude of John toward his fellow soldiers and their families.

"In closing, let me say this with a very heavy heart, I do not believe there is any American of high station, including many of my fellow returned POWs, who are willing to stand in the breach for our missing Americans. I do not believe there is anyone in government who puts in an honorable, honest day's work on the question of live American POWs.

"There are those that feel I have been hard on some of my fellow Americans. In my view, I have ignored their warts and childish behavior concerning everything from live POWs and Smith vs. Reagan, to Private Robert Garwood for too long. I have always felt they were well intentioned, just out of step with the Asian reality.

"I must conclude that the evidence of live American POWs has been constant from the sixties to this day. There is no denying it and the above should provide more than enough proof. . . The last few months have taught me a sad lesson. When dealing with the lives of American POWs and trusted agents/operatives the rule is, no one can be trusted completely. I would like to thank those so-called icons of 'American Patriotism' for teaching me that lesson. I will never forget it. In the end, the families, a few soldiers and a handful of concerned everyday Americans will be the keys to the gulag. Perhaps there is no man on a white horse. Maybe there never really was, but as I look at all those who have participated in this cause down through the years, I continue to hope and pray that the man on the pale steed still lives in Texas."[26]

THE MYTH

I was moved by an H. Bruce Franklin article I read in 1992. Here are several quotes I think are important to consider when we talk about the POW/MIA issue.[27]

- "The POW/MIA myth has had a profound political, cultural, and psychological influence on American society that continues to deepen. . ."

- "Sooner or later the myth that there are still live American POWs in Southeast Asia must fade away."

- "In the final analysis, the POW/MIA myth must be understood not just as a convenient political gimmick for rationalizing various kinds of warfare and jingoism but also as a symptom of a profound psychological sickness in American culture."

- "But the disease can never be cured so long as we fail to confront the true tragedy of the missing in Vietnam. We certainly need a 'full accounting,' but one far more painful than the kind demanded by our government."

1999 POW/MIA STATUS UPDATE

At the beginning of 1999, the National League of Families updated the numbers of missing Americans from the Vietnam War. They reported that 2,072 were still missing and unaccounted for. This figure included 561 in North Vietnam, 984 in South Vietnam, 444 in Laos and 75 in Cambodia.

The League once again stated that its highest priority was to resolve the live prisoner question. The update included information that joint field activities in Laos were allowing greater flexibility for U.S. teams to find remains of Americans. Agreements between the U.S. and Indochina countries at last allowed Vietnamese witnesses to participate in joint operations in Laos and Cambodia, since over 80% of U.S. losses in Laos and 90% in Cambodia occurred in areas where the Vietnamese forces were in control. Previous to this time, the local Vietnamese were threatened not to reveal what they knew about missing or dead Americans.

"The League supports steps by the U.S. to respond to concrete results, not advancing political and economic concessions in the hope that Hanoi will respond."[28]

This same report included statistics provided by the DOD POW/MIA office.[29]

Live Sightings: As of December 21, 1998, 1,896 firsthand live sighting reports in Indochina that have been received since 1975, 1,832 (96.62%) have been resolved (see Chapter 5).

Sixty-seven percent of those, or 1,283, were supposedly now accounted for, such as returned POWs, missionaries or detained civilians.

Five hundred and eleven Americans have been accounted for:

1974-1975 Post war years: 28
1976-1978 US/SRV normalization negotiations: 47
1979-1980 US/SRV talks break down: 1
1981-1984 1st Reagan Administration: 23
1985-1988 2nd Reagan Administration: 155
1989-1992 Bush Administration: 113
1993-1996 1st Clinton Administration: 136
1997-2000 2nd Clinton Administration: 7

By country, the 511 accounted for Americans broke down to:

Vietnam 379
Laos 125
China 2
Cambodia 5

ACCOUNTABILITY FOR MIAs

The Department of Defense used two categories to define missing Americans in Southeast Asia. One category was casualties that were labeled KIA/BNR. Those cases have an "evidence criteria" that strongly suggests the servicemen could not have survived. This designation was given to Jim after he spent 2 ½ years on the MIA list.

The other category was "statutory presumptive finding of death." That means a specified amount of time had passed allowing the government to change the serviceman's MIA status to KIA without having physical evidence.

Whenever remains were returned from Southeast Asia, they were identified against military men in those two categories. The U.S. Code permitted, in those times, "secretaries and/or heads of agencies to declare an individual dead after the person has been missing for 12 months under circumstances indicating he or she may have died. Each case is decided on its own merits and cases may be reopened if sufficient evidence is presented indicating the individual may still be alive, although not physically returned to U.S. control."[30]

More than one case has been noted where live sightings were disregarded, due to this method of accounting, because the American sighted was on the KIA/BNR list. Therefore, the sighting couldn't be authentic.

One U.S. serviceman was declared KIA/BNR after a year, only to be discovered in a Viet Cong prison camp through a letter he smuggled out. His status had to be changed to POW at that point.[31]

Identification of remains has always been a problem. Sometimes all the DOD has to go on are bone fragments or a tooth. On October 5, 1990, four servicemen were buried at Arlington National Cemetery with full military honors. Their caskets were to have held some of their bones which took their names off the unaccounted for list. However, two of their families discovered that the caskets were empty. DOD admitted that there was never any physical matter returned for those men. "This burial charade was based on specious deductive DOD procedures."[32]

The casket for POW Milton James Vescelius, Navy, contained one tooth. As late as 2001, April, a Vietnam MIA was buried in Goleta, California. The only thing in his coffin was a tooth--the upper front left molar found in a dry streambed in 1998. Lt. Col. Roscoe Henry Fobair's tooth was "wrapped in a blanket, fastened to a full-dress Air Force uniform." He had been shot down in 1965, his 55th and last mission before he was due to be shipped home. Along with the tooth, investigators found "zipper tabs from a flight suit, a 1964 penny and remnants of a watch."[33]

I would say that this was a great way to reduce the list of unaccounted for Americans in order to make the DOD look good and to cover the truth for the American public. I have even heard of some caskets that families opened only had bricks or stones in them, airplane parts, and empty uniforms, instead of the remains as they had been told the caskets contained. Shameful! Deceitful!

One identification problem our government ran across was the practice Vietnamese had of warehousing remains for the purpose of bartering. They even had a government official whom we call The Mortician, who was "personally responsible for preserving and storing in excess of 400 remains of American servicemen,"[34] according to his testimony.

It is obvious that many of these remains are still in Hanoi, even if all of the ones that the U.S. has received from the Vietnamese (255) came from The Mortician's 400. "While this policy of doling out remains of U.S. servicemen, one set at a time, in an on-again, off-again fashion, may be repugnant to Americans, it accurately reflects the Vietnamese government's ideology, history, and the repatriation policies of its Communist allies."[35]

The fact that they stored remains was confirmed through forensic examination both by CILHI, and Dr. Michael Charney, a board certified forensic anthropologist.

So many questions flood my mind. Jim was declared KIA/BNR after 2 ½ years as an MIA, but they found no sign of him – not bones, not a tooth, not a piece of his uniform, not a boot, not anything.

On top of this, I have found no other cases that's status was changed prior to the end of the war without any new information after going through two review boards. I've asked numerous other members of POW/MIA families, Army Casualty, and DPMO. None of them knew of another case.

How can I be assured that he really died in that dense Vietnamese jungle?

If Jim was captured and became a POW, has he been one of those live sightings that our government officials have shrugged off because he is on the KIA/BNR list? Or, if he was captured, did he die in one of those camps, somewhere in Southeast Asia or Russia or China? Are his remains one of those that the Vietnamese are holding in Hanoi, preserved and stored? Or did something else happen to Jim?

"The government, in its zest to cross names off the POW/MIA list, has positively identified remains without sufficient scientific evidence and information about POW/MIAs is so highly classified that the people who could act on it never see it."[36]

* * *

"Those who deny freedom to others deserve it not themselves, and under a just God, cannot retain it."

Abraham Lincoln[37]

* * *

PRISONERS OF WAR, Nigel Cawthorne[38]

Orbis Publishing in Great Britain sent Nigel Cawthorne to the U.S. to seek some answers to the complex POW/MIA issue. After Operation Homecoming, many people wondered about the speculation that hundreds of Americans had been left behind. Prisoners of War is the result of that investigation. The book became a part of the series, Eyewitness Nam, produced by Orbis.

"When one American is not worth the effort to be found, we as Americans have lost."[39]

Following are some of the quotes in the book that need no explanation. They say all there is to say about the abandonment of our American men after the Vietnam War ended.

"I will tell you this. . .we are holding tens of tens of American pilots whom we have shot down."

"Taken to police headquarters, she says she repeatdly overheard her guards discussing American prisoners and their problems with them."

"American prisoners have not only been seen alive in Laos, which never negotiated a peace, they have also been seen in Vietnam, which did."

"They were all white and in their forties and a sorry-looking group. They were thin, with long hair and beards, and dressed in pyjamas."

"There was no routine interrogation of refugees – – even of those who had been resettled in the U.S. - - about who or what they had seen."

"It was common knowledge among Hanoi's ruling elite that American servicemen were being held as bargaining chips."

"There were any number of pieces of evidence that these 80 had been alive and in captivity. But the Vietnamese denied all knowledge of them."

"Slowly, the full enormity of the situation dawned on Kissinger. After five years of bargaining, he realized that he had been taken for a ride."

"None of the American servicemen taken prisoner by the Pathet Lao was returned. None of the 566 men missing in Laos was ever accounted for."

"Some were kept naked for months. Their diet consisted of vegetables smeared with human excrement."

"Jane Fonda asked him to cooperate and make a statement condemning the American war effort. He refused. When she left, the guards came in and broke his legs."

"The Vietnam war was the Soviet Union's best chance to get its hands on the latest U.S. weaponry, weaponry that might be used against it some day."

"Watergate was breaking. Vietnam, missing men or no missing men, was old news. The public was not interested in Southeast Asia anymore."

"The families of the MIAs and POWs formed themselves into a pressure group called the National League of Families. This now took up the fight."

"Reagan and his advisers decided that it would be wrong to pay for hostages, as it would appear that the U.S. could be blackmailed."

"She later saw reports that her husband had killed three Vietnamese guards with his bare hands when they had tried to chain him to a desk."

"It wasn't just airmen. There were other players in the secret war, people who should never have been in Laos and who were not even listed as missing until years later."

"The last thing the State Department wanted to hear was that there was someone being held prisoner in Vietnam."

"He concluded that it was impossible to tell whether the shards of bones were even those of a human being, let alone a single individual."

"Our Party and our State are not stupid. We have spent a large amount of money to feed and guard those men, we want to use them to bargain."

"The North Vietnamese accused the U.S. of exploiting the POW issue in order to divert attention from the principal problem - - that of ending the war."

"Every time the U.S. officially decides that there are no more Americans being held in Vietnam, Hanoi releases some bones, or sends back some dog tags or an ID card."

"Witnesses are intimidated by JCRC personnel, embassy staff and CIA operatives. Refugees coming forward with information are accused of lying."

"It would reflect badly on both political parties in the U.S. if the fact that the MIAs had been abandoned for political reasons ever came out."

On page 37 of Prisoners of War, there is a hand written note, showing support from an Alexander Solzhenitsyn. It reads:

"If the government of North Vietnam has difficulty explaining what happened to your brothers, your American POWs who have not yet returned, I can explain this quite clearly on the basis of my own experience in the Gulug Archipelago. There is a law in the Archipelago that those who have been treated the most harshly and who have withstood the most bravely, who have been the most honest, the most courageous, the most unbending, never again come out into the world. They are never again shown to the world because they will tell tales that the human mind can barely accept. Some of your returned POWs told you that they were tortured. This means that those who have remained were tortured even more, but did not yield an inch. These are your foremost heroes who, in a solitary combat, have stood the test. And today, unfortunately, they cannot hear it from their solitary cells where they may either die or remain for thirty years. . ."

"Who gives a shit about the MIAs anyway?" (Reported to have been said by Attorney General Edwin Meese at a 1981 White House meeting.[40])

A long believed fact, by many Americans, is that some of the servicemen missing in action were held by the Vietnamese long after the peace settlement. Still others believe that many of the MIAs were never found because no one looked for them, alive or dead. And another thought by some is that a lot of MIAs were declared KIA by our government to keep the number of missing down to a minimum.

Stories abound from our soldiers, Vietnamese defectors and those who have returned to Vietnam seeking information.[41] Henry A. Kissinger, Secretary of State during President Reagan's two terms in office, maintained a list of 80 men who might have survived but later died in captivity. One belief is that this could have accounted for the high ratio of MIAs to prisoners between 1966-1968.[42]

According to Malcolm McConnell, author of Inside Hanoi's Secret Archives, "Most of the Laos MIA cases dated from the intense bombing of the Ho Chi Minh Trail in 1968 and 1969. . . In fact, of the 354 Americans originally listed as MIA in Laos, the DIA later determined that a 'significant number' should have been listed as KIA/BNR.

One important reason for the government to want the MIA status changed to KIA/BNR is the pay allotments. When a serviceman was declared KIA, his wife and children would receive a one-time payment of death benefits. If he was listed as MIA or POW, his family would continue to receive his pay and allotments and medical privileges until his status changed to KIA/BNR or he was declared PFOD (Presumptive Finding of Death).[43]

President Richard Nixon, on January 23, 1973, promised that all of the American POWs would be released and that there would be "the fullest possible accounting for all those who are missing-in-action (MIAs)." In Monika Jensen-Stevenson and William Stevenson's book, Kiss The Boys Goodbye, Monika says that her "60 Minutes" report at Christmas, 1985, stirred up "a hornet's nest." She states in the book, "In many cases, I found later, their capture (MIAs) and imprisonment was monitored by U.S. intelligence."[44] A great American scandal had been uncovered on a large, powerful news network.

Congressman Sonny Montgomery, D-Miss, a decorated war veteran, formed the House Select Committee on Missing Persons in Southeast Asia. Angry and frustrated veterans and MIA families were largely responsible for this. Secretary Kissinger suggested to Montgomery that his committee members discuss the issue with the Vietnamese 'in the context of normalization' rather than in terms of the Paris Peace Accords.[45]

The committee sent delegations to meet with Vietnamese and Laotian Communist officials in 1975 and 1976. Nothing much came from the Montgomery Committee except that Congressman Montgomery concluded there were no American survivors in Southeast Asia.[46]

This remained the general conclusion for the next twenty years. The MIA situation was a stalemate. Attempts to discover what happened to our MIAs were doomed to failure. Until 1991, the DIA's investigation of the MIA issue remained unchanged. The DIA continued to be indifferent to the MIA familys' needs and to continue their mind–set of not validating any intelligence on live sightings.

At this point, a new committee, the Senate Select Committee on POW/MIA Affairs, was established through the efforts of Senator Bob Smith R-NH. Pressure from the general public was building (69% of the people surveyed in a Wall Street Journal/NBC News poll believed that POWs were still being held in Indochina). President George H. W. Bush's administration was under a good deal of pressure to seek some kind of breakthrough before the 1992 election. The DIA, charged to resolve the MIA mystery, did no such thing. Instead, the DIA continued business as usual.[47] Nothing! Or rather I should say, they continued to prey on the MIA families, as any disreputable con men would do.[48]

In March of 1991, Army Col. Millard A. "Mike" Peck, resigned as chief of the DIA's Special Office for POW/MIAs after only seven months. Among his reasons for giving up the position were his accusations of "gross misconduct, including a possible cover-up among the government officials who had managed the MIA issue for the past twenty years. He also accused Ann Mills Griffiths, Executive Director of the National League of Families of American Prisoners and Missing in Southeast Asia, of blatant interference in the intelligence process."[49] Mike Peck's memo stated that there were "'unscrupulous people in the government, or associated with the government' who manipulated the entire POW/MIA issue for 'personal or political advantage.'"[50]

In January, 1987, Jerry Mooney, U.S. intelligence analyst who broke his silence after 20 years, went public in a television documentary, "We Can Keep You Forever: The Story of the MIAs" in association with the BBC. He waited for the devastating story to break, but instead a blanket of government denials erupted, killing the story. As a result, Mooney decided that he would tell everything he knew--to heck with secrecy and possible prosecution. As quoted in the Los Angeles Times Magazine article, "On The Trail of the MIAs," by Edward Tivan, October 27, 1991, Mooney said, "For the government to say 'we have no evidence' about POWs and MIAs is absurd."

There remained no possibility of access to MIA information until Senator Bob Smith's Senate Select Committee was formed in 1992. Even then, the executive branch of government continued to resist giving intelligence data on POW/MIAs to the Senate.

What is interesting is that for the first time in the history of U.S. wars, the status of KIA/BNR has been changed back to MIA for one of our Americans.

Lt. Cdr. Michael Speicher was shot down in an F-18 fighter in the 1991 Gulf War, and he was declared MIA. The Pentagon decided, within 48 hours of when he was shot down, that he would be carried as KIA/BNR.[51]

Senator Bob Smith (R-NH) spearheaded the challenge to the Pentagon, for there seemed to be enough evidence to suspect that Speicher had survived the crash and had been captured by the Iraqi government. Both Senator Smith and Senator Rod Grams (R-Minn.) convinced Navy Secretary Richard Danzig to change Speicher's status back to MIA.[52]

So, on January 10, 2001, days before the end of the Clinton presidency, that is what happened. A great victory for all those who have fought so long to keep the government from presuming that a serviceman was KIA/BNR, instead of keeping his MIA status until proven otherwise.

A "60 Minutes II" TV show on September 19, 2000, explained a lot more about the Michael Speicher story. According to "60 Minutes II," Speicher was declared dead without anyone checking to see if that were true. The file was "closed and forgotten." No one even bothered to look for the F-18. That was because the Iraqi government said they were doing everything possible to find the pilot of the downed aircraft.

But they didn't. And when they returned POWs at the end of the Gulf War, Michael Speicher was not among them.

Treating MIAs, as they had during the Vietnam War, the government, of course, declared Speicher KIA and had his wife sign-off on him, even though there was no evidence of his being dead. Then, the Pentagon wouldn't talk about it.

The F-18, according to "60 Minutes II," was discovered three years later, but no one looked for the pilot for two more years. Why was the Navy so reluctant to look for their fallen comrade, the show asked? Why did the DOD "finally acknowledge, grudgingly" the possibility that Speicher could be a POW--could still be alive? Why did they want to keep him listed as KIA all those years when they had no evidence to substantiate that? It wasn't because, through those years, there were no volunteers among his Navy buddies who wanted to go look for him in Iraq.

* * *

". . .Hanoi has given the Americans fake cake on the MIA issue by not returning even one MIA. Conversely, the Americans still patiently promise everything and give everything - - fake cake, including Most Favored Nation fake cake!. . ."[53]

POEM
(Author Unknown)

While the others were sitting at home, I was in Vietnam.

While the others were washing their cars, I was cleaning my weapon of death, my M-16.

While the others were talking to their girl on the phone, I was calling for dust-off choppers and air strikes on the radio.

While the others were sitting with their families at the dinner table, I was eating C-rations from a can deep in the jungle.

While the others were at the movies watching the big screen with their girl, I was watching the red and green tracers of death.

While the others were shouting for a stop to the war and burning the flag, I was screaming for the medic.

While the others were sleeping in their warm soft beds at night, I was huddled under my poncho in the rain with the bugs in the jungle.

While the others were out for a walk on the beach, I was walking point looking for the enemy.

While the others were killing time just hanging out, I was killing people, the enemy.

While the others were deciding what college to attend, I was trying to get an R & R.

While the others were having a snack late at night, I was checking my men, the claymores and the wire.

While the others were taking out their trash bags, I was putting brave young dead soldiers into body bags to send home to their loved ones.

While the others were hoping their girlfriends would keep their date that Friday night, I was hoping just to survive the night.

Now you know why I'm different, set apart from the others.

PART II

Reawakening

"Never before in the history of mankind has any nation done what we are doing. The effort of JTF-FA to honor the U.S. commitment to our unaccounted for comrades, their families, and the nation is unprecedented."

Pete Peterson

The nightmares I was having in 1988, plus the fact that my son David was considering joining ROTC in college, led me back to the National League of Families meetings after fifteen years. It was time for David to go with me to a League meeting so he could experience, firsthand, the way the government works regarding its commitment to its service personnel.

I hadn't attended a National League meeting for years. David went with me so we could ask questions about the dog tag sighting document I had received and he could see all the craziness about the POW/MIA situation that was going on in our country.

The days were packed with government briefings by the DIA, CILHI, DOD, JTF-FA and so on. Family members were being filled with propaganda, which is the way I perceived the information. But, what startled me the most was that the press was allowed into the meetings. They actually had a platform in the back of the room where their cameras rolled as long as the government people were making their presentations. When the quorum was opened to questions, the press had to leave. I could not figure out what the deal was. I was really baffled.

I finally found someone to ask who had been attending the meetings for years. She told me that the questions would be controversial and the government didn't want the world to see this. They wanted to be portrayed as doing everything possible to get resolution to this issue. My immediate thought was how weird! These weren't classified briefings. Why wasn't the press angry about being thrown out?

One of the panel members that day was a man by the name of Bill Bell. He was retired military and had a job with the DOD, working out of the embassy in Bangkok for an agency named Stony Beach. Their mission was to go to Vietnam, and with the approval of the Vietnamese government, to follow up on live sighting reports of Americans who had not yet been found or who had not yet been turned over to the United States. They also questioned the Vietnamese refugees, as they exited the Republic of Vietnam (RVN), about our missing men.

In 1988, there wasn't much going on with information gathering. We didn't have diplomatic relations with Vietnam so Americans couldn't travel there, legally. As Bill Bell made his presentation at the League meeting, he talked about interviewing many of the refugees coming out of Vietnam who might have information that could be pertinent to the Stony Beach cases, specifically those Americans last known to be alive. A lot of these people were ex-military who wanted to settle in the States.

After the panel's presentation, and the question and answer session had finished, several people approached the head tables to ask questions, one-on-

one, with specific panel members. I kept to the back of the line of folks who wanted a word with Bill, as I was a little intimidated by what was going on.

When it was my turn, I said, "My name is Barbara Birchim."

Before I could say anything else, Bill Bell said, "Yes, your husband's name is Jim Birchim," and he proceeded to tell me the whole story of how Jim became an MIA.

My mouth fell open in shock. I asked him how could he remember that, and why would he know Jim's story in the first place.

"Oh, I remember your husband very well."

How odd! In fact, I was flabbergasted.

After I mumbled a few "Uh. . . uh. . .uh," noises, I said, "How do you go about interrogating these refugees? I mean, do you have a room where you put all these pictures of the lost men up, you know, and do you march the refugees through the gallery, and ask them if they remember any of those faces?"

"No, no," he said. "As they come out, we ask them if they have any information. If so, we write the information down and we call it a dog tag sighting."

With that statement, I got the answer to the question David and I had come to Washington D.C. for.

"Originally, people gave us dog tags and so we called that a dog tag sighting. Now, we call any information we get a dog tag sighting. You know, like I saw this American on the corner, or working in the field, or my mother has an American body in a jar out on the porch, and we want to give it to you. Things like that."

"Wow!" I was still very curious about how he could recall Jim's case on the spur of the moment.

"Well," Bell said, " He's the only man who was declared missing in action on that particular day. And he's the only man who had that kind of an incident. Most of the MIAs are pilots or they're people on the ground. I believe Jim is the only MIA who had been hanging on a rig and fell off."

Okay.

"Your husband's case is very unique and that's why I remember it."

I must say I got a feeling from his demeanor that he was being quite CIA-ish. And I only say that because my vision of the CIA is of very cold, calculating, chain smoking, no expression, always looking around, 'I have my space, don't invade it' types of men. That was Bill Bell.

On my first trip to Vietnam, who should I bump into in Hue but Bill Bell. He and some other men came walking into the little hotel our tour group was staying in. He still looked like the CIA. But that story comes later.

Chapter Four

Seeking Closure

"Nothing in Vietnam is ever straight forward or simple."
Ted Schweitzer 1994[1]

I made a promise to Jim that, when the children were old enough to be on their own, I would go to Vietnam. By 1989, I was ready to fulfill that promise.

I just knew that everything would be fine and that the bad dreams I was having at that time would go away, once I got to Vietnam. I wasn't searching for answers at that time. I only wanted to see what the country was like, and to find the place where the reports said Jim had disappeared.

While I was preparing myself for the task of finding a way to get to Vietnam, since United States citizens weren't allowed to travel there from the U.S., I became aware of numerous articles in newspapers and magazines about Vietnam. Some of the headlines were:

> "American POWs Reportedly Sighted in Vietnam"
> "U.S. to Study Monk's Stories of American POWs in Vietnam"
> "700 Americans Are Still Rotting in Vietnam Prisons"
> "Mujahids to Negotiate Recovery of Americans"
> "Five Forgotten Heroes"
> "Hendon Initiates New Plan For Release of POWs"
> "Freed Vietnam Captive Reports Seeing U.S. POWs"
> "The Men They Left Behind"
> "Americans, Soviets, Mujahideen Trying to Cook 3-way POW Deal"

What was that all about? My curiosity became aroused.

I found that, as an American, I would be able to visit Vietnam if I joined an Australian tour group. So, I set that possibility in motion.

I flew into Bangkok to meet the group. There were several other Americans, too. Our itinerary called for us to go to Vientiane, Laos, as our first stop. When we gathered in the Bangkok airport, our luggage was piled in the middle of the floor in a circle. Our tour guide was supposed to have told the airline officials that our luggage needed to get on the plane with us.

As it turned out, the bags never arrived in Vientiane. Bags for 24 tourists remained in the middle of the Bangkok airport. It seems no one was curious about why the bags were there, stacked in a circle with nobody attending them. That sure wouldn't happen today!

At that time, there were only a few flights a week to the places on our itinerary. So, the airline officials said they would put the bags on the first flight out of Bangkok for Hanoi since there were no other flights to Laos before our departure for Hanoi.

That meant we had to go to the local marketplace and try to find things like toothbrushes to hold us over till we reached Hanoi. Although it was inconvenient, I didn't mind too much because I'd carried my camera, film, medications and toiletries with me.

As it turned out, our bags were never sent to Hanoi or to Da Nang. We didn't see them again until we arrived in Saigon nine days later.

I'll tell you, the members of our tour group were furious. We had nothing to wear. All of us dressed for the hot Bangkok weather, but when we arrived in Vietnam, we were freezing since Bangkok is so much closer to the equator than Hanoi. We tried to buy clothes in every marketplace we came to, but the Vietnamese people are small compared to the Australians and Americans. A retired National Airline pilot in our group was 6'4". He was carrying a little weight, too. He didn't let this inconvenience bother him, like it bothered some of the others, because he was a seasoned traveler.

We were quite a sight--a motley crew. All of us ended up with a lot of souvenir T-shirts to take home. Everyday, at breakfast, I'd say to the 24 bedraggled men and women, "Okay, who needs medicine?" Everyone needed malaria pills. I'd say things like, "Betty, you owe me five. George, I've got you down for two," and on down the line. I kept track of who was borrowing medication so that they could repay me when we finally got our luggage.

Before I went on the trip, I was given the name of a lady who had been in Vietnam as a missionary, and who was interested in POWs. When I spoke to her, she mentioned she had passed out leaflets on the sly when she was there.

I said, "Well, gosh, I guess I could do that, too."

"It's very risky. You can't let the Vietnamese know you're doing it." Then she went into a long explanation about how she distributed the leaflets.

So I had some stickers made with a reward message on them. Anyone who responded to my message would be eligible for reward money if they brought out a live American prisoner of war. Some congressmen and businessmen generated the reward money. They had put together 4.5 million dollars in an account hoping that at least one live American would be returned.

I had the message translated into Vietnamese and Laotian. The stickers looked sort of like return address labels. They were a size that I could stick on the local money. That way, whoever found the money, could still use it by pealing off the sticker. I hoped they'd read and maybe act on my message before they threw the sticker away.

While we were in Vientiane, I went outside our hotel, walked across the street, and pretended my shoelace was untied. I put some of the money with stickers in the bushes. I folded the money so no one could see the sticker, and then found places where I could leave the money so it would not be found until our group was gone. I did the same kind of thing all the way through Vietnam.

When we visited the temples and pagodas, I sort of lagged behind, and would stick one of the bundles of money behind a Buddha. Or in a collection plate. I even left them under trashcans in what they called the "Ladies Room." I didn't leave any in my hotel rooms because I was scared to death of getting caught with them.

And that was the beginning of my counterinsurgency. Or, whatever you'd call my scheme.

Only once did I almost get caught. I was in the Bangkok airport when a Thai security woman stopped me as I went through the metal detector. She indicated, by hitting me in the stomach, that she wanted to know what was in my money belt. I knew I didn't have any metal in the money belt, but I did have the stickers.

Oh shit! What was I going to do? I was wearing a skirt, so in between the woman's pats on my stomach, I reached in the top of the skirt, unzipped the money belt, and pulled out one of the Laotian stickers.

I hoped she couldn't read Lao and so she wouldn't know what the sticker said. "Stickers. . .that's all I have in here. . .stickers," I said.

She looked at the piece of paper like what the hell is this? The people in line behind me were getting quite impatient, so I suppose she decided this tourist was crazy to be carrying paper in her money belt instead of cash. She let me go.

Meanwhile, another customs inspector was going through my carryon and pulling out the $1,200 in cash I had. As he waved the money for all to see, and jabbered Thai to his cohorts, I'm sure he thought I was a nutty tourist.

That made me feel like a fool. The last thing I wanted was for everyone around me to know how much cash I had with me.

When I joined the Australian tour group, I was up front about my husband being an MIA. When the tour leader gathered us together in Bangkok to lay the ground rules before we took off on our trip, I got her aside.

"Look, my husband's an MIA, and I want to ask questions, if that's okay. If it's not, if it's going to get everybody in trouble, I won't do it. You have to tell me when it's okay."

"I don't see anything wrong with that," she said.

So, what I did was talk with local people as we walked through the marketplace, if I could find someone with a little knowledge of English. I would say, "You know, I was wondering if you could tell me where I might find an American who stayed here after the war, took a Vietnamese wife, and had a family. Because, I'd love to say hi and tell them who's winning the baseball games."

I'd make up all kinds of statements like that to try to get someone's attention, and to show that I was just a tourist, not part of the government.

Almost every time, the person's response was, "We can't talk about the Americans." And that was that.

I noticed, though, each person would seem to break out in a sweat, turn around and leave, or shake his head no, no, no.

When I spoke with villagers in remote areas, I couldn't help but wonder how they all seemed to be aware of Americans. Often, the villagers seemed afraid of my questions. I later discovered there were always undercover government people watching the villagers I spoke with, and those villagers would get a visit from the agents afterwards, asking what they had said to me.

Oh, my God, was my reaction after talking with a few of the villagers! There really were Americans alive in Vietnam. In my naivete, I decided that if I brought back this information to Washington D.C., the government would jump on the bandwagon and take care of the situation. Truly those were my thoughts.

Once in awhile, as our bus traveled through the countryside, I would see someone who looked like a Caucasian. I wish I could have pulled a cord and made the bus stop so I could talk with the Caucasian. Of course, the person could have been from any one of a number of different countries, not just the U.S. Each one I saw looked like he lived there as he worked the fields. In other words, he didn't look to be under guard like a prisoner would.

The only reaction I ever got from the light-skinned men I noticed as our bus passed by, was one man who saw me and seemed to have a startled look on his face. But then, that was understandable, I suppose, since Vietnam didn't let too many tour groups in the country at that time. And, of course, no American tourists.

I was given a map of Vietnam by one of the tourists in our group. I found Kontum and the tri-border area, which was where Jim was last seen. My plan was to try to get to Kontum, if at all possible. Kontum is in the Bla River valley, east of Dak To.

From the information I found in Jim's papers, I noted Dak To and Dak Sut by putting arrows on the map. Dak To was a heavily entrenched Special Forces base near the Laos border. Dak Sut is just north of Dak To, minutes away from both Laos and Dak To, if you are flying.

During the war, Kontum was the headquarters for what they called CCC, or Command and Control Central. CCC worked Laos and Cambodia as opposed to CCN, which worked North Vietnam, the DMZ, and Laos. CCS worked Cambodia and South Vietnam.

Kontum is south of Dak To by quite a ways. Dak To was considered part of CCC. Some pilots had told me that sometimes they would fly from Kontum to Dak To to refuel before they'd run their missions across the border.

In other words, the story in Jim's file made no sense when the reports said the plane had flown for such a long time. Why didn't the helicopter pilot land in Dak To? Better yet, why didn't the pilot land at a nearby clearing and get those guys inside the aircraft ASAP?

Also, the reports about Jim's disappearance said they had flown at an altitude of 2500'–8000', depending upon which document I read. The question in my mind was whether the report meant an altimeter setting or were they talking about the number of feet above the ground?

When I studied my typography map, the elevations on the line of flight were such that the helicopter would have been flying at 1000' underground in some locations. Those guys really needed to get their stuff together.

The town of Hue (pronounced Way), north of both Kontum and Da Nang, was where heavy fighting and heavy American losses took place during the war. Hue is the last Imperial capital of Vietnam, and the center of Vietnamese culture, with lotus ponds, temples, magnificent tombs, and the Thein Mu Pagoda.

While we were in Hue, I bumped into Bill Bell in our hotel restaurant. I had met Bell for the first time during the previous summer's National League of Families meeting. Bell worked for the DIA in Vietnam at the time, was a former infantry reconnaissance NCO, and a "member of roving intelligence teams with multiple tours of combat duty in Vietnam."[2] The long war, and Vietnam's continuing importance after the end of the fighting, became the basis for Bell's future career. He was fluent in the Vietnamese language so he became important as a translator during the exchange of prisoners in 1973. He had "a near-encyclopaedic knowledge of the most troubling MIA cases..."[3]

I couldn't believe it when Bell walked into that dining room with several other men. He was wearing civilian clothes and a serious look on his face. I'm sure my surprise showed. He looked at me and said, "Well, Barbara, what are you doing here?"

I explained that I had made a promise to myself, twenty years before, that I would come to this country to see what it was like. I asked Bell if he was on a tour, too.

"No," he said. "We've come down from the North. We've traveled from Hanoi. They've allowed us to go this far south, and we're trying to get access to certain other areas."

"Oh, really? I'm hoping to get to Kontum."

He said, "Well, I'm going to be meeting with the minister of that province. Would you like me to ask if you can travel there?"

As soon as he asked me that question, in walked the provincial minister. Because Bell was fluent in Vietnamese and some of the Hmong dialects, he was able to plead my case to the provincial minister. I watched, without understanding, as the two spoke. But the expression on the minister's face told me he was surprised a woman would go to such great lengths to find her husband in Vietnam.

According to Bell, the minister said, "Yes, that's fine. I'll make way. . .I'll make it possible so she can go."

I thanked the minister with a smile and a nod, and off he went. As this conversation was taking place, in walked four or five of Bell's compadres on this foray. I would say they were all in their mid-twenties. They sat down at the end of a long table next to the small, square table at which Bell and I sat.

When they were settled, Bell said, "I'd like you to meet Barbara Birchim. Her husband's name was Jim . . .Jim Birchim."

One of the young men spoke up. "Oh, yeah. He was the Special Forces guy who was hanging on the rig. Yeah, he's one of us. He's one of the good guys."

He used Jim's name in the present tense? Alarm bells went off in my head.

By this time, my tour group started to gather at their table to eat, and they said to me, "C'mon, we've gotta eat. Forget this stuff."

This whole incident took me off guard. Bell leaned over to me, as I began to excuse myself, and looked me square in the eyes. That was something he was not prone to do. Most of the time, Bell swept his eyes around a room, from here to there to here, and back again. He said, "If I were you, I'd want to go to Kontum, too."

Just like that. . .with no expression on his face or in his voice. From his body language, and his remarkable knowledge of Jim's case, I supposed that he was telling me I would find some answers in Kontum, but he couldn't tell me what they were.

Holy mackerel! At that moment, I determined to take advantage of what the minister said and go to Kontum. I would arrange my travel in Da Nang.

As an aside, I found many years later, in an unclassified confidential document, a report about my meeting with Bill Bell. It's dated 2/17/89, and titled "General Report Concerning Joint Search/Investigation Activities Conducted by Team Four During the 12–26 Jan 89." It was concerning JCRC Liaison Bangkok and was sent, among others, to

"WHITEHOUSE WASHDC"
"SECSTATE WASHDC"
"SECDEF WASHDC"
"JCS WASHDC"
"DIA WASHINGTON DC"
"USCINCPAC HONOLULU HI"
"CDRUSACILHI FT SHAFTER HI"

On page 5, it reads, "IN HUE CITY THE TEAM WAS BILLETED AT THE HUONG GIANG HOTEL FOR ONE NIGHT BUT THEN MOVED TO A SMALL GUEST HOUSE WHEN THE HOTEL BECAME FULLY BOOKED DUE TO DELEGATIONS AND TOUR GROUPS FROM THE US. THE FACT THAT THE TEAM WAS ABLE TO SPEND ONE NIGHT AT THE HOTEL WAS PROBABLY DUE TO A PREVIOUS PLEDGE BY BINH TRI THIEN PROVINCE CHIEF OF STAFF NGUYEN MINH KY DURING THE PREVIOUS EFFORT THAT THE TEAM WOULD NEXT MEET WITH HIM AT THE HUONG GIANG HOTEL RESTAURANT ON THE NIGHT OF THEIR ARRIVAL. SINCE THE HOTEL WAS CROWDED WITH TOURISTS AND MEMBERS OF DELEGATIONS FROM THE US INCLUDING ONE GROUP OF VETERANS AND ANOTHER GROUP OF PUBLIC HEALTH PERSONNEL FROM BOSTON, MASS, KY DECIDED TO TAKE THE TEAM OUT ON THE TOWN. ACTUALLY, KY TOOK THE TEAM AROUND THE CORNER TO A NIGHT CLUB WHICH WAS A PART OF THE HOTEL AND PROBABLY SUBORDINATE TO THE PROVINCE CULTURAL OFFICE. THE TEAM HAS SEEN SIMILAR 'CULTURAL' ARRANGEMENTS IN OTHER CITIES WHERE HOTELS OR LARGE GUEST HOUSES ARE LOCATED. THESE ARE APPARENTLY DESIGNED TO GIVE FOREIGN VISITORS THE IMPRESSION THEY ARE ACTUALLY GOING OUT TO A PRIVATE ESTABLISHMENT AND MEETING WITH ORDINARY VIETNAMESE CITIZENS, WHEN IN FACT ACCESS TO THE FACILITY IS CLOSELY CONTROLLED AND ALL EMPLOYEES OR 'GUESTS' WHO HAVE CONTACT WITH FOREIGNERS ARE SCREENED IN ADVANCE. WHILE AT THE HOTEL MEETING WITH KY, THE TEAM WAS

APPROACHED BY MRS. BARBARA BIRCHIM, THE WIFE OF 1LT JAMES D. BIRCHIM (REFNO 1322). MRS. BIRCHIM SAID SHE WAS IN COUNTRY AS PART OF AN AUSTRALIAN TOUR GROUP AND ASKED FOR ASSISTANCE IN GAINING SRV APPROVAL FOR HER TO VISIT KONTUM WHERE HER HUSBAND WAS LOST. THE TEAM CHIEF COMMENDED HER FOR HER SPIRIT AND REFERRED HER TO MR. KY SINCE HE WAS A MEMBER OF THE PROVINCE PEOPLE'S COMMITTEE. MR. KY SAID HE WOULD ARRANGE FOR HER TO MEET WITH THE FOREIGN AFFAIRS OFFICE THE FOLLOWING DAY. THE TEAM DID NOT SEE HER AGAIN, AND THE OUTCOME OF HER EFFORTS IS UNKNOWN."

In a way, I should feel honored that my unexpected meeting with Bill Bell was important enough to be sent to the White House. But I'm not. As far as I can tell, that was the beginning of "their" keeping track of me all through the nineties and into the 21st century.

Back to my story.

In order to change my travel plans, and get to Kontum, I had to go through either Saigon Travel Agency or Vietnam Travel. They were the only travel agencies in Vietnam and both were run and controlled by the government in 1989.

I knew that our itinerary included a full day and a half of extra time in Da Nang, so I told the guide in Hue that I wanted to take that time to go to Kontum. I would connect with the group when they arrived in Saigon. They were going to take a side trip before they flew to Saigon, and I thought that would give me time to get to Kontum, to see the area, and to connect back with them before our departure to Cambodia, which I didn't want to miss.

"No, you can't do that," was the guide's response. "You have to arrange that when you get back to Da Nang."

I said, "Okay."

Da Nang is the third largest city in Vietnam, famous for Marble Mountain and its grotto. When we got to Da Nang, I went to the travel agency's office and told them what I wanted to do.

"No, can't do it from here. Have to arrange it from Saigon."

Since Saigon is in the southernmost part of Vietnam, I tried to convince the government travel agency in Da Nang that once I got to Saigon, I would have to spend a lot more time and money to travel all the way back north to go to Kontum. They continued to say that an adjustment in my itinerary had to be made in Saigon. It couldn't be made in Da Nang. I later discovered, when our tour group reached Saigon, that the trip would cost $2300 cash, U.S. dollars only. I'd have to extend my travel visa and the time off from my job. I didn't have the cash and they didn't take travelers checks or credit cards. Besides, my boss had been gracious enough to give me three weeks off as it was.

In Saigon, I said, " No, I can't do that. I'll tell you what. I'll come back next year."

"Okay, no problem," the travel agent said.

"Just make sure when I return that you book that trip for me," I added.

So, at that point, I had no doubt that I could travel to Kontum without any trouble. I'd gotten permission from the provincial minister, and confirmation from the travel agent.

It wasn't until we reached Saigon that our bags caught up with us. It was like Christmas that day. We were little kids opening our suitcases and discovering all the clean clothes we'd packed for our trip.

I had stuffed my suitcase with granola bars, crackers with peanut butter, and a whole lot of changes of clothes. It was amazing that we had been through two-thirds of our trip before we got our things. And amazing, too, was the fact that we realized we didn't need all those things.

Off to Cambodia we went.

Cambodia has been famous for over 1000 years for its temples at Angkor Wat, the most impressive man-made ruins on earth, one of the wonders of the world.

We had been told, the night before we left for Angkor Wat, that Pol Pot's infamous Khmer Rouge were within several miles of the main temple there. "We're not sure you'll be able to go there," was the comment.

But, we got up the next morning at 5:00 for a 6:30 flight, and called ahead to see if we could get into the Siem Reap airport. They said we could.

Before we even got off the plane, our guide told us that we would be leaving the airport at 2:15, after visiting Angkor Wat. If we were late, the bus back to the airport would not wait for us. It was too dangerous. The guide really put the fear of God in us.

The Cambodian military was everywhere. We were instructed to stay with our guide, and we were not to wander anywhere on our own. The Khmer Rouge was about five kilometers from our destination.

I guess danger was indeed there, for during the tour of the temple, one of the ladies in our group jumped off a ledge and took several steps backwards in order to take a picture of the carvings and bas reliefs on the walls.

The guide, walking ahead of us, turned and went crazy! He yelled in Cambodian and waved his hands while pointing in a certain direction.

"Betty, don't move," I said. "I have a funny feeling that he's telling you there are land mines out there."

She froze.

I said, "Put your foot in the same print that you made getting out there. Do not make a new trail."

Several of the men in the group helped pull her back onto the ledge.

The guide had taken us outside of the main entry in Angkor Wat, figuring we'd follow him in a perfect line, I guess. He didn't count on an American tourist picture taker.

The next day, we were taken to Toul Sleng, the school that Pol Pot had used for interrogating, torturing, and killing his own people. What a horrific sight!

From there, we visited the "killing fields." The enormity of that genocide is incomprehensible! And we knew that Pol Pot was still alive, and active in the area around Angkor Wat.

When we returned to Bangkok, the Australian members of our tour group went home, and I came back to America.

I must admit, at this point in my story that all the emotions from the first few years of Jim being missing came flooding back. I had not heard anything from the government since 1974, but now, almost twenty years later, I had once again become confused, angry, and disillusioned. I began to feel that maybe I betrayed Jim by not working on the issue during those years I spent raising the children, and trying to keep my life together.

I didn't discover that Jim was alive when I was in Vietnam, but I did discover that the issue was not dead. The more I learned, the more curious I became once again after the government started the paper flow.

The shock of finding evidence that Americans were left behind in Vietnam was the hardest for me to handle. How dumb could I have been to believe my government!

My Return Home

Not long after I returned to the States, The National League of Families held a regional meeting at Fort Huachuca in Arizona. I decided that I would go so I could share my photos from my trip, and tell people about my reactions to Vietnam. I had no thoughts of going back at that point, even though I'd told the travel agent in Vietnam that I would. So, I didn't fear the possibility of repercussions as a result of what I planned to say at the meeting.

Forty-fifty people attended that meeting, plus a lot of folks representing the various government agencies who were involved in the Vietnam "issue."

During the first break, I found the moderator and told her that I had just returned from Vietnam, and I wondered if she could mention that to the audience in case anyone was interested in looking at my pictures. She was quite receptive to the idea, and asked if I would say a few words about my trip. That was just what I'd hoped would happen.

The briefings ended 30 minutes earlier than scheduled, so the moderator went to the podium and introduced me. At this point, I thought the military and government personnel were leaving the room. Because of the bright lights in front of me, I couldn't see the back of the room where they had lined the walls in the darkness.

As I stood at the microphone, I told the audience about my trip and invited them to take a look at my pictures. Then I hit my punch line. I spoke of my encounter with Bill Bell. And my reaction to our meeting. I also told them of the villager's reactions to my questions about Americans.

The audience seemed glued to my words. What I said was short and sweet. "The Americans are there. They are alive. And even the villagers know about it."

When I stepped down from the platform, a woman came rushing toward me. She introduced herself. "Sara Bernasconi," she said as she grabbed me and took me aside. "What's wrong with you?"

I could tell she was wondering who this bumbling nutcase named Barbara Birchim was.

Sara, who became my best friend, told me later, "Barbara, if you could have seen all those government guys! Their antennae went up so fast. They were glued to every word you said about your meeting with Bill Bell."

For years, Sara had been going to the League meetings, and she'd seen all of the propaganda stuff that was going on. She was also following up on a lot of information she'd been given that made her think maybe her husband had survived his plane crash in Vietnam. She knew a lot of cover-ups were being perpetrated year after year. I was brand new to that kind of skullduggery.

It seems there were ramifications resulting from my opening my big mouth, including the beginning of the government keeping an eye on me.

I still had not decided for sure that I would return to Vietnam the next year, so I didn't care if my passport would be flagged as a result of the things I said. The farthest thing from my mind was that my words about Bill Bell might get him into trouble. As I look back on it, I can't help but wonder if my words helped seal his fate.

Not long after this League meeting, Bell was forced out of his government position, which led to his retirement.

* * *

SARA

As I stated earlier, I met Sara at The League of Families meeting at Fort Huachuca in 1989, after I returned from Vietnam.

Sara had been married to Air Force Major Tommy Gist, who was a navigator in an RF4C when it was shot down off the coast of Dong Hoi, North Vietnam.

Terry Uyeyama, the pilot, ejected over the water and was floating in a flotation device when some Vietnamese paddled out in a sampan to pick him up. His injuries were severe, but he remembers one of the very first guards trying to communicate with him. When Terry would ask about where the other American was, the guard would draw his finger across his throat. As an American of Japanese descent captured by the North Vietnamese, Terry withstood horrible treatment by his captors for 5 1/2 years. He never heard anything about what happened to Tommy, his backseater, while in captivity.

The Vietnamese have told several different stories about Tommy's whereabouts, however. The first story was that the plane burned up so there was no body. Another was that the plane went down just off shore, and they buried Tommy on the beach. But, when Sara received Tommy's ID card in pristine condition in 1991, the story changed again.

Through the years, Sara and I have had some enlightening conversations. We've cried together, we've gotten angry together, we've tried to help each other with our particular MIA issues.

Some of our talks revealed these words from Sara that are worth sharing.

"There is no blueprint or handbook to tell us (wives of MIAs) what to do or feel. . .no maps on how to navigate.

"There were times when I thought I should share what Tommy was going through. How could I be comfortable when he was suffering? I'm sure this is something all family members experience at one time, like not buying a new car because the husband/father/brother/son was living as a captured war criminal in Vietnam under terrible circumstances. What right did someone have to be happy and buy nice things when the loved one was suffering.

"I'm not content with my feelings, even now. . .I guess the thing that feels right for me is to think that Tommy is alive. Beyond that, this whole miserable thing doesn't feel right until I can make it concrete in my life."

Those of us who are POW/MIA family members have been asked to bear our burden graciously. For the most part, the wives have done this. And so have the children. It's just too bad that the accounting of our servicemen have to be at the whims of politics.

It's hard enough to lose your husband, and it's bad enough to be lied to by the government, but the continual lying that goes on makes it so bad that it affects every part of one's life.

And to put that burden on my kids isn't fair, for they are naïve to the fact that they may have to experience this one of these days. I don't think it's right.

When your children are kids, you have to warn them not to touch the hot iron because it's going to burn them. And not looking both ways when crossing the street means a car might hit them. But the odds of being untouched by all of the government's lies and deceit, in the scheme of things, is very remote for the kids of Vietnam War POW/MIAs.

It's disgusting that POW/MIA families have had to live this way. . .with this distress.

You know, there's a tremendous turf battle going on between Stony Beach intelligence and DPMO. Stony Beach is the intelligence branch of DIA. . .the good guys. Those men and women are qualified linguists and have the training to interview witnesses that DPMO and JTF-FA (now known as JPAC) don't have. Why? They often don't pick the right people because of ego and politics. After the war, Stony Beach was formed under the umbrella of JCRC for the purpose of interviewing refugees and collecting data.

During the 1998 Annual National League of Families meeting, Pete Peterson, then Ambassador to Vietnam who was a retired U.S. Air Force officer and returned POW, had the audacity to say to the members regarding MIAs, "We all need to be patient." He also said that the only thing we Family members were interested in was "instant gratification."

How could he stand up in front of a bunch of family members who are attending a League meeting, some for their 30th year, and say they are just too impatient?

I remember that meeting. I had to get out of there or I would have done something really foolish. Pete . . . try 30 years, I wanted to say to him. After all, what's the description of patience in the dictionary?

"Let the diplomatic channels work," he said. I felt like saying, "Have you ever studied the history of the Vietnamese people and their culture? The result we need is not to look at how many remains have been identified by CILHI over four or five years, but how many remains were returned."

The man I was sitting next to in the meeting whispered to me as I left, "If I were in your shoes, I would be a raving maniac by now."

Through the years, I have made a chart or graph according to what the Republican and Democrat Administrations have done. Republicans are the ones who held out a carrot and a stick. . ."You do this and we'll do that" (to get POWs and remains returned).

The Democrat Administration, under eight years of Clinton rule, were giving away the farm and waiting for the magnanimous Vietnamese to come up with a deal. The results? Nothing! Except to return a lot of coffins to loved ones without bodies.

Since the French left Vietnam, they have found a way to bargain with the Vietnamese to get some of their POWs, and the remains of some of their dead, returned each year by paying Vietnam to maintain the French cemeteries. Clinton offered nothing in exchange for giving the Vietnamese government virtually everyting they wanted.

I read recently that Clinton had the highest body return of approximately 269. The problem with that is, about 150 remains were brought to CILHI ten years ago. And they've been sitting there all this time. I ask you, why would it take ten years for forensic pathology to make even one identification? Granted, sometimes it takes a while to track down family members, but that is just an excuse, as far as I'm concerned. If the IRS wants to get a hold of you, they get a hold of you. So that's not an argument. Besides, they have DNA matching now, which cuts a lot of the guesswork out of remains identification.

It's just so unfair. Not that life ever promised to be fair, but it is misleading for the next generation. Let me tell you something else that just hacks me. Those of us, who have lived through this for so many years, have done numerous things to make it better for future generations of POW/ MIA families. At least, we thought, something good has come out of all this. History won't repeat itself.

But. . .I happened to be in Washington D.C. at the time when two flyers were shot down in Kosovo. Those of us in The League, and others, had worked for 13 years to get missing person legislation in place that would provide protection for those men classified as POWs.

It took a gaggle of lawyers over 48 hours to come to the decision that our government should declare the two men shot down in Kosovo as POWs. Forty-eight hours! They haggled and haggled over the classification, even though we had been assured, when working on the legislation, that the interest of our men would always come first, and the best classification would be made for the greatest benefit to the men.

I was incensed!

(I remember Lt. Cmdr. Michael Speicher, who was shot down in an F-18 fighter on the opening night of the 1991 Gulf War. His wingman saw the plane go down and he knew the loss coordinates, but nobody bothered to look for Speicher. He was declared dead. And it took ten years for the Department of Defense to reclassify him as MIA instead of KIA.)

I've been told that we lose 5% of all service personnel in combat situations. We lose them or the enemy loses them. Anyway, they can't be found. That's not good. The government says that they're sorry, but they are not going to spend any more money around the world trying to find them because it is only 4%-5% of our fighting men. It's not economical. Too bad!

I would have respected our government a helluva lot more if someone had told us that, instead of stringing us along for 30 years.

It kills me, now that I am a little bit involved with the Army's Special Forces as well as the Special Operations men in the other services, that I continue to run into some who feel they know it all. They seem to think that just because they belonged to Spec Ops, they know the government has told them the truth, for sure, and that there are no more POWs left in Vietnam.

I told one guy I met, "Do you really think that you knew about every Special Forces operation that went on in Vietnam while you were there? Just because you knew about the missions in FOB2 doesn't mean you knew about everything."

He said, "Yeah, but I'm sure that if anything went on out of the ordinary, I'd have heard about it."

Then I said, "Did you ever work with the men who worked undercover?"

"Oh, yeah. You may be working with Dick Frank but it turns out to really be Bob Jones, an alias."

"Yeah? Then, what's that all about?" I love it when somebody's light finally goes on and when someone stands up and says, "Oh, my God!"

It's enough to drive you frickin' crazy. You have to get them to understand what you're saying, by using examples unrelated to the POW/MIA issues, before they get the point.

The other day I was talking to two military friends, telling them some of the things that I've learned about the war through the years. They kept saying, "You're kidding."

What I was telling them had nothing to do with POW/MIAs, but it did have something to do with other information tied to the POWs.

I said, "I've got documents and a bunch of other stuff if you want to read it."

They acted like they knew everything that could possibly be in a sealed document.

I said, "Okay, Misters Know-it-all. What about Nick Rowe?"

"Who?" they said in unison.

"You're kidding me. Where have you been?" I proceeded to tell them about Colonel James N. "Nick" Rowe, a member of the Special Forces who was ambushed and captured by the Viet Cong on October 29, 1963. After five years as a prisoner, he escaped, was picked up by American forces on

December 31, 1968, and brought back to the U.S. to teach at the Sere School at Fort Bragg, North Carolina.[4]

(In 1985, Nick Rowe was a colonel in charge of special intelligence operations, and an expert on prison survival techniques. That year he told Monika Jensen-Stevenson, author of Kiss The Boys Goodbye, that rescue-operations for POWs had not been carried out for many years.[5])

Col. Rowe, who had been shackled in bamboo cages every night during his 5-year captivity[6], became very helpful in the Bobby Garwood issue--prisoner vs. traitor. Since he had been in eight prison camps, Col. Rowe knew the Vietnamese prison system, and felt strongly that Garwood had been a prisoner along with all the other Americans who had been left behind.[7]

In 1989, Col. Rowe was a military advisor to the Philippine's armed forces and U.S. advisor on how to counter Communist terrorists. He was a strong believer in the fact that the Vietnamese still had many of our country's POWs, and that we should be looking for them. On April 30th, 1989, he was gunned down in Manila by communist terrorists, at the age of 51.[8]

There was a lot of scuttlebutt after that about Col. Rowe being assassinated because he had information about the POW issue, and was going to bring it forward and make it public. I think that was why he was killed.

The last time I was in Washington D.C. and went to Arlington Cemetery, I went by Col. Rowe's grave. On his headstone, where it gives his date of birth and death, was a sticky note that read, "Assassinated by his own government."

It's not just people involved in The League and groups like that, who believe there were some shenanigans and funny business related to his death. A lot of authors have also discussed what Col. Rowe knew, and his outspoken stand on POWs being left behind. He spoke up about this situation even while on active duty. I believe that the government couldn't afford to have Col. Rowe reveal the information he had.

THE MAZE

What Sara did for me, in the years following our first meeting in 1989, was to fill me in on so many things I did not know and that I was oblivious to because I had not been active in the POW/MIA issue for a number of years.

I learned from Sara that there were some people deep in the government who knew what the truth was. But they were not going to let this information get out. Even though there were people in government whom I might have access to, they would not always have the information I was seeking.

It took me a while to work through that. Sara said, "You have to realize that unless you have a need to know, you won't get this information. They will only tell you what is in Jim's chart, and what is in the chart is incomplete."

All this type of activity takes a lot out of a person. I've seen it in Sara through the years. I've felt it in me, also. All I can say is, thank goodness I met Sara, and thank goodness she filled me in on a lot of information before I went back to Vietnam the second time. My search for Jim and the truth through the years would not have happened without Sara.

Chapter Five

Monkey Business

"I knew wherever I was that you thought of me, and if I got
in a tight place you would come - - if alive."[1]
W.T. Sherman to U.S. Grant

Families seeking lost loved ones have always been concerned by live sightings of POW/MIAs in Southeast Asia. Reports have been recorded since the early 1960s. They have been turned over to the military, the White House, congressional committees, newspaper/magazine reporters and the like.

One of the purposes of my traveling to Vietnam was to see if I could find anyone who might have seen Jim somewhere/sometime during the years. I have never received a live sighting report regarding Jim, but I felt it didn't mean there weren't any. Considering how I received other information about him, nothing would surprise me.

I have copies of many dog tag reports. I have articles written about pictures of our servicemen taken many years after they disappeared, which family members say the pictures resemble their men. I have looked and looked through all of this material to see if there could possibly be a picture of Jim or a description of someone who might resemble Jim.

So, the next question is, what has the government done to follow up on these live sightings, and what have they done to let the families know of the government's findings?

HEARSAY OR TRUTH?

Live sightings have come from Laos, Cambodia, North Vietnam, and elsewhere. They have come from Vietnamese, Montagnards, American citizens, military personnel, missionaries, and foreigners. Some of the information has included a name, some a description, some hearsay.

Some of the reports of live sightings come from prison camps in Laos and North Vietnam. Other live sightings come from people who have allegedly seen Americans in villages, caves, and fields. Some have even come from prison camp guards.

A group of congressional members went to Southeast Asia in February 1986. On their return, Rep. Gerald Solomon, R-NY, said there was an "'overwhelming amount' of evidence that Americans are living in the region."

He continued. "We've received so many live sightings from so many different sources that there just cannot be any question but that they're there. The question is, who are they, how many of them are there, and in what categories are they there? Are they prisoners of war being held against their will? Are they people, Americans, who just stayed there after the war? Or are they deserters?"[2]

The National League of Families has received live sighting reports, also.

LAOS & CAMBODIA

As of 1991, some 528 U.S. military personnel were reported lost in Laos, of which 449 were "downed in areas totally controlled by the North Vietnamese Army (NVA)." Even though this was true, the Vietnamese insisted that all of the POWs in Laos were under Pathet Lao (PL) control.

The Laotians charge the U.S. to accompany the American investigators when they search the Laos crash sites. They have promised 100% cooperation. As of 9/29/02, 391 Americans are still missing in Laos, according to the National League of Families update.

Because of political problems in Southeast Asia, the CIA requested in 1991 that U.S. agencies stay away from Laos.[3]

Even though there might be live sightings? Yes!

THE PHOTOGRAPHS

In 1991, a flyer was printed with pictures of five Vietnam POWs, three of the five were taken from a photograph the Pentagon received in June of 1990. Their military photographs were compared with the prisoner pictures. The families positively identified them. A year later, no action had been taken to find these men.

The response from the military was as follows:

For Col. John L. Robertson, U.S. Air Force, Pentagon officials said in reports "the photo was probably a hoax."

For Maj. Albro L. Lundy, Jr., U.S. Air Force, the Air Force insisted he was dead.

For Lt. Cdr. Larry J. Stevens, U.S. Navy, his mother was denied access to Hanoi. She wanted answers to why her son's picture appeared in that Vietnamese photograph.[4]

All three of these men have been declared KIA. Their bodies have not been recovered.

The Pentagon received fingerprints and palm prints of these three men, but according to the flyer, the Pentagon claimed that they had none on file with which to verify the prints.[5]

Forensics expert, Dr. Michael Charney, Professor Emeritus of Anthropology at Colorado State University, analyzed the photo of Maj. Donald G. Carr, U.S. Army. He reported, "I can tell you that it is Carr, but I don't have the hot proof in my hands right now."[6]

Jerry Richards, chief of the FBI's specialized photographic unit lab division in 1991, said that they needed the photo's time, place, and authenticity to make a positive identification.

The other two pictures on that flyer were of Lt. Daniel V. Borah, Jr., U.S. Navy and Maj. Carr. The photo of Borah, that was in a set of 17 color photographs obtained by a Lao-American in Tennessee, is claimed by our government to be of a Laotian. But, Borah's family has compared it to his grandfather's picture and his Navy photograph, and they say that all three of the pictures are of the same person.

SOME FAMILIES ARE MISLED

Nashville Circuit Judge Hamilton Gayden declared in 1991 he had evidence that U.S. servicemen are being held in Southeast Asia--photographs, hair samples, fingerprints, coded maps, and messages. He received all of this through the Laos-American who was his bailiff.[8]

As for Maj. Carr, a Laotian courier took a picture of an American he saw in Laos, and it was identified as Maj. Carr when it was laid beside his father's picture and Carr's 1962 wedding photograph.

The message written in this flyer is, "If we allow our government officials to succeed in their devious attempt to discredit these photographs, it sends an extremely dangerous message to the Vietnamese, Laotian, and Cambodian governments who are holding these men and many more."[9]

Unfortunately, there have been some instances of people who have taken advantage of POW/MIA families, trying to sell them bogus information, and getting their hopes up. But, was the photo of those three men in that category? Soldier of Fortune editor and publisher Robert K. Brown said in 1991, he didn't think those three men were Americans. "I regret having to dash the hopes of the families of these soldiers. But the people creating these POW hoaxes are vermin."[10]

OFFICIAL REPORTS

There had been 1,400 reports of live sightings by 1991, which have been found to be wrong, or so I have read.

How can all of these reports be that wrong?

The most common (standard) statement, from the military to POW/MIA families regarding live sightings, has been, "I (We) regret we are unable to determine the veracity of this information."

One document says, "In the regard, your attention is directed to Para 2-L0B, AFM 30-4, which stipulated that conclusive evidence of death is considered to exist when available information indicates beyond any reasonable doubt repeat reasonable doubt that a missing person could not have survived. CDS 1980 DPMSCA PMSCB"[11]

I have copies of some reports sent to families that are sanitized to the point that very little information is left. If a family member wanted to visit the live sighting area to look for her loved one she wouldn't be able to.

One report has a note attached that says, "This intelligence report comes out of Danang Regional Intelligence in 1969. The camp described here was 20 miles south of Hue and about 40 miles northwest of Danang." The family would never have gotten that information from the sanitized military report.[12]

The part of the report that wasn't sanitized said, "Attached are a list of U.S. prisoners positively and tentatively identified by (blacked out) from photographs, list of Viet Cong Huong Thuy District Committee and sketches of the committee's headquarters. List of U.S. personnel identified by (blacked out) from photos, on 11, April 1969." The date this report item #4 was released was on April 16, 1984.[13]

On the Positive Identification list, there were 22 names, of which 12 were noted as MIA. On the Possible Identification list of 32, 22 were MIAs. From both lists, 9 names were marked "released."[14]

An article in The San Diego Union in 1986 stated that the DIA was collecting live sighting reports of Americans either considered missing or unaccounted for in Southeast Asia. The reporter quoted the following statistics: 838 Americans were held after 1973, but they were hearsay reports. Some 320 additional reports were from incarcerated South Vietnamese from communist re-education camps. It was inferred that those people could not be believed.[15]

Another 871 live sighting reports interested the DIA because they were made after all POWs were to have been returned in 1973. Of those, 547 had been resolved, they said. And 191 of the reports were fabrications. According to the article, that left 133 factual reports that Americans were being held prisoner in 1983.[16]

One of those reports reads, "The source of this report spent 15 years in communist prisons in North Vietnam after serving as a CIA-trained Special Forces paratrooper. At the end of 1978, he and 130 American POWs were transferred to Thanh Hoa (North Vietnam). While in Thanh Hoa, the former paratrooper said he saw about 30 Americans held in three separate camps about seven kilometers from each other. . .when we went to work we passed by their (the Americans') place of detention, we saw them at a distance of about 20 meters; therefore, I do not know their names and addresses. The POWs I saw were very thin; they were covered with scabies; there was just skin and bones left on them. They could hardly walk, yet they were forced to carry wood from the forests distant about 500 meters. They often fell down. Sometimes they were beaten by the guards. These things I saw with my own eyes."[17]

The National League of Families released that live sighting report.

I could go on and on with additional information that basically reads the same.

But, I think you can understand some of the frustration on the part of family members, especially when they have pictures authenticated by authorities in the private sector or they have received information about live sightings from non-military sources. In some cases, the information is so specific, as to a particular individual, that the family members would be the only ones to recognize it. This lends to the frustration when our government dismisses the information as bogus.

* * *

"You go into combat prepared to die, to be wounded, to be taken prisoner. But not to be abandoned. It might be impossible to get our men out, but if it's impossible, let us at least acknowledge their sacrifice."
          Navy Captain Eugene B. (Red) McDaniel
          Six years a POW in North Vietnam[18]

* * *

The "DOD has been able to construct a rationale to discredit 'officially' nearly each and every live sighting report" according to a 1991 Examination of U.S. Policy Toward POW/MIAs by the U.S. Senate Committee on Foreign Relations. "Staff found instances where DOD merely excluded from its analysis certain details of a valid sighting, such as a source's statement about the number of POWs sighted, their physical condition, a description of the camp or cave they were held in, whether they were shackled, or, whether they were gesturing for food. By the exclusion of such corroborating details, the report could – under the convoluted DOD bureaucratic process – be labeled a fabrication." The DOD "appears to be geared toward disproving each live-sighting report, rather than each report receiving, as proscribed by official DOD policy, the 'necessary priority and resources based on the assumption that at least some Americans are still held captive'."

A meeting was held on July 18, 1991, with General John W. Vessey, Jr., Col. Frank Libotti, Senators John Kerry, Frank Murkowski, Hank Brown, and Representative Lane Evans, (plus directors from the VFW Washington office, American Legion, Vietnam Veterans of America, Senate Foreign Affairs Committee staff members, and the VFW Director of National Security, and Foreign Affairs). The opening statement was that "an exchange of views was important to maintain the momentum gained from the recent visit of veterans to Vietnam."

They stated in their report that live sightings were "passed along a lengthy and time consuming bureaucratic chain until it is too late for the Government to react to the information if it were accurate."

They also discussed the fact that these live sighting reports became months and years old, but they shouldn't be ignored just because they are not time-sensitive.[19]

Nice words but no results. Do you find this insulting?

TODAY'S LIVE SIGHTINGS

According to the Personnel Recovery and Accounting Report, dated June 2001, printed by the Defense POW/MIA Personnel Office, all live sightings are evaluated today by 3 decades of historical knowledge. The sightings are correlated, if possible, with returned POWs or other Westerners who are known to their analysts. At that point, an investigative plan is developed, if necessary, to obtain and clarify details. "Some reports require travel to the site in question."

Even in the Gulf War, live sightings became important. Take the incident of Lt. Cmdr. Michael Scott Speicher who was first declared KIA/BNR within 48 hours after he was shot down by enemy fire on the first day of the air war over Iraq in 1991. However, through the years, there have been reports of seeing him alive as a prisoner in Iraq. Could he still be alive?

Senator Bob Smith, R-NH, is quoted to have said, "What we need to do now is get answers from Baghdad. This pilot, if he's alive, has been there for 10 years, with nobody looking for him. That's just plain outrageous. . ."[20]

Thanks can go to both Senator Bob Smith and former Senator Rod Grams who suffered a great deal of criticism for their stance on the POW/MIA issue.[21]

It is general knowledge that the Defense Department, and its POW/MIA Office (DPMO), have operated on the basis that there are no POW/MIAs from World War II, Korean War, Cold War, Vietnam War, or Gulf War. So, for the DOD to declare that there is an MIA in their records is extraordinary.

The MIA status now offers Lt. Cmdr. Speicher the legal protection that no other MIA has ever received. I weep for all the other MIAs through history who did not have this.

(NOTE: As of March 12, 2002, U.S. intelligence agents are working on information that maybe Lt. Cmdr. Speicher is alive in Iraq, a prisoner of Saddam Hussein's regime. The information came from a defector. It seems that Lt. Cmdr. Speicher was moved to a "military facility on Sept. 12, the day after Islamic terrorists hijacked American airliners and drilled them into the World Trade Center and the Pentagon."[22])

In response to Lt. Cmdr. Speicher's status change to MIA, Roger Herrick, brother of Capt. Jim Herrick, MIA 10/27/69, wrote on 1/13/2001,[23] "Finally!!!!!! The Pentagon and DOD finally admit what much of the country (and secretly, the government) has known for several years – that Lt. Cmdr. Speicher did NOT die when his F-18 crashed in the Arabian dessert during the Gulf War. He was abandoned, admittedly by mistake at first. But the mistake was continued by design – through official denial of the facts for almost 9 years after Michael was taken prisoner to Baghdad! I just hope to God that Michael is still alive and will be brought home alive. This could open an ugly sore that's been a festering part of the American anatomy for over a century. Could we possibly be on the road to some kind of healing? Pray to God we are!"[24]

It is ironic that, as I'm wrote this book, I heard an interview show on KSFO, San Francisco, where the talk show host, Barbara Simpson, interviewed Bill Gertz from The Washington Times. The discussion involved the latest information about Lt. Cmdr. Speicher. According to Washington Times. com, there was evidence that he was still alive. More intelligence reports were coming in so the White House issued a request, according to Gertz, that Speicher be returned to the United States.[25]

There was no response, Gertz said.

(I have heard for years that the military is supposed to take care of its own. What happened?)

So far, Gertz reported, the Iraqi's misled and deceived our country several times. Once they said it was an animal that our intelligence thought was Speicher. Another time they put off our government.

The discussion led to the question about what the designations of first MIA, then KIA/BNR, and then MIA again meant to his family. His wife has remarried and she and her husband hired an attorney to settle the issue.

The whole thing must be very disheartening. "When is our country going to get angry enough to do something about this? I don't feel the outrage," in our country, Barbara Simpson said. She noted that the media seemed to downplay this whole issue. She continued. Since there's "no evidence that he's dead, so if he's not dead, then he's got to be alive. . ." There seems to be a "tremendous resistance to doing anything about this issue."

Perhaps there are more MIAs to come off the KIA/BNR list--maybe from the Vietnam War?

Perhaps it's too late.

If not, the status change could mean that many of our military would no longer be considered dead, like Jim, and the opportunity for further investigations would be opened up once again.

CAN THEY STILL BE IGNORED?

Under the new status, live sightings gathered by special intelligence would no longer be ignored. Maybe Vietnam, Laos, Cambodia, and the other countries involved would not hold back the information they have had all these years. Perhaps healing for the MIA families could finally take place.

As Nigel Cawthorne writes in his book, The Bamboo Cage, "But the sheer volume of the live-sightings reports cannot be discounted. The administration, and others, believe the live-sighting evidence to the extent that they have mounted rescue missions to release American POWs, but murky political considerations have got in the way at every turn, not the sort of thing that makes a snappy item on the six o'clock news."[26] Cawthorne wrote this in 1991.

At the National League of Families meeting in June 2001, a family member asked the panel how they could in good conscious shrug off the 32 live sightings she had of her husband in 2000, and the additional 14 live sightings she'd had in the past six months. The response from the panel was gobblygook.

From a statistical standpoint, after taking into account those matched up with our returnees, it seems to me that it would be impossible to discredit every single live sighting report to come out of Vietnam, period.

DOG TAG REPORTS

Through the years, the DIA has received hundreds of dog tag reports, most of them from Southeast Asian refugees. At one time, the DIA had a wall covered with charts following all of the dog tag reports, and checking on things like whether the report was the same handwriting or made on the same machine.

The year Americans and veterans were allowed to travel in Vietnam, the dog tag reports increased. A lot of this was due to dishonest villagers who thought American tourists would buy their stories because the tourists were so anxious to find evidence of MIA remains and POWs.[27]

Only about 57 dog tag sightings remained valid as unresolved by 1991. That's 57 out of 1,672 refugee reports, 3,000 hearsay reports of American prisoners, and 4,000 reports of crash and gravesites.[28]

The DIA handled over 15,000 refugee statements from the fall of Saigon to 1991, due in part to pressure from The National League of Families and members of Congress.[29]

When I was looking at microfiche from Jim's folder at the National Archives, in 1995, I discovered a lot of documents that I'd never seen before in the hard copy file. One of them was a dog tag sighting.

The report came from a Vietnamese military person in Vietnam who said he remembered stumbling across a scene, in May or June 1971, where 30-40 dead Vietnamese and one dead American lay.

He described the height and insignia worn by the American, saying he didn't take anything from the bodies. His commander told him to put the American in the mass grave since they didn't know who he was.

Why was this report in Jim's file? I made a copy and took it back to the Casualty Office. When I questioned the casualty officer, he said that anybody killed or missing in that area would have the same report in his file.

JUNE 2001 NATIONAL LEAGUE OF FAMILIES MEETING

During one of the sessions at this National League meeting, I was able to ask some hard questions of the military panel sitting before us.

One: Isn't it true that in fact, Lt. Cmdr. Speicher is not the only MIA from the Persian Gulf War? Aren't there 10 Special Forces men listed as MIA, also?

Two: When investigators find a jungle cemetery, do those at Stoney Beach take all of the bodies or just the one they are expecting to find? How do you approach this type of situation?

Three: I think it's now safe to say that those men in Special Forces never gave the correct map coordinates because of the type of missions they were running. We can also agree, I believe, that because no one actually witnessed when or where Jim fell off the rig, some of the loss sites were SWAGed (Stupid Wild Ass Guess).

My question is, for those cases that are now in a "no further pursuit" category, meaning our government has no avenues left to investigate, will you (my U.S. government) consider them beyond the boundaries of those SWAGed coordinates?

In this instance, Dickie Hites, then Deputy J2 for Operations, JTF-FA, answered me with ". . .we never really close anything and yes we do extend the possibility of those lost beyond their recorded site."

Four: It's safe to say that the only live sighting reports that we would hear about would be high-profiled stories covered by news organizations. If you consider a quick response to be like the response you made toward the case of the Japanese "monk," then I can only assume that any other live sighting report would be done at less than a snail's pace. Do you automatically discount these testimonies because it's too difficult to stand up to a foreign regime, which you'd rather not upset? If that is the tact, please be honest with this audience and say that.

(Note: When the Japanese "monk" was released from a Hanoi prison in 1989, he said that the only reason he was alive was because American POWs were feeding him. He reported that five or six Americans were still alive when he left the camp. "I heard all of them were beaten and tortured as I was," he said. (Reported in the L.A. Times, 6/8/89.)

Again Dickie Hites responded. ". . .we strongly take into account the country we're dealing with before asking and pressing for answers."

* * *

Roni Shanley, a friend of mine as well as a POW/MIA family member, wrote a letter to the editor that was published in the San Diego Union, 3/12/91. In part, she said, "The Union's article (Feb. 25) on POW bracelets misrepresented the issue of live American POW/MIAs being held in Southeast Asia. Although it mentioned the Reagan administration's policy statement, it failed to present the live sightings of American POWs held in Vietnam reported by a Japanese monk (June '89), Stan Cottrell, the American runner (July '89), and the October 1990 U.S. Senate Foreign Relations Committee's Interim Report on the Southeast Asian POW/MIA issue."

Stan Cottrell, a long distance runner and a member of the Billy Graham Crusade, had an interesting story to tell when he returned from a good will run in Vietnam, the summer of 1989.

The Vietnamese had planned his route from Hanoi to Da Nang, and provided military escorts to keep him on track. Since the trade embargo was still in place at that time, American tourists were almost nil. So, this event was staged to try to open the way for others to visit that country.

One day, as Stan was running just north of Hue, with his Vietnamese escorts and support staff in tow, a strange thing happened. He saw some 20 Caucasians in prison attire being led back into a well-hidden cave.

Almost at the same time, his escorts scooted him away in a flurry of activity. That night after dinner, one of Stan's escorts approached him and asked if he'd like to know more about the American POWs he'd seen on the road that day.

Stan was nervous about getting into a political conversation with the man, so he said he wasn't interested. That seemed to surprise the Vietnamese man.

When Stan returned to the States, a small article appeared in the newspapers telling what I've just described. To my knowledge, our government never did anything about the POWs Stan saw. It's my belief that this may have been an attempt on the part of the Vietnamese to show the U.S. that they did in fact hold POWs, and that maybe the incident would reopen talks about the money the Vietnamese felt the U.S. owed them.

* * *

"There is no longer any question that there are live Americans in SE Asia. The question is who they are and how many of them there are. There could be Americans in the mountains, in the caves, in areas beyond their control. For God's sake, bring them home."

Congressman G. Solomon – 1986

* * *

"WHY DIDN'T YOU GET ME OUT?"

As I finished writing my book, I bought another one to add to my library of Vietnam War tales. Written by Frank Anton, Why Didn't You Get Me Out?[30] is about a POW's nightmare in Vietnam. Frank Anton was one of those POWs who knew his government was aware of his existence and location almost all of the five years he was imprisoned in Vietnam.

When he was in Da Nang, after his release, he saw CIA planes more than once, the same ones that hovered so many years ago "over that muddy rice paddy"[31] where he struggled to escape his captors after his chopper crashed during the Tet Offensive in 1968.

Anton made a number of comments in his book that confirmed my thoughts about what had gone on in Vietnam. For example, he mentioned that he never saw a single U.S. serviceman with physical problems while he was in captivity. He wrote, "In fact, of the 591 men who returned during Operation Homecoming, none was missing any limbs or had any serious disfigurement. . .Nearly thirty years later, those (wounded) men - - and others - - have not been accounted for."[32]

One of the revelations Anton had, about the fact that his country knew where he was during those five years, was a picture shown to him during his debriefing after he was released. It was a picture of Anton marching along the Ho Chi Minh Trail. When he asked his debriefer who took it, he was told, " 'We really can't tell you that.' Once again, I'd learned that my country knew exactly where I was."[33]

As the daily debriefing continued, "In hoarse amazement I asked, 'If you knew where I was, why didn't you come and get me out?' One of them looked me right in the eye and responded, 'We don't know. That's not our job. I can't give you an answer'."[34]

Another time[35], Anton mentioned to a debriefer that he was stumped as to how his father, an Air Force Colonel, knew about his capture by the Vietnamese within a week after his chopper crashed in January 1968. The families of the other men with him didn't get that information until late 1969.

It seemed incredible to me that such a horrendous thing happened to Anton, and others in our military, but here are Anton's words to make the "live sighting" by the CIA, or whomever, a fact.

"As I limped in pain along the Ho Chi Minh trail, someone was there keeping an eye on me. From somewhere behind the concealment of jungle foliage, a camera captured my image, a curious, unrecognizable image that was to stare me in the face more than two years later after I had returned home. Someone knew where I was.

"For three years, I was held in four jungle camps, each shrouded by the central highland forests that I thought were hiding me from the rest of the world. I felt swallowed up, lost, never sure exactly where I was. Yet I returned home to see the photographic evidence - - each picture taken during the times that I was in each of the camps - - that someone knew where I was."[36]

Anton didn't realize then, but Ho Chi Minh ordered his men to capture as many Americans as possible so he would have more leverage with the U.S. government to get money for his hostages. So they did.

Anton remembered, once he was home, that one of his guards told him, smiling, "We like you very much. Maybe the war will start up again and we can keep you several more years."[37]

Anton's continual question of "why?" was finally answered many years after the Vietnamese released him. His source told him the following, after he learned that one of MACVSOG's operations was to monitor POWs.

"Frank, they didn't get you out because they didn't want to tip the fact that they knew where you were. The NVA would then begin to identify their sources, which included people within the Viet Cong and very likely the NVA structure. They chose not to compromise their sources because the information was more valuable than you were."[38]

In other words, those POWs were expendable. Anton said that if the prisoners in those Vietnamese jungles had known how their government felt about them, "the despair from that betrayal would have caused virtually every one of us to die."[39]

In 1973, after Anton had given a speech at a college in Ocean County, New Jersey, where he stated that there were men left behind in Vietnam, he was told by a Colonel in the Pentagon, "Look, we know we left people back there. We're doing everything we can to get them back, but your talking about it doesn't help us get them back."[40]

Later, Anton was told by a General in the Pentagon that if he wanted to stay in the military until retirement, ". . .stop talking about the MIA issue."[41]

It's interesting that live sightings were not only made by individuals in Southeast Asia, but by our military. When they were denying authenticity of most live sightings reported to them, our government was guilty of conducting live sightings of their own--in secret.

Anton wrote, "official signal-intercept surveillance was continuing at least three years after Operation Homecoming. Indeed, a U.S. satellite image taken in June 1992 of the Dong Mang prison in northern Vietnam showed a man-made signal stamped out in the grass: GX 2527. Pentagon analysts tried to argue that the image was a 'photographic anomaly,' but the combination of letters and digits matched the unique authenticator code of Peter Richard Matthes, the copilot of a C-130 transport shot down in Laos in November of 1969 and still listed as missing in action at the time the satellite snapped the picture."[42]

It became apparent to Anton, once he had time to think about everything he'd experienced as a prisoner in Vietnam, plus all of the information he'd picked up later, that "if the United States wanted its POWs back, it would have to pay a ransom, reparations, reconstruction assistance, or whatever other term it chose to use."[43]

And the United States chose not to heal those wounds!

* * *

"With malice toward none; with charity for all; with firmness in the right, as God gives us to see the right, let us strive on to finish the work we are in; to bind up the nation's wounds; to care for him who shall have borne the battle, and for his widow, and his orphan – - to do all which may achieve and cherish a just, and a lasting peace, among ourselves, and with all nations."

President Abraham Lincoln[44]
Second Inaugural Address
March 4, 1865

At Colorado State University, in the 1980s, a prominent physical anthropologist conducted extensive reviews of the remains of missing Americans from the Vietnam War.

Dr. Michael Charney, Professor Emeritus, was internationally known as an expert in the science of forensics. He had worked in the field since the end of World War II, and he had developed a theory for identification of human remains.

Dr. Charney became interested in reviewing some of the remains that the U.S. Armed Forces personnel, who worked at the Central Identification lab in Hawaii (CILHI), had identified.

A number of MIA families had questioned the identifications they received from CILHI, especially when it was nothing but a tooth, or one small bone, or such. For example, how could CILHI be so sure to whom the tooth belonged, when dental records were missing.

As a result of the cases Dr. Charney reviewed, he concluded that it was scientifically impossible to identify the bone fragments that had been returned to the next of kin. This is how he came to that conclusion.

First, he found that CILHI had not used a scientific basis to make any type of identification. Therefore, the misidentification of the MIA remains had to be intentional.

He found that as many as eighty separate sets of remains of U.S. servicemen listed as MIA or KIA/BNR were falsely identified. He had reported this in 1986 to the U.S. House of Representatives hearing on the CILHI facility, and as a result, the Army hired recognized experts with doctoral credentials in an attempt to correct the situation.

Then, between 1985 and 1987, Dr. Charney reviewed thirty sets of repatriated remains from North Vietnam and found that they had been wrongly identified as U.S. servicemen from the MIA or KIA/BNR lists. In each case, the bone fragments and bone parts were not sufficient to identify a "specific individual by sex, race, height, weight, physical peculiarities and so forth." In some cases, the technicians used forensic methods not recognized by professional forensic anthropologists.[45]

Dr. Charney came to the conclusion that the only reason these misidentifications were made was to remove more names from the list of accounted for MIA servicemen in the Vietnam War, and to placate MIA families. In other words, to deceive them.

He reported, to the general public and to the U.S. Senate Committee on Foreign Relations Republican staff on May 23, 1991, that "This facility (CILHI), entrusted with the analysis of mostly skeletonized remains of our servicemen and women in the identification process, is guilty of unscientific, unprofessional work. The administrative and technical personnel have engaged knowingly in deliberate distortion of details deduced from the bones to give credibility to otherwise impossible identification."[46]

In addition, Dr. Charney told the committee that CILHI lied about a large number of the remains they identified. He considered this to be blatant and deliberate. Some of the remains or other material, he said, were not capable of providing identification. Many of the technicians lacked training in the forensic anthropology field and some, referred to as doctors, had never been awarded doctorates in any field.

DOD has not refuted his report and there appears to be no evidence to contradict him since 1991.

Dr. George W. Gill, former secretary of the physical anthropology section of the American Academy of Forensic Sciences, and a member of the Board of Directors of the American Board of Forensic Anthropology in 1991, agreed with Dr. Charney's conclusions. Dr. Gill publicly stated, "It is clear from the bones that the problem in the CILHI reports results either from extreme carelessness, incompetence, fabrication of data, or some combination of these things."[47]

One of the more famous cases that Dr. Charney became involved in was his identification of Army Cpt. Donald Carr of East Chicago, Indiana. For the first time, someone was able to find proof that, after twenty years, an American prisoner was still alive in Vietnam.

One of Dr. Charney's skills was to scientifically match skulls to photographs. Cpt. Carr was one of 528 military men lost in Laos. A photograph, reported to have been smuggled out of Laos where it was taken in 1990, was identified as Cpt. Carr. The picture was of a man grinning in what seemed to be a metal cage in a jungle setting.

Dr. Charney took one look and felt the picture was of the same man as Cpt. Carr in his wedding photograph taken in 1961. To be sure, Dr. Charney enlarged the prints to the same size, and studied the ear lobes. Then he superimposed one face on the other. The ear lobes and the faces matched.

But that wasn't enough. Dr. Charney took the pictures to the mechanical engineering department at Colorado State University, and an associate professor, Patrick Fitzhorn, used a high-tech image digitaliser. Bingo! A match.[48]

At the time, those who knew of the positive identification thought this evidence of a live MIA would have extraordinary political implications. But nothing happened. No attempt was made to find Cpt. Donald Carr or to negotiate with Vietnam for the return of their prisoner. It must have been hard for his family to know that he was alive, but that they would never see him again. Today, our government continues to state that the photograph taken in 1990 is a fraud.

"The military was lying over what they saw, trying to clear up the books on the war," charged Dr. Charney about the identification of the remains of Col. Thomas Hart who was shot down over Pak Se, Laos, in November 1972.[49]

Ann, Col. Hart's wife, received 12 bone pieces in July of 1985. She was told that they were her husband's and if she didn't accept them, they would be buried in a mass grave in Arlington National Cemetery.

According to a Task Force Omega bio on Col. Hart, dated October 10, 2002, several familes, including Ann Hart, employed two forensic anthropologists to examine the bone fragments reported to belong to their loved ones. The only thing the experts could conclude was that the bone fragments were human, but maybe not from the same person. Ann Hart and George MacDonald's family sued the government. In doing so, they discovered that search and rescue personnel had found, and photographed five deployed parachutes and two piles of bloody bandages at the crash site of the Spectre gun ship that Col. Hart and Capt. MacDonald had been on. Six months later, and 200 miles north of the crash site, a satellite photographed a symbol stamped out in nearby elephant grass, believed to have been made by Thomas Hart, or another member of his air crew. The symbol was "TH 1973" or "TH 1573."

The government was forced to rescind their identification of Hart's and MacDonald's remains when the families won their suit. However, once both men's names had been removed from the list of POW/MIA's, our government considered them "remains recovered" no matter what the court ruled.

It seems that everything Dr. Charney did to identify remains, as well as photographs of live Americans, has been filed away along with all the other reports concerning POW/MIAs.

* * *

When the armed services first began to bring bodies back from Vietnam, family members questioned whether the body in the casket was truly their loved one.

They were told it wasn't necessary to open the casket to verify the body.

"No, I want to look," many families said. And when the families did open the caskets, they found things like airplane parts or bones from a pig or rocks, or other such things to add weight to the casket. That was before DNA tests. And so, Dr. Charney became important if a bone or two happened to be included in the casket.

Sometimes the bones would be of a tall man when the soldier, whose name was on the casket, was short, or a woman when the body was supposed to be a man.

And what kind of responses did the families get at that time? "Our staff is very qualified to do this kind of work."

Some families refused the remains they were given, like maybe a finger or hand. When that happened, the government wrote the soldier's name off the missing list and said they had proof the body was recovered. That meant the end of their search for the real remains of the soldier.

If a tooth sat in a casket, as proof of a missing serviceman's body, the family would often be told, "This is your husband's tooth. We know it is because we've matched it to his dental records. So, he is dead."

No consideration was made of the fact that the tooth could have fallen out or been knocked out. People lose teeth all the time. To say a person is dead because a tooth was found is incredible! That person could be alive in a prison camp, yet the records declare him KIA/BNR.

There's another problem with finding a tooth or jawbone. Some dental work was done in Vietnam during the war, which would not show up on the dental records in the soldier's file in Washington, D.C. And missing teeth from combat would not, either. Jawbones, with a tooth or two, are not the same as fingerprints, unless there's a full set of teeth and nothing happened to those teeth since the last record was made in the States.

From the October 5, 1990 Congressional Record – S14623, comes this sub-head, "The Mock Burial of MIAs."

The discussion was about an announcement by the DOD that the remains of four MIA servicemen (missing since March 5, 1971, Laos) would be interred in a military burial at Arlington National Cemetery. The remains of the four were recovered during a January 5 to 10, 1990, excavation by the U.S. and Lao governments.

"The families will at last be comforted by the knowledge that they know where the bodies of their loved ones lie," the record says.

However, that was not the case.

"There were no remains whatsoever for" Sp4c Joel C. Hatley or for Capt. David L. Nelson. For WO Ralph Moreira and Sp4c Michael E. King "there were minuscule fragments of bone and a tooth not positively identifiable by any objective forensic analysis. Yet, four coffins will be buried with full military honors."

The families were "thrilled when they first got the news that their sons had been found; but they were shocked when they were told, upon further inquiry, that no actual remains were being returned, just four empty coffins."

The record stated, "Why does the department of Defense put the families of MIAs through this kind of charade?"

It seems that the DOD has a different definition of "remains" than the rest of us. Instead of referring to actual physical remains, they use an abstract meaning "deduced from circumstances." If remains are found in an appropriate place where more than one military man should have been, the DOD declares all of those men's remains found and closes the case without trying to resolve the identity of the bones or other findings. "Thus empty caskets are returned as symbolic remains."[50]

* * *

I can't help but ask myself if having nothing under Jim's marker isn't better than a bone or tooth or fragment that CILHI said was Jim, when it really wasn't.

Sure, those MIA families, who were lied to, could finally have closure to the awful situation they found themselves in. And someone could say, what difference does it make whether the bone belongs to a certain MIA, or not.

But, I have to go back to what this country is all about. It was established on truth and honesty, not rule by lies. Wouldn't it have been much better for the MIA families if the various branches of the armed forces had just said, "We're sorry. We have no evidence to confirm your son's death. We don't know whether the bone fragments we found are his or not. We will probably never know."

And then, is it so terrible if the KIA/BNR list is long? It is generally understood that a war is not a situation in which all bodies or identifiable body parts are going to be found. What the MIA families wanted was to know that their son's buddies made a serious attempt to look for him. I can't imagine any family wanting to receive a bone fragment that was not their son's, just to have something to bury.

* * *

Lt. Cmdr. Larry J. Stevens was another military man, a Navy pilot, whom Dr. Charney identified. An Associated Press article appeared on November 4, 1991, in The San Diego Union, in which Dr. Charney said he had examined a recent photo that was of the pilot. He had been missing in Laos since February 1969.

Charney said, "People say, 'You're 100 percent certain but we want you to be 200 percent.' If you want me to swear on five Bibles and on my mother's grave, then to hell with it."

The article had a most interesting quote from the Lt. Commander's mother. "And now that I know he's alive, I'm very angry and I want to shout to my government, 'Damn you, you've left them and you know they're there.'"[51]

* * *

Every once in awhile, the Vietnamese "find" another set of remains, even though they continue to declare that there are none. These remains are often in excellent condition, as though they had been warehoused, for example, in a box on a shelf in Hanoi. The Vietnamese answer is always that some villager brought the remains to them--the bodies had just been found. After all of these years, you'd think there might be bits of dirt or something on the bones if they'd been sitting in some village all this time.

According to Monica Jensen-Stevenson, in Chapter 21 of her book Spite House, the Mortician (named by the Vietnamese), testified before the Senate in 1979, saying that he had been in charge of processing and storing American remains in a Hanoi warehouse. The Mortician knew of more than 400 boxes. He also testified that he saw three American POWs, one of which he identified as Bobby Garwood.

Yet, holding those bodies for leverage with the U.S. did not work for the Vietnamese because they didn't get their 3.2 billion as Nixon promised. And, when President Clinton lifted the trade embargo, the U.S. no longer had leverage to get the boxes of bodies back, much less the return of live POWs. Vietnam was then free to trade with other countries, as well as the U.S., thereby achieving their economic goals.

When Senators John Kerry and John McCain visited Hanoi several years ago, the Vietnamese government told the Senators they had turned over all the information they had about Americans--POWs, MIAs and bodies. A few days later, thousands of pictures showed up of Americans that the Vietnamese said they just happened to find.

Senators Kerry and McCain, with straight faces, told the American public that the Vietnamese were doing the best they could.

That's a lie!

And based on my experience in Vietnam, and years of dealing with this issue, the lie is on both sides of the fence.

* * *

Maj. Jessie Massey Jr., team leader of five outreach missions to recover service personnel remains, said in 2002, ". . .the outreach could continue until the very last set of remains - - sometimes merely bone fragments accompanied by dog tags - - is found. 'This mission will transcend your generation and my generation and probably my children's.'"[52]

> "And seek the peace of the city whither I have caused you
> to be carried away captives, and pray unto the Lord for it:
> for in the peace thereof shall ye have peace."
>
> Jeremiah 29:7

Russia played several roles in the POW/MIA issue during the Vietnam War. First, the Vietnamese took a page out of Soviet POW treatment, and classified many POWs as war criminals, men who committed crimes against the state. That way, they could take away the POWs citizenship and rights under the Geneva Convention. And of course, the Geneva Convention didn't apply since we were not in a declared war. The Chinese used the same trick after the Korean War in order to keep Americans in Asia.

If Americans weren't POWs, then the Vietnamese could do whatever they wanted with them. Some even said that since America didn't declare war on Vietnam, then there couldn't be any prisoners of war. Therefore, these particular men became criminals in Vietnam, instead. Of course their names were never placed on any Vietnamese list of American POW/MIAs.[53]

The other role Russia played was to keep prisoners of war from other countries, like Korea and Vietnam. According to former Czech General Major Jan Sejna, first shipments of U.S. POWs to Russia took place in August 1961 under Vietnamese guard.

In 1999, the Special Forces Association publication, The Drop, printed an article about General Jan Sejna. It seems he was the highest-ranking Communist to defect to the U.S. Among other things, Sejna organized POW shipments to Prague and the Soviet Union.

Sejna testified before the Senate Select Committee on POW/MIA Affairs in 1992, and again in 1996 before the House National Security Subcommittee on Military Personnel.

According to the article, "It is only natural to assume that our government officials who have worked on this issue as employees in the DOD, DIA and DPMO knew, and have known this information since 1968, especially since Mr. Sejna was an employee of the DIA."

After passing five CIA polygraph examinations, Congress decided that he was not lying or deceiving them.[54]

The Soviets also set up two hospitals in Laos for biological tests on U.S. POWs. Most of these men ended up in Russia, often being shipped through Prague.[55]

China got into the act, too. They acted as "bankers" for 600 U.S. POWs in North Vietnam as evidenced in Moscow. A KGB agent reported this in a London Daily News article in 1973.[56]

In a 1992 June summit meeting between President Bush and Boris Yeltsin, Yeltsin admitted that our U.S. servicemen had ended up in the Soviet Union from Vietnam. He told NBC, "We don't have complete data and can only surmise that some of them may still be alive."[57]

Edward Tivan wrote an article, "On the Trail of the MIAs," for the Los Angeles Times Magazine, October 27, 1991, p. 9. In the article, he discussed how Jerry Mooney and Terrel Minarcin, former U.S. Intelligence Analysts, divulged clues to the MIA puzzle after 30 years of silence. Jerry Mooney gave secret testimony before a Senate committee in the late '80s. He appeared on national television stating that the U.S. government had abandoned hundreds of American prisoners in Vietnam, too. "He also claimed that U.S. Intelligence officials knew not only that Hanoi had withheld American POWs as 'bargaining chips' for future negotiations, but also that the North Vietnamese had handed over scores of American airmen to the Soviets for interrogation; 50 or so POWs, he charged, had disappeared into the hands of the Soviets."

On page 39 of that article, it says that at the time the article was written, there was no good access to MIA information. Neither Mooney nor Minarcin knew until 1991 that Nguyen Cong Hoan, a Vietnamese national assemblyman, had defected in 1977. The significance of that defection was his testimony the next year before a closed session of Congress. He testified that it was general knowledge in North Vietnam that Hanoi kept American prisoners as "trump cards" because the Soviet Union wanted some of them for interrogation.

Today, the DPMO is still involved in an aggressive program, interviewing Vietnam War veterans from Russia, and other Eastern Bloc countries. After three decades, they're still trying to find out if U.S. POWs were sent to the former Soviet Union. And, what was the Soviet Union's involvement with U.S. POWs in Southeast Asia?[58]

* * *

A well-known story involving Russia, China, Canada and Vietnam is about Richard Barker, a so-called spook or what we might call a freelance investigator. I have a transcription of Richard Barker's 59-page statement dated April 2, 1986,[59] and I have read Chapter 17 of Nigel Cawthorne's book, The Bamboo Cage, that condenses Barker's story.[60]

In short, Douglas Pierce hired Barker in 1985 to get Pierce's son, and other survivors of the oil drilling ship, Glomar Java Sea, freed from the Chinese.[61] (See footnote for more details.)

In the end, many people and countries made up a web of intrigue and espionage that saw the failure of the plan and the imprisonment of Barker.

Remember, this statement was written in 1986. Under Hanoi's Political Position, Barker said,[62] ". . .Hanoi's present official government sold out to the Soviet Union in the mid-1970s in exchange for Soviet promises of rebuilding Vietnam. . .The war against the United States was supposed to make Vietnam into a communist self-determined nationalistic country. After more than eight years of occupation by the Soviet Union, this has only become another false hope. . .The Hanoi government today is almost to a point where it has become a government in exile in its own country. Yet, the United States still insists on dealing with this government to get information on the POWs, when in reality, as I am sure U.S. intelligence must know, this government has little or no control over the fate of POWs, much less any real power over the leaders of Laos. . .The only thing Hanoi does have control over is the 400 some odd caskets containing American bodies held in Hanoi, which they release periodically in groups of less than ten. They also have the power to allow the United States officials to excavate crash sites (of course with Soviet approval) and in the name of cooperation with the western world. The actions of the United States government only helps to prop that government up in the eyes of the world as being in control of Vietnam, which is in line with the aims of the Soviet Union.

The 400 caskets of expired Americans can be verified by going through the testimony of an ex-Vietnamese mortician during the Senate Subcommittee hearing on east Asian affairs on the POWs and MIAs, held periodically in Washington, D.C. or by contacting Bill Hendon, U.S. Congressman in Washington, D.C. for this information."

In the section of Barker's statement titled Soviet Political Position[63], he writes, "The United States had felt beaten in Indochina and had made it perfectly clear that Indochina was something that it wished to forget, like a very bad nightmare. This action by the United States allowed the Soviets a free hand in shaping Indochina into whatever it pleased."

According to Barker[64], in 1986, 100,000 Soviet troops occupied Vietnam. They had a naval installation and air installations and a "puppet army of Vietnamese and Laotian regulars." POWs became an excellent source of intelligence information, and a KGB training encampment was set up across the railroad tracks from Yen Bai, a prison camp northwest of Hanoi.

"The potential release of American POWs from Vietnam would focus attention on the expansion of Soviet domination of Indochina, and possibly cause the Soviet Union to lose its newly acquired naval installations in Indochina. Also, the shadowy attack on air stations such as Clark in the Philippines by the insurgent uprising of the NPA would be in jeopardy, and the fall of Marcos would have all been for nothing as far as the Soviet Union would be concerned. For these reasons, the possibility of Soviet intervention concerning the destruction of our plans to release American POWs and coup the puppet regime in Hanoi would be of paramount importance to the Soviet Union."

One little known fact in this whole story, at least the U.S. media has not spent time on this, is Canada's involvement in Vietnam, the rescue of Americans during the Iranian crisis, and the plan to rescue POW/MIAs and the Glomar Java Sea people.

According to Barker, the Glomar Java Sea, owned by a corporation in Texas, was "partially financed by the Canadian Development Corporation, a government of Canada institution." When the "global marine went bankrupt in January (1986), Canada, the largest investor, took the biggest loss. To add insult to injury, Canadian people were aboard that drill ship and their bodies were never recovered."

If Canada could develop better relations with China, then "the largest untapped market in the world," and if Canada could see that American POWs were released, then they would have "great leverage with the American government."

"Finally, the release of POWs and the Glomar Java Sea people by the Canadian government would create a nationalistic pride." That, Barker said, was why the Canadian government agreed to help him in his attempt to get POWs released.

It didn't turn out that way, however. The Canadian government members changed their mind, Barker was set up on a drug charge and put in jail, one of his cohorts was bludgeoned to death, and his business partner disappeared off the face of the earth.

In Barker's handwriting, he wrote from his jail cell, "If Canada were to go through with the original plan, the risks and profits would potentially be detrimental. Humanitarianism plays no role. I feel Canada has decided it's better, more profitable and wiser to stop our plan and do nothing concerning the human rights issue at hand."

As it turned out, Barker's plan was killed by the Canadian government-- and so were some of the men involved. International intrigue! At its highest, wouldn't you say? And this is a very condensed version of the Richard Barker story.

Regarding the American Political Position and Ramifications part of Barker's statement[65], "Another possibility which has occurred to me and to others is the matter of national security. If prisoners of war are released, in some cases 20 years after their capture, it will certainly have a damaging effect upon all volunteer arm(ed) forces, as no one would want to join a military service in the United States with the knowledge that if captured, the government would do nothing for years to effect their release. . .The United States could not afford to gain the release of prisoners of war and hold the lid on the cover up implications which would reveal a government unconcerned for the prisoners for so may years. . .

"I have never had any intention of embarrassing the United States government, but I was and am still concerned with the release of the 475 prisoners of war left in Vietnam today."

All of this adds up to the fact that there were attempts by some people to negotiate the release of U.S. POWs, at least in 1986. And some of these attempts were made through international channels. I now ask myself, why would someone from our country have to go through Russia or China or Canada to try to find our POWs and return them home to the United States?

* * *

In March, April, May and July of 2000, Mike Blair wrote articles that were published in The Spotlight. One headline read "U.S. POWs Kidnapped, Tortured by Communists," another was "Former POW Files Suit to Reclaim Good Name," a third was "POW Lawyer Told to Halt Probe," and a fourth was "Army Agents Conceal Fate of POW."

It seems that Sp4 Ernie Fletcher, a 19-year old American soldier, was abandoned in 1959 by our government when the Russians abducted him, and then tortured him for 22 years.

When he was released on November 17, 1981, he returned to Fort Dix, New Jersey, to be discharged from the Army. Only one American visited him all those years, a U.S. military official. The Red Cross was not permitted to contact him to determine if he was starving or being beaten. The government's story was that Ernie wanted to stay in prison. Two British soldiers, who later escaped from East Germany, confirmed Ernie's abduction story.

An even more startling bit of information is that Army Command Sargeant Major Joseph P. Nevin Sr. (ret.), who decided to help Ernie present his case, had his life threatened, by what he believes to be CIA agents, on two different occasions.

The July article revealed, "U.S. Army intelligence officers violated orders issued at the highest level at the Pentagon to conceal the fate of American servicemen taken as prisoners by the East German communists and Russians during the Cold War."

I guess the government would rather save face and go along with reports from STASI, East German secret police, that Ernie had defected, than believe Ernie's story and clear his name.

How many others, one has to ask, had their freedom taken away from them in the same way?

* * *

Even some TV shows are questioning the Soviets involvement with our American POWs from the Vietnam War.[66] On 1/11/02, PAX TV's program, "Encounters With The Unexplained" featured an entire half hour on "Where Are The POWs?"

At the end of the program, after discussing American POWs in both Korea and Vietnam, the narrator said, "Other long silent mysteries remain. Did the Soviets secretly transport American POWs to the former Soviet Union from Korea and Southeast Asia and even from German POW camps in World War II? And, is it possible that Americans ended up in Soviet slave labor camps, many in even more horrific circumstances as guinea pigs for Soviet-run medical experiments?"

Thank God we are finally talking about possibilities like this! There have been too many reports to ignore this situation any longer.

* * *

In March of 2002, I received e-mail about a "Trip Report for TDY to Moscow, Krasnoyarsk and Irkutsk, Russia, 9-26 September 2001.[67] The purpose of the TDY was to "thoroughly investigate the eyewitness sightings of U.S. servicemen in the Gulag."

The result of this TDY was that "New information on Americans in the Gulag was garnered, and the circle of academic and historical sources was greatly expanded. As the Gulag research effort grows, more research trips will need to be conducted to strengthen and exploit current information sources and establish new ones."

Now, what kind of conclusions should we draw from this bit of information? Hm-m-m?

> "Washington bureaucrats will never voluntarily acknowledge a problem they don't know how to solve."[68]

In 1993, President Clinton's top deputies refused to meet with relatives of POW/MIAs, while at the same time the President was telling them of his devotion to the POW/MIA problem. This was just the latest in a string of contradictions by the presidents in office during and after the Vietnam War.

In 1990, Theodore G. Schweitzer III, believed he had the answer to the MIA issue, so he approached the DIA with a plan to write a book based on research he wanted to conduct. He planned to use a Fujitsu optical scanner to copy the secret prisoner archives and a central record index (The Red Book) that Colonel Pham Duc Dai, then director of the Hanoi Museum, had shown him.[69] He needed the U.S. government's approval as an agent or snoop since the trade embargo had not been lifted, yet. He would gain access to the Vietnamese archives based on his background as a librarian.

After months of getting nowhere, Schweitzer was told by a Pentagon civilian, "We could never fund anything this . . . irregular." In desperation, Schweitzer turned to Texas billionaire H. Ross Perot after months of searching for other funding and a publisher. His belief remained steadfast--he had the answer to the MIA situation.

Perot's response to Schweitzer's project was a firm "No" when he learned that all American's in The Red Book were dead. Perot was interested only in bringing home live POW/MIAs. He also felt strongly that if he was able to get any of the POW/MIAs out, they had to be real prisoners, not defectors or involved in drugs.[70] He was also convinced that there was a conspiracy abroad involving our government, drugs and the POW/MIAs.[71]

> "The Pentagon will never admit there is 'evidence' of U.S. POWs in Southeast Asia. Yes, there's information. But there can never be evidence. Because the existence of evidence would require the bureaucrats to take action."[72]

In 1969, Ross Perot led an intensive campaign, United We Stand, to do something about the MIAs left behind in Vietnam. His objective was to make the public aware of their plight. McConnell's book, Inside Hanio's Secret Archives, goes into more detail in Chapter 10.

A special Congressional Commission was set up under Ross Perot in April 1985. He had already done a study on the MIA problem for President Reagan. He was on the President's Advisory Council on Foreign Intelligence. One of the conclusions he came to was that the DIA, being military, was looking for "usable Intelligence," enough to be able to rescue an MIA.[73] What friends and families were looking for was, is anyone still alive over there?

In addition to his leadership regarding MIAs, Perot helped finance some U.S. Intelligence for a number of years and maintained a staff to work on Vietnam prisoner data.

The consensus of opinion is that our government tried hard for several years to keep Perot from going to Hanoi to conduct his own private negotiations at his own expense. He was determined to get POW/MIAs out of Southeast Asia even if he had to pay for them. This, of course, would embarrass almost everyone who had been involved in our foreign policy since the seventies.

In 1987, a White House memo from Vice President Bush is supposed to have stated that if live Americans were found in Southeast Asia, after 14 years of denying there were any, ". . .can you imagine what would be asked for?" According to the book, The Men We Left Behind, it would have been embarrassing to almost all of those who had been involved in American foreign policy for the past 20 years.[74]

President Bush asked Perot to stop all of his negotiations with Hanoi. Perot had become upset, as had many POW/MIA families, that the discussions by our government with the Vietnamese never seemed to include our live prisoners. Perot's insistence on talking about missing Americans brought the following statement: "White House officials say they have tried to cooperate with Perot for some time on the MIA issue. But they say there is strong disagreement among Perot, MIA families, and responsible officials of the National Security Council staff. They say what Perot seems to be asking for is the prime role in the overall effort and although the President wishes him well, officials here say that (the prime role) he won't be given."[75]

"Imagine a returned U.S. POW asking Bush whether he did enough while Director of the CIA and then President to recover U.S. POWs. What would the POW say when he saw editorials and stories in the major media urging America to get past the POW/MIA issue and mocking POW activists? How would Christopher explain his top State Department job in the Carter Administration, when the U.S. government offered Hanoi recognition with no strings attached and no POWs required? What would a returned American prisoner want to tell Scowcroft[76], who helped negotiate the Paris Peace Accord, then years later sneered at the possibility that any prisoners remained in Southeast Asia while at the same time ordering that key POW records be kept secret from the American people?

"Finally, how would a U.S. POW react if he met the Pentagon and State Department officials, many in POW-related positions for the last twenty years, who since 1973 have said there was 'no evidence' that any U.S. POWs were retained by the communists after Vietnam?"[77]

During President Clinton's first term, a lot of people urged him to stay with the POW/MIA "status quo," for they found lots of reasons why pushing the issue would cause problems.

"'See, that's not the issue,' Perot said. 'The issue is they're our men, they went into combat for us, we left them, we owe it to them to bring them home. It won't look pretty back here, but we can build a consensus here that it's the right thing to do.'"[78]

Grieving Families

"We're committed to all of our warriors, past and present, we're committed to their families, whose pain has endured for decades. America's fallen heroes did not face the horror of battle for us to turn away from their sacrifice. They didn't fight for us to forget."

William S. Cohen
Secretary of Defense

Several years ago, Michael S. Clark, a graduate student at the Graduate School for Social Research in New York City, wrote his Ph.D. dissertation on "Grief Reactions in the MIA Families."

His father, Colonel Stanley S. Clark (USAF), was shot down over Laos in 1969 and listed as MIA.

Very few studies had been done on the continuing trauma that POW/MIA families had endured through the years. Research on this subject was the first goal of Michael Clark's dissertation.

The second goal was to look into why the Armed Forces and the Department of Defense had continued to give much more attention to the returning POWs and their families than the MIA families.

And third, he wanted to consider the impact of his father's loss on his own life. He hoped that the results of his research would help other MIA families who had relatives missing.

"What we all share is the uncertainty and ambiguity surrounding the loss of a loved one and the inability to bring finality to our grief."[1]

Michael Clark's pilot study was conducted on 63 MIA family members. In comparison with individuals who suffered a normal or expected loss, the data Michael gathered "demonstrated that the MIA families as a group are exhibiting intense levels of grief reaction. The levels of grief intensity are higher than those of the comparison group of relatives who had lost a loved one 18-months earlier--the normal death group."[2]

He found that even though the MIA family loss is still unproven, their grief has not subsided because the loss of their missing man has not been finalized.

". . . it is difficult to confront the loss when one does not know if the missing man is dead or alive."[3]

The agreed upon length of time a person should grieve is six months to two years. This is not valid for MIA families. The agreed upon result of a person who grieves longer than that period of time is determined to be negative and that person can experience pathological grief. This, also, is not true when it comes to MIA families because they have no body to bury.

"In fact, many of the family members are functioning at relatively normal levels when compared to individuals experiencing pathological grief."[4]

FREEDOM OF INFORMATION ACT

Through the years, hundreds of families have pressed the government and the Armed Forces to give them information about their MIA loved ones. Despite the unclassified documents that became available when the Freedom of Information Act was instituted, most MIA information is still being withheld. And the information that is provided the families is most often such that would not be considered detrimental to national security.

Many of these families have resorted to legal battles to obtain the MIA information. To no avail. Some of these ordinary citizens have been put under surveillance because they exercised their legal rights to do so.

THREATS

Many organizations have cropped up through the years to act as POW/MIA activists. A few of the MIAs were returned after their families paid huge amounts of money to Vietnam officials.

Our government returned other MIAs only after the families were told to never speak about the incident, for if they did, a disaster of some kind would occur to one of them.

Still others were told that if they pursued their quest to find out what happened to their MIA men, the MIAs would be killed.

Some families were threatened with a variety of things if they continued to talk about their MIA son or husband or brother.

Others found strange things happening in their homes: doors unlocked, items missing, mysterious calls in the night, disappearing papers, gas turned off then on again without lighting the pilot, veiled threats, barbecues lit in the middle of the night, cars tinkered with, strange men breaking into their homes when they were not there--scare tactics to shut them up. Some homes have been bugged it seems, so the government can find out what the families know.

"The secrecy that cloaks this issue has led many people to conclude that there are some in the government who don't want the truth to come out."[5]

That is certainly an understatement!

OUR GRIEVING CONTINUES

I ask, after having experienced a lot of these tactics and talking to others who have, too, how can our grieving not continue? If the government and the military keep doing and saying things that are questionable, even to an idiot, how can we MIA families believe that our loved ones are really dead? Not knowing is killing us!

Some stories stand out among those that I've heard about through the years. For instance, a man named Liam Atkins, who worked for CNN in Vietnam, was charged with a criminal offense and sent to jail because he talked too much about the POW/MIA issue.[6]

Another American, Ann Holland, told Monika Jensen-Stevenson (Kiss The Boys Goodbye), "The pain the families have had to live with. . . The nights, the sleepless nights. . . Two of my sons now serve in the Air Force. If I quit asking questions now, who will be there for them if their time comes? This is our country and if the people running it aren't doing their very best, then they need to be reminded of what this country stands for. We do not leave men behind who gave all they had to give when they were asked, believing we would give all we had to give to get them back."[7]

There were families of POW/MIAs shot down in Laos and Cambodia who have received information that their men were indeed alive, but they have been declared KIA by the military. This, after Kissinger said in 1976 that there were no American prisoners in Cambodia.

According to some intelligence analysts, our government knew that many of our men were kept in remote prison camps, even though they had been listed as MIA.[8] Some information, declassified at one time, was re-classified when it became apparent that it contradicted other documents already made available to the public.

Do you think that certain bureaucracies in our government are afraid to declassify information about MIAs because it might reflect on their department's performance? Do they hope that in time, all POW/MIA families will forget, die or give up on finding out what happened to their men? And in which parts of government are these bureaucracies?

YEARS AND YEARS OF NOT KNOWING

I received a letter in 1991 from an acquaintance, Carolyn Reed-Shaw, whose father had been on the Glomar Java Sea. Her mother had just died when she wrote, "She enjoyed your mutual interests in Vietnam. For. . .years she was tormented with the question of whether my father was dead or alive. She wanted to believe that he hadn't survived the accident after all this time, but couldn't . . . because of all the unanswered questions. And to think of all the families who have been going through it for so many years, too."

In the American Legion magazine, March 1992, there appears an article entitled, "POW/MIAs - The Men We Left Behind."[9] The authors quote Richard Christian from the Legion's Washington office, who said, "These people want to know what happened to their sons, their husbands, their fathers, and their brothers. . .All they get from the Pentagon is a sheet of paper that's all blacked out except for three lines. It's a cold process devoid of compassion."

The 18-page article continued. "There is evidence of the following: U.S. government officials didn't take the hunt for POW/MIAs seriously; the government's effort to find POW/MIAs was destined to fail from the beginning; and military secrecy buried the truth about America's missing men--in Pentagon files and on the battlefield."[10]

And the grieving goes on and on and on.

> "WE HAVE the sensitivity of a pile driver in dealing with families."[11]
>
> Gen. John W. Vessey Jr.
> Presidential Emissary to Hanoi

Mrs. Marion Shelton's husband, Col. Charles Shelton, was the only American serviceman listed as a POW until 1994. In my estimation, the U.S. continued to carry Col. Shelton as a POW because of an overwhelming amount of evidence to support his survival. It also gave the impression that the U.S. government kept the POW issue as a national priority even if there was only one POW to find.

Col. Charles Shelton was shot down in 1965 over Laos. Marion was told not to talk about the information she was given re: the CIA's failed attempts to rescue him. Her phone was bugged to make sure she followed the CIA instructions. But, on her own, she spent years in secret gathering reports, 200 pages worth. She even traveled to Laos to try to find him.

Marion raised her five children by herself and worked almost 24 hours a day on the POW/MIA issue.

I remember the last thing Marion said to me about the information she had just received about her husband. Live sighting reports were showing up on a continuous basis at that time. People would come out, some of them Vietnamese refugees, and Marion told me they would say things like, "I worked in such and such a prison, and we had a man, an American, a big man, real big, and taut, and tall, and strong, and bull headed, who lost a lot of weight. He would take so much and then he'd punch out some guard. Of course he was beaten up pretty bad and slammed back in prison."

Marion had an inventory of names and contacts she'd kept through the years and a chronology of the way things progressed in her attempt to find her husband. I wish I knew what happened to those lists. They would be more than valuable in tracking down people who could have maybe helped me and/or others in their quest for information about POW/MIAs.

One time, Marion told me I was welcome to read through her documents, but I never did. I wish I'd been quicker to ask her family about her records.

She also told me, around the middle of 1989, that she was having trouble with a local person who was trying to get her to be chairman of his POW group. It was quite common for such groups to ask a POW/MIA family member to be on their board. But, Marion didn't like that. She said there was something about this redheaded guy, named Gregory. She didn't want to be involved with him in any way.

Her daughter decided to take the job of treasurer, just to keep an eye on what he was doing, but he got more and more pushy. He kept asking Marion for more and more things and tried to get into her personal life. She shared with me that he was annoying her a lot, which made her most unhappy.

I wasn't the only one who disliked and didn't trust Gregory. Was it a coincidence that he was intruding in both Marion's and my life? Was he really a Vietnam Veteran biker trying to do good or one of "them?"

What's interesting is that the government paid Marion through the years as though her husband was on active duty, which was contrary to Nixon's policy based on the fact that all POWs were either returned or dead.

She was considered one of many POW/MIA wives who were paranoid or just wacky, and she was not to be taken seriously by the media and others. "Even the National League of Families, who were supposed to be on her side, said that her husband was only listed 'alive' for symbolic reasons, despite the huge amount of evidence she had accumulated over the years."[12]

Through years of stress and pressure over the POW/MIA issue, trying to get her husband returned home, Marion developed problems with drinking and prescription pills, and had several episodes of being in rehab. But when I knew her, she had conquered all that and was living in San Diego. As a way of starting over, she thought maybe moving to a new location-- a place in Texas--might help her. She had found a house and was looking forward to moving. When I last visited her, she was fine and upbeat in her attitude on life.

Marion Shelton was found shot to death in her home on October 4, 1990. The autopsy report said she had committed suicide.

(Just a note: this was the same time intrusions began in my home).

The whole story of her suicide is iffy, if you ask me. She was too upbeat at that time. She had been asked out to a movie with her daughter and some friends, but declined saying that when they got back, she'd have dinner waiting for them.

When they returned, the front door was locked and she wasn't answering the doorbell. The side gate was locked, too, which struck them as odd. When they got inside, they called her and looked for her. They thought maybe she had started drinking again and had gone to bed. They even began to look in closets, thinking she had become paranoid. She was nowhere.

Then they went to the sliding door in the back of the house. It was locked. Upon opening it, they stepped on to the patio and looked in the hot tub. Nothing!

At that point, someone looked up. Marion had a terraced backyard, and there on one of the terraces was Marion, dressed in a cocktail dress, dead, with a gun in her hand.

All of the doors were locked from the inside.

Besides, most women don't use a gun to kill themselves. A bottle of pills, a jug of vodka, the hot tub--maybe. But a gun? And what was it with a cocktail dress?

Her family struggled with the POW issue after that. It was not long before the now grown children asked the government to change their father's status to KIA. They were unable to cope with the responsibility and the publicity needed to keep the entire POW issue alive, any more, which is what Marion had done for all those years. Of course, the government didn't object when the Shelton children requested their father's status be changed to KIA. It got the only POW off their list without having to account for him. Amazing how things happen, sometimes.

Marion made some incredible contacts with some people high up in our government as well as others in the world. She was getting information from behind a lot of backs.

By knowing Marion, I was introduced for the first time to the serious venue of spy stuff. She was taking huge risks. She couldn't name her contacts because she was afraid for their lives. She needed to protect them. The first time I met her, I sat awe struck. She made my little forays look like peanuts. I was involved in a Girl Scout Camp compared to what she was dealing with in the real, grownup world.

Marion even went to Afghanistan to try to get them to release Russian POWs with the stipulation that the Russians, in turn, negotiate the return of American POWs in Vietnam.

Following is a tribute written to Marian Shelton by Ann Holland.

FREE AT LAST

She was just a young wife and mother when her life was plunged into a hell she never asked for.

When her beloved Charles was chosen to represent the thousands of men who were left behind, it fell on her shoulders to be the one to carry his candle and keep the Light of Hope burning for all of us. It was a position where she gave up her right to a "normal" life. She was not a widow, nor was she a wife. She served that position willingly, always with grace and dignity. Many times over the next quarter of a century, her body got tired but she knew she had a job to do and even though ill and in pain, she would carry our Candle of Hope to the far corners of the world.

In the end, the one constant factor in her life, her love for her children, was not enough to sustain her. The young woman who only wanted to love and be loved, got too tired and became another casualty of the Vietnam War.

May God in His infinite wisdom and mercy, grant her the wings she earned here on Earth. She served her Charles and her country, above and beyond the call of duty.

Thank you, Marian Shelton. Soar with the eagles, Dear Lady. Your chains have been broken and you are Free at Last.

(Pictures of Charles Shelton and his family appear at the beginning of Scott Barnes book, Bohica.)

THE CALLOUS MILITARY

"To say that the wives and families of the missing men had been treated callously by the military and the American government would be an understatement. . . They have given the families only the information that they needed to know. They have kept them apart and prevented them from checking out what they have been told. And they have relentlessly snuffed out any spark of hope they might have had."[13]

Col. Charles Schraf, US Air Force, was shot down over North Vietnam in 1965. He was listed as MIA. Even though he was seen in pictures of American prisoners in Hanoi, his status was never changed to POW.

His sister, Barbara Lowerison, never gave up on trying to get her brother home. She has written to everyone she could think of through the years--United Nations, His Holiness the Pope, the Queen of England, Mr. Gorbachev, the Vietnamese and the Chinese. She also sends telegrams to her brother (in care of Hanoi), on Christmas, his birthday, the anniversary of his shootdown and at Thanksgiving. She gets an international call a couple weeks after each telegram. The call lasts about two minutes and no one speaks but she can hear planes taking off and landing. In 1988, during one of those phone calls, she heard three words, "Barbara, help me."

Air Force Intelligence officers listened to the tape, took a copy with them, but it was somehow blank. They asked for several more, but they said those tapes were blank, too. When they asked for the original, Barbara refused. I wonder why?

Barbara Lowerison has been trying to deal with the military for over thirty-six years. She has never given up.[14]

Her story and picture appeared in the January 13, 1992 TIME Magazine. " 'I think they've known all along where he is,' she says. 'They've made grave, serious mistakes leaving so many men behind. Now they want to cover it up.' But like some other MIA family members, she has become so distrustful of the Pentagon that she may never be satisfied by any official sifting of the evidence that does not lead to her own conclusions."[15]

In The Bamboo Cage, author Nigel Cawthorne writes that this waiting to hear what happened to their MIA loved ones has taken a terrible toll on the wives. Some have almost gone crazy over the government denying the MIA's existence and the leaked documents the wives have received saying the men are alive.

Most wives have become bitter with the government as well as the military. A lot of ex-military men have become disillusioned with their country. Wives and mothers go to the empty graves of MIAs, still wondering where their loved ones are.

And then there are wives like Kathryn Fanning who have fought the government. In 1985, as Patty Hopper, chairman of Task Force Omega told me, the Defense Department gave Kathryn some remains, identified by dental comparison, saying they were her husband's. She accepted and buried his remains.

Eighteen months later, Kathryn obtained the CILHI paper work, proving there were no teeth among his purported remains. She had her husband's remains exhumed and sent to Dr. Charney. He documented the fact that the small amount of remains in the casket could not be scientifically identified as Hugh Fanning, or anyone else for that matter.

As a result, she said the identification given her was circumstantial, so she wouldn't accept the government's findings, afterall.

According to a 1991 Newsweek article, Kathryn Fanning spent six years trying to get people to pay attention to her. " 'People ask me why I don't get on with my life,' she says. 'This is my life.'"[16]

Many relatives have had con men and pranksters prey on them. They are given false stories and misinformation, along with a request for money, to get their MIA back.

MEMORIAL DAY

On the front page of the Sunday, May 30, 1993 Parade Magazine that appeared in most large newspapers across the country, pictures of a lot of our POW/MIAs from the Vietnam War, were displayed. Explaining the Memorial Day photo spread was, ". . . it is fitting that we give special thought to the POWs and MIAs of the Vietnam War. Their fate remains in doubt, and their families continue their vigil."

All of the pictures were labeled "missing" and out of the 53 faces, four were Special Forces and two of those became MIA in 1968. I continue my search for any information I can find that might lead me to discover what really happened to Jim. Unfortunately, the two 1968 MIAs disappeared in May, not in November when Jim was listed MIA.

Ann Holland, wife of an MIA, is quoted in that same article as saying, "Families of the missing men are the living casualties of the war. We don't know whether or not we will ever see our loved ones again. But, at the very least, we would like an honest accounting."[17]

Too many other families have tried to put the whole MIA issue out of their minds.

But the grieving goes on.

WHY MIAs LIVE ON

In 1991, Cokie Roberts was a special correspondent for ABC News. She wrote an article that The San Diego Union published on September 25. "Why MIAs live on: how it feels when one of the family is missing" was about Cokie's father who was an MIA, not from Vietnam, but from an air crash in Alaska.[18]

Cokie wrote, "While focusing on whether some MIAs might still be alive, we fail to understand why it's crucial to solve the mystery of the missing. . ." The MIA families have suffered "indignities" while "thousands of miles from where their loved ones are lost, with their government only occasionally showing any interest in their cause and the Vietnamese government proving totally untrustworthy, first saying all bodies have been located, then suddenly producing some remains."

She noted that it seems to be the MIA women relatives who contact the reporters at ABC, insisting that something be done to return the missing or the POWs.

"And though it's important to know if some soldiers survived, it is just as important to identify those who died. Their families are entitled to the peace of certainty; they deserve to mourn without fear that their mourning somehow implies they have abandoned hope; they are due the dignity of burying their dead."

And Cokie's mourning, although her father was not lost in Vietnam, sounds just the same as POW/MIA families. "I know my father is not alive. . .But still I catch myself hesitating before changing the kitchen wallpaper, fearing that he will come home and think strangers are in the house."

Although all of these stories, including mine, are heart-rending, can you ". . . imagine for a moment what it must be like to be one of the missing men: to be abandoned for ever in an enemy prison, to know that your government has declared you dead, your wife is getting on with her life and has probably married someone else, your kids have grown up without you and that you will probably never see your homeland ever again."[19]

POW/MIA BRACELETS

The first POW/MIA bracelets with name, rank, and incident date, appeared in 1970, before the war ended. Robert K. "Bob" Dornan, former Air Force fighter pilot, and later a Congressman from California, came up with the idea. VIVA (Voices in Vital America) had the bracelets made and distributed.

The bracelets became an instant hit. Hundreds of Americans were looking for a way to demonstrate their concern and support for the POWs/MIAs, and the bracelets were perfect.

By January 1973, when the Paris Peace Accords were signed, five million Americans wore bracelets. Like the POW/MIA flag, the bracelets are a remembrance that the POW/MIA issue is still unsolved--still not concluded--still unfinished.

There are bracelets now for the missing men in World War II, the Korean War and the Persian Gulf War. Memory bracelets are also available for those who want to honor the servicemen whose remains have been returned to the U.S.[20]

Over the years I've had several bracelets with Jim's name on them. When the occasion arises, I find myself removing the bracelet and giving it to someone who shows an interest. Usually this is that person's first introduction to the POW/MIA issue. The bracelet somehow allows the wearer to feel connected to that serviceman. The bracelet becomes a daily reminder that someone is still unaccounted for and needs the wearer's help to be able to return home.

I've discovered, over the years, that I am unable to wear Jim's bracelet on a continual basis. It represents my feelings of futility, heartache, depression and disappointment in our government. To stay in a constant state of turmoil would surely drive me crazy.

After more than 30 years, the grieving process continues for thousands of families whose servicemen are still unaccounted for.

PART III

Chapter Six

Searching

"Breathes there the man with soul so dead
Who never to himself hath said,
This is my own, my native land!
Whose heart hath ne'er within him burned,
As home his footsteps he hath turned
From wandering on a foreign strand? . . ."[1]

Sir Walter Scott

After I returned from Vietnam in 1989, I began to discover, as a home health nurse, that doctors threw away hundreds of pounds of medications and supplies that I realized a lot of countries could use, such as Vietnam, Laos, Cambodia and Thailand. In fact, bells and whistles went off in my head when I saw how I might be able to swap medical supplies for information on the humanitarian level.

So, I began asking various doctors I knew, "Can I have those things you throw away that are still useable?"

The answer was always, "Oh sure. No problem."

Several newspapers and television stations contacted me when I returned to San Diego. I did a TV spot about my trip to Vietnam at this time and I said I was planning to return to Southeast Asia in the near future.

As a result of the TV spot, two Vietnam veterans called the TV station to get my name. I returned their call since the station was instructed not to give out my phone number. We made a date to meet at a local restaurant.

Both of the San Diego men were friends and they said they were interested in making a trip back to Nam. They wondered if they could tag along when I went. Their names were Bill Evans and Sam Van Alystyne.

My friend, Veronica (Roni) Schanley, whose brother was an MIA, had said she'd like to go with me, too. Roni was a clinical social worker at Scripps Hospital at the time. I thought a group of four would make a nice number--two women, two men. But, I wasn't too sure about having two veterans along who might be suffering from post-traumatic stress disorder (PTSD). The other doubt I had was whether I could handle three other people on "my" trip.

I also felt that the four of us needed to get to know each other before we traveled together. So the four of us met and I laid the ground rules, "according to Barbara." I told them about the problems we might run into with the Vietnamese government and how we would handle that situation. We also explored the possibility of our own emotional problems and what we would do to help each other.

What would I do if one of us got arrested? If one of us got sick? If one of us went bonkers? Besides, I had to get us there--and home again--safe. I couldn't depend on some tour company to handle all those details.

In February 1990, Mademoiselle magazine ran their usual horoscope article which said, under my Capricorn sign, "With six planets in your sign, you'll be able to accomplish a great deal. One of these planets, Venus, gives magic to the way you handle people. You're more confident and in command than you've been in awhile. You know what needs to be done and you don't hesitate to take the lead. Your vitality returns as well, so when all the problems stop at your desk. . .you'll know exactly what to do to get your show on the road. Some unusual situation brings a cherished wish closer."[2]

If I followed that reading, then I was on the right tract. I decided to do just that.

We spent six months meeting once a week, getting to know each other, and talking, talking, talking. During those six months I spent almost every evening on the phone, networking to get names of people in Vietnam I might be able to use if something happened. For instance, what if we found an American? How would we get him out without our government killing him before we got him to a safe place?

* * *

I need to stop here for a moment to explain that last comment. You see, I have papers that describe how the government tasked a man while he was still on active duty, to go into Laos from the Thai side to look for POWs. He did. And he found live Americans across the Mekong River.

When he returned he told of a deal the Laotian government was willing to make for the return of the Americans. And our government, the specific person I don't know, said to "liquidate the merchandise." The man was ordered to do away with the Americans. It would appear our government didn't want live POWs returned at this time.

The man wouldn't do it, so his career ended. Not only that, but the IRS hounded him from then on, and he was made to look like a turncoat. His name is Scott Barnes and he wrote the book, Bohica, about his experiences. There still is controversy about whether his story is true or not.

There have been a lot of ideas as to why our government didn't want POWs returned. I think the most plausible one is that from the beginning, the Vietnam War was not a popular war. Nixon wanted to look good as the savior, so our people in power decided to just chop everything off. End everything. No loose ends. Soon there was a policy--those who didn't come back in Operation Homecoming were dead. Over and out.

From that point on, the government put up a wall between the answers and the families, no matter how much the POW/MIA families screamed, "How can you say they're alive one day and then say they're all dead the next. Does that mean the Vietnamese lined them up against the wall and shot them all? If that's the case, we want the bodies."

By now, the Vietnamese were saying, "We're not giving you anything." This was their response to the Paris Peace Talks where Nixon had promised the Vietnamese 3.25 billion dollars in reconstruction aid in a secret communiqué, through his representative, Henry Kissinger, according to Chapter 3 in the Bamboo Cage.

However, Congress denied the appropriation.

I could just see the heads of the Vietnamese government ticking off numbers, reducing the list of POWs they would return to us.

So it was like there was a price on the head of each POW, just like the Vietnamese did with the French. They held back the French prisoners after France left their country in 1954. And every year, when France donated money to care for the French cemeteries, another few Frenchmen were released from some jungle camp in the boonies. And that continued fifteen or twenty years after the French occupation, which was around the mid-fifties.

According to the chairman of Task Force Omega, she discovered through research that France had paid the ransom for 1000-1500 French Legionaires, between 1954 and 1976. The last two Frenchmen we know of who made their way out of Southeast Asia did so in 1982. That was nine years after the Vietnam War ended. One had been held captive in North Vietnam while the other was held in Laos.

Knowing this pattern of leveraging prisoners for money existed among the Vietnamese, the POW/MIA families began to say that it wasn't unusual for the Vietnamese to barter, so let's barter. But, as the years went by, and we couldn't seem to get past the policy that the POW/MIAs were dead, only one person, to my knowledge, was tasked by our President to negotiate with the Vietnamese to get live Americans out. And that was Ross Perot.

Perot was actually tasked by President Reagan to go to Vietnam to see what he could do about the whole issue. Being a person who handled everything in a very business-like manner, I think he went to the Vietnamese and said something like, "This is what we want. What do you want?" And they probably said something like "We want this money."

Knowing Perot, he no doubt said, "Well, I can do that."

The story goes that Perot came back to President Reagan and said, "This is the deal. We can get this number of POWs out. Here's the money. Here's what we have to do. I'll supply the planes. It's a done deal."

For years Perot had supplied the planes that carried Red Cross boxes to the POWs in Hanoi, so it wasn't unusual for him to jump into this deal. He was a real supporter--a real gung-ho supporter of the military.

I understand that the President said, "Can't do it."

I think that was as much as Perot could take. So he backed off.

There were a few family members who have gone to Southeast Asia who wanted to negotiate, but they were not successful. They spent thousands of dollars trying to get information, thinking they could buy the answers to where their loved one was held in a POW camp, or where his remains were. No such luck.

I've had a fantasy for years that somehow I found Jim and got him home. Other than standing at the top of the Empire State Building, screaming at everybody, I would take Jim on my arm and walk into a National League of Families meeting. I'd wait until the last day when all of the panel members were in front of the attendees, answering questions, and all the Generals and their staffs were sitting there on stage under the hot lights. And I'd go up front and say, "Excuse me, I'd like to introduce you to somebody. This man you say has been dead since. . ."

I would love that.

But, if they came to me and said, "To get you off our backs, we'll let you have your husband, but you can never say anything about it," then I'd accept that, but I'd be very angry knowing that Jim probably wasn't the only one being kept under wraps.

If it meant his freedom, I would do it. So, it's possible that some families have succeeded in getting their men back and have sworn to never speak about the cover-up.

There have been times when I have been flying home from one of The League meetings when I've sat next to an active duty military person. I can remember one, a Lieutenant Commander, who said, "Why were you in Washington?"

I told him about The League meeting.

"Oh, what's that about?"

"Well, my husband's an MIA. What do you think about the POW/MIA situation?"

He said, "I've got no doubt we left them behind. I bet you'd find that 80% of active duty personnel believe there were men left behind."

But, I digress.

I think another reason why our government would not buy back the POWs was because as a country, we don't pay for political prisoners. I call them that, because there's been a whole change in titles. The Vietnamese don't call the POWs "prisoners of war" but "criminals against the state."

The result of the title change is interesting. When someone talks to the Vietnamese about POWs, they can say with a straight face, "We have no POWs."

I'll tell you another story. I found out that when speaking with the Vietnamese, I had to be precise. No general questions. Everything I said had to be very specific.

So, if someone from our government were to ask the Vietnamese today if they still had POWs, and they said no, we'd believe them. Why? Either we're bent on wanting to believe them, or our country is too trusting of another country's government speaking the truth.

But I ask, why believe your enemy? Did you believe your enemy when you stood in front of them with a gun? Or did you treat them like the enemy they were? Did you shoot first, or did you ask them if they wanted to shoot you and then took their word for it? I don't think so.

There have been six administrations since the Vietnam War. We've got a real snowball going here. What a can of worms it would have been if the truth came out, if anywhere along the line, the people had said, "Gosh, wouldn't that be a real plume in the President's cap if he brought all the Vietnam POWs home?"

If that had happened, I can't imagine how many people in those six administrations would have had to stand in the line of those responsible for keeping the policy alive-- "there were no POWs left in Vietnam after Homecoming II."

The word treason comes to mind.

And I can't imagine how many wives would be bigamists, thinking their husbands were dead, or how many illegitimate children there would be as a result of the wives remarrying. Or how many mothers and fathers died during these many years, thinking their sons were dead but having no bodies, no closure. Would families have to pay back the death benefits they received from insurance companies? And what about the serviceman's back pay?

So, there are a lot of reasons why our POW/MIA situation doesn't change. We didn't want to be in Vietnam, we wanted to get out as fast as we could, and we made it policy that we hadn't left any military men behind. When it's policy, that's it.

And that's it.

* * *

Now back to our 1990 trip.

It was important that Bill, Sam, Roni and I agreed on the itinerary for our trip to Vietnam and how we would conduct ourselves. We should not be at cross-purposes, either. I also needed to feel comfortable with our arrangements, since I was the leader.

I wanted to impress the three of them with how important this trip to Vietnam would be. I was determined to work this sucker out. I had the name of a Tokyo news reporter who was interested in this topic and said he would get me help if I needed it. I had names of people who lived in Thailand. I searched for veterans who lived in Southeast Asia who might be able to hide an American. As was true for my first trip in 1989, Americans still could not make travel arrangements from the U.S. to Vietnam.

I sent the following letter.

Honorable Nguyen Co Thack
Ministry of Foreign Affairs
Hanoi, Socialist Republic of VietNam

Dear Mr. Thack:

In July of 1989, I collected approximately 600 pounds of medical supplies for Humanitarian International who planned to go to China Beach to start construction of a new medical clinic. Unfortunately, they were unable to get funding for the trip at this time. I had heard that an organization named East Meets West was traveling to China Beach for the same reason, so I decided to give them what I collected so that the supplies could be used without delay for this project.

I have again collected medical supplies, but this time plan to deliver them myself with the help of three other people. . . We are planning to arrive in Ho Chi Minh City on February 16 and travel north arriving in Hanoi on February 28. . .

My husband has been missing in the Kontum area since 1968, and the lady traveling with me has a brother that has been missing since 1969 in the Bong Son area. We both hope to visit the areas that our relatives were last seen in. If you could offer any insight as to how this can best be accomplished, please let us know.

We are looking forward to this trip and the possibility of meeting with you.

Sincerely,
Barbara Birchim

I sent the following postcards on January 9, 1990. The first one went to the Peoples Committee Gialai, Kontum.

Dear Mr. Quang:

I have collected about 500 pounds of medical supplies which I will be delivering to several facilities. I would like to leave some with your medical facility. We hope to be in Kontum about February 22. It would be a delight to have the opportunity to meet you. I will also be looking for any information on my husband who was last seen in Kontum in 1968.

Sincerely,
Barbara Birchim

Dear Mr. Hoang Lien:

I will be in Da Nang about February 26 delivering medical supplies and would like to meet with you if possible. My husband has been missing in the Kontum area since 1968 and I thought that you might have an idea on how I might go about locating any information on him.

You help is greatly appreciated.

Sincerely,
Barbara Birchim

The itinerary I set up began with our flying to Bangkok and staying there for three days to get used to the weather and the time change. We also needed several days to process our visa at the Vietnamese Embassy. In order to do that, we had to bring extra pictures.

Then, we were to fly on to Saigon to begin our trip through Vietnam.

Here is the letter I submitted to Vietnam Tourism regarding our itinerary.

Dear Sir:

These travel plans are based around our need to deliver medical supplies to the hospital in Da Lat, Ky La and Hanoi. Also, Barbara Birchim wishes to go to Kontum to see the area where her husband was last seen 21 years ago, and Veronica Schanley wishes to stop in Bong Son to visit the area where her brother was last seen.

Fly to Ho Chi Minh City on 2/16 - 2 days
Drive to Da Lat, deliver medical supplies – 2 days
Drive to Ban Me Thuot – 1 day
Drive to Pleiku – 1 day
Drive to Kontum – 3 days
Drive to Bong Son – 1 day

Drive to Da Nang – 2 days
Fly to Hanoi on 2/28
Fly to Bangkok on March 4

We will be carrying approximately 400-500 pounds of medical supplies. Any help that you can give us would be most appreciated as we wish to make this a successful humanitarian trip.

Thank you,
Barbara Birchim

Let me explain why we chose certain cities to visit. Ban Me Thuot was where Sam was once based during the war and he wanted to revisit it. Roni's brother's helicopter went down near Bong Son and she wanted to see the area. Of course, I wanted to get to Kontum. And we needed to deliver medical supplies to Da Lat, a mountain resort considered to be the gateway to the Central Highlands, Da Nang and Hanoi.

Because tourism was so new in Vietnam and Saigon, we would have to have a government guide and an interpreter wherever we went.

I could only hope that the six months of getting to know these three new friends, along with endless hours on the phone making contacts, would be enough to prepare us for whatever might happen. Each of us came with our own mental baggage and it was going to be up to me to keep the group together. I made it quite clear from the beginning that this was "my party" and if they didn't like the rules, they couldn't come with me.

They had to agree to my agenda, or no dice. I'm a very flexible traveler, but the goals were clear. We were looking for information about Americans who were left behind after the Vietnam War. I figured that if I showed my government "pals" how to get information while in Vietnam, then maybe they would hop to and find the errors of their ways. After all, if a single person, an unknown nurse could do it, then the government should be able to find some way to do it, too. How could the U.S. cower to the Vietnamese when everyone I met in my travels from other counties knew the Vietnamese were holding POWs?

I guess my anger and frustration along with my stubbornness was at play at this point. You tell me I can't do something and by George, I'm going to do it.

Friends of Sam and Bill came to the airport to see us off on February 12, 1990, along with some of the local media who took lots of pictures of the ten boxes and duffel bags that were stacked on the curb waiting to be processed by the airline.

The boxes were full of the medical supplies and medications that we were going to personally deliver to hospitals and clinics.

Each of us carried our personal clothing, cameras and toiletries in backpacks on to the plane. Quite a send off!

We had two more boxes than allowed and the airline wasn't being gracious. They wouldn't wave our overage even though it was for humanitarian purposes, so I had to pay an additional $177 before we left San Diego.

Our first stop was Tokyo where we had to change planes, which made me nervous about the possibility of our medical supplies getting lost in the shuffle.

But, upon arriving in Bangkok, all of the supplies came off the conveyor belt in good shape. While the other three took care of our bags, I talked to customs and got the okay to walk straight through, which was a great surprise and relief.

Our tour agency greeted us and suggested that we check our medical containers at the airport. That turned out to be a fabulous idea. We didn't need three cars to take us to the hotel, after all.

Our adventure had truly begun. The jitters of getting things together for this trip, and the contacts that needed to be made, were behind us. If we didn't have what we needed now, it was too late.

I had small stickers with a 4.5 million-dollar reward message written on them in Vietnamese left from my first trip. We planned to put the stickers on the local money and leave them in places where they could be found. We would do this in high traffic areas so the government wouldn't know we were dropping them, we hoped. It was risky, but we all agreed to do it.

I also had some flyers made up with information about Jim on them plus a picture of him that an artist drew of what he thought Jim would look like in 1990.

We took a vow before we left San Diego, to support each other when the locations and the memories became too much to bear alone. The test of whether or not we could pull this off successfully had started.

The first order of business in Bangkok was to get our visas for Vietnam and take care of last minute details. We went to the Vietnamese Embassy, but they didn't have our paperwork. We wondered where our $30 application fee had gone as we proceeded to fill out the paperwork again, and give them more money. Of course, we couldn't get the visas then so we'd have to return the next day.

We discovered there was a possibility of getting our freight shipped free to Saigon, so the next day Roni and I went to Thai Air. I gave the lady copies of letters I had from Humanitarian International, East Meets West Foundation, and Frances Carroll, Chairman of the American Legion Vernon Hill Post 435. The lady would not allow all of our boxes to go free, but she gave us 100 kilos free. We were ecstatic since that was about the amount of our excess baggage. When I presented the letter to the ticket agents, as we checked in for our flight to Vietnam, they allowed all our bags without a charge.

It was important to meet with Bill Bell at the American Embassy, so that was next on our agenda. Several months before we left, I wrote a letter to Bell and told him when we would be in Bangkok. I had a feeling from my '89 trip that he had more information about Jim and so I hoped he would meet with me. He sent a hand written note back, saying, "Oh, I'm glad you're coming. That's wonderful. Just call me when you get in and we'll do dinner."

Roni and I spent 2 ½ hours with him at the Embassy. The flavor of his response in Bangkok was 180 degrees different from his note. He was standoffish, and not sure he could fit us into his schedule.

At one point, he talked about the dangers of our going to Kontum. I was taken aback at his comment because he told me in 1989 that I should go. When I reminded him, he said he didn't remember telling me that.

Don't you believe it!

As during my earlier trip, Bell told me he remembered Jim's case because it was the only one like it. I listened to him as he mentioned things like the numbers of men being extracted via McGuire rigs, the long length of the flight, the adverse conditions, and the fact that Jim was the only serviceman declared MIA on November 15, 1968.

It still puzzled me how he could remember Jim's case so well when there were over 2400 men still missing in action.

One bit of information Bell gave us shocked me. He said they were getting a lot more live sighting reports from Laos than from Vietnam, a country where we American people were told none of our military men fought.

He also said there was a popular story floating around about a blind American living in the Highlands.

I was concerned that all my various activities might hinder my ability to get to Kontum, but Bell said he doubted that. He planned to be in Hanoi at the same time as we, so I invited him to have a drink with us then, even though he had just told us he could not have dinner with us, after all. There was no "Sorry," or "Let's do it next time you're here."

Had someone gotten to Bill Bell?

On the 16th, we got our medical supplies out of storage, through the X-ray at the airport, and checked on our Thai Air flight to Saigon.

SAIGON

We were quite a sight, arriving in the Saigon airport with all of the medical supply boxes and duffel bags.

I had color-coded padlocks and their keys, and I made an inventory for every box and duffel bag, with each item numbered. I took duct tape and scissors in case I needed to open the boxes.

Our group was the last one through the line. When it was our turn to go through customs at the Tan Son Nhat airport, I walked up to the customs person and said, "I know you want to open these, so which one do you want to go for first?"

He looked at me in utter shock. Then he ran around, talking in Vietnamese with the other customs officials. They seemed to be trying to figure out what the heck to do with our entourage.

"I've got them all ready to open. Let's go," I said.

The customs man I spoke to first, became very angry then, and finally after 45 minutes, he waved us on as the whole group of officials shook their fists at us and went stamp, stamp, stamp on each box and duffel bag.

A representative of the Vietnam Tourist Agency met us and took us to our hotel. We found out, when we arrived at the hotel, that there was no elevator. We couldn't lug all of those medical supplies up three flights of stairs. The hotel clerk said they had no storage rooms for our use, so we stacked everything at the far end of the check-in counter and covered them with several tablecloths.

Sam and Bill shared a room, and Roni and I had a room together. As I put the key in the door, I heard the phone ringing. An American voice said to me, "I'm with the Christian Science Monitor and we want to interview you. Would you mind?" His name was Ed Fitzgerald.

I said, "How did you get my phone number? How did you know I was in Saigon?"

"Oh, we have our ways."

He explained that they paid people at the hotels to watch for American tourists who fell within a certain age range. What they were looking for were GIs returning to Vietnam whom they could interview. He asked if we could meet with him the following evening.

The phone rang again before I got a chance to open my suitcase.

It was Greg from World Vision, calling to set up a time for an interview. He, too, was interested in veterans who were returning to where they had been stationed in Vietnam.

I explained that we were there on a humanitarian mission and we'd be asking questions, as we traveled, about the Americans who chose to stay behind.

I made an appointment with him for five o'clock that evening because we had to go to Vietnam Travel to get our itinerary worked out during the day.

The travel agent took us to his office after we were settled in our rooms. There they told us that the Highlands were closed to tourists. Needless to say, we were all upset. That meant that we could not deliver our medical supplies to Da Lat and I couldn't get to Kontum. I'd have to telex Dr. Thein in Da Lat to arrange for him to pick up the supplies, which he did before we left Saigon. I also needed to call Mr. Tach in the morning to see if he could pull some strings and get us into Kontum.

Things were not going well.

The interview for the Christian Science Monitor was held in one of the famous old hotels in Saigon, The Majestic Hotel, located on the waterfront in the center of of the city. The once elegant hotel stood proud, across from the harbor.

We had a hoot. The Christian Science Monitor reporters had rented a room that looked like a bordello, including red velvet wallpaper. It was a scream!

The lights and cameras were all set up ready for us when we arrived. None of us were used to the heat from so many lights, but the heat hit Sam the hardest. They had to stop filming to mop off his face and neck with towels more than once.

The reporters were very interested in why Sam and Bill had returned to Vietnam, and their feelings at seeing this country some twenty years later. They asked each of us why we came and where we were going. We gave them our itinerary and told them about the places we were going to drop off the medical supplies. But we didn't mention the stickers.

Ed Fitzgerald, the reporter, said, "You're going to Da Nang? So are we. Can we tape you when you go to the hospital up there?"

He wanted to film us meeting the staff of the hospital and our handing over the medical supplies. I liked the idea of being visible to the world. I felt like the more people who knew where we were, the safer we would be and the less likely we'd be to disappear.

I didn't feel that we could go to the U.S. government for help. After all, look what they'd already been doing to the MIAs. My strong feelings about my government were what prompted me to collect so many names and phone numbers just in case we needed help in a hurry. I'd tried to think of every possible problem and its solution.

I'm not sure how Christian Science Monitor edited the interviews taped that evening, because the footage was aired before we got home.

We stayed in Saigon several days, taking in some of the sights, including the tunnels of Cu Chi. These were an amazing network of underground tunnels no taller than a person could crawl through in places. Yet, hospitals and sleeping quarters, kitchens and gardens were all created in this underground network in which some of the Vietcong lived for years during the war. The Vietcong were right underneath the U.S. troops and they would come out at night to attack, disappearing into the darkness much to the dismay of our military.

Bill had one of his horrific wartime experiences there, so all of a sudden we began to see some stress in one of us.

One night we went to the Rex Hotel where officers used to stay in Saigon. This hotel became famous during the Vietnam War from the newsreels shown in the U.S. of officers sitting on the hotel roof, under balmy skies, with the moon and stars shining over the Mekong River. It was our turn to experience that, now. We looked down on the streets below, watching the crowds of people milling around, while we passed the evening sipping cold drinks, amazed that we were really there.

I would guess that 80% of the people traveled by bicycles, 15% by scooters, and about 5% by cars. I never saw a traffic light, so it was a surreal scene to watch hundreds of bicycles/scooters/cars go through intersections without anyone directing traffic. And there was no noise. I was mesmerized each time I watched this scene unfold during my entire stay in Vietnam.

One day, as I stood on the curb outside the hotel, trying to cross the street without success, because of the traffic, a man came from across the street, took my hand and led me through the maze. He must have been watching me for some time and took pity on me.

Even though we had been assigned a guide and an interpreter when we arrived in Saigon, they were pretty good about giving us some free time for shopping, having dinner or going to the marketplace.

So, when we were at the Rex Hotel, unbeknownst to our guide, we happened to meet a Captain of a freighter that was offloading in the harbor. Sam and Bill had a great time doing their male bonding thing like "Let's have another Vietnam beer." As the evening ended, and we were walking back to our hotel, Sam said, "We've been invited by the Captain to have lunch on his ship tomorrow."

"No kidding," I said. I felt pretty excited. We had no other plans, so I said, "Let's do it."

I can't remember what nationality the Captain was, but I think he was from India.

When the four of us arrived at the Port Authority at noon the next day, we had to go through a mini-customs. Would you believe that the port police would not let us in?

The Captain of the ship was there to meet us, so when the customs official became irate, even though we insisted that we were not going to take any pictures of the ship or the port, the Captain pulled out a bottle of Jack Daniels and gave it to him. Then, the guy looked the other way while motioning us to "Hurry, hurry, hurry."

The Captain said, as we hurried toward the ship, "Keep your cameras hidden. Don't take them out until we get on board. Then you can take pictures of anything you want, including me."

We had a delightful time on the ship. The Captain was a great host, served a wonderful spread and seemed to enjoy entertaining us. I did have a slight twinge of paranoia at one point, so I asked Sam, "How do we know he's not in cahoots with the Vietnamese, and we're now going to be in a place where we can't get off?" He was a lot more trusting than I. But, everything turned out well and we had a great time.

We took a half-day trip to Lai Khe. That was where Bill went through a great deal during the war. He became very quiet. The guide drove him crazy by asking why he was so sad. We had lunch at the River Front Restaurant overlooking the Saigon River.

Our tour guide, Mr. Huong, told us the next day that the Highlands, including Da Lat, were closed only to Americans. Since that bit of information agreed with what the travel agent had told us, we went to the Department of External Affairs to try to get permission to travel to Da Lat. We got nowhere.

The government sent two guides and a driver to accompany us. One of the guides, Mr. Dung, was supposed to be a guide-in-training, but we figured out that he was sent along to stick to me, like the KGB. The official guide was Mr. Huong.

Both Roni and I had been forthright when we filled out our visa documents. Even though this was a humanitarian trip, we both said that we would be asking questions about her brother and my husband. I think they wanted to keep an eye on me in particular, because I was the leader of the group. I don't know, maybe they knew I had dropped leaflets during my trip the year before.

Our destination that first day of our tour was Nha Trang. We all piled into a van and began our trip heading north along the coast.

While the seven of us were getting acquainted, since we would be together for quite some time, the guide-in-training said to Sam, "What did you do yesterday?"

"Oh, we had lunch with a Captain on his ship."

I couldn't believe Mr. Dung's reaction. "You did what?" he yelled at us.

"We went on a ship and had lunch with Captain."

The guide screamed, "You can't do that...you can't do that!"

"Well, we did," I said.

The two guides and the driver went crazy. I guess they realized that they shouldn't have left us on our own in Saigon.

NHA TRANG

The scenery was beautiful on the way to Nha Trang, but not the roads. There were potholes everywhere and no right or left or wrong lanes. . .just whoever got there first had the right of way. Puddles of water that had formed during the monsoons filled the potholes so that when the van hit one, our backs not only screamed from the jarring, but dirty water splashed all over the brand new Toyota van.

On the way to Nha Trang, we stopped for lunch at a nice little seaside place that specialized in seafood. I didn't know until then that Roni was allergic to shellfish. She had to keep telling the waiter, "No seafood, no shellfish. No, can't have." That was so hard for everyone in the place to understand. So, they finally brought her a meat dish that was swimming in greasy juices and wasn't cooked all the way through.

I was not allergic but I was leery of the lobster and the humongus prawns they served. Being a nurse, I was concerned about getting hepatitis from the shellfish. So, I stuck to veggies and a chicken dish.

Sam and Bill sure didn't worry. They raved about the food. "This is wonderful. You should eat it." Yeah, right!

Through the day, we made stops to take pictures and stretch our legs. Mr. Dung stuck to me like glue. Since we'd all agreed that he was more than a guide, we dubbed him Mr. KGB Man.

Within an hour after eating lunch, Roni started to feel ill. By the time we got to Nha Trang, I asked Mr. Huong to find a doctor.

The local medical man came to our motel room. I was concerned because I knew Roni was getting dehydrated and we weren't close to a hospital. I'd brought a liter of IV fluids in our medical supplies, tubing and butterfly needles, so as the doctor started asking questions, I went through my inventory lists in search of those supplies.

As luck would have it, they were in the box in our room. I offered them to the doctor, but his puzzled expression told me he had no idea what they were.

Mr. Huong, who had been interpreting for us, left the room and came back in 20 minutes with a few pills wrapped in a scrap of paper, and a packet of ORS (Oral Re-hydration Salts) with "donated by Save The Children" stamped on it.

It was time for me to have a serious talk with God.

I needed to know what to do, and fast. I told Roni that I'd give these pills one hour to take affect, and if we didn't see any results, I was starting the IV fluids and making arrangements to get her transported back to Bangkok. At least there, she would have a chance to get medical attention. And from there, she could be flown back to San Diego.

I was torn between wanting to stay with her until she got medical care, and completing what I needed to do in Vietnam.

The strange pills began to take affect and for the first time in almost 12 hours, one of her symptoms seemed to let up.

As Sam and I stood outside her room, we talked about the possible change in itinerary. It was late at night and Sam asked me to wake them up at five in the morning. With a "goodnight" we went to our rooms. I didn't get much sleep since I needed to give Roni her medicine every two hours.

At five, there was a tapping on my door. A voice told me it was five o'clock and time to get up. Then, I heard the same message delivered to Sam and Bill's room. Within seconds, Sam pounded on my door. With excitement in his voice, he announced that he'd gotten a wake-up call and it wasn't from me.

I said, "I told you our rooms would be bugged while we were in Vietnam."

After that, Sam and Bill became believers.

Although the violent symptoms Roni experienced were almost gone, she was wiped out by morning. She refused to consider the idea that we send her back to Bangkok, or on to Hanoi.

At breakfast, I spoke to Mr. Huong and Mr. KBG Man to see if we could stay one more day to give Roni a chance to rest. After they spoke to their boss in Da Nang, they agreed. That meant we would have to shave off a day from one of our other destinations.

While Roni rested between four-hour medications, Mr. Huong took us for a ride around Nha Trang.

It became apparent that we were never going to be given permission to travel into the Central Highlands. But we didn't give up hope that we'd find a way, somehow.

Nha Trang is a beach resort northeast of Da Lat with a fine harbor and a 10th century temple. I knew that Jim had taken some Special Forces training there. The white sandy beach and the clear blue water made me wonder what it was like when Jim was in Nha Trang. It was hard to believe that just 22 years before, that beautiful seaside town had been bustling with military personnel and that the pictures Jim had sent home to me were actually taken where I was walking.

At times during the day I could almost feel the presence of those men who had passed through there. I wondered how many would live to see that beach area a second time. My feelings of betrayal, of youth lost, of fear and disgust and excitement, pain and total disbelief all seemed to swim on the surf as it crashed to the white sands beneath my feet.

For a moment, my guard was down and the rush of those emotions overcame me. A heavy sadness filled me.

But, there was work to do. I had to stay focused on the trip's mission so I couldn't let my emotions take over. My talks with God became more frequent that day. I needed His help to keep me strong.

I found myself looking at faces and hoping that I would find an answer to what happened to Jim. There were lots of stars that night and as I looked up at them, I couldn't help but wonder if Jim was in Vietnam and looking up at the stars, too.

We continued our journey north the next day. At a certain point along the road to Quin Nhon, we came to a place where, if we turned left we would be going to Pleiku and Kontum. We had joked about it, until we reached that fork in the road. We had confused the driver with our joking, so he started to make the left hand turn until Mr. KGB Man yelled at him. The driver corrected his course.

We'd failed.

Our van became very quiet as we passed the turnoff.

Roni had been lying on the back seat throughout the day. I knew she needed to see the area where her brother's helicopter was last seen, so when we got to Bong Son, I woke her up and we stopped to take pictures.

When we climbed back into the van, I began to cry. I had heard Jim's voice screaming at me from the direction of the mountains that bordered the coastline. He kept saying, "Don't leave me! Don't leave me!"

I felt like I was abandoning him. He seemed so close. But, I couldn't get to him.

My tears turned to anger. I'd worked so hard to put this trip together, to make it possible for us to get to Kontum. And because some officials decided that Americans couldn't go there, I was not going to be able to find the area where Jim was last seen.

I had deserted Jim, again. I knew that if I was allowed to spend some time in Kontum, I could somehow find a clue to help me discover what had happened to him.

For miles my tears came and went. I was surprised that so much hurt remained inside me after 24 years. The other night Sam had said he admired me because I didn't give up. That's great, but how long would I be able to go on? The question overwhelmed me.

We dropped off some medical supplies at Le Ly Hayslip's The Mothers Love Clinic in Ky La, which was opened by East Meets West, and toured their facilities on our way to Da Nang. It was good to see some of the medicines I'd sent before, sitting on the shelves. Everyone in the village turned out to greet us. I was gratified to know that I could make even a small difference in the villagers' lives.

HUE (pronounced Way)

Hue was our next stop, the original capitol of Vietnam, and where the Citadel is located. This was the sight of a large battle during the Vietnam War in which both sides lost many men. As we walked through the majestic walled city, Roni and I were struck by the history and beauty of what was left standing. Bill and Sam reflected on the battle that took so many lives.

After checking into Huong Grang, the same hotel I'd stayed in the year before, we spent some time talking with travel writers, travel agents and an Australian agricultural man working in Laos.

The Australian told me he didn't think there were any Americans in Laos, Cambodia or Vietnam. One of the travel writers, who was taking the train through Vietnam, said he was interested in talking with me when he got back from Laos. We never re-connected.

Bill happened to meet a man named Frankie on one of our walks. He made an appointment to meet Frankie at eight that night, on the street outside our hotel. As the time got near, Bill got nervous. I kept telling him to relax. It was probably a ploy for getting money. Lots of people wanted to sell bogus information to Americans because they knew that's what the Americans were in Vietnam for.

As it turned out, Bill and Sam walked together. Roni and I walked 25 feet behind them. It became apparent that we were being followed. We were playing a game of not letting Bill and Frankie be alone. I figured that at least one of us would be watching the other's back. Frankie showed up as arranged, and spoke with Bill for about 20 minutes. When Frankie left, Bill started walking back towards us as we headed for the hotel. Some guy came up to me and said he had something but it was at his house down the street. At the same time, a young man engaged Roni in conversation. He just wanted to practice his English.

At that point, I decided to see what this guy had to show me.

Roni said, "Okay, I'll stand here at the corner."

I walked down a dark street with him, thinking that it was not a good idea at the time. I hadn't brought much money with me so there was nothing for him to steal.

We kept going farther and farther down the dark street as the guy kept saying, in quite good English, "It's just a little farther, just a little more. . ."

I finally stopped under one of the few lights along the way and said, "No, I'm not going any further. I need to get back to my friends." He argued with me, but then he realized he hadn't won.

He talked about two dead Americans in 1972, but he had no real information. He only wanted money. I pulled out about 10,000 dong and gave it to him.

I caught up with a nervous Roni at the corner. "Why did you do that?" Roni said. "The man who was talking to me said that the man you were following was Vietcong."

"I thought Bill and Sam were watching us." But they weren't.

I was furious. We went to Sam and Bill's room to talk with them about leaving us. Their response was, "We thought you were behind us."

I said, "How could you do that? We walked down the dark street covering your butts and yet when the tables were turned, you didn't watch out for us. Damn it! You didn't even notice we weren't behind you."

Bill told us that Frankie was supposed to have some bones and papers that he wanted to sell to us. It struck us that this was what family members go through when they come to Vietnam seeking information.

The next day, Monday, February 26, we left for the Ho Chi Minh Trail and Hai Bhu village. We picked up a local guide in Dong Ha who was worthless. He didn't tell us anything. So, Mr. Huong and I, from my memory of last year's trip, gave the commentary.

We actually got to walk on some of the Ho Chi Minh Trail. We stopped at the Van Kieu Tribe Village where I hadn't been the year before. Those people had been more exposed to civilization for many of them were wearing western clothes.

Their houses were built on stilts with thatched roofs and woven mat sidings to protect them from the elements. Theirs was a simple way of life with few conveniences. The children played with rocks and string, and they all seemed happy.

From the bag of things we had collected, we gave each of them toothbrushes, which Sam demonstrated how to use. That mesmerized both the kids and the adults. We also had candy for everyone and a bottle of Jack Daniels that came from Sam and Bill's stash, for the head of the community. Lots of the children wore tribal clothing and seemed to enjoy it when Roni and I sang to them in French.

While we were there, a peaceful look came across Sam's face, as if he'd finally come home. These were the people he had bonded with some 20 years before. A healing took place there, between strangers.

As the van door shut to take us away, the villagers crowded around and waved. We were sorry our stop there was so short, but each of us left with a smile.

As we drove through the countryside, we each exchanged our perceptions of our visit with the tribe. It wasn't long before we faded into our own thoughts as we stared out the windows at the passing scenery. All four of us had a sense of accomplishment that day.

Before long, the driver pulled off the road for a pit and snack stop. We were in the middle of nowhere and I guess our guides felt secure about letting us out.

We had just passed a small hut that was surrounded with scrap metal from the war. Spent shell casings, parts of trucks and who knows what had been flattened and stacked high.

I decided to walk to the hut and take a picture while Mr. KGB Man and the guides were using the bush potty. As I focused my camera on this odd sight, out popped several Vietnamese Army men who asked me to take their picture, too.

Thank goodness I was out of sight of the tour bus because that was a no-no. I got away with it because for the first time, I wasn't being followed.

We dropped off the local guide. Then Mr. Huong said he'd take us to the DMZ for free. I didn't know that the DMZ was actually in the middle of the Ben Hai River.

No one was around so the countryside was absolutely quiet. The wide, dry riverbed looked so unimportant. What a change from what it must have looked like twenty or more years ago.

Along the way back, a man named Sven, from Rhodesia, asked if he could hitch a ride back to Da Nang. He said he had one 30-minute videotape left and would take movies of us on the road in payment for the ride. I wish that we had had more movie footage as this tape has become a treasured memory of the trip.

On Tuesday afternoon, Roni and I met with six Red Cross officials. They thanked us for our help and presented us with certificates of appreciation. In turn, for our medical supplies, they agreed to circulate to other Red Cross Committees some of the flyers of Jim I'd had made. They gave us forms to fill out about Jim and his disappearance, and Mr. Huong translated them for me.

Then all of us went to the Da Nang hospital where several doctors met us. Greg, the reporter from the World Vision whom we'd met in Saigon, taped us delivering our supplies. Sven also taped portions of our meeting and our tour of the hospital.

The doctors and hospital administrators turned out to greet us. They were quite excited about receiving our box of supplies. It was quite an event. I'd hoped that we could speak to the doctors about possible American patients, but both Mr. Huong and Mr. KGB Man stuck to us like glue. Another lost opportunity.

This was my first experience seeing a Third World hospital and it was horrible! Yet, it had been given awards for the best hospital in Vietnam. If someone had used soap and water to scrub down the walls and floors, it would have helped a great deal. Nothing was sterile and there were no supplies. Not only that, there were no sheets or mattresses on the beds, just thin straw mats, which the patients' families brought to cover the springs.

The reporter, Greg, said the hospital was in good condition compared to many third world countries. I wouldn't realize the truth of his statement until two years later.

Having visited Marble Mountain the year before, I wanted the other three to see it, too. From the road, it looked like any old mountain. But, when we walked up the small path, hidden from view, was an entry into a vast cavern that actually housed an extremely large Buddha and a temple, along with ample room to have hidden some 1200 Vietcong from the Americans during the war. Standing in the center of the carvern, we could look up at the sky through a large hole cut in the top of the mountain that was the source for fresh air and light. Yet, from the outside, the top of the mountain didn't seem to be missing.

That day was beautiful. But Sam had to leave us and return to the van. His memory of a bad experience in that area during the war, with a grenade and some children, put him in bad shape for hours. Even though Sam and Bill wanted desperately to return to Vietnam for their own closure to the war, it was very hard on both of them.

We'd been careful about dropping our money with reward stickers attached in high traffic places where the locals would find them, we hoped. This was to be our last night in Da Nang, so I told everyone to dump any stickers they still had, because I had a bad feeling about dropping any in Hanoi. "If we don't dump the rest of these stickers, then we'll have to destroy them," I said. Everyone agreed. I got rid of the last ones I had under the trashcan at the airport.

HANOI

Hanoi is considered a city of lakes with broad boulevards, yet the streets are filled with people dressed in black, riding lots of old, rusty, dirty bicycles. The contrast between the north and the south of Vietnam became quite evident to us when we arrived. The northern Vietnam economy had appeared depressed to us, the people seemed without hope compared to the south of Vietnam where the economy was quite different, even to the bright color of their clothes and the shiny, new bicycles they rode.

As we got off the plane, Bill discovered he still had some stickered money, much to my dismay. In fact he had a wad of money. "Oh, I forgot to get rid of these," he said. All of the money he had was wrinkled, dirty and torn. Since the exchange rate at that time was like 3000-4000 dong to the dollar, it was like having Monopoly money.

I was so mad, I said, "Hand me some of those bills. I'll get rid of them before we get to our hotel in Hanoi."

So, I sat in the back of the van, cracked the window a little bit, and started dropping the money out as we drove along. It was dark so while the other three were keeping our new tour guides busy I was shooting rolls of money out the window.

Mr. Tine was our guide in Hanoi. He remembered me from the year before. Amazing! I told him I was still trying to get to Kontum. He suggested that I go to the Immigration Department to request passage.

The government guesthouse was actually a large compound on the river with several big buildings, and was enclosed with a fence and guards. It was obvious that they wanted to know our every move.

The rooms were big, clean and had tall ceilings. The French influence was everywhere. We strolled about the buildings and out towards the river, all the while reminding each other that the only safe place to talk was outside.

Mr. Tine had arranged a trip to Nam Dinh for us so we could see a pagoda in a rice paddy and could take a ride in little sampans. The next morning we were in the van on our way.

Much to my dismay, Bill and Sam found a few more stickers. They decided to drop the last of the stickers in the collection box at the pagoda. The little Buddhist nun bowed and said, "Oh, thank you. Thank you."

Whew! I was very nervous knowing that one of us still had some stickers on our person.

The sampan ride was most interesting. We sat in small woven basket-like rafts and were paddled around and through outcroppings of mountains that jutted out of the water. It was quiet and eerie.

As we came out of a tunnel, through one of the mountains, we could see little shacks with smoke coming from a cooking fire, stuck on the sides of the limestone monoliths. I couldn't help but think what a perfect place to hide POWs.

The Majestic Hotel where we were taken, was a real dive and we at once dubbed it the Bates Hotel. The electricity kept going off so we resorted to candles. There were no heavy blankets for the extreme cold. Besides, everything was damp, even the sheets. The smell of mold was unreal. As we walked along the outside corridor to the dining room, we watched rats play in front of us.

There was a little room off the reception desk with a small television set against one wall. Since the four of us could not stand to stay in the dark, smelly, damp room, we decided to go for a walk in the outside courtyard. As we passed the TV room, I noticed that it was crowded with Vietnamese people sitting in chairs in the dark, staring at the blank TV set.

I thought, "I'm in the Twilight Zone. . .a twilight zone without power." We started to laugh. The more we laughed, the funnier it got.

Just by chance, the electricity came back on and it was like the people hadn't missed a beat. They didn't flinch. Their Vietnamese soap opera was on again.

That night at dinner, we were served five or six different dishes. We tried everything as we passed each dish around the table. Sam bit into this thing he thought was a chicken leg, then said, "Man, these are the scrawniest chickens I've ever seen."

About then, Bill took his chicken leg and pulled it open. It was a bat wing.

All I could think of, being a nurse, was my nursing manual. What did it say about tropical medicine and bat rabies? Did cooking a bat kill rabies? Oh, my God, what had we done now? How many days would it take before we all began foaming at the mouth?

When we sat down for lunch the next day, we thought one of the dishes was another of those "chickens." We passed on that one.

OUR INTERROGATION

As we were getting ready to leave the "Bates Motel," I noticed an official car rolling into the driveway. There was a flurry of activity and lots of chattering between our guide and the person in the car. All of a sudden, our guide began waving to us to come. I yelled at Sam and Bill and Roni to "Come here, now!"

I pointed to the excited Vietnamese down by the car and said, "I think we've been caught and we're up shit creek without a paddle. We're done ducks."

I told everyone of my fear and then we discussed the strategy we should take. "We're not gonna lie. Don't anybody lie 'cause if they separate us, we're in even bigger trouble."

I explained that I was going to take the fall for this because I had the best credibility with the Vietnamese authorities due to the fact that I was giving away all of the meds.

We were informed that someone from immigration wanted to see all four of us. Just as I thought, someone had seen us leaving our stickers at the pagoda. Boy, were we in trouble.

We were ushered into a sitting room at the Majestic Hotel. Then, a big man in uniform walked in with another man. The gist of an hour's conversation with them was that three bills with stickers on them had been dropped at the pagoda the day before and the four of us were the only people to visit the pagoda that day.

The tension was so thick in the room we could have cut it with a knife, to use a cliché. The uniformed man wanted to know which one of us had dropped the bills. I knew that we weren't going to get out of this, so I decided that I had a better chance than the other three. I confessed.

Immediately, Bill said he did it. Then Sam said he was the one. Bill insisted that he was the only one, so Sam and I backed off. It was scary--a hair raising experience!

The uniformed man gave us hell, through his interpreter.

At the end of the hour, we were made to sign a statement saying we would never do that again. The uniformed officer said, "I hope you have a nice journey. Everything is fine now that I gave you my two cents worth, so to speak."

The officer said he had to fill out a report and then led us to believe that this would be the end of the incident.

We had made it! Yet, I had a nagging feeling there was something wrong with this picture.

Our guide was livid. "Why didn't you tell me you wanted to do that?"

I felt like saying, "Because we didn't want you to haul us off to jail to start with." But, I said, "We didn't see a need to tell you. We didn't think we were doing anything wrong."

He went on and on about how we had ruined his life, everything was upside down for him now, his family would be reprimanded for what we'd done and so on.

We had no sooner arrived back at our government house in Hanoi than a Department of Internal Affairs and Immigration representative appeared and gave Roni, Bill and me an invitation to appear the next morning. Sam didn't get one. The representative kept saying that we had to be at the Department of Internal Affairs promptly at ten o'clock, and not to be late. Our anxiety level was at a new high, to say the least. We walked around the grounds of the group of guesthouses, planning how we'd handle the situation.

Before we retired that night, I told them I was going to do my best to get everyone out of the country. If they kept anyone, it would probably be me. They were to leave and get help.

I assigned Roni the job of praying for us. Since Sam wasn't invited to the "party," I said to him, "You've got to keep things going on the outside for us. Get the hell out of Dodge if we get stuck here." I gave him a list of the names and resources I had for back-up support.

The next morning, the four of us arrived at 10:00, sharp, said goodbye to Sam, who had to stay in the van, and walked past the guards and into the government building.

The three of us were introduced to a Mr. Phu Thai when we got inside DIAI.

A Captain, who took notes, was also in the room. Then there was a Mr. Tiwvyen from Immigration who did the interpreting.

We weren't allowed to bring our own interpreter with us which made me very nervous.

The room was cold, dark and bare except for a long table with three chairs on each side.

The next two hours were a roller coaster of anxiety for us. Mr. Thai would start by saying that he knew we'd done a lot for his people by bringing medical supplies with us and giving them to the hospitals and clinics. Then, his expression would change and he'd say, in an accusing voice, that we had violated law #81, Part 1 and 2--using currency for our own purpose and propaganda. That carried a sentence of 3 to 12 years in prison.

Having said that, he would ask in which province Bill had dropped the bills. We had no idea what province we had been in. Mr. Thai thought that was very odd. All three men shook their heads.

Almost all of the questions were directed to Bill. I wondered if the Vietnamese were reluctant to think that a woman could be the ringleader of this venture and so they picked on Bill.

Bill was getting cornered at one point, so I pulled out one of Jim's flyers and said that I'd originally thought I'd leave them all around, but because someone told me not to, I didn't.

"If we'd known that leaving the stickers would be a problem, we wouldn't have left them, either," I said. "We thought the message on the sticker was a general form of what I'd written about Jim on the flyer."

I talked about how in the United States we advertise for missing persons on milk cartons, flyers and such, and how we didn't think we were doing anything wrong since the sticker could be removed from the money.

Bill really needed to regroup for a moment, so it was my turn to get the questions.

146

Mr. Thai commiserated with Roni and me on our situation because he said the Vietnamese had many more MIAs than the United States did. He asked why we hadn't gone to the Red Cross in Hanoi with our questions about Jim and Roni's brother, so I asked him for an address. I told him that the MIA's family members had never been given that information.

All three men seemed to soften.

Then, they started their interrogation all over again. They pounded the table and screamed at us, building up to a crescendo. One time Mr. Thai said, "Don't you realize we are not democratic? You go before our judge, you get three to twelve years in our prison. What do you think about that?"

Were we going to be taken to jail?

Another time Mr. Thai said he was pleased with our bringing help to his people and it was wonderful that we were doing such great work. "And we know, Miss Barbara, that you sent more supplies through another organization."

Each time he said how grateful he was, it would lead to more and more demanding questions. He even asked me what I thought about him sending me to prison for 3 to 12 years.

I went into another dimension. I wasn't scared, or crying, or pleading. I just said, in a flat tone, "You need to follow the laws and do what you need to do. I can't tell you what to do." Then I became quiet and resolute all the while knowing that I could be put into the "Hanoi Hilton" and that would be that. I figured my government would probably be happy if I was put there.

Several times they asked us if we knew we were breaking the law. I wanted to say to them, "How would we know that? Do you know the laws of the U.S.?"

The thought kept running through my mind that at least Sam was on the outside. They didn't have all four of us.

Roni sat there the whole time, terrified. Sometimes she just closed her eyes while she prayed.

Bill, on the other hand, kept making up little stories, not lying, but embellishing the truth. When asked once where he got the stickers, he said, "Well, I can't remember. I think it was someplace like a magazine or something."

"What kind of magazine?"

"I think it was in a Harley magazine."

For some of his answers I found it hard to keep a straight face.

At one point, Mr. Thai mentioned their laws again, and said that we should have read all the laws of his country before we traveled there. He went on another tirade about this. It was all I could do to keep from laughing. All

I could think of was going to the library in my neighborhood and asking for a copy of the laws of Vietnam. Right!

Then Mr. Thai brought out a book, about the size of a small paperback. It had pages in it as old as Ho Chi Minh, probably. He slammed the book down. "These are the laws!" He slammed the book down again, three more times. Did he think I could read Vietnamese?

I answered him with, "Well, no sir, I hadn't thought about reading your laws."

"We're going to tell your embassy about this. What do you think of that?"

My thought was that I hope you do. Please?

The final relief came when Mr. Thai said that he wouldn't send us to criminal trial because we'd promised not to drop bills any more with questions about American POWs on them, and because he was grateful for our humanitarian works in his country. He knew about the certificates of appreciation that Roni and I had received from the Red Cross in Da Nang.

When I had a chance, I told Mr. Thai about the World Monitor reporter to whom we had suggested that everyone should visit Vietnam. He seemed to like that.

Another thing he kept asking us, during the interview, was our opinion of how we were treated. Once he said he might have to tell the Hanoi police department, which was better than what they started out saying about putting us on trial.

During the entire time of our interrogation, we were served tea, but the room was so cold, I didn't think we would ever thaw out.

Mr. Thai never looked me in the eye, which is a typical Vietnamese trait. He asked all of his questions through the interpreter.

Before we were allowed to leave the interrogation, Mr. Thai began asking me questions that were really tough. First, he wanted to know did I think that my husband was still alive?

I knew I needed to be careful with this answer--to be more cautious about the things I said. I told him I thought it was possible he had survived the incident surrounding his disappearance and he had wandered in the jungle not knowing how to get out or who he was. That was why I brought the flyers.

Another question he asked me was why is it that when the Vietnamese government complied with the demands of the U.S. in regard to lifting the trade embargo, the U.S. then put another obstacle in the way by raising the requirements?

I told him I wasn't a politician and I had no way of knowing why that was happening. "I'm sorry I can't answer that," I said.

The third question he asked was why we didn't go through their MIA office in Hanoi. He also said, "Didn't you know that you were supposed to contact our Red Cross, our Department of Missing Persons here in Hanoi, and give us the information so we could look for your husband?"

"No," I said. "No one in my government ever mentioned that."

Mr. Thai listened to my answers with rapt attention. At last he lifted his eyes and looked straight at me. And, in perfect English, he said, "You family members will have your answers when the time is right."

I couldn't believe what I'd heard. It took all my strength not to reach across the table and grab him by the throat. He might as well have poured kerosene on the fire, for crying out loud.

He then apologized for having to do this to us "but it is my job." That was the end of his speaking English. He lowered his eyes again, and said in Vietnamese, "You will have no trouble getting out of the country. We hold no animosity. I hope the rest of your trip is delightful. Goodbye."

I couldn't help but think that Mr. Thai knew right where Jim was and that was the reason we'd been denied access to Kontum.

When the interview was over, we had to sign a transcription of what the Captain had written in Vietnemese during the two hours. We had no idea what we were signing. After that, I asked Mr. Thai where he thought we should leave the last container of medical supplies. He said, "The Department of Exterior."

The last thing Mr. Thai said to us, through the interpreter, was that he wanted us to tell others to come to Vietnam but never to bring propaganda. And that we were welcome to come back.

What an unbelievable experience! I've never been so scared in my life. The whole time I hoped they wouldn't throw us in prison, but I knew they could do anything they wanted to. We were at their mercy. Thank goodness our good works and connections seemed to have worked in our favor.

All I could think of was to get out the door as fast we could before they changed their minds.

Sam was a wreck by the time we appeared and I was never so glad to see him. I got into the van, grabbed the seat and said, "Dear God, get us out of here."

The driver said, "Well, where do you want to go?"

I said, "Remember that Friendship Store, whatever it was called? We're going there." It was the only western store they had, sort of like a duty free place. The others asked me why I wanted to go there.

"I saw some bottles of rum there, before." Then, to the driver, I said, "Make it snappy."

We needed to play the game a little longer. So, after picking up the rum, we headed straight for the Department of Exterior. I didn't even want to deal with the last container of supplies, but I knew we weren't out of harms way, yet.

I tried to hand over the container and leave, but that didn't work. Once again we were ushered into a reception room, treated to tea and formally introduced to several dignitaries. It was hard to smile and be polite after what we'd just gone through, but we did it.

Once out of there, we headed back to our government guesthouse. We replayed the events of the day with each other, filling Sam in on what had happened.

This time our feelings started coming out. We knew the room was bugged but I didn't care if they heard how frustrated and let down I felt. Again, my tears started flowing as I realized that all those months of hard work had been for nothing.

Jim's voice was still calling me to "Come now before it's too late. Don't leave us." It was so haunting and pleading. How could I leave him behind?

Sam, Bill and Roni tried to make me feel better by saying that I'd done everything possible. It didn't work.

On top of that, the adrenaline that I'd been running on was beginning to crash. We weren't out of the woods yet, but I was crashing fast.

It was amazing that Thai Air found four seats for the following day, since they'd screwed up our reservations and 48 hours earlier had told us they didn't have four seats available. I have a feeling that Mr. Thai called them and had them bump people in order to get us out of the country. I wondered if we'd make it through customs.

BANGKOK

On Sunday, March 4, we were picked up at 11:15 to go to the airport. We actually got through all of the checkpoints without a hitch. They didn't even want the receipts for the medical containers. We were so relieved when the plane took off.

I wondered if someone from the U.S. Embassy would greet us at the Bangkok Airport. No one showed up. We had planned to make a side trip to Chang Mai, but we cancelled our flight for the next day. Instead, we checked into The Menam Hotel that had lots of clean towels and hot water. And no mold on the walls. We had a wonderful French dinner at the hotel. No oriental food! Needless to say, we were all in heaven. We slept like rocks that night.

After an American breakfast the next morning, I began to feel sick that I not only did not get to Kontum, but that I'd never get to go back to Vietnam. After the sticker incident, it would be too dangerous to return. They'd probably throw me in jail or would not grant me a visa to begin with.

I consoled myself by remembering that I had brought medical supplies and made some humanitarian contacts, so that was good.

I always like to set things up for myself so I have a chance to win. This time I worked hard for Jim and lost. Maybe it was time for me to let go.

After a day of sightseeing and good food, we left a wake-up call for 3:45 AM. We were packed and ready for our March 6th flight back to the United States and civilization.

I wasn't looking forward to going home to an empty house.

NOTE:

In Jim's DPMO Intelligence Casualty File, dated September 1999, I found the following report on my trip to Vietnam in 1990.

C O N F I D E N T I A L Liaison Bangkok 09680 Feb 90

1. On 15 Feb 90 our office was visited by Mrs. Barbara Birchim, wife of REFNO 1322, and Ms. Ronnie Shanley, sister of REFNO 1533-0-01. Mrs. Birchim and Ms. Shanley said they had just come from the SRV embassy where they were being processed for a visa to visit Vietnam sometime in the next few days. They plan to travel from Ho Chi Minh City to deliver 500 pounds of medical supplies to a hospital sponsored by "Project Concern" in Da Lat. After delivering the supplies they plan to go to Binh Dinh where the REFNO 1533 incident occurred and Kontum, the area of the 1322 incident.

2. Both ladies have leaflets (forwarded under separate cover) in English and Vietnamese with sketches of their relatives, including an artist concept of how the men would likely appear today. Mrs. Birchim said she had recently been troubled by a change in her dependent eligibility enrollment record (DEER) because her husband's status had been changed from "inactive dead" to "retired dead" which reinstated her medical benefits. She said she had applied for information through FOIA, but only the FBI responded affirmatively. She said she had contacted the FBI and learned the information regarding her husband had been transferred to DOD channels, and LTC "ZORN" at DOD was currently working the problem of locating her information. She added she believed there were Americans remaining in Vietnam who have Vietnamese wives and do not desire to return to the U.S. She intends to address this issue with Vietnamese authorities in Vietnam.

3. Ms. Shanley said she had received information that two remains repatriated during the Jan 89 repatriation had been identified as crew members of the same helicopter as her brother. She said her mother was currently trying to decide if she wanted to participate in a group burial and she hoped to gain additional information regarding her brother while in Vietnam.

MISSING

For years I lived with the thought
of his return. I imagined he had ditched
the place and was living on a distant
island, plotting his way back
with a faithful guide; or, if
he didn't have a guide, he was sending
up a flare in sight of an approaching ship.

Perhaps, having reached an Asian capital,
he was buying gifts for a reunion
that would dwarf the ones before.
He would have exotic stories to tell,
though after a while, the stories
didn't matter or the gifts.

One day I told myself, he is not coming
home, though I had no evidence,
no grave, nothing to say a prayer over.
I knew he was flying among the starry
plankton, detained forever.
But telling myself this was as futile
as when I found a picture of him

sleeping in the ready room,
hands folded across his chest,
exhausted from the sortie he'd flown.
His flight suit was still on,
a jacket collapsed at his feet.
I half thought I could reach out

and wake him, as the unconscious
touches the object of its desire
and makes it live. I have kept
all the doors open in my life
so that he could walk in, unsure
as I've been how to relinquish
what is not there.

Gardner McFall[1]

PART IV

"Vietnam, brought to you by. . ."

Chapter Seven

The Turning Point

"Now we're off to bombing these people. We're over that hurdle. I don't think anything is going to be as bad as losing, and I don't see any way of winning."

LBJ to Robert McNamara
February 26, 1965

By 1956, the U.S. military had been active in the Pacific region for fifteen years. We'd seen World War II and the Korean War. So, the buildup of our Special Forces in that area should have been no surprise.

Unconventional warfare or guerrilla warfare became the term the Army used for the Special Forces training in those days. They were supposed to organize, train and control various Asian groups that might be involved in wartime activities at some time in the future.

Many of the Army commanders felt the Special Forces were not necessary and they didn't like their unorthodox methods of fighting, even though there was an all-out threat of war.[1]

One of the groups, the Special Forces was assigned to work with in 1961, were the Montagnards in the highlands of Vietnam. "In 1962 the war (with the Viet Cong) was still a backwater affair, and local Vietnamese military commanders often treated the Viet Cong haphazardly, as more of a nuisance than as a formidable threat."[2]

Many of the Special Forces in Laos had been involved in CIDP (Civilian Irregular Defense Program), but instead they were ordered to report to Vietnam where their CIDP training was put to work. The CIA funded the program. By July 1963, ". . .the Special Forces had, in one way or another, become involved in almost every conceivable Vietnamese paramilitary activity. Seven years after the first detachments had been organized in Hawaii and Japan, the Special Forces had evolved from a small, specialized guerrilla warfare cadre into the spearhead of an all-out American military training and advisory effort in a major combat theater."[3]

Those at the Pentagon thought that CIDG was the answer to stabilizing South Vietnam by controlling the borders and training the tribal groups. "This may have been true if the Vietnam battlefield was confined to a simple struggle between partisans and government police. Instead, the civil war exploded into a major confrontation between national armies, which hopelessly outclasses the ability of rifle-toting local natives to influence the outcome."[4]

The war was on. John F. Kennedy was President.

In 1963, President Kennedy was assassinated, Lyndon B. Johnson became President and we were in a full-blown war that was lasting much longer than the American public was told it would.

"Lyndon Johnson took us step by step, often by stealth, into Vietnam. While boasting in public that there will be victory in Vietnam, in private he moans that the war can never be won and that it will crush his presidency."[5]

According to President Johnson, "We started the day after we got back to Washington after Dallas to try to bring peace to Vietnam. We avoided the course this thing took and continued to avoid it until July 1965. At Tonkin Gulf, we got authority from the Congress. Anything we think 'necessary.'"[6]

And that was the open door to prolonging the war.

Michael Beschloss has written a book, Reaching For Glory, Lyndon Johnson's Secret, which is based on 1964-1965 White House Tapes where he talks about the Vietnam War.

For example, on pages 181-182, LBJ is speaking with Everett Dirksen (February 17, 1965). He had just spoken to President Eisenhower about Vietnam strategy earlier that day.

"We've had nine changes of government (in Saigon) because all of them are afraid we are going to pull out. Afraid we are to negotiate. Now President Eisenhower said this morning. . .'You don't negotiate until the other side must want to negotiate. . .When you are dealing with these people, you must have a self-enforcing treaty. They do not keep their word, so whatever you agree on is of no value.' That we know, from Munich on, that when you give, the dictators feed on raw meat. . . (Eisenhower said we should) do everything he could with the CIA to create better morale and, if necessary, to almost buy it with that government . . .He said, 'You must push South Vietnamese participation. You've got to put your own boys with them' . . . (He) said when they go on a raid like they went on the other night... each one of those men come back and they tell their families about what they did, instead of what the Americans did. And that makes them want to fight."

In chapter nine[7], LBJ said to Robert McNamara, Secretary of Defense, on June 21, 1965, "It's going to be difficult for us to. . .prosecute. . .a war that far away from home with the divisions we have here. . .I'm very depressed about it. Because I see no program from either Defense or State that gives me much hope of doing anything, except just praying and gasping to hold on. . .and hope they'll quit. I don't believe they're ever going to quit. And I don't see... any. . .plan for a victory - - militarily or diplomatically."

Previous to that date, on June 7[8], Gen. Westmoreland cabled McNamara from Saigon saying he needed 41,000 more combat troops right away and 52,000 more to bring the number up to 175,000. He wanted to move from a "defensive posture" to "take the war to the enemy."

This meant that LBJ and McNamara had to make a decision. "We could no longer postpone a choice about what path to take." McNamara said, "We're in a hell of a mess."[9]

LBJ sent General Andrew Goodpaster to discuss Westmoreland's request with President Eisenhower, who "flatly approved it, saying, 'We have got to win.'"

Then, on June 10, Secretary of State Dean Rusk, McNamara and the President met with Senator Russell at which time, the Senator said he "would like to find a way out of Vietnam but didn't see how without losing face."

"WE KNOW IT'S GOING TO BE BAD"

Special Assistant to the President, Bill Moyers, began to worry about LBJ in July 1965. "LBJ had been prone to paranoid outbursts and depression. But 'it was never more pronounced than in 1965, when he was leading up to the decision about the buildup in Vietnam.' Years later Moyers . . .(said) Johnson's depression came from 'the realization, about which he was clearer than anyone, that this was a road from which there was no turning back.'"[10]

On July 2[11], LBJ had another meeting with Eisenhower. The conversation went this way.

"LBJ: . . .You don't think that we can just have a holding operation, from a military standpoint, do you?

EISENHOWER: . . .You've got to go along with your military advisers, because otherwise you are just going to continue to have these casualties indefinitely. . .My advice is, do what you have to do. I'm sorry that you have to go to the Congress. . .but I guess you would be calling up the Reserves.

LBJ: Yes, sir. We're out of them, you see. . .(The State Department says) we ought to avoid bombing Hanoi until we can see through the monsoon season whether, with these forces there, we can make any progress. . .before we go out and execute everything. . .

EISENHOWER: . . .(you must say) 'Hell, we're going to end this and win this thing. . .We don't intend to fail.'

LBJ: You think that we can really beat the Vietcong out there?

EISENHOWER: . . .This is the hardest thing (to decide,) because we can't finally find out how many of these Vietcong have been imported down there and how many of them are just rebels.

LBJ: . . .How many they're going to pour in from China, I don't know...

EISENHOWER: . . .I would go ahead and. . .do it as quickly as I could."

By July 27, LBJ had made up his mind.

"LBJ: . . .We don't think that we can leave these boys there inadequately protected at these bases. . .Now . . .we're. . .giving (the military), in our own way, what they say they have to have. But, we're not (letting) them . . .go with any new adventures. And we're hoping. . .to get through the monsoon season. . . .Hoping that maybe the other thing will work. If it doesn't, then by January, you may have to appropriate and appropriate and appropriate. And you may have to do other things. But I'm doing my best to hold this thing in balance just as long as I can.

I can't run out. I'm not going to run in. I can't just sit there and let them be murdered. So I've got to put enough there to hold them and protect them. And. . .if we don't heat it up ourselves, and we don't dramatize it, we don't play it up and say we're appropriating billions and we're sending millions and all (those) men, I don't think that you (will) get the Russians. . .or the Chinese worked up about it. That's what we are hoping."

The next day, LBJ told reporters in the East Room that "'our fighting strength' in Vietnam would rise 'to 125,000 men, almost immediately. Additional forces will be needed later, and they will be sent as required.' He would double the monthly draft call and 'step up our campaign for voluntary enlistments,' but he would not call up the Reserves. Sending 'the flower of our youth' into battle, he said, was the 'most agonizing' duty of 'your President.' But 'we will stand in Vietnam.'"

In the Appendix of Reaching for Glory[12], the author lists several conversations that LBJ taped of himself discussing his career and life as President in 1969.

In talking about Vietnam, he said the following:

"Until July 1965, I tried to keep from going into Vietnam. Nearly 85 percent of the people in the Congress said, 'We're not for your poverty program, but we're sure behind you on Vietnam.' If I'm the only man left in this country to say 'Aggression must not succeed anywhere in the world,' I'll say it."

* * *

"Nothing fully prepares a young man to go to war, but every soldier carries with him some expectations, or at least preconceptions, about what is expected of him and what he expects from the government that has sent him into battle."[13]

159

Chapter Eight

Finally The End?

"War is a contagion."
Franklin D. Roosevelt

On January 27, 1973, the Paris Peace Accords were signed, the same day the first American POWs were released by the Saigon government and the Provisional Revolutionary Government (Vietcong) in the South.[1]

The talks had broken down in the preceding December so President Richard Nixon and Dr. Henry Kissinger, his chief negotiator, decided to perform an all out attack on Hanoi and Haiphong. The bombing lasted for eleven days. At last, a withdrawal was negotiated. Part of that agreement included the return of all prisoners and the bodies of those who had died in captivity. This return was to take place within 60 days. The U.S. was to withdraw from Vietnam within that 60 days, as well.

In The Bamboo Cage, author Nigel Cawthorne writes that everyone knew the Paris Peace Accords "weren't worth the paper they were written on."[2] What the Accords did was allow the U.S. the opportunity to withdraw from Vietnam to save face.

"More than 450 American POWs held in North Vietnam were scheduled to be released in three groups by the PAVN. These repatriations would coincide with releases by the Saigon government and the Provisional Revolutionary Government (Vietcong) in the South. A total of 120 American POWs in the South would be freed by the PRG, beginning with a group of twenty-seven turned over to U.S. officers in Quan Loi, north of Saigon."[3]

When criticized about the terms of the Paris Peace Accords, Dr. Kissinger said, "Look, you don't understand my instructions. My orders are to get this signed before the inauguration." As it turned out, he was seven days late.

Right after the talks, the Vietnamese gave lists of American prisoners to the U.S. that they acknowledged having under their control--one from the North Vietnamese and one from the Vietcong (PRG). These lists were later refined by making two new lists--one identifying live POWs and the other identifying those Americans who had died while in captivity.[4]

When U.S. personnel compared the lists with their own, they discovered that many, many names of men the government knew had been captured were missing from the Vietnamese lists. In fact, eighty of those men's names had been broadcast on Hanoi Radio through the years, or their pictures had appeared in Vietnamese newspapers, or in East German propaganda films. Some pictures of these prisoners even appeared in Paris Match and Life magazines and on NBC news programs.

Dr. Kissinger traveled to Hanoi to discuss these 80 men, among other things. Vietnamese Foreign Prime Minister Pham Van Dong told Kissinger he would look into it. The result was that Dong said our government was mistaken. Those 80 men simply did not exist.

The U.S. expected 400-500 more men returned whom they had reason to believe had been captured. The eighty men were not a question. The rest could have been refutable. (See The Bamboo Cage, p. 48.)

"After the last American prisoner was released, various classified lists of men known to have been captured alive or suspected to have survived their loss incidents were drawn up" by the DOD. However, the list varied between 67 and 83. "But no senior official of the Nixon administration ever demanded that North Vietnam, the PRG or the LPF release" them.[5] It seems that the powers-that-be decided all of those men were dead because the intelligence they received was mighty thin.

Many also thought that a lot of the MIA survivors had been held back by the PAVN or the Pathet Lao. Still others figured that some of the captured Americans were going to be returned in body bags or coffins.

Two days after the signing of the Accords, Kissinger met with a group from the National League of Families. One of the questions they asked him was "What happens if they (Vietnamese) welsh on one or another of the (Paris Peace Accord) provisions?"

Kissinger's answer? "They know that if there is any welshing on one issue, it is over for the rest too. . .We will brutally enforce the release of the men on the lists."[6]

Famous last words, as the expression goes. Wouldn't that have been wonderful if Kissinger's words had turned out to be true?

We now know, from the San Diego Union Tribune, ("Nixon On Tape Proposes Idea Of Nuclear Bomb On N. Vietnam," Associated Press, Deb Riechmann, March 1, 2002, p. A17), that "The war weighed heavily on Nixon's mind." Nixon is quoted as saying, "The point is, we have to realize that if we lose Vietnam and the Summit, there's no way that the election can be saved."

Could Nixon's dream of re-election have had something to do with the downfall of our POW/MIAs coming home?

Robert L. Leggett, California, spoke to the House of Representatives on March 23, 1971 regarding the American POWs.[7] He said, "We won't get out (of Vietnam) until we're sure they'll give the POWs back. They won't settle the POW question until they're sure we're getting out. So why not do both at once?"

Rep. Leggett had developed a plan, along with Donald W. Riegle Jr., Representative from Michigan, that they called "proportional repatriation." The plan was designed to enable the U.S. to withdraw our troops and recover POWs at the same time. They said it was "feasible, and nearly foolproof and cheatproof as a settlement of this kind of war can be."

The proposal included the following words. "It should be understood that this approach in no way implies a willingness to let our men suffer one additional moment beyond the earliest possible time we could otherwise secure their safe return. We make this proposal only in the hope of achieving a breakthrough in the negotiating deadlock caused by the apparent unwillingness of the other side to return any substantial number of prisoners in the foreseeable future."

Twenty-five Members of Congress endorsed the plan and sent it to President Nixon on January 2, 1971. He had not responded by the time Representatives Riegle and Leggett spoke on March 1971.

In April, I received a letter from Congressman Leggett. By then he had 40 Congressmen co-sponsoring his resolution. He urged me to write to newspapers, other news media and to public officials about his resolution, hoping that the pressure would convince President Nixon to adopt the plan.

According to the above article by Deb Riechmann, in the San Diego Union Tribune, Nixon had thoughts about using the nuclear bomb. In fact, she wrote, his thoughts could "have reflected mere frustration with the war or been part of a strategy to make the North Vietnamese believe he was a madman and could not be restrained--and so they should negotiate peace."

* * *

Before long, the U.S. came to terms with the fact that this situation was enormous. Five years later, our government realized that we had been skunked. The Vietnamese never had any intention of returning our military men. This included the MIAs. From the very beginning, the Vietnamese and the Americans were deadlocked. What Vietnam wanted was reparation and aid, or in other words, money.

In secret, President Nixon pledged four and one-half billion aid dollars to Vietnam in a letter to Prime Minister Dong on February 1973. The promise was not kept because Congress never granted the aid. They were angered by the tricks the Vietnamese were playing with their lists of POW/MIAs and also by the reports of torture and mistreatment of U.S. military men they received upon the POW's return.[8]

"The Americans were expecting the return of literally hundreds of burn cases and amputees. By the end of Operation Homecoming those hospital beds still lay empty. So where were the burn cases, the amputees, the disfigured, the mutilated?"[9]

As a consequence, the Vietnamese government was angry because the monetary aid was not forthcoming. So, they responded by not returning the Americans, they called "pearls,"[10] whose names they had furnished the U.S. Of course they said later that they did not have.

The Vietnamese were also angry because our government had not lifted the trade embargo, which the U.S. had put into effect at the war's end.

" What started as possibly an error in judgement, or an act of political expediency, grew with the passing years into a conviction that national security would be hurt by the disclosure that U.S. intelligence capabilities, which were formidable, had failed to serve the men" who fought in Vietnam.[11]

In effect, the lives of our American servicemen were being used as pawns or bargaining chips by both sides.

On page 148 of The Men We Left Behind, the authors wrote that in truth, ". . .Kissinger wasn't attempting to get back POWs, or even obtain an account of the MIAs--he was soliciting Le Duc Tho's assistance in writing them off."[12]

As it turned out, the Paris Peace Talks ended our country's involvement in the Vietnam War. But, the U.S. withdrawal caused our country to face the most humiliating defeat in our history. "A small South-East Asian country had brought the world's mightiest superpower to its knees. Withdrawal, however, did not wipe the slate clean. It soon became apparent that many U.S. servicemen had been left behind. Some had certainly been taken prisoner. Others were simply missing. Their families were naturally anxious to learn their whereabouts--or their fate--and were amazed to find the U.S. authorities were not merely unhelpful but positively obstructive when they pressed their inquiries."[13]

We can even find references to that situation in novels. James Lee Burke wrote the following paragraphs in his novel, Bitterroot, published in 2001.[14]

"If Nick Molinari's life and violent death had any significance, it probably lay in the fact that he had volunteered to fight for his country and had been left behind in Laos with perhaps four hundred other GIs, whose names were taken off the bargaining list during the Paris Peace Negotiations at the close of the Vietnam War.

"But those are events that are of little interest today."

As it turned out, the Vietnamese held some POWs for reasons not discussed at the Paris Peace Talks. Those reasons included a particular technical knowledge an American might have that the Vietnamese could use, knowledge of communist secrets, the value an American could be as a trade for Vietnamese held by American troops, or as means toward making diplomatic concessions.

"But the fate of most U.S. servicemen was linked to ransom."[15]

Every presidential and congressional commission since President Nixon has chosen in some way to ignore the evidence that there are American POW/MIAs still being held in Southeast Asia. As one person said, the problem has been swept under the rug year after year. It seems that the result of the Paris Peace Accords, signed almost thirty years ago, has turned out to be too dangerous to tackle. Even now.

Chapter Nine

The Charade Continues

"On March 29, 1973, President Richard Nixon announced to the nation, 'For the first time in twelve years, no American military forces are in Vietnam. All of our American POWs are on their way home.' This was a message the American people had awaited for many years. One of the most painful chapters in our history had finally ended. Or so it seemed."[1]

It is hard for one who is not in politics or in the military, or is not attuned to what the CIA is capable of doing, to understand how our servicemen, labeled as MIAs, could have been forgotten at the end of the war. Through the years, I collected hundreds of newspaper clippings, read numerous books and attended as many national meetings as I could, regarding our MIAs in Vietnam.

The political games that our government played during the war escalated after the war ceased. Yet, most of us not only were unaware of that, but we believed our government when we were told that there were no more MIAs left in Vietnam. We were told that the only POW was Col. Charles Shelton, USAF, and that all the other POW/MIAs were dead and their remains were missing.

How could that be, I kept asking myself. Year after year, as my children grew up without knowing their father, I kept wondering how the government could tell me that Jim was declared dead after being MIA for only a few years. Yet, I am not sure they made any effort to find his body, so I was labeled a KIA/BNR wife, forcing me to place a marker in the military cemetery without a body or a grave.

As I began to research documents issued by our government, I found that there were as many answers to my questions as there were people to answer them.

For example, on January 19, 1989, the Department of Defense and the Department of State published a Final Interagency Report of the Reagan Administration on the POW/MIA Issue in Southeast Asia.[2]

The document indicated the Reagan Administration had inherited a report in 1982 stating that there had been no remains turned over to the U.S. by either the SRV (Socialist Republic of Vietnam) or the LPDR (Lao People's

165

Democratic Republic) for several years. The conclusion this report came to was that no Americans "could have survived the war and little accountability was possible."

The obvious meaning of this statement was that our government was no longer interested in looking for MIAs. However, statistics showed that 2,383 Americans were still missing or unaccounted for -- 1,747 in Vietnam, 547 in Laos, 83 in Cambodia and 6 in China.

By 1982, the "powers that be" decided that, upon reviewing those numbers, the Americans should be presumed dead in all cases except one. This presumption was made for "administrative and legal reasons."

Between 1976 and 1978, both the U.S. and Vietnam looked for ways to negotiate their differences, but those discussions ended when Vietnam demanded war reparations. The U.S. government hoped that they could get an accounting of the missing Americans as a by-product of the negotiations. That did not happen.[3]

During the years between 1978 and 1981, the Vietnamese officials stopped all contact with our government about returning the remains of any Americans they might have had, as well as any discussion about POW/MIAs.

Between 1981 and 1989, more soldier's remains and material evidence was returned than at any other time since the war ended. The Reagan Administration saw that joint U.S.-Vietnamese teams met on a regular basis and an agreement with Laos was reached to set up a year-round program of cooperation.

The POW/MIA issue became a matter of the highest national priority.

Unfortunately, progress was slow during those years. Negotiations were often halted because both the Vietnamese and the Cambodians tried to connect the POW/MIA issue with political issues. However, the administration continued to put on pressure to seek the return of our country's dead and missing.

Too bad they didn't apply the same pressure to return living Americans.

The National League of Families, through its Executive Director, Ann Mills Griffiths, became quite involved with the White House at this time. Delegations were sent to Hanoi, also, to try to resolve the political issues with the Vietnamese, to no avail.[4]

Finally, in February of 1987, President Reagan appointed a special Presidential emissary to Hanoi, headed by former Joint Chiefs of Staff, General John W. Vessey, Jr. (Ret.). General Vessey was able to obtain, from Foreign Minister Thach in Hanoi, an agreement of cooperation on humanitarian issues, including POW/MIAs. As a result, the Vietnamese turned over 140 remains for U.S. inspection and they agreed to joint field investigations for the first time.[5]

In 1982, a public awareness campaign was started by the administration, with the help of the National League of Families. They felt it was very important for the American public to know more about what was going on with the POW/MIA situation.

Media interest was initiated which helped to affect the attitudes of the American people. They also set up programs to make sure the POW/MIA families were not only informed of the administration's current efforts, but that Congress, active-duty military, veterans groups, the media and the general public were encouraged to take an active part in seeking an end to the POW/MIA problem.[6]

LITTLE GOVERNMENT INTEREST

Along that line, The San Diego Union Opinion section ran an op ed piece on August 17, 1986 by Robert J. Caldwell, entitled "Vietnam POW reports must be pursued." Here are the first four paragraphs.

"Imagine a jungle prison camp in Laos or a closely guarded compound in Vietnam's capital city of Hanoi. Now imagine a dozen, or a score, or a hundred American servicemen, dressed in rags and hunkering in cells or shuffling through a mind-numbing routine of menial chores and debilitating hard labor.

"Thirteen years after their country's armed forces withdrew from Indochina, and 13 years after all U.S. prisoners of war were to have been repatriated, the men in this terrible vision are still being held.

"They wonder whether their country knows they are still alive and still prisoners of war. They wonder whether, even if their government knows or suspects that they are alive, they have been abandoned nonetheless.

"They wonder. They wait. They despair. . ."[7]

Caldwell writes that the Reagan Administration had tried several attempts in 1982 to find and rescue American prisoners in Laotian jungles. The attempts involved Laotian irregulars that the CIA recruited. They failed.[8]

A policy since 1982 states that "Actions to investigate live-sighting reports receive, and will continue to receive, necessary priority and resources based on the assumption that at least some Americans are still held captive. Should any report prove true, we will take appropriate action to ensure the return of those involved."[9]

I wonder how they defined "true" and "appropriate action?" Such general terms leave a lot of room for interpretation. And as far as I can tell, that is just what the various presidential appointees and bureaucrats have done through the years--invented their own definitions.

POW/MIA RECOGNITION DAY

Each year, during the Reagan years, the Congress passed a joint resolution establishing a National POW/MIA Recognition Day now observed on the third Friday of September. In 1988, 46 of the 50 states also declared POW/MIA Recognition Day at the same time.

In the 1989 Final Interagency Report of the Reagan Administration on the POW/MIA Issue in Southeast Asia report, the following statement was made.

"We have yet to find conclusive evidence of the existence of live prisoners, and returnees at Operation Homecoming in 1973 knew of no Americans who were left behind in captivity. Nevertheless, based upon circumstances of loss and other information, we know of a few instances where Americans were captured and the governments involved acknowledge that some Americans died in captivity, but there has been no accounting of them . . . because of such discrepancies and the lack of knowledge about many cases, the Reagan Administration has concluded that we must operate under the assumption that at least some of the missing could have survived until we can jointly conclude that all possible efforts have been made to resolve their fate. In human terms, return of remains ends family uncertainty and, in terms of the live prisoner issue, it permits us to focus on unresolved discrepancy cases, thus moving us closer to answering the highest priority question. In addition, the United States has placed a high priority on resolving 'live sighting' reports received from a variety of sources . . ."[10]

"After resolving the discrepancy cases, achieving the fullest possible accounting in Southeast Asia will still be a long-term process; crash site excavations and remains recovery could continue for years. . .

"Resolving this issue of highest national priority is on track. The effort now is to keep it there."[11]

The effort now is to keep it there? Little did they know in 1989 how prophetic that statement was. Nor did I.

* * *

THE BUSH YEARS

"When men go to war they are prepared to die, to be
captured and tortured, but not to be abandoned by the
very government that sent them!"

Eugene "Red" McDaniel
Captain, U.S. Navy (ret.),
Former POW.[12]

In 1991, the Chief of the Special Office for POWs and MIAs, Colonel
Millard (Mike) A. Peck, resigned. He stated, in his 5-page memorandum,
that the government's highest officials were "committing a travesty" and "a
cover-up." He believed that there was enough evidence available to prove that
American POWs were alive in Southeast Asia. He concluded that, "Everyone
is expendable. I have seen firsthand how ready and willing the policy people
are to sacrifice or 'abandon' anyone who might be perceived as a political
liability. It is quick and facile, and can be easily covered."[13]

The harsh reality for Colonel Peck was that he had never really been in
charge of his office. He was just a "figurehead or whipping boy" for a group
of conspirators outside the DIA.[14] "It appears that the entire issue is being
manipulated by unscrupulous people in the Government, or associated with
the Government. Some are using the issue for personal or political advantage
and others use it as a forum to perform and feel important, or worse . . .the
entire charade does not appear to be an honest effort, and may never have
been."[15]

He wrote of "Smoke and Mirrors" and "High-Level Knavery", "fall guys"
and "patsies to cover the tracks of others", "a political legerdemain", "puppet
masters" and "The Mindset to Debunk".

The totally disillusioned and frustrated Colonel Peck gave up his career
with the following statement. "So as to avoid the annoyance of being shipped
off to some remote corner, out of sight and out of the way, in my own 'bamboo
cage' of silence somewhere, I further request that the Defense Intelligence
Agency, which I have attempted to serve loyally and with honor, assist me in
being retired immediately from active military service."[16]

To support Colonel Peck's allegations, Harry V. Martin, in a series of
articles in the Napa Sentinel (Napa, California), wrote in 1992 that "There
is a split in government — many military insiders know there are still POWs
in Vietnam and support any effort — government-financed — to repatriate
these long-held prisoners. Yet, the highest echelon in government does not
support the military contention."[17]

Colonel Peck was not the only person working for the DIA who had that reaction to the cover-ups. Richard Armitage, a key figure in POW negotiations on behalf of the Defense Intelligence Agency (DIA) had the job of finding and repatriating POWs. Yet, he was falsely accused, by the Golden Triangle's biggest drug lord[18], of being the top U.S. drug dealer in Southeast Asia. The drug lord said that U.S. POWs were being used as slave labor in drug trafficking. According to Harry Martin, "Approximately 90 percent of the heroin trade between the Golden Triangle and the United States was sanctioned by the Central Intelligence Agency."[19]

Apparently, in direct violation of Congress, a secret military slush fund was being established from the drug sales in order to finance the covert military operations in Central America.

Former Director of the DIA, retired Air Force Lieutenant General Eugene F. Tighe, Jr. also agreed with Colonel Peck, that POWs still remained in Vietnam.[20] A six-man Tighe task force was created to overhaul the DIA's POW/MIA office. They found it was "self-evident that a large number of MIAs may never be properly accounted for."[21]

In 1981, General Tighe testified before the House Subcommittee on Asian Pacific Affairs that "American servicemen are alive and being held against their will in Indochina." He suggested that the "DIA holds information that establishes the strong possibility of American prisoners of war in Laos and Vietnam."[22]

Nigel Cawthorne's book, Bamboo Cage, published in 1991, was written to tell the stories of the military personnel who fought for their country in Vietnam, only to be left behind at the end of the fighting. Cawthorne wrote about how General John Vessey had visited Hanoi a week before Cawthorne did, in the late 1980s, when he was doing research for his book. General Vessey spoke of only bones remaining in Vietnam when he was leaving Vietnam. Upon returning to Washington, he said he was satisfied that there were no live Americans in Vietnam. President Bush repeated General Vessey's report and indicated that Vietnam now had an openness that showed their willingness to cooperate.

Jerry Mooney spent most of his 20-year career in the Air Force working for the National Security Agency, the world's largest and most secretive intelligence operation. He eavesdropped on radio communications, broke codes and got information about American POWs from hundreds and hundreds of North Vietnamese communiqués. He was not to break his vow of top secret silence. Ever!

Yet, in 1987, Jerry Mooney went public, the first person in the intelligence community to talk about the POW information that crossed his desk. He testified before a Senate committee and appeared on national television. What did he have to say? "The U.S. government had abandoned hundreds of American prisoners in Southeast Asia after the Vietnam War . . . U.S. intelligence officials knew not only that Hanoi had withheld American POWs as 'bargaining chips' for future negotiations, but also that the North Vietnamese had handed over scores of American airmen to the Soviets for interrogation."

The government officials reacted to his testimony by ignoring Mooney. He was told to "shut your mouth." No one else from the NSA spoke up to support his testimony. Congress was told that he was "a flake" and his testimony was "off the wall."

Presidents Reagan and Bush had called the accounting for MIAs the nation's highest priority, but "Mooney's allegations, along with the entire MIA issue, slipped back into history as the country accepted the idea that all that could have been done to account for the nation's MIAs had been done."

According to Mooney's testimony, he had "tracked more than 300 POWs on the ground in Southeast Asia, of whom only 5% came home." The families of an EC-47 8-man crew had been shot down.[23] The families were told that the men on that "electronic intelligence gathering flight" were dead. "The remains of the entire" crew "had been found."

Mooney said, "I personally wrote the message that these men had been captured alive."[24] But the DIA decided to declare these men dead and their names were removed from the list of POWs. But the men weren't dead. "The names were scratched from the list because they were an inconvenience that would have complicated Henry Kissinger's life."[25]

There was another time when President Bush told someone involved in the POW/MIA situation to "shut up and sit down." The time was President Bush's campaign for re-election. He was speaking before the annual National League of Families convention on July 24, 1992. Unfortunate for the President, many of the POW/MIA families had lost their patience, and when he proceeded to tell them the same rhetoric that the members had heard for years and years, "It was more than many families could take."[26]

As a response, many of those in attendance stood and demanded that the President be serious in negotiating with Vietnam and that he open all of the POW files to the families.

And what did President Bush say to "No more lies! No more lies! Tell us the truth!"

"I know there's doubt and I know people are saying. . .right from the heart, go over there and bring them back. Do you think if I knew of one single person and where he is and how it was that I wouldn't do that? Of course I'd do that."[27]

"While U.S. leaders knew their fate, the Pentagon chose to deceive the families, and the American public, by declaring all their sons and husbands dead."

The Men We Left Behind

* * *

Among my many questions at this point were things like, could Jim have been captured instead of killed? Could Jim be a POW? Did our U.S. military abandon the search for him because he was considered one of those "expendable" men Colonel Peck spoke of?

Not only was I sick at heart over the possibility that he died in that Vietnamese jungle where no one had returned to try to find his body. But, I was also thinking that he may not have died, but was captured instead and had spent all those years in a POW camp somewhere in Vietnam, Laos, Cambodia, Russia, China, or heaven knows where.

If that was true, and he was still alive, did he remember me? Did he wonder about his daughter who was only 3 months old when he last saw her? Did he know that I delivered his son in March 1969? Did he still speak English--remember his mom and dad--dream about the American flag and apple pie—wonder why no one had come to rescue him—pray for God to give him strength to live through his ordeal, day after day, year after year?

Some days I hoped and prayed that he was not alive, living in a dreaded POW camp away from his loved ones and the country he had fought for.

* * *

AND OTHER YEARS

It is unbelievable that under President Nixon, our government had two lists of MIAs as a result of the Paris Peace talks in 1973. The Vietnamese list of MIAs based on the 1973 "Operation Homecoming" was much shorter than the list our negotiators brought home from Paris.[28]

During President Gerald Ford's three years in office, he was "not informed that the five year 3.25 billion dollar reconstruction program was actually Nixon's offer of aid . . ."

"This lack of information produced a non-movement toward an accounting of those men still missing.[29]

Four years later, when President Jimmy Carter was elected[30], his administration began to look at the MIA cases to reclassify them as "presumed dead."

President Carter formed the Woodcock Commission, an ad hoc committee of men who were supposed to help relations between the Vietnamese and the U.S. The response from Vietnam was that they would talk about MIAs if the committee talked about money. But, the committee had no power to negotiate or sign agreements. They were to present the President's views to the Vietnamese and try to get information about U.S. MIAs.[31]

What they did was visit Vietnam, return with 12 sets of reported American's remains, and announce that they found nothing to believe that Vietnam was holding POWs.

So, Leonard Woodcock stated that all of the POWs were dead, which some think was what the Carter Administration wanted the committee to do.

If all of the POWs were dead, then the Vietnamese, who wanted money, would have no prisoners to bargain with. By the same token, the U.S. would not have to bargain with the Vietnamese over POWs who might still be there.[32]

How could it be simpler? No POWs--no money. So, declare all POWs dead! End of subject. What logic!

Later, President Richard Nixon and Secretary of State Henry Kissinger said the United States would not leave Southeast Asia until all of the POW/MIAs were accounted for. When the Vietnamese government declared, "We have no more live Americans here," two American commissions (Woodstock Commission and the Montgomery Committee) confirmed that statement after visiting Southeast Asia.

Marine Private Robert Garwood, who escaped in 1979, blew the whistle on them. However, he is the proof that there were POWs. He claimed to have seen "live men, our men, still being held live in Southeast Asia." As of 1987, the U.S. government still had not thoroughly debriefed Garwood, as though they didn't want to know what he knew. President Nixon and Secretary Kissinger had never been asked to testify before Congress regarding their alleged misstatements.[33]

One month after then Representative Robert Smith, Republican from New Hampshire, revealed the above information in the Washington Times (July 17, 1987), the L.A Times carried the story, "U.S. to Discuss MIAs and Some Aid to Hanoi."[34]

Unfortunately, the Vietnamese cancelled that meeting. General John W. Vessey Jr., President Reagan's handpicked emissary and former chairman of the Joint Chiefs of Staff, had hoped that the meeting would lead to an accounting of the 2,413 missing Americans in Vietnam.[35]

According to The Bakersfield Californian, (August 4, 1987), "For the past several months, Vietnam has not returned any remains of U.S. servicemen and has refused meetings with American technical experts."[36]

Lieutenant Colonel Robert Howard, a highly decorated soldier in the U.S. Army, with 30 years of active service who was engaged in 300 battles with the enemy, testified before the Senate Committee on Veterans' Affairs that there were American POWs alive in Southeast Asia. He told the committee that he had seen photographs to verify his statement. He had seen live-sighting reports and other information that convinced him of that fact. At the time, he was chief of the combat support team to the Special Forces Detachment stationed in Korea, and gathering this kind of information was his responsibility. He had passed this information on to the DIA and Military Intelligence.

Lt. Col. Howard's military superiors showed no interest at all in his findings. Some of his reports were even destroyed. He felt it was not so much an attempt to cover up as not wanting to be involved.

A CIA report dated 1969, had 30 names marked on it as positive identifications. Lt. Col. Howard saw this document. Yet, in 1973, at the end of the war, a majority of the men did not come home. ". . . this Class A, number one Intelligence suddenly is considered bogus bullshit. . . and these guys cease to exist."[37]

One of the most lasting controversies of the last half-century is the conspiracy theory of how our U.S. government abandoned, on purpose, hundreds and hundreds of American military men in Vietnam, Laos and Cambodia.

Military and government documents, as well as individual servicemen's records stamped Top Secret or Classified, have troubled POW/MIA families, some legislators, and the general public when they've been made aware of it. After all these years, is there information they won't let us see in these documents that would throw our country into a political or moral crisis? If none of these men are alive, then why the need to keep the records and the files classified in the first place.

I am not the only person who knows of servicemen who were in Vietnam in 1975, making raids across the border from Vietnam into Laos and Cambodia to extract POWs. There is no evidence in their service records of these servicemen having ever been there--their records have been sanitized. Some of them now have health problems from being in Vietnam. They are unable to get medical benefits from the Army because they can't prove they were there.

I wonder what would happen if the truth were really known about our Vietnam War POW/MIAs and the lengths our government has gone to keep the truth contained.

Chapter Ten

Bubba Gets To Vietnam At Last

"The President is ignoring the facts. There is no question, based on our own government's assessments, that Vietnam can take unilateral action - - right now, today - - to resolve individual cases. As happened too many times in the past, the U.S. Government has decided to reward them on their rhetoric, not their actions. This is a political move to justify full normalization of diplomatic and economic relations."
Press release, 1996, Executive
Director John Sommer, The American
Legion.[1]

During the nineties, or better known as the Clinton Era, changes took place in the relationship between the U.S. and Vietnam. We began hearing rumors concerning the possibility that the U.S. might lift the embargo we had established with Vietnam. The embargo was based on their insisting we pay them millions of dollars in return for the bodies, live or dead, of our Americans they still held.

Senator Hank Brown, Senator from Colorado, issued a memorandum from his office on October 16, 1991 that explained some of the thinking that took place then regarding the embargo.[2]

The memo said, in part, "The embargo will not be lifted until Vietnam has completed all requirements in stages one and two and is making progress in the third stage of the 'roadmap.' In fact, our relations with Vietnam will not move from one stage to the next until all of the requirements for that stage have been accomplished."

And then there is a surprise. "Oil exploration with the Vietnamese government is currently illegal. It is only near the end of the second stage of the agreement that U.S. businesses would even be permitted to sign contracts with the Vietnamese government. However, these contracts cannot be executed until the third stage of the 'road map,' by which time Vietnam must have resolved all discrepancy cases."

When President Clinton announced in February 1994 that he was going to lift the embargo, Robert J. Caldwell wrote a response to that in The San Diego Union-Tribune. Even though Vietnam was still declaring that they had no POWs, evidence was to the contrary.[3]

"Potentially, the most explosive evidence was said to be contained in top secret photographs taken by spy satellites and aerial reconnaissance. The photos were taken over Laos and northern Vietnam and extend over a span of years from 1973 to 1992."

Anthony Lake, Clinton's top national security aide, "was told the photographs clearly show ground markings of names, distress symbols, and authenticator codes correlating to more than two dozen American servicemen missing in Indochina. Nearly all were pilots or aircrew members downed over Laos or Vietnam. With one or two exceptions, the men are still unaccounted for.

"In two cases, ground signals correlating to the same MIA appeared up to six times over a period of years. In one case the latest sign was photographed in 1988. In a second case, the most recent photograph of a clear signal is supposed to have been taken in 1992. Some distress signs, codes, and names were reportedly photographed first in northern Vietnam and later in Laos, suggesting that some POWs were moved from Vietnam to Laos during the mid-1980s."

Caldwell ends his article with, "Clinton no doubt hopes his decision to lift the trade embargo against Vietnam will begin closing one of the most painful chapters in modern American history. Don't count on it."[4]

President Clinton started making comments, such as the one in 1996 where he claimed "full faith" cooperation by Vietnam in our getting "the fullest possible accounting for our prisoners of war and missing in action."[5] There was no mention of the money Vietnam had been holding out for since 1971. So, with what did Clinton have to bargain?

The embargo.

When Clinton lifted the embargo, he blew any kind of leverage we had to get to the real truth. Hope of having any of the live MIAs returned went down the drain. At times, Clinton liked to brag about how many sets of remains the Vietnamese government turned over to us during his watch. But the fact is some are not American or even human remains. It's all a numbers game.

Disabled American Veterans National Commander Thomas A. McMasters, III, stated in response to the embargo situation ". . . President Clinton's pronouncement that the Vietnamese government is 'cooperating in full faith' is premature and unverified."

National League of Families Chairman of the Board, Jo Anne Shirley, made this statement that same year. "It appears to us that President Clinton's promises are nothing more than empty rhetoric and a dishonor to America's POW/MIAs, our nation's veterans and those now serving and will choose to serve our nation in the U.S. Armed Forces. The Clinton Administration's real priority with Vietnam has been and is full normalization of economic and political relations."

Congressman Bob Dornan (R-CA) said, "The Vietnamese could return tomorrow a minimum of 400 remains of American heroes. In addition, they could immediately hand over essential Politburo and Central Committee records that would finally divulge the truth that would end the suffering of the families of hundreds more missing men."

Senator Bob Dole (R-KS) helped found the National League of Families in 1970 and was instrumental since then in furthering the POW/MIA accounting effort. In response to Clinton's pronouncement, Senator Dole said that, "Once again, President Clinton has placed his desire for normalization with Vietnam before his repeated promise to achieve the fullest possible accounting of POW/MIAs."

I read in The League's July 10, 1996 newsletter, that "Although the League appreciates such statements of commitment, the words rang hollow since the certification, itself, is inaccurate and unwarranted."[6]

On the same day (May 29) that President Clinton made his statement about "full faith cooperation," James Wold, Deputy Assistant Secretary of Defense, DOD's POW/MIA Office, was named to form a new Office for Missing Personnel. The League considered this "window dressing" and a "bureaucratic 'camel' directing operations of an office that may continue to be nearly dysfunctional, as it is now."[7]

In a box ad that The League ran in its July 10, 1996 newsletter, they printed "POW/MIA FAMILIES STILL WAIT FOR ANSWERS . . . 2,150 Americans are still missing and unaccounted for from the Vietnam War. Nevertheless, the U.S. established economic and diplomatic relations with Vietnam . . . without getting the fullest possible accounting . . . answers that the U.S. knows Vietnam could locate and provide. We need your support to continue our mission; the return of all POWs and the fullest possible accounting for the MIAs, including the repatriation of all recoverable remains."

In August 1998, The League passed a resolution that I seconded. "Resolved that members present at the National League of Families of American Prisoners and Missing in Southeast Asia 29th Annual Meeting reject as invalid the President's March 4, 1998, certification to Congress that the SRV is 'fully cooperating in good faith' to account for Americans still missing and unaccounted for from the Vietnam War."[8]

Seven years later and the Vietnamese are still not cooperating and the Americans are still not accounted for. My how time flies!

In Home to War[9], author Gerald Nicosia writes about a 1999 Department of Veteran Affairs report that tells of terrible conditions in veterans' hospitals, due in part by Congressional budget cuts. He further writes, "But even in the face of so much wrong done to this nation's veterans of every color and stripe, one would err to assume that there is some depravity or malice at the heart of our government, which leads to such unconscionable acts. Inherent in government is a paradox, in that what is created to serve men often takes on a life of its own, and ends up serving only itself."

I was amazed to read that last sentence. What has happened to the POW/ MIA issue couldn't be described better. So much of my criticism in this book is not based on my anger with specific individuals, but what these people have allowed to happen through the years. The issue has taken "on a life of its own and ends up serving only itself."

Further, Gerald Nicosia states, that "Not only do governments sometimes make mistakes, but they sometimes stubbornly pursue actions they know to be wrong. There could not be a better case in point than the Vietnam War, followed close after by this government's shabby treatment of the veterans of that war."

Our nation's guilt over the Vietnam War continues on and on, year after year and each new president "stubbornly" pursues the wrongs of his predecessor, not wanting to "open the can of worms" left for him and his administration.

On the front page of the February 1999 National League of Families newsletter, is the following headline--PRESIDENT AGAIN CERTIFIES VIETNAM AS FULLY COOPERATING. Clinton's words had not changed. The news media must have used the same news release copy from three years before.

As it happened, three months later, nine Americans were accounted for who had been missing from the Vietnam War. That brought the missing number down to 2,063, over 90% who were unaccounted for under Vietnamese control at the time they were lost. Those families of the 2,063 still longed and hoped for records and remains from the Vietnamese government.[10]

Lo and behold, by April 2000 the National League of Families newsletter stated that "The Clinton Administration's policy since 1993 was evident to all: move toward normal diplomatic and economic relations, and base the steps on perceptions of vast cooperation. In reality, results on POW/MIA accounting would again be the 'hoped-for-by-product,' as family members will recall that U.S. Ambassador to the United Nations Richard Holbrooke saying during the Carter Administration when he served as Assistant Secretary of State for Asian & Pacific Affairs. Though the words were changed, we were back where we were in the late 1970's, except that the joint accounting process would continue."

It seems that the Clinton administration began using such words as outstanding, superb, tremendous and unprecedented in 1993 and continued to do so throughout the nineties when speaking to Vietnam's cooperation. However, the POW/MIA families knew that in reality, Vietnam officials were not providing our government with information or remains[11], with but a few exceptions.

Guess what? On February 18, 2000, President Clinton issued another certification to Congress. Vietnam is "fully cooperating in good faith" he said. And once again he stated "that the central, guiding principle" of his "Vietnam policy is to achieve the fullest possible accounting of our prisoners of war and missing in action."

As The League newsletter reported, "Our question is why is it necessary to destroy perceptions? Isn't it more logical and honorable to stick to the facts and state the obvious - - U.S. policy in the Clinton Administration was to normalize relations and hope that results would increase? Yet, some administration officials continue to maintain that normalization steps as early as 1993-95 were based on increased Vietnamese cooperation when it was obvious to all the unilateral action had ceased."[12]

As vacancies come up on The League's Board of Directors, men and women who run for that position make statements as to why they should be elected. Among the published 1999-2001 Board of Directors Candidates' Statements, Gail Innes, from Illinois, wrote, "I strongly supported the priority established by President Reagan and continued by President Bush, but recognize and am angered by the Clinton Administration's policy. I am impatient for answers; we've waited too long!"

Mark L. Stephensen, Idaho, ended his statement with "The current Administration is prepared to sweep us aside. I will not let that happen without a fight."

"I advocate continuing to live dangerously (vis-à-vis finances) because we must continue to learn and tell the truth, knowing the difference between fact and fiction," wrote David F. Gray, Florida, returned POW.

"Our primary objective must continue to be returning any who might still be alive, with a secondary objective of returning identifiable remains to prove that the first is not possible and to provide closure for the family involved." This statement was made by Wayne O. Jefferson, Jr., from Virginia.

Michael S. Clark, New York, said that "Though President Clinton assured us that in normalizing relations with Vietnam an increase in unilateral action would occur, many of us have long since ceased to hold our breath. Predictable, Vietnam continues to drag its feet by providing limited and incomplete information about our Last Known Alive cases provided by the

1994 League Delegation. Furthermore, the ongoing pattern of remains that are meted out continues when it is in the best interest of Vietnam."[13]

* * *

Clinton's empty words continued on. There was no progress in getting information and remains from Vietnam. I am now looking at the turn of the century–2005. As far as I'm concerned, Clinton's words were used for stringing along families, vets, concerned citizens and some politicians, to keep them quiet from year to year--nothing else. Because Clinton's words could be interpreted that he cared, most people did not question his motives. He was working very hard, so he said. Getting a full accounting of our POW/MIAs was the nation's highest priority, he said.

But, when his administration lifted the embargo (opened trade with Vietnam), it blew any kind of leverage our country had to get the real truth.

Now came Clinton's visit to Vietnam as his second term of office came to a close. In November 2000, the newspapers were full of front-page stories about this historic visit. Pictures of Clinton accompanied each article, showing him with throngs of Vietnamese children wearing their cone-shaped hats. There were pictures of Clinton receiving flowers from beautiful young Vietnamese women, visiting rice paddies, reaching out to touch young Vietnamese men's hands, watching as little Vietnamese boys and girls tried to shovel thick mud where an American pilot might have been buried 33 years ago, and so forth.

And Clinton had the gall to talk to the Vietnamese about working hard to make a better life for themselves. It seems to me that Clinton's going to the crash site outside Hanoi was a weak attempt to say that it was the nation's hightest priority, and that "he cares" and was doing everything to get the fullest possible accounting.

David Brunnstron, Reuters News Agency, wrote in The San Diego Union-Tribune on Thursday, November 9, 2000, Hanoi would not demand during Clinton's visit that Washington pay billions of dollars to "help repair the damage of the Vietnam War." This is a reference to the $3.25 billion that Nixon had promised in a secret annex to the 1973 Peace Accord signed by Henry P. Kissinger and Le Duc Tho.[14]

On November 13, 2000 I received an e-mail from Anna Campbell with a message she thought everyone should read. She said, "People just don't realize what effect stuff like this (see below) has on soldiers, sailors, pilots, and Marines alike, and everyone should be a little more cognizant of that fact, because it's the only way it is every going to be stopped." I agree, so I've copied the e-mail she received.

"President Clinton reportedly plans to visit China and Vietnam before the end of his term, and, according to high-ranking Navy officers, the commander in chief will alter long-standing naval regulations to allow the American flag to fly below that of Vietnam when he sails into the Communist nation's territorial waters on a U.S. Navy ship. Highly placed Navy sources, who spoke on condition of anonymity, believe this action on the president's part would further devastate already tenuous Navy morale.

"As part of his swan song, Clinton reportedly intends to visit two ports aboard Naval vessels. Trip one takes him to the People's Republic of China which has a regulation that no war ship of any country may enter its territorial waters flying a flag higher than that of the People's Republic of China. According to one Navy source, China and the U.S. have effected a compromise whereby both flags - - the U.S. and the PRC - - will be flown from U.S. naval vessels at the same height. But visceral outrage is resulting from a proposed change to Navy regulations that would result in the American flag being displayed subordinate to the flag of Vietnam.

"Navy regulations and tradition prescribe that no country's flag will be displayed in a superior position to the U.S. flag. However, Vietnam's rules reportedly demand that the Vietnamese flag shall always fly in a superior position to any other country's flag. High ranking naval officers, speaking on condition that their names not be published, say the reason for all the alarm, anger and career-threatening rhetoric is that Clinton allegedly has either ordered, or is about to order, the Secretary of the Navy to amend regulations to permit the Vietnamese flag to be displayed over the U.S. flag."

"I'd like to blow the @#*% thing up!" said one frustrated officer.

The United States Navy Regulations began with the enactment by the Continental Congress of the 'Rules for the Regulation of the Navy of the United Colonies' on Nov. 28, 1775. So a long and proud history bolsters the long-held Navy tradition that no country's flag will fly higher than that of the United States. Commenting on the report, Col. David Hackworth, America's most decorated living war veteran, said, "What's new? Clinton has done everything else to dishonor the flag, why not make it number two?" He added, "Congress ought to pull this traitor's travel plug . . . now."

Calls to the Navy Staff operations and Special Events office were referred to the Public Affairs Office, which then referred to the radio station WND to the news desk. When WND outlined the scenario, the spokesman whose first comment was, "Wow"--later called back to say, "We haven't been able to find anything on it yet, but we're trying to run the story to ground."

Adm. Thomas B. Fargo, Commander in Chief of the U.S. Pacific Fleet, is reported to have visited the People's Republic of China recently, although the reason for the trip is not known. (This was blocked by all major news media.)

The media did report, I understand, that the Vietnamese-Americans hoped President Clinton's trip in November 2000 would highlight human rights and bring Vietnam closer to democracy. The Vietnam veterans, however, were reported to want Clinton to make accounting for all of the war dead as his top priority. They wanted closure to the POW/MIA issues.

Clinton, who protested the war as a college student, planned to question the Vietnamese government on America's MIAs. The visit was more political than fact finding. Some hoped the trip would focus on religious freedom and human rights. Many Americans were not hopeful of the visit having an affect at all. Clinton was a lame-duck president at the time and the next president hadn't been elected.

As it turned out, Clinton called for more openness while in Vietnam and scaled back his human rights message. In fact, the New York Times News Service reported that Prime Minister Phan Van Khai stiffened when Clinton brought up the human rights message. "Both men, according to U.S. officials, said 'We may have different definitions of human rights,' and said they had to worry about the rights of Vietnamese to eat and get an education before they moved toward America's agenda."[15]

Did that mean that the Vietnamese want money from us to feed and educate their citizens before they'll talk about more information and the return of our POW/MIA remains?

According to an article in The Oakland Tribune (California), November 19, 2000, three more sets of human remains were given to the Clinton visiting party for which a military honor guard took possession after a repatriation ceremony. The coffins were sent to Hawaii for forensics work.[16]

This, of course, was wonderful. Three more of our missing men had been found. Three more families could have closure. That is, if they were American remains and if they could be scientifically identified. But, weren't they but a token from the Vietnamese to keep us satisfied for a few more months, at least to make Clinton's trip worthwhile in American minds?

The West Contra Costa Sunday Times (California) ran the same syndicated story about Clinton's visit on November 19, but their sub-head said, "A sad but cathartic harvest of soldiers' remains, both U.S. and Vietnamese, testifies that once-warring nations are working together."

There was one reported resistance to Clinton's visit and that came from the Communist Party's general secretary, Le Kha Phieu. He said, "Where did the cause of our resistance war against invaders come from? Fundamentally, it came because imperialists invaded to get colonies. Why did the United States bring its army to invade Vietnam when Vietnam did not bring an army to invade the United States?"[17]

From the Florida Times-Union article, published November 19, 2000, written by Terry Dickson, I found the following reprint on the e-mail.

"I think it's wonderful, Mr. President, that you visited Vietnam. I cannot agree, however, with your decision to come home. Let's see now. More than 30 years after you dodged the draft, you go spend a few days. Al Gore spent four months. That gives each of you about two months. Vietnamese officials said they consider you a friend because you didn't fight against them; and that those of us who did are criminals. It was too late to go, Mr. President.

"You should have been there when enemy machine-gun fire - - that would be friendly fire to you - - pinned down some Marines on a hill near the DMZ. Ernie Tuten, a big old boy from Brunswick, stood up, charged forward and opened up with his M-60 machine gun, pouring rounds into the bunker until his buddies took it out. I asked Ernie what he was thinking while he was standing there blazing away. "I thought, 'I hope I don't run out of ammo,'" he said. He got a Silver Star a few years ago for doing that. Better late than never, I guess.

"No, that wasn't another reference to your visit. You should have been with me sitting on a fire base somewhere west of Marble Mountain in 1971 under a sky full of stars and a little sliver of a moon. Then across the river, on the other side of the Purple Heart Trail, a firefight broke out. Tracers were going everywhere; there were white and yellow flashes. And not one bit of sound ever reached us. It was beautiful and sickening. We sat watching silently, somebody else's war, brave men and scared men dying across the river.

"You should have been there in the bush that night when Cowboy, my absolutely fearless point man, sat crying over a letter and a Polaroid picture of his wife and little boy. He said he was losing her and I couldn't find any words. Maybe you could have felt his pain.

"You should have been there for one of the good times, when we waded up a little creek on patrol until we hit a rock wall with a waterfall tumbling down into a deep pool. Those who couldn't swim stood guard. Those of us who could stripped down and dived in.

"You should have been there to help carry Stein. I wasn't in the country yet, but his buddies said the choppers couldn't get out in the rain. They had to carry his body around for days in a poncho. They could have used another hand.

"And it took a long time for a chopper to fly out to pick up Graham when he took four AK-47 rounds in the legs on Charlie Ridge. He was the only man I had who got shot. I know it wasn't his fault, my fault or anyone's fault. It was the war. But 29 years later I still wonder if I could have done something different.

"You should have been there when the med-evac chopper hoisted him up from his own blood - - Lord, there was so much blood - - up through the tree limbs and the swirling fog. It was the last time I saw him. We know you couldn't be there. You had other things to do to. You were at Oxford protesting the war.

"Although you thought the war was wrong, you said you wouldn't apologize to the Vietnamese. I appreciate that.

"You know what I wish you'd do when you get home, though? Get up before dawn sometime and go to the wall. You know the one I'm talking about. Walk along, read a few names and then say, 'I'm sorry, guys. I should have been there.'"

As I read the progression of these newspaper articles about Clinton visiting Vietnam, I became increasingly angry. How could this Vietnam-dodging President even hold his head up to not only the Vietnamese and to the veterans in this country, much less those who lost loved ones?

It seems to me that all he tried to do was to see as much of the world as he could on the taxpayer's money. And Hillary! How thoughtful of her to spend twice as much money by going to Vietnam on her own Air Force plane with her own staff and extra security. Gosh! Why didn't she invite us to go along? Why didn't our government give the Vietnamese the money Hillary spent on the plane and make her travel with her husband? I wonder how many MIAs we would have gotten back if she had given the money to the Vietnamese instead?

Of course, he didn't mention the outrageous price the Vietnamese government charges the U.S. for doing anything in their country. I feel the Vietnamese are taking us to the cleaners, getting whatever they can as part of what Kissinger promised them at the end of the war, but couldn't deliver. In return, Clinton told us back home, "And look how wonderful the Vietnamese are being at doing everything possible to help us find our POW/MIAs."

The Vietnamese must have been very confused during Clinton's visit by what he said since they knew what the real story was. I wonder if we'll ever know the truth about who has been making the deals and passing monies to get our POWs out. It's all so insidious.

Written in the June 13, 2001 statement from the National League of Families, "Vietnam's Ability to Account for Missing Americans" is: "The League supported a policy of reciprocity - - steps by the U.S. to respond to efforts by Vietnam to locate and return remains and provide case-specific archival documents. In the League's view, important leverage was lost without commensurate results during the Clinton Administration."[18]

I couldn't have written it better than J.D. Wetterling did in an article, published on Memorial Day, 2001. "I have forgiven those flawed national leaders. . .I served, my Asian enemies and even myself for tragic youthful hubris. God willing, I will one day find it in my heart to forgive Bill (Clinton)."[19]

This roller coaster of emotions never really stops. I can get so mad that I want to rip some statesman's head off, and then I tumble back off that adrenaline rush and feel--what's the use?

* * *

(The following information comes from "The Untold Story of Baron 52 - - Their Flight Was Supposed to be a Secret, Not Their Fate" by Alfred Lubrano, Philadelphia Inquirer, Sunday January 11, 1998, Part I, D Section, page 24, and January 14, 1998, Part II.[20])

Mary Matejov, the mother of Sgt. Joseph Matejov, cursed President Clinton for removing Vietnam's incentive to give the United States vital information about her son. "You know," says Matejov, "my late husband used to say, 'They don't do this in America.' But you learn the hard way. They sure do. There isn't anything my country wouldn't do. We're just as dirty as any other nation. It breaks your heart."

Matejov's family had joined other Americans to make up the Bamboo Pipeline. They believe that our government has buried men in the wrong graves and declared men dead when there is evidence that they may still be alive.

Sgt. Matejov was one of four men in the back end of Baron 52, an EC-47Q converted cargo plane that was the last one to be shot down in the Vietnam War. The lumbering Baron 52 was to eavesdrop on a convoy of North Vietnamese tanks moving along the Ho Chi Minh Trail into Cambodia.

A search team reached the plane four days later and reported they saw three or four bodies in the front section of the plane. But what happened to the four in the back section? Did they parachute out and were they captured? That is what the families believe.

But our government declared everyone dead. The proof was a dogtag and half a tooth found in a 1993 excavation identified as belonging to one of the back-enders, Sgt. Peter Cressman. However, according to a declassified NSA report, our air and ground "spooks" heard North Vietnamese officers say in code that they were "holding four pilots captive" not long after the plane was shot down in the general area.

Then, there were intercepted messages such as "four pirates" being moved north, "The people involved in the south Laotian campaign have shot down one aircraft and captured the pilots." The Vietnamese seemed to interchange the words "pirates" and "pilots" for any rank.

Jerry Mooney, then a National Security Agency analyst, was in the room when the Baron 52 was shot down. He read those messages. "There was no other plane shot down that day, and the code systems they were using pertained only to that area," Mooney said.

Congressional records show that a 6994th Security Squadron communiqué read, "Believe . . . crew members could have bailed out and possibly been carried north by the winds. . ."

A message from Air Force headquarters in Nakhon Phanom, Thailand, to Washington D.C. said, "There is a chance. . . crew members . . . bailed out and landed safely on the ground . . . There is not conclusive evidence of death."

Roger Shields, Assistant Secretary of Defense in 1973, wrote an internal memo that reads, "DIA. . . feels there is some reason to believe that the four may actually have been captured."

According to a former security analyst with the 6994th, Robert Wilhelm, members of that squadron received a message from a very reliable, friendly Laotian who reported seeing "four clean-shaven Americans in flight suits" being led by North Vietnamese soldiers through the jungle in Laos after the crash.

None of the families of these four men were ever told any of the above information.

Instead, a priest and an Air Force Officer visited the four families, who said words such as, "We have conclusively established that your son could not have survived."

For five years, none of these four families doubted the information they were given. They just grieved.

Then things changed. The Cressman family became obsessed with the fact that Peter Cressman may have survived the crash. Two of the brothers visited Laos, brought back six sets of KIA remains but saw no live prisoners. They tried several "hair-brained" schemes, to no avail.

They even visited a Chief Master Sgt. Ronald Schofield in Texas, in 1991, who "examined the crash site" days after the crash, because they heard he had information for them.

"I've been waiting for you guys for 18 years," Schofield said. "The parachute door was missing. Those men got out of the plane alive. I knew it from that day."

In his deposition, Schofield said he didn't think the back-enders bodies burned in the crash because he recognized the front-enders bodies. They had worn Nomex fire retardant suits. There should have been eight bodies. He testified that he believed the men kicked out the door and bailed out before the plane crashed and burned.

"People say we can't handle death. Garbage," Steve Cressman says. "What we can't handle is knowing that the government left them behind."

Sgt. Joseph Matejov's father was a Lt. Col. (ret.) when all three of his sons went to war in Vietnam. His daughter was a West Point graduate. "We believed in duty-honor-country," he said, "But what they teach you at West Point, they don't practice." He vowed to get some answers about his son, Joe.

Lt. Col. Stephen Matejov soon found enough information to believe that the United States didn't want to admit that they were sending spy planes to Laos when the war was over. This also took place just before 591 POWs were about to be released by North Vietnam and Matejov believed that the U.S. government didn't want to have anything go wrong with that. So they sacrificed four men for 591 men.

Roger Shields, Kissinger's POW/MIA specialist, met with Lt. Col. Matejov. Mary Matejov remembers Shields saying that he always "meant to go back to get" the men but "I'm sorry, I dropped the ball."

Shields remembers saying, "I'm sorry we didn't get back in to investigate."

Lt. Col. Matejov died in 1984. His wife, Mary, was active in speaking around the country about MIAs, but not so much any more, the article says. She stated that the government is "trying to wait me out. . . I hope I irritate the government for the rest of my life."

It is ironic that the POW-Missing Personnel Office in the DOD states that all eight members of the Baron 52 died and burned in the crash. "Early speculation and uncorroborated theories have unfortunately given false hope to the family members."

Senator Bob Smith attacked Robert DeStatte, senior analyst for the DIA for being dishonest in his interpretation of what happened. Jerry Mooney, who read those decoded messages when the plane went down, called DeStatte "a bald-faced liar." Senator Smith even asked Attorney General Janet Reno to "go after DeStatte for perjury" but nothing happened with that.

Bill Bell, President Bush's chief of the U.S. Office of POW/MIA Affairs in Hanoi, said he found it bizarre that after 20 years, a search party would find one tooth and a dogtag just laying around at the sight of the crash in the jungle. The Vietnamese are known to be able to create phony dogtags for sale.

Mary Matejov had her son's dogtag tested but there were no conclusive results.

Resigning his post with the Bush Administration gave Bill Bell an opportunity to declare his belief that the government was "more interested in commerce with the Vietnamese than learning the whereabouts of MIAs." He wasn't sure, after so many years, that there were still live prisoners in Southeast Asia, but he said, there were "after Nixon said all prisoners were out in April 1973. And we never mounted a serious effort to find out because we couldn't live with the truth. The Cressman case is a good example."

In March 1996, at Arlington National Cemetery, a single coffin was draped with an American flag, with 29 pieces of bone inside. No one was sure if they were all human bones.

The names of both the four front-enders and the four back-enders were engraved on the headstone. The Cressmans and Matejovs had tried to keep this event from occurring, until they had proof of their loved ones' death. To honor the feelings of the other two families, they attended the ceremony. The members of the Bamboo Pipeline wore yellow armbands. They did not go there to say goodbye.

When Evelyn Cressman began to cry, her daughter, Pat said, "It's not him, Mom. There's nothing in the box. They're just trimming the ends off their package." Later, Pat said, "It was a beautiful funeral. The only thing missing was the corpse."

* * *

How can I add anything to that? Jim's funeral was beautiful, also. The only thing missing was his corpse. And it still is, as nothing sits beneath his engraved headstone in the cemetery at the Presidio, San Francisco.

Chapter Eleven

Picking Up The Pieces

"Poor is the nation that has no heroes, shameful is the one having them . . . forgets."[1]

While George W. Bush was campaigning for president in the fall of 2000, he made several remarks about what his administration would do, if elected, to revive the MIA situation as top priority. "I will place this matter high on America's diplomatic agenda," he said. "I'll make it clear to all countries concerned that this is a test of good faith in their dealings with the United States."

The prior June, during his campaign, Governor Bush wrote in a letter, "I will work with Congress to ensure that those departments and agencies have the necessary resources, including intelligence capabilities, to carry out the POW/MIA mission."[2]

Lionel Van Deerlin, an 18-year representative to Congress from San Diego, California, responded to Governor Bush's campaign promises with an opinion piece in the San Diego Union-Tribune on September 20, 2000. His response, among many comments, was that "If he deems the MIAs still a viable issue, it can only mean the Texas Governor has not been paying attention. Since Reagan's 'top priority' promise nearly 20 years ago, not one of those 2,300 missing men on the Pentagon's list has been located and brought home.

"Two Americans who may be thought to hold a keen interest in this subject - - Sen. John McCain and former Rep. Douglas 'Pete' Peterson, now the U.S. ambassador to Saigon - - both are satisfied that no MIAs remain alive, and that the Vietnamese government has dealt with us in good faith. (Between them, McCain and Peterson spent 12 years as prisoners of what was then North Vietnam)."[3]

I became so irate when I read Van Deerlin's column, that I sat right down and addressed the following letter to him, via e-mail.

Mr. Van Deerlin:

You obviously didn't do your homework when you wrote this article! There was an American who did come out of a Hanoi prison some 5 years AFTER the end of the war. That's after the Vietnamese denied holding any other Americans prisoner, and after our government declared all the unaccounted for POW/MIAs dead. Surely, you don't think that our government would go back to war with Vietnam just because one man did escape and was able to get to the press. No way! To save face, the only answer was to declare him a deserter. I'm not going to argue either side of that issue. But the fact remains--he is an American, he was left behind against his will in prison, and our government never did anything about it except to crucify him when he got back to the States. They refused to debrief him for almost 10 years, and he kept trying to give them the names of other Americans that he'd been held with and knew of.

"Why the concentration on Vietnam's lesser MIA toll, and not those others (WWII and Korea)?" That's an easy answer. Americans didn't question the government's integrity during those two wars. We were a nation of believers then. It wasn't till the formation of the National League of Families for POWs and MIAs in Southeast Asia took place in 1969, that there was any organization that was asking the government to be accountable for their statements. Had Nixon not made it a "policy" that they were all dead, I wonder if we'd be dealing with this today?

Answer this question. If Senator John McCain or Ambassador Pete Peterson were as vocal and dedicated at getting to the truth of this issue, do you think that they would still be holding office? I doubt it! Why? Because it's not a popular topic.

Here's another reason. "We don't leave our men behind." Ask any soldier from an elite group if that isn't their motto. I've actually heard Generals say it. So the obvious way to get around it, is to deny that there were any men left behind. It amazes me how they put blinders on when it comes to sworn testimonies in front of Senate Select Committee hearings about men that were in fact left behind. To top this off, "we don't pay for political prisoners."

Make my day, and learn more about the real issues that seem to be behind this country's lack of interest in resolving the fate of all the men left behind from the various wars.

Until then, shame on you for falling for the "party line" on this issue.

Barbara Birchim
Wife of Cpt. James D. Birchim
MIA since November 15, 1968

* * *

"It was no accident that Texas Governor George W. Bush used the term 'prisoners' alongside the word 'missing' in his speech before the Veterans Museum and Memorial in San Diego on September 15, 2000 (National

POW/MIA Recognition Day)," wrote Cdr. Chip Beck, USNR (ret), two days later in 2000.

"For eight years, the Clinton-Gore administration, and its front office appointees at the Defense POW/MIA Office (DPMO), virtually eliminated the term 'POW' from the official lexicon, purposefully burying the mystery of America's 'unrepatriated POWs' under the more politically advantageous term 'MIAs,' or missing in action."

Cdr. Beck is a former POW Special Investigator and a retired CIA officer in the clandestine service. Through his work, he gathered insights into operations and programs and modus operandi of the Soviet KGB, as well as its communist allies.

His definition of MIAs is "combatants who were killed in battle." His definition of POWs is "those who were captured alive, secretly held without full knowledge of the U.S., and not returned to America after the conflicts ended."

He further explains that a serviceman held as a prisoner is a POW, whether our government knows his true status or not. He is not an MIA because the country holding him prisoner knows he's not missing. If the POW dies in captivity, he's still not an MIA. He's a dead POW. The enemy can account for him. Nine thousand unrepatriated "American POWs from 20th Century conflicts fall into that category.

"The difference as to why the POWs have been ignored, and the MIAs attended to, is that our foreign adversaries have been offered financial incentives to help U.S. teams dig up the remains of service personnel killed in combat. President Clinton's announced trip to Vietnam, after the election, is part of the economic payoff involved for this 'half' of the accounting equation. . . the POW side, is far more embarrassing to the governments and intelligence services of Russia, China, North Korea, Vietnam, and even former Warsaw Pact countries."

In 1997, Cdr. Beck and Norman Kass, then Executive Director of the Joint U.S.–Russian Commission Support Directorate, provided Vice President Al Gore with the above information/definition. "Mr. Gore failed the test. The Vice President never responded, which clearly demonstrated his indifference and lack of caring regarding the POW issue."

The opposite was true of Governor Bush. He responded in public and private, clearly stating his plans to do something about the POW/MIA situation when he became President. "First," he said, "should I be elected president, I will direct all relevant departments and agencies to make it their own priority. Second, I will work with Congress to provide all the necessary resources to carry out that mission."

Cdr. Beck stated, "Governor Bush's remarks, and the access channels that he has allowed to be opened to him and senior advisors, represent the best opportunity in three decades for competent and professional investigations to be applied to the mysteries surrounding an estimated 9000 un-repatriated POWs from the North Russia Expedition (1918), Depression era Soviet retention of American agents (1930s), 7000 Americans transferred from the German Stalags to the Soviet Gulag for permanent holding (1945), 2000 Americans transferred to Siberia from North Korea and China (1950-1953), Cold War shoot downs (1948-1962), and the First and Second Indochina Wars (1954-1975)."[4]

At the National POW/MIA Recognition Day, 2000, in San Diego, Governor Bush stated that he was most aware of the POW/MIA families. "Theirs is a daily burden - - not knowing, even now, what has become of their husband, or father, or brother, or son. We owe them something, too. We must have the fullest possible accounting. This must be a high priority - - a presidential priority - - and it must come soon."[5]

The League members were pleased to hear those words. They felt that Bush's commitments, when elected, would be carried out with a "strong sense of purpose." One of the commitments Bush made that pleased me the most was ". . . my administration will share what we learn with the families of the missing - - every fact we gather, all the evidence we find about their loved ones. This is a duty we owe to the families, and to those who served."

Hallelujah! I only hope that this will come true.

Then, Bush added, "It is also our duty to the men and women who currently serve - - a signal that those who wear our country's uniform will never be abandoned."

Do you suppose that he can really change a pattern that has existed with our governmental powers for well over 50 years? I wonder! President Reagan's documents due to be declassified in 2001, were reclassified by Bush, doomed now to never come out from hiding. What could possibly be so important that the family members of our POW/MIAs couldn't be privy to the information held in those papers?

The League reported in its March 20, 2001 Newsletter how pleased everyone was with Vice President Dick Cheney's remarks at the Salute to Veterans on January 19, 2001. He said, "Today we also remember those who are not so near - - those who never came home - - those whose fate is still undetermined. We honor the memory of the fallen soldier. We have not forgotten the missing soldier, and we pledge to their families our best efforts at the fullest possible accounting."[6]

Even though President George W. Bush said, before he was elected, he agreed with having a trade agreement with Vietnam, he made it clear that he was not going to let the Vietnamese government get away with not furnishing the U.S. with all of their records regarding POWs and MIAs. The League responded that the members supported "steps by the United States in response to unilateral and joint actions by Vietnam, not steps in advance in the hope of responses."[7]

* * *

"Kennedy's Wars," by Lawrence Freedman, hit the bookstore shelves in spring 2001. In the book, the author "attempts to cut through mythology to assess John Kennedy's performance in the four foreign crises he faced as president, in Cuba, Laos, Berlin and Vietnam."[8]

Freedman brings the reader's attention to the fact that Laos was where much of the trouble started in Southeast Asia. He says that it was "about Laos, not Vietnam, that President Eisenhower warned Kennedy during their transition meetings." It seems that Ike never mentioned Vietnam to Kennedy.

The book asks, in so many words, what Kennedy would have done in Vietnam if he had lived? As other books and movies have suggested in the past, Kennedy was ready to write off Vietnam as the "wrong place to fight another Asian land war." He was ready to withdraw the 16,000 U.S soldiers from Vietnam. It seems that "Kennedy had asked for a plan for troop withdrawals in early 1963" but no one knows why.

"The Camelot myth helps us to believe Kennedy would have spared the country the agony of Vietnam; that no president with his intelligence, style and sound political instincts could have created such a mess; that it was the fear and loathing caused by his assassination that sent us reeling toward disaster under Johnson."

After all these years, we want to believe that Kennedy would have ended the U.S. involvement in the Vietnam crisis without war. Yet, there is the opposite thought on that dream. Without a good policy, we would have probably become involved in a Southeast Asia war nightmare, no matter who was president.[9]

* * *

The Bush Executive Order 13233, signed in November 2001 has a lot of people, historians, journalists and members of Congress concerned. This Order stopped President Reagan's confidential and private communications with his advisers from being released by the National Archives after twelve years, which is the existing law, as I mentioned earlier in this chapter.

This determination for secrecy is but another sign that our government is knee-deep in misinformation, lies and questionable actions. Or, so it appears.

On November 9, 2001, John Dean, former Counsel to the President of the United States and author of The Rehnquist Choice: The Untold Story of the Nixon Appointment That Redefined the Supreme Court, wrote the following--

"The Bush administration would do well to remember the admonition of former Senator Daniel Patrick Moynihan in his report on government secrecy: 'Behind closed doors, there is no guarantee that the most basic of individual freedoms will be preserved. And as we enter the 21st Century, the great fear we have for our democracy is the enveloping culture of government secrecy and the corresponding distrust of government that follows.'"[10]

I can add nothing to that statement, but check this out. At a White House Briefing, broadcast on CNN, the 13th of March, 2002, President Bush was asked by a reporter whether or not Cdr. Scott Speicher's MIA status would impact our aggression towards Iraq. President Bush shook his head in disgust. "Any government that would hold a prisoner without notifying his family. . ."

Letters from the Birchim Family

"Please take care of yourself, and don't be a hero. I don't
need a Medal of Honor winner. I need a son. Love Mom."
Letter engraved
on Vietnam War Memorial
in New York City

Through the years I have received many letters from Jim's parents and his
sister, Jean. Here are some excerpts that are quite significant as to how MIA
families have felt during the last forty-plus years.

My letter from Jean Birchim, in 1994, follows:

". . . God, all the anger! I cannot believe what our government
has done to those men! I cannot believe they can get away with it so
easily! But how can they be stopped?

I pray the men are dead. I cannot bear the thought of them
knowing we left them on purpose! They are probably better dead
and not knowing.

. . . I have had more luck locating some of the people who were
supposedly with Jim. I spoke with Steve Sherman[1] (Special Forces
veteran) again. He was much more informative this time than
the last. He knows a lot of the people involved with the Belletire
questioning.

. . . Both Brooks[2] and Sherman said we would probably never
know what really happened to Jim. Brooks (Lt. Col. Mack Brooks)
confessed to Mom that Jim was teaching biological warfare and was
into atomic weapons - - said Jim was into some nasty business, all
CIA, and they do not give out their papers. What I cannot understand
is, if we, the families, need to put it all behind us, then why doesn't
the government?

Why do they get to keep our loved one's papers? If we are to be
so understanding and brave, why don't they have to do the same?
Why is it always so one-sided?

. . . I just need to talk to those men who were with Jim that
day. We will never learn anything from the government, we need to
talk to them before they get too old and die. (Col.) Jack Warren[3] is
already dead.

. . . By the way, there was no commanding officer for FOB#2
for 45 days, the same time of Jim's disappearance. This is interesting.
Remember in the beginning the Army told Mom over the phone that

Jim was with a man by the name of Smith when they were attacked - - going in, not coming out - - and one of Jim's letters mentions how he went with a Smith to some blown up village. Now I find out that Jim's commanding officer at FOB#2 was Col. Smith. Smith was in command from Nov. 67 to Oct. 68, he was moved up to D.C.O., or some title, under Col. Warren. No one else is in command until Dec. of '68. . .Smith is just everywhere in this thing. Also, there was a lot of other activity going on in Laos on those same days as Jim . . .

Did you happen to catch the fact that the helicopter, which went in for Jim, had only 3 McGuires on it? Pissed me off! . . . But if you look at Hoeck's[4] (pilot) statement, it says 'all 4 ropes seemed taunt in climb out.' The document you sent also says they could not land in the LZ because of heavy artillery fire, not that they moved to another one and could not land because there were too many trees. There never was a rig tangled in the trees, because there were only 3 to begin with and the Montagnard's is the only one which says there were three ropes. But I do not like the way it just sort of stops short and states, 'it was dark, Birchim fell somewhere' or something to that effect.

Sherman said I probably would not want to know what really happened to Jim. He is wrong! Dead wrong! Why are all these knowledgeable people so willing to protect all of us family members? If everyone would stop trying to protect us from the truth, then maybe we could really 'put it behind us.' Don't they realize that our imagination is worse than the truth? And who are they to protect us? It is our business to protect ourselves.

. . . I am always afraid I say too much. I am afraid to send this letter for fear someone else may read it before you. Ridiculous!"

Jim's dad wrote many letters to each of the presidents after Jim disappeared and was presumed dead. He sent a copy to President Nixon of a letter he wrote to General Kenneth G. Wickham on March 14, 1971. "I don't believe I would be so concerned about getting the details if it weren't for so many puzzling and suspicious events prior to and after his disappearance. The thought of foul play didn't occur to me until perhaps a year after his disappearance. I began to consider certain events and facts that made me suspicious, and believe me, this is a bad experience for anyone. . .You suddenly begin to question what you have always believed - - just took for granted. Our faith is shattered.

". . .Of interest also, is that shortly after his disappearance, the Army wrote his wife requesting a recent photo of him. They explained his file had been lost (?). They had no records. Rather peculiar? Also, when his personal effects were sent home, all there was were some socks and underwear. That's all. Peculiar?

"My son only wanted to help America - - and I think he died or is missing, doing what he thought America really expected of him. He was a brave boy and may have served some purpose if he died resisting some of these terrible charges against our country. I am very proud of him. I miss him. I know, if he died, he 'stood tall' as all Green Berets are taught and as we taught him. He was a great kid."

On May 15, 1971, Jim's dad wrote to President Nixon, asking for more information on Jim's status. He also wrote, "I wish the Army would write his grandmother and explain he is dead. She writes Jim every week through the Paris Viet Cong Delegation, and she insists he is alive."

He wrote, dated May 11, 1971 after finding out how the Air Force treated the parents of their MIAs, "The Air Force was proud, but this Army feels mysteriously indifferent about my son. . .We have never gotten any letters from those who knew Jim and soldiered with him. This is disturbing. Jim was a wonderful, popular boy who easily made friends wherever he was." The only letters Jim's folks received were form letters. In the same letter to President Nixon, Jim's dad was curious why Jim and Belletire had to hang from the chopper. "Why didn't the helicopter crew hoist the McGuire rig. . .into the chopper? The Army won't say. Even Bowers calls the rig a hoist. Two wounded men are expected to hang onto a rope, upside down, for apparently an hour? Plus ride? Why couldn't they hoist them up? Why? God, if they had only of hoisted them up."

In 1974, Jim's dad wrote to President Gerald Ford, another of the many letters I found in Jim's file at the Casualty Office.

"A month ago I wrote you expressing concern that the plight of the MIAs is being considered less and less by our government. I had hoped that in someway I would be reassured by you that this was not the case.

My son has been missing 6 years. The Army declared him dead several years later, apparently they do this . . . they review his case and evaluate his chances of survival. I appreciate that they permitted him this extra time. It gave us hope.

(My contact with the military) has always been unsatisfactory, frustrating and painful. They absolutely care nothing about me or my son. It took me years to find out what really happened to my son. They never once contacted me directly or have ever offered to help. They have answered my letters as briefly as they could (often incomplete) and that's all they've done. . . I wish to God I'm wrong.

197

I've always been very proud of the Army, until I experienced their attitude, with the loss of my son.

The reply (from my letter to you last month) was essentially a form letter sent to me, signed, or forged, by a machine using a general's name. I feel this is hypocrisy and certainly in no way reassuring.

Does anyone really give a DAMN?

. . . The pain of Vietnam is within everyone in this country. One wonders if it can ever get back to those good days, pre-Vietnam, again - - when the government was so well respected, but until honor and love can again be felt by us all, it's an uphill climb."

My father-in-law wrote to the President, the Secretary of the Army, the Joint Casualty Resolution Center and the Department of the Army in 1973, to say that he was dissatisfied with the poor service he had received from the Adjutant General's office regarding his son's disappearance.

The six page letter outlined all of the things Jim's father was upset about. One thing was that he was always kept in the dark about everything.

"I don't know anything about what's being done to locate my son's remains. Nothing! . . . Why have we never received any progress reports or any information on what is being done to locate Jim? (Or is it again just because you call him dead . . .)

. . . Why have you never contacted me personally, phone or otherwise? Why have I had to search out all I've learned about my son? . . . The war is over, my son is gone, and the past is the past. But it is my hope that in future wars your office will be more understanding in helping families of boys lost. . . This is a great country and I hope my son died for its greatness in some way."

In 1971, Jim's father also wrote to the Department of Defense.

"In answering my letters, many of my questions are ignored, some are misinterpreted and some pre-answered. Why won't they answer me. If they can't answer a question, why don't they say so? They even increase the anxiety by being mysterious. They appear to have little if any concern for the families. I don't think they should consider me a pest--I think I've written only four letters to them in the three years. I haven't asked much of them."

James Birchim wrote his first letter to the Adjutant General's office on June 20, 1970. In this five-page letter he asked for help for the first time.

"My son was a very bright and wonderful boy with a great future outside the Army, and so I hope that if he is dead that it wasn't due to the Army's failure to use every means to rescue him. . . We pray that every means were used to expedite him, but as I say it appears minimal. Another big wasted life."

To quote Jim's father, "the Army evaluates my son's performance and expresses sympathy and regret, but not pride or respect." Our Army didn't used to be like that.

Following is another letter Jean Birchim wrote to me, this time on February 22, 1994.

"Not too sure about Hoeck's story. Did answer some questions I had, but he said a different version to Belletire's story. I have found three different versions to Belletire's story . . . the pilot's written testimony and what he told you. Maybe he was just scared. Pilot said he read Belletire's statement right after incident, he said--Jim was upside down. Belletire held on until he was down to Jim's 'bloody boot' when his hands became so cold he could no longer hang on and Jim was gone. Pilot said when he landed at Kontum all the men dangling from bottom of chopper were passed out and almost frozen because of the storm and flying at 100 knots. The reason he didn't go to Dak To was because he became lost in the thunderstorm and almost lost the chopper--he was almost out of fuel when he broke through the storm, headed for beacon at Kontum. Can't remember any other crewmember's names. Said he would meet with us whenever we may want him to.

Not much--still working on it."

One of the most startling things about these letters is the discrepancy of information that filtered down to each of us from various departments of the government. Everyone told us something different. Either no one knew how to answer our questions or no one could tell us because of secret and/or classified information. If the latter were so, then what on earth was Jim involved in?

PART V

Chapter Twelve

The Last Hurrah

"Did you leave me behind?" the voice asks. "Have you forgotten your promise? Am I still alive in your hearts?"[1]

My files are full of articles that I collected during 1991, when there seemed to be a new surge of interest in the POW/MIA issue. Just look at some of the headlines:

"MIAs – The Lingering Fallout of the Vietnam War"
Albuquerque Journal, 11/10/91

"POWs Sent to Moscow and Beijing U.S. Spies Say"
The Street News, Albuquerque, NM, October 1991

"Vietnam POW Search Hindered by Support Group Leader, Says DIA Colonel"

"General Tiche Confirms Colonel Peck's Accusations"
Air Commando Association Newsletter, June 1991

"Photo is Match with MIA: CSU Expert's Study Indicates Navy Man May Be Held in Vietnam"
The Sunday Denver Post, 11/3/91

"POW Panel Urged"
Associated Press, 7/29/91

"The MIA Mystery – One Man's Journey" – 8/25/91

"Senate Votes To Create Own MIA Panel" – 8/3/91

"Why MIAs Live On: How It Feels When One of the Family Is Missing" - 9/25/91

"U.S. Official Admits Americans Were Abandoned in Vietnam" – 11/7/91

"Hanoi Radio Reports Pilot's Remains Found" – 12/11/91

"Case Builds for a Senate Probe of POW/MIA Issue" – 8/4/91

"Cheney Sees No Firm Evidence of Live MIAs" – The San Diego Union, 11/6/91

"Cover-ups About POWs a Betrayal of Liberty and a Threat To Us All." The Orlando Sentinel, 1/22/91

"New Probes on MIA Leads in Vietnam Unproductive, U.S. Claims" San Diego Tribune, 11/5/91

In February 1991, the Persian Gulf crisis had ended and the feeling throughout the country was of jubilation that we were the winner. To me, and many of those involved in the Vietnam POW/MIA issue, came a feeling of sadness and depression. Our Operation Desert Storm heroes were being honored, as they should be. The welcome home parades were appropriate, but as the weeks drew on, it seemed that we were trying to make up for what we had not done back in 1973 at the end of the Vietnam War. It became obvious that we were trying to lick our wounds and rid ourselves of guilt by spending millions of dollars on parades to honor our veterans, something we had not done for our returning troops from the Vietnam War.

I was asked to be in a parade in San Diego, which turned out to be a very large one. I just couldn't do it. If I participated, it would mean to me that I would be saying the Vietnam POW/MIA issue was over. Besides, the parade I needed and wanted to be in, was the one to honor all the POWs and MIAs who had come home at last.

On the other hand, I hoped that all the vets I knew, including Sam and Bill, who went with me to Vietnam the year before, would understand that I couldn't force myself to be in the parade. I wasn't belittling the returning soldiers. I just couldn't do it.

THE NATIONAL LEAGUE OF FAMILIES ANNUAL MEETING

On July 10, I took a COIN Assist flight from North Island, near San
Diego, to Washington D.C. for the annual National League of Families
meeting.

Roni, my friend from our trip the year before, and I shared a room in the
hotel. I had an appointment the next morning for us to meet Duncan Hunter,
U.S. Representative for my district about a bill that was before the Senate.
And Roni was meeting with Senator Seymour at 2:00 to get his support for
the POW/MIA issue. After that, our plan was to "hit the hill" and see Senator
Alan Cranston from San Francisco, and as many other folks as we could. And
that's exactly what we did.

Compared to when we walked around the hill in 1990, Roni and I found
a lot more interest in the POW/MIA issue. Perhaps it was the way in which
Colonel Peck had resigned his position as the DIA's top POW/MIA expert
in February. A lot of press followed that story, which brought to light the
continuing cover up.

While talking with Duncan Hunter, we told him about our trip to
Vietnam and the two agendas we had. We discovered that he was one of
the money backers behind the reward we had printed on the stickers we
gave out in Vietnam. He seemed pleased with our efforts to disseminate that
information.

We also told him about being interrogated for three hours and how we
had problems getting our medical supplies where we wanted them to go.
Duncan introduced us to John Palafoutas, his administrative assistant, who
said that we could always call or fax him if we ever had problems like that
again in a foreign country. He suggested that next time, we should get in
touch with the U.S. Emissary, or whomever, when we were in places like
Saigon or Hanoi so we would have some support for our endeavors.

Roni and I both chuckled as we left Duncan's office. The antiquated
phone system in Saigon, for example, is so poor that I could just see me
grabbing a telephone and calling Washington D.C. I don't think I'd ever be
connected, even if I tried for a week.

That evening, we went to the Vietnam Wall. It was after 9:00 so there
weren't too many people. I sat there, looking at Jim's name on his panel, 39W,
for quite some time. I don't know whether it was the tension I was feeling
about the League meeting, my weariness from the long flight, or just the
power of the Wall itself, but I began to cry.

I was amazed that I could cry after all those years. I couldn't understand
why such a tremendous feeling still lay deep inside me when I looked at Jim's
name etched on that monument.

The next day at a luncheon hosted by the Army, Roni and I were late, so we had to sit at a front table where there were still two seats available. One military or government person was seated at each table. Dick Childress, National Security Council (NSC), charged with the POW issue, was that person at our table. We had a nice, non-threatening conversation during the meal, until I opened my mouth and mentioned that Roni and I had been in Vietnam the year before and it was quite obvious to me that there were still lots of Americans being held there. And that not only does our government deny it but, so did the Vietnamese officials I met.

All of a sudden, the mood of those at the table changed. Antennas went up. No one said another word until lunch was over, except Roni and me, as we talked to each other.

During the meeting, one of the bits of information I learned through non-government channels was that 20 American POWs had just been flown into Virginia on a MAC flight (Military Assistance Command) from Vietnam. The POWs were to be in Virginia for awhile and then were to be split up into Safe Houses.

During the entire time I was at the annual meeting, I heard stories like this. Live sightings, photographs, verifiable evidence, and more stories--a bombardment of information. With all of this, I couldn't help but wonder why the government wasn't acknowledging it.

During the DIA briefing that afternoon, a four-star General stood at the lectern and proceeded to tell us that he was the one who fired Colonel Peck. Of course, everyone in the room knew that Army Colonel Milliard A. "Mike" Peck had resigned as head of DIA and the POW/MIA committee, and why. I guess the General felt he needed to explain his statement, so he said he fired the Colonel because he was not appropriate for the office. Right!

The truth was, Colonel Peck had "had it" after only seven months in that position. He made "sweeping allegations of gross misconduct, including a possible cover-up among government officials who had managed the MIA issue for the past twenty years. He also accused Ann Mills Griffiths, Executive Director of the League of Families, of blatant interference in the intelligence process."[2]

Once the briefing was over, the press was asked to leave, and at that time those in the audience could come forward to ask questions of the panel members.

I was the first one on my feet. I had never spoken out before at an annual meeting. I was wearing my jazzy pants and shirt, looking like a typical Southern Californian--not hard to miss in a crowd.

I stepped up to the microphone and told them that I would like to make an observation. I said, "For the past 20 plus years, all of you on the panel, and a lot of your constituents on the hill, have worked very hard to convince all of us sitting down here in the audience, that we are basically crazy to even consider that there might be a live American POW being held against his will in Southeast Asia. You've done a fine job at trying to convince us, and unfortunately, you have convinced a few.

"Here is my dilemma. I need some help with this. Maybe you can do that. Now, all of a sudden, you are going to open a little office in Hanoi and it is going to be specifically set up to look at the 1400 reported live sightings. Now, if they've been dead for 20 plus years, how then can we be looking for them as live POWs all of a sudden?"

Dead silence filled the room.

"You know," I continued, "I am only a nurse. I'm not a diplomat and I'm not a politician. But here I am to tell you that I've been to Vietnam twice in the past 24 months and I'd like to challenge all of you sitting up there on the panel to take off all your fancy buttons and bows, and leave all your diplomatic passports at home. Go to Vietnam as a tourist. Get away from the local guide and go ask the villagers about Americans. Then, draw your own conclusions. There are American POWs being held against their will in Southeast Asia as I speak, and even the villagers know about it.

"I do not understand what is so difficult here. Those of us in the audience do not have the technology that you do, yet we know there are Americans still alive over there. It is so simple. All you have to do is go and look."

With that, I turned around and walked back to my seat.

My God! I got a standing ovation! Somewhere between 300-400 people stood and clapped. My determination to speak my piece turned out okay, much to my surprise. My adrenaline was on super high at that point.

Needless to say, the only response to what I'm sure the panel considered a tirade was to reiterate that the Hanoi office would be responsible for checking on their list of 1400 live sightings.

Several people came up to me later and thanked me for speaking out. They asked that, if they went to Vietnam themselves, could they find some kind of completion or at least find some answers? I told them that if they could go to the countryside and meet the people it might benefit them by giving them some answers to their specific questions. Of course, both The League and the government discouraged POW/MIA families from doing that.

Another question several people asked me was if I would take them to Vietnam, now that I'd been there twice. This went on for a few days after my comments to the panel.

The next afternoon I bumped into Billy Hendon, former Republican Representative from North Carolina, a dedicated advocate for the POW/MIA issue. He had spent time at the Pentagon so he knew where a lot of the skeletons were in a lot of closets. He told me that we were almost on top of a POW camp last year when we were on highway 9 at the Laotian border. Billy kept asking why I didn't let him know before we left in '90. And I kept telling him that I had asked him for all that type of information but he never answered me.

"When you give me a job to do," I said to him, "I do it. Now, next time I ask you for information prior to going to Vietnam, I expect you to. . ."

"Darlin'," he said in his southern drawl. "I will give you everything."

What's interesting is that the only contact I had ever had with him was to tell him about my trips to Vietnam after Sara introduced him to me.

He is a wonderful man, extremely helpful and supportive of the POW/MIA issue.

About one in the morning, after our Saturday night banquet, I decided I wanted to go back to the Wall. Several of my friends discouraged me, but after promising that I would be okay, I left them at the hotel.

The construction of the Wall is such that as you walk along, it seems like you are going down into the ground, creating the feeling of entering a grave. As the small lights from the ground illuminate each panel in a V formation, you are enveloped in a deep sense of awe and sadness.

I found Jim's panel and sat on the ground beneath it, Indian style. I focused on his name, at the same time rubbing his MIA bracelet that I wore. I began to rock back and forth, and then the tears came. They came in waves, over and over again.

I kept looking at the names that surrounded Jim's on the Wall. I couldn't help wonder if any of them had known Jim. I had the feeling that they wanted to talk with me. Their souls were in pain, crying out to me to do something, to put them at rest, at last.

After a long while, I told those names, screaming at me from the Wall, that I was doing as much as I could. I didn't know what else to do. They had to show me.

I started to cry again, so I said, "I have to go." I turned around and forced myself to walk away. It was five in the morning. Where had the last four hours gone?

One of the guards, named Cody, whom I'd met before, found me and said I must go to the top of the monument. I said I would another time. But he insisted. He said the Park Rangers would not allow anybody on the top and the only time the Rangers weren't there was between midnight and 6:00 AM.

So, I accompanied Cody to the top and we sat there, talking for some time. He spoke of the souls who played out in front at night, and how the Wall was structured so that one wing pointed to the Washington Monument and the other to the Lincoln Memorial. He told me that he took care of the Wall and the walkway in front, and how he couldn't really stop to look at the Wall anymore because it was too painful.

Cody told me that one night, when his platoon was in the field, he walked away from camp to relieve himself and when he came back, everyone was dead. And so he feels a huge responsibility for being alive. He now stands guard at the Wall for all his buddies who died that day.

The walk back to the hotel was a blur as I kept reliving the past four hours trying to figure out why the Wall was so mad at me.

HOME AGAIN

Several days after I returned home from the annual meeting, I received a call from Bob Sioss, Channel 8 in San Diego. The picture of three POWs, (Lundy, Roberts and Stevenson) had just hit the newspapers and Bob was interested in talking with me. (See Live Sightings)

I did an interview for Bob the next morning, as well as one for Channel 10, in the afternoon. Channel 10 also did a perspective that night which was excellent. When I got home, I had a call from John Dikkenberg from Asia Magazine in Hong Kong about that picture. I referred him to Billy Hendon.

Five days later, I attended a news conference at the Naval Training Center in San Diego. Two of the three men in the picture were represented by their families, along with Barbara Lowerison, an MIA's sister, and me. As we were leaving, Albro Lundy Jr., who was about my son David's age, spoke to me. He said he and his family had thought all those years that his dad was dead until the week before when he saw that picture for the first time and he recognized his father.

I told him to please call me anytime and I'd be happy to talk with him, to share our experiences. This is the one part of the POW/MIA issue that is so horrible and ugly, so up and down, so full of adrenaline highs and terrible crashes.

I went to my first Task Force Omega meeting early in August, an organization compelled to work on the Vietnam War POW/MIA issue. Several nights later, Vicky Gloor, assistant producer for Inside San Diego, invited me to dinner. I ended up being the entertainment for the evening. Everyone wanted to hear my stories.

You can see, by the succession of people and events at this time, that there was a strong undercurrent of information in regard to POW sightings and movement. Information was coming from a number of different directions about live POWs being moved under cover. Something was going on.

PLANS PUT IN MOTION

In mid-August 1991, I spent the weekend with Sara and her friend, Terry, a Vietnam POW veteran. He had expressed an interest in returning to Vietnam and said he thought he'd like to travel with me, if I went again, since I knew my way around. I had a chance to get to know Terry a little bit and to get a feeling for whether or not we might be compatible.

I was concerned about going back to Vietnam for they certainly had my name on their "list" and I might be stopped from doing anything or going anywhere.

I suggested that I go alone and stay in Hanoi as a decoy, while Terry went to Saigon to try to get access to the Central Highlands and information on Jim's case. Terry had made a promise to himself to help the Americans who had been left behind, in any way he could. He had been incarcerated for quite awhile at the "Hanoi Hilton." He spent a total of six years as a prisoner in Vietnam.

We spent quite some time on the phone after that, laying ground rules, planning our itinerary and when we would leave. I had decided that he would be an okay travel companion, except for one thing. How would the Vietnamese deal with an ex-POW?

In mid-September I called a tour company in Australia to see what kind of tour packages they had for Vietnam. They told me that Americans were being denied access to the Central Highlands where Kontum is located. Any other nationality could go anywhere in Vietnam. Great! Of course, Kontum was where I still wanted to go.

During this period of time, I was interviewed for a full-page spread in a Sunday paper. I also went to a candle light ceremony at Mt. Soledad in honor of National POW/MIA Day and gave a presentation at the Westwood Club in San Diego.

At the end of September, I met a man by the name of Bob Rosalee. He was retired military and had been in Kontum for five years, including 1968, with Special Forces. He gave me some information about the Special Forces at that time. He doubted very much that Frank Belletire was telling me the truth about what happened to Jim. Rosalee said that nobody would come into Vietnam and be automatically placed in Special Forces, as I'd been told. Belletire said he'd never been trained at Fort Bragg in Special Forces, and after only a couple weeks worth of training in Vietnam, he'd been shipped to Kontum to go on the mission with Jim. I agreed with Rosalee. Was Belletire lying? Or was this another government snafu?

There were other reasons I was being drawn back to Vietnam. Contacts I'd made and continued to make kept my need to get to Kontum alive. Some of those contacts were people who could hide the POWs being extracted from Vietnam.

I had met Father Su on my last trip to Vietnam, and I felt that if I returned with much needed medical supplies, my good faith would cause the people Father Su knew, in turn, to give me information about Jim. I also hoped Father Su, who had been a contact of mine for three years, would come up with some important information for me.

In the middle of December, the Bush administration lifted the ban on U.S. organized travel to Vietnam, an easing of some sort of the trade embargo. That meant travel agents could book individuals and group tours, even though it was still possible for U.S. citizens to go through a third country, like I did the first time I went to Vietnam. It didn't mean, though, that the U.S. could have direct flights to Vietnam.

I had requested the JCRC biographic/site report from their Bright Light data concerning Jim. Originally, the term Bright Light was the code name for teams whose missions were to go in and get POWs out of Vietnam. Now, the term Bright Light refers to the biographical data, on all POWs and MIAs from Southeast Asia, which is housed in Bangkok.

Also, in early December, I got a letter from Lt. Col. J.G. Cole, U.S. Army Chief of POW/MIA Affairs, in response to my request for a copy of Jim's fingerprints. He sent me a key to the Bright Light codes, and then added, "A review of Jim's file did not reveal any fingerprint cards. I have submitted a request to the FBI to see if they have fingerprint cards on file."

Can you believe that? Another bit of Jim had disappeared from the files. I began to wonder if there was ever a Jim Birchim according to the government!

MAY 25, 1992

The months leading up to the trip were filled with establishing more contacts and renewing old ones.

I discovered that, when Terry and I arrived in Bangkok, a lot of changes had taken place since I'd last been there. I no longer could get my tourist visa from the Vietnam embassy. Diethelm Travel, in Bangkok arranged it for $150 (3,500 baht) or $80 if we waited five days. What a change! And the taxi fare to the airport had doubled.

This time, when we arrived in Saigon, I couldn't get the medical supplies through customs because we had no one to meet us. So, I got a receipt for four duffel bags and left for the hotel. Two days later, we were able to make a contact with a local humanitarian group who helped us get the medical supplies out of customs for $10.65 U.S., plus lots of hassling.

I delivered some of the supplies to a convent in Saigon, and then tried to get permission at Saigon Tourism to travel to the Central Highlands. No, was the answer. So, I went to Vietnam Tourism to see Mr. Hung. He was Assistant Manager, now. He had gotten in trouble when we passed out the stickers during our trip in 1990. He thought that Terry and I might be able to get to Kontum.

However, the next day Mr. Hung told me we couldn't get permission to travel in the Highlands. I asked him if it was because of 1990. He said no. I asked him if Terry could go alone, and he said no to that, too. He said, "Try again. Maybe things will change."

I was numb with disappointment. We refused to give up, and decided to try every way we could think of to get permission to leave for Kontum. The waiting was almost unbearable. I prayed a lot, knowing that there were many people in the United States who were also praying for my success. "Please God, let me have the answer," I kept saying.

During the next two weeks, we not only waited for Mr. Hung, but we canvassed 10-15 other small travel companies. None of them could get us permission to travel to that area.

As we waited, we filled our days by going to local marketplaces, and we continued to search for new leads as to how we could gain access to the Central Highlands. I noticed how the city of Saigon had changed. There were fewer bicycles now, and more motorscooters. Billboards advertised luxury products by big name manufacturers, both of which I'd not seen in Saigon before. Locals wore more western attire than I had noticed on my previous trips. I hope the Vietnamese don't lose their culture in their eagerness to become westernized.

At that point, Terry called home and found out that his wife had fallen, and was in the hospital with a broken leg. Terry flew back to the States the next day.

I was left in Vietnam--all by myself.

No one except Terry knew I was alone. This would be the perfect time for me to disappear. The Vietnamese could deny it, and our country wouldn't do anything about it. I was petrified.

My dialogue with God was more intense. I had to trust that He would lead the way. I became hyper-vigilant because I couldn't afford to miss anything. After all, I was on a mission to get any information I could about Jim, or any of the other men or women still listed as MIA.

Two days later, I arranged for a driver to take me to the small hospital in Da Lat. Dr. Turpin, a former Army doctor stationed in the area during the war, started this hospital. Project Concern, a humanitarian organization now headquartered in San Diego, developed out of Dr. Turpin's ongoing wish to bring health care to the people of Da Lat, the gateway to the Highlands. I spent a day or so, visiting the hospital, speaking with the physicians, and touring the countryside. The doctors were all very nice, and with great pride they showed me around the ill-equipped hospital, so broken down I couldn't believe it. Some soap and water would have helped a lot. Even Ms. Thuy, my guide, couldn't understand why something so simple as basic cleanliness was lacking in the hospital.

Then, off to Vung Tau we went, my driver, interpretor Ms. Thuy, and I, before we headed back to Saigon, a two-hour trip. Vung Tau is a beautiful seaside resort south of Saigon, used during the war for R and R by our troops. I couldn't help but reflect on what it must have been like there during the Vietnam War.

During the drive to Da Lat and Vung Tau, Ms. Thuy and I had lots of time to talk about our families. Our conversation was fairly constant. I listened as she told me how difficult it was for her to raise a small son by herself. She and her husband were separated. Although she was grateful for having a job that paid quite well by Vietnam standards, she was in an emotional turmoil.

My trust and admiration for her grew, and as she asked me questions about my life, I decided to take a chance and tell her why I came to her country.

There was no accusation or anger in my voice as I explained I was only looking for a resolution. If I could find where Jim was buried, then I could bring him home. She was shocked and dismayed, but understood what my intentions were.

I told her I was being denied access to the area where Jim was last seen after I had been promised permission to travel to the Central Highlands in 1989.

Ms. Thuy was struck by and sympathetic to my plight, and offered to help. She told me her husband was a policeman and said she would ask him if he could help me gain access to that area.

The next day Ms. Thuy called to say that her husband's contact whom I believed to be a member of a police-run organization, had granted me permission to travel to Kontum.

The travel date they set was for four days later. I was concerned because my visa would run out the day after we were to return back to Saigon. This allowed no room for car trouble or bad weather to the Highlands. But that is when we left.

The delay in my departure seemed to me to be a stall tactic on their part for reasons I could only guess. It might have been the movement of POWs out of my line of vision, among other things. No amount of coercing could get them to change the departure date.

After giving it a lot of thought, I decided to ask Ms. Thuy to come along as a friend/translator/traveling companion because she now knew my story, and had a good command of the English language. I also felt that having an additional person join me on this trip, someone who seemed to be on my side, might make the possibility of my disappearance more difficult. And that was a strong possibility, since Terry was not with me, and I had already had a run-in with the Vietnamese government in Hanoi two years before.

I offered to pay her way, and asked if she could get time away from Saigon Tourism to accompany me. Ms. Thuy, her boss at the travel agency, and those at the police travel agency couldn't understand why I would pay extra to have another interpreter come along when one was included in the price of the travel package. A rich American, (ha, ha), I wasn't, but they must have thought me quite foolish.

I was really scared again. I made a quick call to Terry in the States before I left Saigon to tell him of my new itinerary.

Little did the Vietnamese know I was trying to protect myself from being another MIA that our government wouldn't give a rat's ass about.

THE ROAD NORTH

We left the Que Huong Hotel in Saigon at 7:15 in the morning, and arrived in Nha Trang at three. I discovered that the tour guide and driver had not been to Kontum before, when they stopped a block from the hotel to buy the same map from a street vendor that I had purchased two weeks before.

I was surprised that the road north had had some repair work done since the last time I traveled it. The road went through areas ranging from tropical vegetation and rice paddies, to arid countrysides. We also drove along the ocean that resembled the Northern California coastline with its rocky formations and deep blue water.

As we drove through the villages, I enjoyed stopping to sample some of the local fruits like Dragon Fruit, Logan's Eyes, and Custard Apples. Although I was careful about what I ate, I was not bashful about trying packaged foods or food I could watch being cooked at the local stands. The people seemed amazed and pleased that I would even consider doing that.

Mr. Phuc, the driver, was joined by a tall and slender Ms. Mai, the guide who spoke little English, made up our group. And, Ms. Thuy, who looked forward to visiting this area for the first time, was able to join us as my traveling companion.

Half the time, I felt like I was leading the group, especially after the driver took two wrong turns. Who was leading whom on this trip? I had more information on road conditions and the route.

That first night we checked into the Thang Loi Hotel. I found I needed to be careful what I said when I was with my three companions. They talked amongst themselves most of the time, and sat together for their meals. I began to wonder about people who said they wanted to practice their English.

I noticed the absence of Russians who vacationed in this area when I was there in 1989 and 1990. Ms. Thuy told me that I was the first non-Vietnamese American to be granted permission to go to Kontum and Dak To. I decided I'd better be on my best behavior so the government would let more Americans travel the Highlands, in the future.

At the end of that first day, I thought I'd better write a letter to Jim, just in case. It struck me that maybe the reason they were letting me into the area, at last, was because I was by myself. Or, did they move Jim so they could take "this lady to the Highlands to satisfy her quest, hoping she wouldn't bother them any more. Or, was Jim dead?

The following day we drove from Nha Trang to Qui Nhon to Pleiku where we checked into the police Guesthouse #3, and waited for the officials to show up. When they met us, they said we could travel to Kontum, Dak To, and Dak Sut the next day, with a police escort.

I became a little antsy when Ms. Mai said we'd be staying in Pleiku for three days because there was no hotel in Kontum. We'd have to drive there and back each day. I was hoping I didn't have to stay in the guesthouse more than one night. The floor had never been mopped, and the bathroom was gross, at best. It had never been cleaned, and the showerhead was right above the sink. The water went out a hole in the floor, but not all of the water. Thank God the weather was a little cooler because I'm sure if I had turned on the shower I'd only be calling every mosquito in the area to dinner.

We spent till 11:30 the following morning, at the police building in Pleiku, getting permission to travel to Kontum the next day. They kept talking around me, making me feel like I was on display. I didn't know whether to smile or look somber.

I thought this had all been okayed when I got permission in Saigon to travel to Kontom. Not so! Each province has the power to allow or disallow one to travel on the road, much less spend the night. I was getting perturbed. This was seriously eating into the time I'd planned to spend in Kontum.

They finally gave me permission to go on to Kontum, which we did. We moved to the People's Committee Guesthouse to wait. If the Minister of External Affairs in charge of MIAs, Mr. Trung, said it was okay, then I could progress to Dak To and Dak Sut.

When Mr. Trung showed up, he said it would be a problem if Jim's name did not show up on the list of dead or missing American soldiers in their area.

"If only you contacted the new POW/MIA office in Hanoi, they would have verified with us," Mr. Trung said.

I told him I had their telephone number and I'd be happy to call them. Mr. Trung wasn't sure what to make of that. I'd played a trump card and won that hand. He asked me for some information that would identify Jim, like his birthdate and military ID number. Then, he took Ms. Thuy and Ms. Mai to look at the list he had while I sat in the room waiting for them.

They returned an hour later with a JCRC Bright Light printout on Jim, plus a synopsis of Jim's MIA report. I thought I was going to get some new information from the Vietnamese list, but the only information they had was what our government had furnished them, and it was written in English. Mr. Trung had no idea what it said.

I had to explain each word and symbol to Ms. Thuy who then wrote it out in Vietnamese for Mr. Trung.

We got the okay to journey on to Dak To and Dak Sut in the morning, plus we were invited to stay overnight in Kontum at the People's Committee Guesthouse so we could get an early start the next morning. What a victory! I was elated.

Back to Pleiku we went to pick up our belongings, and then we returned to Kontum to spend the night. Because the road to Dak Sut was bad, we were going to have to rent a Russian jeep and a local guide in Kontum. That was only going to cost me $60 more. Then Ms. Thuy told me about all of the presents I would have to buy for everyone who helped us. She had the impression that I was rich, since I was an American.

I was livid! I'd paid dearly up front, and brought just enough cash with me to cover incidentals. I'd left the rest of my money in Saigon in case I got robbed on this portion of my trip. I set her straight right away.

The guesthouse in Kontum that night cost me only $20.00. What a bargain considering it had an outhouse for a bathroom and if we wanted to bathe, we had to do it out of a well in front of everyone. And, I had to sleep with the two interpreters on top of it all.

It was a good thing that Ms. Thuy came because the next morning, Ms. Mai was sick and unable to go with us. This meant that Ms. Thuy was my interpreter during the most important part of the trip.

Now I had a new driver, a Minister of MIAs, and a policeman along with Ms. Thuy and myself, all crammed into a Jeep for a 3-½ hour trip to Dak Sut.

The road to Dak Sut started at the old U.S. airbase runway outside Dak To (30 minutes from Kontum), and was full of ruts and huge holes. I'm amazed we didn't get stuck. We stopped at three different locations, and through Ms. Thuy, I talked with five families asking questions and showing Jim's picture.

It seemed that all, but a few of the people who were there in 1968-1970, had moved because they couldn't work the land due to Agent Orange. The people I spoke with were from Laos or further north.

One man, the area nurse, said his 50-year old father, who was working in the jungle that day, was at Dak Sut in 1968. He would show Jim's picture to his father.

My guides were anxious to get back to Dak To before dark. They were afraid of snipers. Mr. Trung told me he made regular trips to Dak To, and he would show the villagers Jim's picture. We stayed in the guesthouse with its outhouse and well, again that night.

I was not allowed to take any pictures while I was in Kontum. God only knows why. I decided that night to burn my letter to Jim and leave the ashes there. It seemed fitting, somehow. Both Ms. Thuy and Ms. Mai kept telling me that if they were me, they couldn't have survived--couldn't have gone on with their lives.

That night, I realized I couldn't think of anything else to do for Jim except pray he was not suffering. I had done my best.

On the way back to Pleiku the next morning, Ms. Thuy told me she had a dream the night before. Jim was standing at the foot of her bed. She seemed to worry a lot. I felt that everyone on this trip had tried hard to help me, and I appreciated that. However, I couldn't help wondering if my trip to Kontum had been a show. Even Dak Sut's name had been changed to Dak Lak. Who knows?

I arrived back in Saigon on the 25th. I saw a lot of old U.S. military trucks and tankers along the road. Ms. Thuy spent much of the time that day telling me I should forget Jim. That was hard to take, but in the middle of her "sage" advice, she said she'd have her sister check some kind of POW list her sister seemed to have. That night I had a nightmare about a man in my room. I felt like I was cracking up.

Ms. Thuy and her son took me to the airport the next afternoon. After four refusals and three weeks of waiting, I had reached my goal at long last--to get to Kontum.

ANTI-CLIMAX

As I sat in my hotel room in Singapore, I began to feel a great sense of sadness at not having found any new information about Jim. The adrenaline I had been running on for over a week was fading, and I was crashing fast.

A sense of despair set in as I reflected on what had taken place. Why me, again ran through my mind.

Then I realized I was being given the opportunity to make this journey possible for others who might follow me, and I couldn't afford to do anything to jeopardize their chances.

For four months after leaving Saigon, I traveled through Indonesia, New Zealand, Rarotonga, Cook Islands, and Tahiti. All the while, I tried to decide what was important in life, and what my course should be in the future.

> "Far and away the best prize that life offers is the chance to work hard at work worth doing."
>
> Teddy Roosevelt

I'd run out of ideas on how to pursue Jim's case. The last trip to Vietnam left me feeling hopeless over finding any additional information. I wanted to run away from this issue, at least for a while, and do something on a humanitarian level that would give me a sense of accomplishment.

I was back from Vietnam for only a few months when the news media started broadcasting the plight of the people living in Somalia, Africa. The faces of starving children I kept seeing tugged at my heart. It was then that I decided to leave my good paying job to help these children. As a secondary motive, I also wanted to leave the POW/MIA issue behind me for a while to escape the anxiety I kept feeling.

I left for London on December 15, 1992, flew to Nairobi and on to Mogadishu, arriving five days later. I noticed the beautiful blue waters and coastline as we landed. The U.N. troops had arrived just a couple of days before I did. I noticed the Pakistani soldiers guarding the airport as I disembarked, a big clue that fighting was still going on there.

The streets and buildings in Mogadishu were bombed out, and inoperable vehicles lay strewn everywhere. After lunch, I was taken to Digfer Hospital where the International Medical Corps staff (a humanitarian group) was working.

Here I got my first taste of what I would be doing. The emergency department was filled with gunshot wounds, broken limbs, and eviscerations. I almost fainted when I was asked to hold a leg in traction with one hand, and keep the bone together in an open wound with my other hand.

The oppressive heat, the strange smells, the hoards of flies, and the uncommon quietness created a surreal scene. No one screamed or cried. There was only a doctor and a physician's assistant from IMC working in this entire area, and one Somalia interpreter. No running water was available to even wash our hands. Because of my experiences in Vietnam, I thought I was prepared to see horrific sights, but this topped it. I was a home health nurse, not an ER nurse.

DIGFER HOSPITAL
(Somalia 1992-93)

Poverty
>> destruction
> filth
>>> stench
>>> darkness
> Beautiful smiles
>>> endless handshakes
>>> inquisitive children
>>>> questioning adults
>>>> extended families
> No crying
>>> hideous wounds
>>> missing body parts
>>>> families destroyed
>>>> acceptance of death
> People alone

Barbara Birchim

Also, during my introduction to Somalia that first day, grenades and bullets flew all day long, and very close to our compound. I realized patients and squatters living in the hospital all had AK-47s, knives and grenades, and would use them if they felt personally threatened. The shock was almost too much for me.

On the third day, with the logistician waving at me and saying, "They haven't shot a white woman, yet," I was told to sit in the front seat of a lorry between a driver and two armed guards. We took off for Baidoa.

Because we were stopped numerous times by bandits, my trip to Baidoa took six hours. To add to the "fun," none of the Somalis I rode with spoke English. I must say, the compound I was to stay in made the Que Huong hotel in Saigon look like the Ritz.

Two days after I drove to Baidoa, I learned that an aid worker, traveling on the same road, was shot between the eyes in her car when bandits held her up. Those whom she was driving with escaped.

The hospital that IMC ran in Baidoa was much smaller than the Digfer Hospital in Mogadishu. When I reported for work the next day, I trailed behind Jane, who was responsible for the 100 patients in the hospital. I found that 99% of the patients had gunshot wounds. But the situation was much more manageable than what I encountered in Mogadishu. The area around Baidoa was extremely hot, dry, and without any vegetation--quite a change from the tropical climate and plant life of Mogadishu.

As we finished the day at 5:30, two bombs went off just behind the hospital where the airport and the military were. We had to leave at once. The night was full of helicopters, Newsweek press, CARE people, a U.S. embassy man, and a CBS man. No rest for anyone.

I wasn't sure I was going to be able to make it in Somalia at that point.

When the staff learned I was going to be there for more than a day or two, they grilled me at dinner each night about who I was, where I came from, and what I was doing there.

Once again I was perplexed about what to say in regard to my past. Somehow I just couldn't ignore that I was an MIA wife. Numerous questions followed the staff's blank looks that led me once again to share my story about the POW/MIA issue.

On December 24th, I turned 46 years old. I was quite moved to be a part of history in the making in Baidoa. That night, some of us from the hospital went to the U.N. compound for midnight mass. There were no lights on as we made our way past the security to the outdoor chapel. A camouflage net hung over the makeshift altar, and GIs filled the place.

As I gazed through the netting at the sky above, I couldn't help but wonder if Jim was looking up at the same stars that night from somewhere else in the world. Odd as it may seem, I felt connected, for the first time, to what it must have been like for our soldiers on a Christmas Eve during the Vietnam War, so far away from home, alone. I had a sense that every man who had ever been in a war, was with us, joining in the celebration of Christ's birth. A joyous occasion, yet sad at the same time.

As we sang Christmas carols, and greeted each other after mass, all I could say to the soldiers was, "Stay safe." I was looking into the eyes of young men who were my son's age, no doubt, and the age Jim was 24 years before when he was involved in a war.

My feelings of being away from my family in a strange and dangerous place on my birthday, which was on Christmas Eve, were now a part of my life's experiences. I was grateful that I could have a better understanding of what was going on, as well as have a part in it.

Early in January, I was transferred back to Mogadishu and assigned to Digfer Hospital. A Canadian ophthalmologist, who was on his way to Laos, decided to volunteer with IMC until February. I was interested in what he did and how he got around in Laos. I told him about my trips, and that I wasn't able to travel freely because of my U.S. passport, while other nationalities didn't have that problem. We talked about the POW/MIA situation, and this

70-year-old man said I could marry him in order to get a Canadian passport. I said thanks, but no thanks.

The experience of living in a compound with nowhere to go, and not being able to leave without a guard even if there was someplace to go, was scary and almost claustrophobic. I often wished to have more work to fill my time when I wasn't at the hospital.

Toward the end of February, I was standing in the nursing office when a patient from Room 3 came in. By now, I could only speak a little Somali, but one of the Somali hospital aides had a fair command of the English language. In front of several of us, the patient asked if I was a Muslim. I told him I was a Christian. He raised his crutch and tried to hit me. The others in the room pushed him out. Later, he appeared in the hallway with a knife. For three days, this man would appear from the crowd with his knife raised to attack me. I felt a strange calm each time, as I said to God, "If this is my time, so be it."

It's funny how the anticipation of seeing this man again was scarier for me than when he actually pulled out the knife.

On the fourth day, when a co-worker was confronted by the same knife-wielding man, she cried out, and without even looking up, I said, "Don't worry. He's only out to get the Christians."

She said, "Oh," and then left.

It dawned on me two seconds later that I was becoming quite flippant. That place was getting to me.

ALONE WITH THE ENEMY

Hands constantly touching you
Hordes of people circling close around you
Wondering if you're looking at the person
    who's going to raise his weapon
    and pull the trigger.

Always listening for gunfire
Dark stairwells full of unknown Somalis
Your radio goes out
    no communication with the base
    you're alone with the enemy.

Barbara Birchim

On February 25, we couldn't leave our rooms to go to work for heavy gunfire began early that morning. Shells fell around and into our compound. The night before, a girl from DART (Disaster Assistance Relief Team) was almost stoned to death walking across our street.

Again, all hell broke loose the next morning. We were stuck in our rooms for two more days after that. I decided to hand in my resignation. I had had it.

SIGHTS AT TWILIGHT

Beautiful sunset from the roof
Blue skies filled with puffy clouds
Shorelines once crowded with ships, now empty
U.S. flag waving atop the old Embassy

Streets with children and adults wandering somewhere
U.S. and U.N. vehicles headed back to base
Drivers and workers getting ready for dinner
A city settling in for the night

Friendly Somalis start making obscene gestures
Gunfire echoes outside our compound
Guards thread the bandolera into our machine guns
Night has fallen in Mogadishu

Barbara Birchim

While watching CNN on March 2, I learned that the Vietnamese were planning to turn the "Hanoi Hilton" into a real hotel. I couldn't believe it!

On March 17, I got a call from stateside. "Get out of there, ASAP," I was told. The news about Somalia was not good at all. Two mornings later, for the first time, tanks started rolling down the street. That was 6:45. Cobras flew by around 7:15, almost as if to wish me a found adieu. I left for the airport.

I felt guilty, like I was deserting my fellow workers. I was leaving everyone behind, and I was feeling a sense of being a traitor. The logistician, who drove me to the airport, said that I shouldn't feel that way. In fact, he also felt it was time to leave.

Exactly three months to the day, I left Somalia. I understood, in my own way, why men in war had a hard time leaving their buddies behind.

Within a month after I left, the U.S. fired a rocket into Digfer Hospital, thinking one of the chief warlords was hiding there. And, the Somalis burned down IMC's warehouse with all the supplies in it, in retaliation for our pulling out of Digfer Hospital, and because we were Americans.

Not long after this, the infamous Blackhawk Down helicopter incident took place when eighteen U.S. servicemen were killed trying to extract hostages from an area in Mogadishu called The Green Line. That event gave me a sense of connection with our fighting men and our Special Forces that I wouldn't have had unless I had gone to Somalia.

TO HONOR MY BROTHER

My Dear Brother, Greg,

If I had written this letter to you 32 years ago, I would have said to you . . .

How proud I am of you, my hero, for the person you had become. To be willing to go to another country to help preserve freedom in a war torn country so that we could be one person closer to freedom.

The Yaqui Indian has always fought for the "Mother" earth they hold so sacred. You didn't grow up learning to hate and fight and kill. You grew up with an inborn instinct to protect and preserve what you inherited and that is what you tried to do.

I am 7 years older than you, my beloved brother, and I helped you through the tough times at home when you were growing up. I tried to keep your spirit strong like mine even through the difficult times. . .and there were many.

I loved you so much and enjoyed having you as my "little brother." You were the light of my life.

I miss not having you around to be my best friend, and the main uncle in my children's life. Ron, Kim and Tori got to be part of your life for a few short years. Charles and Greg never got to meet you. February 1, 1969 is the last day I got to see you and hug you before you left for Vietnam. You came to see Charlie the day he was born.

When we celebrate Charlie's birthday each year, I try very hard not to be sad because I don't want to take away from Charlie's birthday. . .but, it is difficult. You never knew I had one last son and I named him Greg. . .for you. You were only 18 and did not have children so I wanted to carry on your name.

One day, I am going to Vietnam to search for you, my brother. I hold no hatred toward anyone for what happened to you. Hatred only burns a hole in the heart and an Indian is not a free spirit without a whole heart. I know your spirit cannot rest until I bring you home. I will spend the rest of my life looking for you. Our soil is the "Mother" of all our people and somehow, my brother, I will bring you home to our "Mother."

I still go to the "Wall" in Washington D.C. each year to leave something for you. I will never take off the POW bracelet I have worn for 32 years. I still find it difficult to touch your name on that "Wall." It is a place to go to feel the spiritual oneness of all those souls. The "Wall" is here forever. . .you are forever. You will never be forgotten by all those in our family who love you as well as those who still contact me for information because they are wearing a POW bracelet.

I will love you forever. . .and one day I shall weep no more forever.

"Big Sis"

Mary

Staff Sergeant Gregory R. Benton, Jr.
United States Marine Corp
1/9, 3rd Marine Division
"The Walking Dead"
Missing in Vietnam/Laos since May 23, 1969
Panel 24, West, Line 81 – The Vietnam Wall

(Reprinted from the program of the 32nd Annual Meeting, June 20-23, 2001, National League of Families of American Prisoners and Missing in Southeast Asia, Arlington, VA.)

PART VI

"What Evil Lurks In The Minds of Men?"

Chapter Thirteen

The Ring Leaders

"They gave their lives so that others might come home."
Donald Rumsfeld
Secretary of Defense

In 1993, the POW/Missing Personnel Office (DPMO) was formed as part of the Department of Defense (DOD). This office established policy on the POW/MIA issue, and worked with many agencies within the government to recover and return the remains of our American servicemen.

The members of the DPMO have provided information to JTF-FA (now known as JPAC) and CILHI as those agencies have conducted crash site and battle site recovery operations in the following places over the past seven or so years:

China
Tibet
North Korea
Vietnam
Laos
Cambodia
Iran Jaya (West New Guinea)
Makin Island (Butaritari)
Great Britain
Siberia and Kamkchatka, Russia

The DPMO records show that the following sets of remains have been recovered:

146 World War II remains
162 North Korean unilateral turnovers
91 North Korean joint recovery operations
18 Cold War remains
591 remains from Vietnam, Laos, Cambodia[1]

In earlier reports, it was thought that there were at least 50-90 American remains in Laos. However, in 1999, the DPMO study found no evidence of any U.S. remains, and no evidence that the Vietnamese tried to collect American remains in Laos.[2]

In the Quang Binh Province of Vietnam, according to the DPMO study, witnesses said that at least 24 remains were recovered and sent to Hanoi in the mid-1970s. The Vietnamese confirmed that number to be 23, saying the 24th was lost. Yet, by 1999, investigators found physical evidence of storage on only nine.[3]

The DPMO study also states that in Northern Vietnam, earlier estimates of America's remains were 365-385. By 1999, their findings were close to 235-240. Many graves have been destroyed, and some areas are too remote to conduct an investigation[4] after so many years.

According to a 1999 Defense POW/Missing Personnel Office accounting report, the DOD will have set up a new "active" method of "conducting the business of recovery and accounting."[5] I guess they seem to feel that what they've been doing about missing personnel and prisoners of war since World War II is not active.

I found out not long ago that the Department of Military Justice was responsible for remains recovery and storage until 1979.[6] What a shock!

I'm glad that they will have a better method of finding our lost and imprisoned servicemen. I regret that it has taken the department all these years, since the Vietnam War, to decide that an "active" method was needed.

MISSING PERSONS ACT

This act applies to all members of the armed forces as well as Defense Department civilians and contractors. The act includes "all actions related to missing persons, from prevention of capture to recovery," and the "fullest possible accounting should there be an incident."[7]

Stony Beach is the DIA's special team charged with collecting POW/MIA information. They have an Oral History Program, and have the responsibility for investigating "first-hand live sighting reports in Laos, Vietnam, and Cambodia."

RUSSIA'S INVOLVEMENT

Within the DOD is a group called "U.S.-Russian Joint Commission on POW/MIAs Vietnam War Working Group." Since 1992, members of the U.S. senior executive branch, and their Russian counterparts, have been interviewing hundreds of Russian and other Eastern Bloc veterans of the Vietnam War--KGB, Russian diplomats, Communist Party, and military officials.[8] This is an ongoing effort.

A joint Commission Support Directorate at the U.S. Embassy in Moscow, under the DPMO's wing, handles MIA activities in Russia. This joint effort covers World War II, Korea, and some Vietnam War losses.[9]

CENTRAL IDENTIFICATION LABORATORY

A part of the DOD office is CILHI, the Central Identification Laboratory in Hawaii. Those at this laboratory perform recovery work such as dispatching teams of forensic anthropologists and other specialists to help locate, recover, catalog and determine the identity of remains from Vietnam, Laos and Cambodia.[10] They obtain DNA samples from maternal relatives if they need help in identifying recovered bones.

Some of the problems these specialists must take into consideration, while trying to locate remains, are acidic factors in the soil, temperature, and moisture conditions, and the decay or fragmentation of the bones.[11] Erosion, overgrowth, missing landmarks, and development make searching for remains difficult. Age, health, memory, and location of eyewitnesses add to their problems.[12]

These specialists always look for enough DNA to help them identify remains.

COMMUNICATIONS WITH FAMILIES

The CEA (Communications & External Affairs), a directorate in DPMO, deals with communication with POW/MIA families. CEA is responsible for family support, casualty liaison, legislative and concerned citizen's liaison, documents management, and declassification.[13]

In addition, the Secretaries of the military departments keep a Service Casualty Office. The SCOs handle all of the familys' questions regarding individual cases. And, the DPMO has conducted family meetings around the country to update their information, and provide an opportunity for family networking. Korean War and Cold War families have joined these meetings, now.[14]

ACCESS TO DOCUMENTS

One of the responsibilities of the CEA, under the Freedom of Information Act (FOIA), is to make case files available to POW/MIA family members. To quote the 1999 DOD accounting report, "DPMO fully supports family access to case files. The family member . . . must initiate the file review process. . . through the Service casualty office."[15]

The file is supposed to be identical to the case file "prepared for an on-site file review. Classified material contained within a DPMO case file pertains primarily to intelligence sources and methods."[16] My comment--Oh, yeah? But more about that later.

JOINT TASK FORCE-FULL ACCOUNTING

Under the DOD is the Joint Task Force-Full Accounting (JTF-FA), established in 1992 by then Defense Secretary Dick Cheney.[17] This group is charged with conducting investigations of last known alive cases, developing an oral history program, conducting oral history interviews, and conducting archival research as needed. Stony Beach members augment this JTF-FA team.[18]

The JTF-FA flag is quite significant as to what the task force is all about.

The Orange color is the international sign of a noncombatant, or humanitarian unit.

The Black Shield is for the solemn thoughts of our fallen comrades.

The White Cross is the Maltese cross. In the 11th and 12th centuries, the Knights of Saint John of Jerusalem wore the cross as their crest. The Knights were known for their great kindness towards the sick and poor.

The White streaks that lead away from the cross are the 'rays of hope.' The map underneath the cross is that of Southeast Asia. The countries of Vietnam, Laos and Cambodia are represented.[19]

VIETNAM'S COLLECTION & REPATRIATION OF AMERICAN REMAINS

I have mentioned but a few of the DOD offices that are involved with POW/MIA affairs. There is one more office I'd like to discuss that handles POW/Missing Personnel Affairs. The Deputy Assistant Secretary of Defense (DASD) presented a study titled, "Vietnam's Collection and Repatriation of American Remains." The DPMO was responsible for the report's contents.

Some of the key results of the report are listed below.

- Vietnamese authorities unilaterally located, collected, and stored approximately 300 American remains.
- Available evidence indicates that 270 to 280 have been repatriated.
- We cannot determine if the estimated 20-30 discrepancy is real or attributable to incomplete data, but Vietnam probably has records that would answer some of our questions.
- Vietnam had the most success in recovering U.S. remains in the North. Results were dramatically lower in the South and Cambodia.
- There is no credible evidence that Vietnam recovered American remains from Laos.

- Vietnam probably completed recoveries in the north by the late 1970s. We believe the last centrally recovered remains from the South and Cambodia reached Hanoi in 1983.[20]

The DASD report also spoke of how many Vietnamese were misled to think, in the 1970s and 80s, that they would receive money or be allowed to immigrate to the U.S. in exchange for American remains. As a result, much illegal trading took place. "By late 1998, Vietnamese and U.S. specialists had examined almost 2,400 such non-American remains."[21]

There has been a lot of speculation as to where the Vietnamese stored American remains after the war. Most of those involved in the POW/MIA discovery-recovery of remains think the remains were taken to the Van Dien Cemetery near Hanoi to be cleaned, then moved to a room in a compound at 17 Ly Nam De Street, Hanoi. Later, the remains were moved to a military prison in Bat Bat district, west of Hanoi. No one knows if American remains still sit there, or if they have been moved again.[22]

Through September 1990, the return of American remains became a political tool for Vietnam.[23] The Vietnamese had something that the U.S. wanted--a way to remind the U.S. that we could take certain actions if we wanted more remains returned.

As an example, the DASD report tells of a list the U.S. sent to Vietnam in August of 1998. The list consisted of 98 individuals whom we believed the Vietnamese knew about as to either their death or the disposition of their remains. "As of May 1999, 19 of them have been identified and returned to us."[24]

SERVICE CASUALTY OFFICE

It is amazing, after writing all of this information about what our government has been doing to answer the hundreds of POW/MIA questions we've had through the years, that my experience has been outside of all this. Along with every other POW/MIA family, I have had to generate questions for the government to answer rather than their "dropping me notes" on their own. That is not what they'd like you to believe. The one exception was the perfunctory form letters they sent during the war.

The government continues to wait for me to discover the illogical pieces of information that filter into Jim's file while they never question whether or not those pieces fit his case.

It's always up to the families to point out the discrepancies. Then it's up to them to continually push for answers. Spontaneity seems to be lacking.

I could write about incident after incident where I was told I couldn't know this, or I couldn't have access to that--even after all documents were supposed to be made available through the Freedom of Information Act.

ANOTHER EXAMPLE

As I started to fill out the numerous forms to attend the 2001 annual National League of Families meeting, I noticed that one form was missing. If any of the family members attending the meeting wanted to review their service member's file, they had to notify their casualty officer ahead of time by sending in a special form. This allowed the casualty office to pull the chart, and transport it to the hotel in which the attendees were staying.

Since that form was missing from my packet, I called Washington D.C. When I explained the situation, the person I spoke with informed me that it was against the law for them to move the charts out of their office. They could copy and sanitize the file, then bring it to me to review.

Of course, I thought this person was kidding me. So, I laughed. I was met with dead silence. The new person to the Casualty Office once again told me the same thing, with a great deal of authority.

Realizing she was serious, I said, "Well, this is very interesting. For thirty years plus, the files have been brought to the hotel for each of us to review. Do you mean to tell me that, for the first time in all those years, it has now just been discovered that your office has been breaking the law?"

With a soft voice, she repeated her previous statement.

I had no one to go to, to by-pass this person, since everyone in Casualty is rotated out on a regular basis.

"If you want to see the original casualty file, you'll have to make an appointment after the League meeting," she said at last. So stupid!

As the number of family members attending the annual League meeting dwindles, so do the requests for file reviews, making the government's job easier.

"Besides being against the law, the files are getting old, and transporting and reviewing them adds additional potential for deterioration," she added.

"Excuse me!" I said. "Doesn't taking all of the pages out of the folder and having a clerk hand feed each page through a copy machine, and then re-affixing the pages in the folder, cause more wear and tear than a family member would, who just wants to look at a certain section?"

There was no immediate answer. So, I continued to push the woman. "This not only doesn't make sense, but it costs money and manpower."

Therein may be the real answer.

I'm sure the woman could tell I was perplexed, so she said she'd copy Jim's file.

"There's no need to kill several trees," I said. I felt like I was caught up in a Laurel and Hardy skit.

I already had a copy of Jim's file up until that year. What I wanted to see was if there were any new documents added to the 3"-thick file I had. The powers that be are prone to insert new papers into the file that they don't send to me.

When I got to the meeting, the lady in the Casualty Office had copied the file, anyway. Go figure!

THE ARMY LUNCHEON FOR LEAGUE MEMBERS

During the annual meeting's four days, each of the military branches hosts a luncheon. In my case, Jim was in the Army, so I'm always invited. Most of the time it is open seating. This year it was different. Place cards were at the tables of eight, to make sure that the Army had each League member sitting where and with whom they wanted. At least that's what I decided.

I was seated next to Brigadier General Harry Axson who was in charge of JTF-FA. Four others at the table were from Army Casualty and DPMO. Two men, who were attending the League meeting for the first time, filled the two remaining seats. Their brother was MIA. They did not say much.

I had to laugh to myself when I realized the seating arrangement was probably set-up to keep tabs on me. Such a dog and pony show! As for me, I saw it as my opportunity to pick Brigadier General Axson's brain.

During the lunch, I mentioned the information that I had discovered when I was doing research in the National Archives regarding Jim's file. Brigadier General Axson seemed interested especially when I reached my punch line.

I told him that for years the Birchims had known that Jim's team was inserted into Laos to try to help another team that was in trouble. Somewhere we'd gotten the name Copley as one of the men on the other team. But, nowhere could I find a mention of this in Jim's file.

"Well," I said, "surprise of surprises, when I happened to roll the microfilm to the next case file, whose name should be there? Copley's! And in Copley's file was information about Birchim and Bellitire having been inserted to try to find him."

Everyone at the table seemed engrossed in what I was saying. I continued.

"The kicker is that the loss coordinates for Copley are hundreds of kilometers away from where Jim was extracted. As a matter of fact, Copley was supposedly lost in the area of Ben Het on the Laos side of the Vietnam border. And Copley was declared MIA on November 16, 1968, the day after Jim's MIA date."

When Brigadier General Axson heard this, he told me to tell Dickie Hites, JTF-FA, my story. He said that the year before, another family member came forward with information, and JTF-FA was able to go to the loss site and recover remains as a result.

As the General said this, I couldn't help but think--why is it that family members have to do the research and digging for information that you guys, with your fancy technology and manpower, should be doing? I kept this to myself, and then I assured the General that I would talk to Mr. Hites.

I must admit that I did have good feelings toward Brigadier General Axson, and what he'd been able to accomplish in one short year as Director of JTF-FA. I'm guessing that he was seen by higher ups as being too "efficient" in regard to POW/MIA issues, and that was why he was being transferred to another post at the Pentagon. The normal length of duty in that position was 2-3 years, so his transfer came as a surprise to The League and to me.

QUESTIONS AND ANSWERS

Each year, during The League meeting, briefings are held by various representatives from the governmental departments that are active in the POW/MIA issue. The briefings are followed on the last day by a Q & A session with The League members in attendance.

This year, all of those who gave briefings were seated at one table stretching across the whole length of the room. There were two microphones on stands for the members to use, one in each aisle.

Anyone can ask a question of the panel, but first the speakers must state their names and who their MIA relatives are. The question cannot be personal, and each person is allowed one follow-up question.

Those of us who have done this for years know that the panel members will only answer the specific question asked. Therefore, it took me a long time to formulate my question on paper before I got to the microphone. I wanted the panel members to know that some heady facts surrounded my question. I would not accept a flippant answer. So, this is what I said:

"My name is Barbara Birchim and I'm the wife of Special Forces Captain James D. Birchim, MIA on November 15, 1968, somewhere in Laos or Vietnam. I'm directing my question to JTF-FA."

As I spoke, I noticed Brigadier General Axson smiling at me from the head table. I think he knew my question was going to put someone on the spot.

"I think it's safe to say for those men in Special Forces, and especially those in Black Ops, that their loss coordinates were SWAGed, or namely, Stupid Wild Ass Guessed."

At this point, not only did the audience start laughing, but everyone at the head table was chuckling and shaking his head.

"With those cases where JTF-FA went to the locations noted in the serviceman's file, and they found nothing. I ask how could they, since these were fictitious coordinates? And as a result, they placed men in a 'no further pursuit' category. Would JTF-FA now make special considerations for those cases by widening the search area and by including those cases as possibilities when investigating other locations?"

I wasn't sure if the panel understood my question, so I asked.

Brigadier General Axson spoke up. He said he understood, and deferred the answer to Dickie Hites, Deputy J2 for Operations, JTF-FA.

Dickie Hites' answer was so short I almost fell over. He said, "Yes," he paused, then he added, "For the first time we're interviewing Special Forces men who are telling us they never gave the correct coordinates because they were on covert missions."

I was astounded.

The very team of experts that had been working to resolve those cases was just now. . . discovering. . .this information?

He continued by saying that it was very important to have DNA samples from all of the MIA families.

As other League members came to the mic to ask their questions, the emotions ebbed and flowed from total sadness to raging anger. All of those in the audience had become a family through the years, not by choice but through happenstance. Each of us feels the sorrows of the other family members as they try with dignity to plead for the answers that have been so long in coming.

At one point, I was shocked by a question asked by the mother of an MIA. I started to formulate a follow-up question of my own. This lady had 32 live sighting reports the year before, plus an additional 15 live sighting reports that appeared from January 2001 to June 2001. The government debunked them all. She wanted to know why JTF-FA hadn't contacted her and asked her if any of the information might actually relate to her son. Maybe some of that information would have been so personal that only the mother would have known, not Stony Beach.

My head felt like it was going to explode as I listened to a long response from one of the panel members that didn't answer her question. My adrenaline and anger rose to a point where I think I could have picked up an elephant.

As I waited for my turn at the mic, I continued to refine my question on live sightings. I watched Brigadier General Axson and the panel members as I once again stepped up to ask a question. They all seemed to have the look of "Oh, God, she's back!" except for the General.

My question went something like this:

"It's safe to say that the only live sighting reports that the public would hear about would be the high profile cases covered by international news organizations or services. You just said that you respond to live sighting reports in a quick fashion. If that definition fits the way you responded to the Monk or to the North Korean POW who escaped to the South, I can only assume that any other non-publicized live sighting report would be done at less than a snail's pace. Do you automatically discount these live sightings because it's too difficult to confront, with venom, a foreign regime? Do you always have to take into consideration the ramifications of confronting a communist country? If that is the tack you take, then please be honest with this audience and say so."

Once again the General deferred the answer to Dickie Hites. This time there was a longer answer. My recollection is that the answer was all fluff until the ending punch line when he said, "Yes, we do take into consideration the political ramifications it might cause."

Bingo!

Finally, they admitted why these live sighting testimonies are debunked.

When the question and answer session was over, we were hurried out the door because a wedding party had booked the room for the evening. This was going to be my last chance to talk to Dickie Hites, so as he came through the doors, I reached him and said that Brigadier General Axson had asked me to tell him what I had discovered in the archives concerning Jim.

We detoured into an adjoining room, and I filled him in on the Birchim/Copley connection that I had discovered in the National Archives. He seemed to show genuine interest and said he'd look into it. Then I said, "There has always been something that has really bothered me about Jim's status being changed from MIA to KIA/BNR after two reviewing cycles and without any new information.

"I have queried DIA, DOD, Army Casualty, plus every MIA family member I've come in contact with," I said. "It seems that Jim is the only one to have this happen. Out of the blue, on May 10, 1971, I was notified that his status had changed to KIA/BNR. It wasn't even an anniversary date of his becoming an MIA and there was no new information to support a status change."

Without a split second hesitation, Dickie Hites looked at me and said, "Well, your husband was Special Forces and in SOG. Right? Well, they killed him off on paper. . ."

He said this matter-of-factly, while he closed his briefcase and walked off to disappear into the crowd. He left me speechless. I stood there with my mouth open, in total shock.

TO LIVE ANOTHER DAY

Going to the annual League meeting always evoked in me a myriad of feelings ranging from hope that I'd find answers to my years of searching, to the deep sadness that I was going to yet another League meeting.

As I reflect on the lies that have been told over the past years, I feel a spurt of energy to go back into the battle with the government, but I am tempered by a feeling of exhaustion for having done this for so many years.

When will this end? I feel the government has the power and knowledge to answer a lot of the POW/MIA family's questions, but they choose not to.

As I left the League meeting in 2001, all I wanted to do was curl up and cry myself to sleep. I couldn't do that, though, because I found no way to turn my brain off as it continued with an endless rerun of the tape.

One thing I knew for sure. I had to try to distract my thoughts because if I stopped and surrendered, I might not get up to fight another day.

MORE LIES

Earlier in this chapter I quoted a 1999 DPMO report that stated there was no evidence of any remains of military men in Laos. I find that very interesting when, on July 22, 2001, the Sunday Times Parade magazine featured a story about a search team going into Laos to reach the wreckage of a Navy plane where 9 men died on January 11, 1968.

Just another example of the government lying to us for more than 30 years.

The article shows pictures of the wreckage and how the limestone mountain, covered in mist, has hidden the evidence on its stony ledges.

According to the reporter, Earl Swift, "After 33 years, their countrymen have arrived to take them home."[25] The team was made up of a forensic anthropologist from the Army's Honolulu-based Central Identification Laboratory, two mountaineers from an Army post in Alaska, a Special Forces medic, a Navy parachute rigger and soldiers "trained to recognize bone when they see it."[26]

Included in the Joint Task Force-Full Accounting are "161 linguists, logistical experts and investigators who scour war records and interview witnesses to pinpoint the places where planes went down, patrols were ambushed or men simply vanished."[27]

Here are some of the statistics reported by Swift. "In nine years, the task force, based in Hawaii, has investigated 3405 cases and conducted 590 excavations. Every year, teams of 30 to 95 men conduct 10 recovery operations--each lasting about 35 days--in Laos, Vietnam and Cambodia. There were 2584 men unaccounted for in the region when Saigon fell in 1975. Today 1966 remain."[28]

Note the mention of Laos, again. And it's listed before Vietnam in importance.

". . . five times a year in Laos, four times a year in Vietnam and once a year in Cambodia, the recovery teams fan out through the countryside to dig."[29]

Lt. Col. Franklin Childress, Joint Task Force-Full Accounting said, "Behind every one of the statistics is a person--and a family--waiting for a loved one to be identified."[30]

Thank goodness these recovery teams are working to find and bring home the remains of our loved ones. I just wonder why it took until 1992 for searches in Southeast Asia to become official and ongoing under a Joint Task Force. And how sad it is that the focus has been on remains instead of on living POWs before they become dead bodies.

Dickie Hites' comment in 2001 bolstered my hope that Jim could have survived the incident. But, if he really did die in the jungle on that fateful day, I held out no hope that a U.S. recovery team would ever return to that spot to look for Jim and bring his remains home like the recovery teams are doing for others lost in Vietnam. Not after 36 years!

Chapter Fourteen

Sneaky Pete

"Men do not fight for flag or country, for the Marine Corps or glory or any other abstraction. They fight for one another."[1]

William Manchester

The OSS, predecessor to the Special Forces, was first created during World War II for sabotage and intelligence reasons. In other words, covert forces--guerilla warfare behind enemy lines. Their connection with the CIA was nebulous during the intervening years before Vietnam. When President John Kennedy came into office, he was fascinated with these guerrilla fighters. They were as close to the French Foreign Legion as the U.S. could get, and the "largest clandestine military unit since World War II's OSS."[2]

The Special Forces were infantrymen highly trained as frogmen, mountain climbers, parachutists and skiers. They were also trained in foreign languages, communications, sabotage, psychological warfare, and intelligence.

These men were smart, fast, bold, lethal, ruthless-- used by the CIA for special missions. They had to deal with physical and mental stress. They needed the ability to deal with ambiguity and the fears that go along with stressful situations such as these.

President Kennedy felt that the Army's Special Forces were exactly what he could use for guerrilla tactics in "a twilight war for democracy."[3] He gave the Special Forces their name, Green Beret, because of their "Terry and the Pirates"[4] headgear, which the Pentagon officials had resisted in the past.

Kennedy then made the Green Berets his "first team at the White House"[5] or as another author wrote, "the shock troops of his 'war in the shadows.'"[6]

President Kennedy is known to have said the Green Berets showed the "mark of distinction, the badge of courage."[7] To this day, the Green Berets still stand for the same symbol that President Kennedy was so proud of.

On the January 25, 2001 "Behind Closed Doors" TV show with Joan Lunden, she said that the Green Beret's invisibility is their key to staying alive. She referred to them as extremely patriotic "warriors."[8]

"Until the president's death (Kennedy) in November 1963, Vietnam would remain nearly a CIA-Green Beret show."[9] In fact, through the years, many have considered that the Green Berets and the CIA were one in the same--a secret relationship, a subversive partnership.

Before long, the Green Berets were used most of the time to build spy teams in Cambodia, and to bring back POWs. When President Lyndon Johnson's term of office was over, the largest command in Vietnam was the 5th Special Forces Group.

Originally in Vietnam, the Green Berets were to train "a U.S. Army long-range patrol and ranger infantry as well as U.S. Air Force airbase defense forces in Thailand." Another of their missions was to train special warfare "contingents in South Korea, Taiwan, Thailand, the Philippines, and South Vietnam."[10]

They were also directed to train the Civilian Irregular Defense Group (CIDG) that fought in the worst regions of Vietnam.[11]

However, one of the most serious jobs they had to do was to hold "key territory and safeguard lines of communication. Special Forces were even charged with controlling the entire length of Vietnam's rugged border, where it actively pursued a campaign of hampering and interdicting the infiltration of main force Viet Cong and regular North Vietnamese Army units. . . (They) established and defended a series of strategic forts in remote areas, which were often deliberately emplaced in Viet Cong strongholds, and formed mobile strike force brigades and battalions to reinforce and back up these citadels. Finally, the Special Forces mobile strike forces were used to assault objectives, such as mountain bastions, which defied regular South Vietnamese Army formations. The Special Forces even launched its own navy to reach otherwise-inaccessible VC sanctuaries and to control the waterways of the countryside."[12]

The actual battlefield destiny of the Special Forces in Vietnam was unforeseen by the original concept of the creators of the Green Berets.

Because a lot of the Green Berets' operations were covert, the money to support their activities came from "black budgets," which were filtered through other Pentagon programs or through money funneled by the Defense Department for the CIA.[13]

I have heard it said that once a man became a Green Beret, he was forever at the beck and call of the CIA. His records were often skewed or erased to prevent his identification as a former covert operator in Vietnam or elsewhere in the world. Sometimes, the records of his having been in the Army were even destroyed. Dental records, social security numbers, fingerprints, photographs, sometimes dog tag numbers were not only classified, or erased, but sanitized--obliterated from all documents.

I found it interesting to learn that inside the Vietnam War, another war--a Secret War was being conducted. This secret war was explained in an ABC News Production for the Learning Channel, called "Secret War, Secret Men--A Vietnam Soldier's Story."

The Secret War, called "A war in the shadows," took place in Laos where Americans were not supposed to be. Since Laos was a neutral country, our military could not go there. So, the CIA solved that by sending our men to Laos with no identifiable names, ranks, unit insignias, and uniforms so that if killed or captured their identities would remain unknown.

The narrator said about the secret men, "If these men are killed, their existence will be denied. They are the unsung soldiers and covert operatives fighting Vietnam's secret wars."

I learned that their records were moved to a Top Secret file so that the men disappeared from regular military records, but insurance and pensions could be covered, if necessary. "In some cases the families of MIAs who were sheep dipped in this way still receive two pensions--one from the military and one from the civilian 'cover' company."[14] I guess that was a good way of keeping the families happy.

The men were chosen by CIA "suits"--technicians who were the best of the best. John Daniel, Radar Technician, described what happened once the CIA chose those men. "They go in, in military uniform, change all of your clothes out, get rid of all identification, dress in civilian clothes, picked up the Lockhead employee identification card, out the other door and on the chopper, going north."

One of the places these men were sent was Site 85, atop a 5600-foot limestone mountain in Laos. Site 85 was "one of a chain of bases in the CIA's war in Laos, where supposedly no war was going on."[15]

Site 85 was built so that highly trained U.S. technicians could guide American bombers to targets around Hanoi, 160 miles east of them.[16]

The narrator on the Learning Channel program said, "The mission is so secret that the men officially retire from the Air Force and then are rehired as civilians under contract to a private company," (sheep dipping). Thai mercenaries and the CIA protected the site.

Ann Holland was the wife of Melvin Holland who disappeared in 1968. He had been one of those technicians at Site 85. Officially, he was based in Thailand and each time he flew into Laos, he was "sanitized" and became a civilian. If he were captured, the U.S. Government would deny any knowledge of him.[17] According to Kiss The Boys Goodbye, "If he had been in uniform, he might have had a fighting chance as a prisoner-of-war."[18]

Melvin Holland, who worked for Hughes Aircraft, ended up missing. Two years after that, President Nixon said there were no men lost in Laos. "Ann Holland asked her case officer, 'If my husband wasn't lost in Laos, where was he lost?'"[19]

In Part 4 of "Secret War, Secret Men," Sedgwick Tourison, former Intelligence Officer who worked for a Senate Committee as an investigator, said, "Special operations . . . covert operations is tough business. You get high losses. And guys don't come home and you expect that. (But) you don't want it to happen."

I tell this story under Special Forces, because the CIA and the Special Forces were synonymous in the Vietnam War. So conversly, the Secret War in Laos, run by the CIA, had to be a Special Forces operation.

I'd like to point out again, that once a member of the CIA, always a member of the CIA, including our Special Forces men.

Isn't it interesting that a man could join the U.S. Army, train as a Green Beret, fight for his country, then, because of where he was sent or what he was told to do, be forced to be a secret operative for the CIA for the rest of his life? If the CIA so chose? And he couldn't prove or disprove any of it for there would be no record of his activities.

He might even have been psychologically re-trained so that his former identity was changed and the memory of his previous life erased forever.

I'm not making these comments because I don't like or believe in the Army's Green Berets--Special Forces. On the contrary. Because I lived with Jim while he was going through all of the Special Forces training, I know how important it is for the U.S. to have men able to conduct guerilla warfare when our country's welfare is at stake. What bothers me is the CIA connection. What Jim did, had to become "highly classified." It was automatic. I guess that means that after all these years, the members of our Green Beret POW/ MIA families still cannot know for sure what really happened to our loved ones.

You can't tell me Jim's recon team did something on that fateful day that would be earth shaking if I was now given the details about what happened to him--dead or alive! At this point in time, I feel like screaming, "Who cares!" at anyone in the Army or the CIA who will listen to me.

* * *

"(Most) of those who died in defense of our country . . . were boys when they died, and they gave up two lives - - the one they were living, and the one they would have lived. They gave up their chance to be husbands and fathers and grandfathers . . . They gave up everything for their country, for us. All we can do is remember."

President Ronald Reagan 1985

The Green Berets are extremely patriotic and professional. In the hour-long program, "The Warrior Tradition," on The History Channel, 1998, the Green Berets were called, "Quiet professionals, warrior diplomats." As the narrator said on that show, "At last their stories can be told" for until then, the "operations remained secret."

For many years the elite Green Berets have been "known as the intellectuals of the battlefield," men who show a "high element of personal courage" as they become involved in "unconventional and psychological warfare."

Army Lieutenant General William P. Yarborough has explained the normal activities of the Special Forces as assisting "in the development of a resistance mechanism which can operate alone or which will supplement, complement, or precede military operations by uniformed conventional military forces, thus bringing to bear against an enemy aggressor the total physical, political, and psychological resources of a friendly state."[20]

To explain some of the training Green Berets went through during the Vietnam War, here is a list of Jim's training:
-   U.S. Army Infantry School, Officer Candidate Airborne Course
-   U.S. Army Chemical School, Chemical Officer Orientation Course
-   Company A, 7th Special Forces Group, lst Special Forces

And these are the decorations and awards Jim earned:
-   Distinguished Service Cross
-   Purple Heart
-   National Defense Service Medal
-   Vietnam Service Medal
-   National Order of Vietnam, Fifth Class
-   Republic of Vietnam Campaign Medal

***

Presidential Unit Citation

***

-   Combat Infantryman Badge
-   Vietnamese Jump Wings
-   Parachute Badge

During the Vietnam War, the Green Berets were highly trained for jungle warfare. However, "as the involvement in the Vietnam War grew, the missions took on different roles."[21] The Pentagon found that the infantry could not handle certain problems that arose, some problems too sensitive for the regular Army. They needed someone to observe the enemy first hand, to work behind enemy lines. Thus was created SOG, Studies and Observation Group. This became the most clandestine of all Special Forces groups.

SOG answered only to the White House and the Joint Chiefs of Staff. Every move the SOG members made was classified. Their operations were so covert that their existence was denied.[22]

Recon teams were formed, consisting of two American Green Berets and up to nine tribesmen mercenaries. They were to gather intelligence behind enemy lines in Laos and Cambodia, but they would also attack, if necessary. They went on these missions with no identification of any kind, not even U.S. made guns. They were "sterile," as the term was defined.

According to "The Warrior Tradition" program on The History Channel, they "played a dangerous game of hide and seek" or "cat and mouse" in enemy territory. They moved in total silence, sometimes for days or a week. They were trained to sense the enemy's presence, thus often labeled as "good in the woods." But, as well as hunting the enemy for intelligence information, they were also pursued by the enemy, which made their job a double hazard.

When a recon team got into trouble in Laos or Cambodia, the Green Beret Hatchet Force went in for the rescue. The recon team would call for air strikes, sometimes endangering themselves, and then the helicopters would arrive to lift them out of their danger.

When there was no place to land a helicopter, in order to rescue the recon team, they would use a McGuire Rig. This had been invented to handle the job, and consisted of four 120-foot ropes and harness affairs attached to the helicopter, and dropped for the men on the ground.

As mentioned several times in this History Channel feature, this type of rescue put everyone in extreme danger. The men were shot at or dragged through the trees while they hung from the "riding strings," as the ropes were called. It was only under extreme circumstances where there was no other alternative but to lose the recon team to the enemy, that this dangerous rescue attempt was made.

After hearing this on the TV program, I realized even more what a tremendous danger Jim must have been in, to have called for his team to be rescued on that fateful day.

By 1968, according to "The Warrior Tradition," there were 100% casualties in those cross-border recon missions. Every American involved in a recon team was either killed, missing, or wounded . . . including Lt. Jim Birchim.

Many Special Forces guys had prices on their heads. "If captured, they weren't prisoners of war under the Geneva Convention. It meant certain death and if not death, the worse torture you could think of," reported one former Green Beret on "The Warrior Tradition."

The Green Berets were among the first to arrive in Vietnam and among the last to leave. "They would rather die than bring any kind of embarrassment or disrepute to the Green Berets." President Kennedy said, "that a nation reveals itself not only by the men that it produces but that it honors." Seventeen Medals of Honor were awarded[23] to the Green Berets in the Vietnam War.

* * *

". . . young Americans must never again be sent to fight
and die unless we are prepared to let them win."
President Ronald Reagan 1988

The patch on the Green Beret uniform has three bolts of lightning denoting land, sea and air--and the conquering of all three. This is truly remarkable.

On January 25, 2001, the viewers of the TV show, Behind Closed Doors starring Joan Lunden, were treated to a series of Green Beret training sessions. One of the most spectacular was when Joan Lunden joined four Green Berets being extracted from a jungle setting.

The helicopter dropped a rope. One man and Joan hooked themselves together onto the rope, about half way up. Two other men hooked on together further down the rope and the fifth hooked on to the bottom. It took them only seconds to perform this feat, and then be lifted above the trees to dangle and swing high above the ground with enemy fire aimed at them.

As stated about the spie rig in Chapter Two, in the TV program, the Special Forces five hooked their closest arms around each other, with their outside arms extended and their legs held apart for balance.

I couldn't help but feel a pang of sadness that these ropes, capable of carrying up to six men, had not been invented in 1968. If so, Jim would not have had to cling to the NCO on a one-man rope, high above the ground, in bad weather, with a broken ankle and other wounds, and with enemy fire aimed at them. An impossible situation, to say the least, as Jim made a desperate attempt to survive the mission. My imagined picture of what happened during that extraction still brings tears to my eyes.

"They died hard, those savage men - - like wounded wolves at bar. They were filthy, and they were lousy, and they stunk. And I loved them."

General Douglas MacArthur

The secret elite group, originally named SOA (Special Operations Augmentation) during the Vietnam War, was later changed to the code name SOG (Studies and Observations Group). The military men in SOG worked in such a concealed manner that even the government denied they existed. SOG was made up of Army Green Berets, USAF Air Commandos and Navy SEALS. This military unit answered directly to the Pentagon's Joint Chiefs of Staff. Some of their missions had to be approved by the White House. General William Westmoreland, and a few non-SOG officers, were the only ones briefed on the activities of SOG.[24] The SOG military men were assigned, for the most part, to the 5th Special Forces Group for cover and for administration purposes.[25]

Though it appeared that SOG members were working for CAS (Combined Area Studies) in South Vietnam, the CAS was really a cover for CIA elements and programs.[26]

The DOD supported SOG with "personnel, equipment, funding and most important, the requisite priorities to . . . support specific operations."[27]

The SOG men were sometimes called "Black Ops" because of the secrecy involved in their operations. The "SOG troopers often wore enemy uniforms and adopted false names, just as Special Forces soldiers in other units routinely used false identities on other sensitive operations they usually had going around the world."[28]

This clandestine warfare involved SOG officers readying and supervising the execution of the attacks, once Washington approved them. The operations were usually carried out by teams of Vietnamese and mercenary Asian saboteurs[29], trained by the Green Berets and the Navy SEALS. These operations were the most dangerous assignments because they called on the members of SOG to go behind enemy lines in Laos and Cambodia, as well as along the heavily defended Ho Chi Minh Trail. Little or no air support was ever available in this last instance.

Among the many heroic feats they accomplished, was to "launch daring missions to rescue downed U.S. pilots from behind enemy lines."[30]

"Despite all of the restrictions placed on SOG and the growing list of naysayers, the SOG chiefs struggled to accomplish as much as their hotly negotiated and heavily restrained authorities permitted. Their efforts evolved into three programs: attempts to create an insurgency in North Vietnam; small-scale seaborne raids on North Vietnam's coasts; and reconnaissance, backed by air strikes, against North Vietnamese forces crossing first Laos and later Cambodia. Each program had its own set of frustrations, almost all of which were American-made."[31]

The men of SOG were brave, heroic and few in number. At its height, there were 2000 Americans.[32] During the war, they were awarded ten Medals of Honor and hundreds of Purple Hearts. They were the war's most highly decorated unit, and the most highly decorated American soldier was a part of SOG.[33]

"Approximately 250 personnel were KIA and 57 MIA/BNR. Because the only two SOG prisoners of war who survived and returned were captured within South Vietnam, there is a suspicion that the North Vietnamese had initiated a loyal program equivalent to Hitler's infamous Kommando Befehl, which directed the execution of any Allied special operators, whether uniformed or not. . .[34]"

SOG soldiers signed a paper swearing to be quiet about its operations and the organization. Until the book, SOG, written by John L. Plaster, was published, most of what the men of SOG did was not discussed.[35]

In 2000, several other books appeared in the book stores about the unclassified SOG records: The Secret War Against Hanoi, by Richard H. Schultz, Jr.; Spies and Commandos: How America Lost the Secret War in North Vietnam, by Kenneth Conboy and Dale Andrade; and SOG: A Photo History of the Secret Wars, by John Plaster.[36]

In 1968, Command and Control North (CCN) lost 18 Americans KIA and 18 MIA, the same number as fifteen recon teams. That meant that every single SOG recon man was wounded at least once that year, plus the 199 SOG Americans wounded in Laos. About half of these men died. "The terrible truth became clear: SOG recon casualties exceeded 100 percent, the highest sustained American loss rate since the Civil War."[37]

ABC News Production made an hour-long video for the Learning Channel called, "Secret War, Secret Men--A Vietnam Soldier's Story." Part 2 was devoted to the story of SOG. The program described how these secret CIA operations worked during the Vietnam War. SOG members were called, "secret commandos" who gathered intelligence and created chaos for the enemy. They usually wore black, and had no signs of identification.

John Cavaiani, SOG, said on the program, that SOG members "saved a lot of our guys' lives by telling them what was coming on down the pike." He said that there were a "whole lot of our guys on that long, black wall" in Washington D.C.

According to General Westmoreland, USA retired, "SOG played an important role during our operations against the communist enemy in Vietnam."[38]

Da Nang, near Marble Mountain, was the CCN headquarters for SOG. The men working out of CCN operated most of the time in Laos and the DMZ. The men working out of CCC headquarters for SOG in Kontum operated in Northern Cambodia and Southern Laos. CCS, which was based at Ban Me Thuot, was the SOG headquarters for missions into Central Cambodia.

Three months before Jim was MIA, those at the SOG CCN headquarters thought that danger was far away. However, on August 23, 1968, more than 100 NVA raiders penetrated the Da Nang compound. Green Berets and Navy SEALS fought the invaders for three hours. By dawn, fifteen Special Forces officers and NCOs had died, the largest single loss of Green Berets in the Vietnam War. It was decided later, that this attack on Da Nang was a deliberate act to cripple SOG, and to disrupt SOG activities across the border in Laos.[39]

It was into this Da Nang situation, that Jim entered the next month as a Green Beret.

The e-mail I received from Darrell Redman, whose name I had been given in 1998, indicated that Jim was a member of SOG. Darrell wrote, "I am sorry for your loss and am glad that you remember those of us who served in SOG. Your husband should be remembered for serving with the finest unit the U.S. has ever produced in its history. Even among the Special Forces, the SOG operators were held in the highest respect and quite often with some awe."

After I received this message from Darrell, I bought the SOG book, and found out about Jim's SOG operations. In referring to the book, Darrell said, "It really tells the story about what we did and separates the myths and BS that have surrounded us for all these years."

In 2000, I found out that in Jim's OCS class in Ft. Benning, Georgia, six appear to have been in Special Forces. Four of those were involved in SOG operations, and three out of those four were KIA. Very sad odds. Jim, originally labeled MIA, became one of those four KIA.

During my research about SOG, I learned that the top-secret world of SOG included an unspoken code of ethics, which was often influenced by the men's duty, loyalty and the danger they might be in at any given time. Each SOG team had a One-Zero, a man who was the most experienced and knowledgeable member. One-Zero would have a One-One or One-Two who could have outranked him, but on the team, One-Zero was in charge. When One-Zero said his team needed to be extracted, he was not questioned or second-guessed.[40] It is my understanding that the One-One and One-Two were often the radioman and the medic.

One-Zero was always the first man off the helicopter during a drop and the last one picked up when the team needed to be extracted. One-Zero was to lead by example, not by rank or force. As Medal of Honor recipient, Bob Howard once said, "It's kind of hard to put into words, but it's like having somebody that you love. If you served in (SOG) and you were willing to die, you wanted to have a person there you would not mind dying for or dying with."[41]

My mind ran away with this information. If a SOG team felt this way and operated this way, then why didn't someone go back to try to find Jim? From the description of a One-Zero, and the other bits of information the government allowed me to see, it sounded to me like Jim had been One-Zero on that fateful SOG mission.

In answer to my nagging question about why I could never find a document varifying that someone had really gone back to look for Jim, I soon found out that another part of the SOG code was--accomplish the mission first, survive second. SOG teams left their American teammates if they had to. The rationale was that they should not give the enemy any more American bodies than necessary. When that occurred, "SOG survivors always felt they carried their teammate's spirit back with them."[42]

All I can hope is that Jim's spirit went back with his teammates, if he did indeed die when he fell from that McGuire rig. My intention is not to place guilt for Jim's disappearance on any Special Forces or SOG member. I just want to know what happened to Jim.

"SOG's legacy is not so much one of lessons-learned as it is one of example. For eight years, despite difficult conditions and impediments at all levels, the SOG Special Forces soldiers, the smaller number of sailors and airmen, and the greater number of indigenous warriors, did their jobs with unfailing dedication, tenacity and all too often, fatal courage."[43]

As Jerry Estenson and I were talking one time, he said, "You are absolutely right--we don't leave our own behind, unless we have no choice. That no choice option is also something accepted by each of us that volunteered for the work. We operated without the protection of military uniforms, military IDs, military dogtags, or any personal items. That placed us outside Geneva Convention protections and we knew it. We also knew that by doing so, we were invisible and our only connection home was each other."

> "One who devotes himself to a cause with his whole strength and soul can be a true master. For this reason mastery demands all of a person."
>
> Albert Einstein

The U.S. government continues to withhold casualty counts from covert or "black" military operations in Southeast Asia, which includes

Burma, Cambodia, Laos, North Vietnam, South Vietnam, Thailand, and the southern provinces of the Peoples Republic of China. Despite the Freedom of Information Act, most of the covert military operations between 1955 and 1975 remain classified. That means that the losses our country endured during the Vietnam War are inaccurate.

According to the May 23, 1991 report, "An Examination of U.S. Policy Toward POW/MIAs", by the U.S. Senate Committee on Foreign Relations, Republican Staff, even when one of those who served as part of a covert "black" military or intelligence operation disappeared, the information remained secure.[44]

Cover stories of a benign nature were sometimes written to explain a serviceman's disappearance. He might have been declared dead immediately (KIA/BNR), or he might have been listed as MIA followed by KIA/BNR twelve months later. This erroneous information would remain in the person's official file, listing a false location of the casualty or circumstances.

Some of the erroneous reports listed battle losses in South Vietnam when the men were really lost in Laos, Cambodia or North Vietnam, and some were listed as training accidents in places like Thailand or Okinawa, which was also false.

Due to the classified covert or special warfare missions, the "presumptive findings of death" were based on faulty data in many case files.

Non-classified and declassified sources have indicated that a large number of military personnel were lost on covert missions. Can you imagine how many were lost who are still classified? It's my feeling the DOD has denied they have a secret list of casualties from those covert operations.

In 1962, the Geneva Pact Accords prohibited any foreign military in Laos. Therefore, it was necessary for the U.S. to deny the fact that our government was conducting black operations there. The files of those who were involved in those operations do not indicate they had ever been in Laos, or their files are still classified, for obvious reasons.

According to the May 23, 1991, report, the operations that the DOD, Department of State, and the CIA conducted in Indochina are still not discussed, openly. However, two books that approach this situation are The Ravens: The Men Who Flew in America's Secret War in Laos, by Christopher Robbins (1987), and The Green Beret at War by Shelby L. Stanton (1985).

As I mentioned elsewhere in this book, certain POWs were returned, maybe even purchased from Hanoi, and placed by our government in some South Seas islands or brought to the U.S. under a witness protection-like program and given new identities. I understand that in a number of cases, the POW returnees were CIA Black Ops spies. You'll never find their names listed anywhere. They seem to have been given new identities and sent to other parts of the world to continue spying for the CIA.[45]

When I read things like this, I can't help but wonder about Jim. His disappearance and his records are so messed up, I wouldn't be at all surprised if he could be in just such a situation. My, what my imagination does to me when I'm left without the facts--when I'm left without the truth.

I watched a JAG television show on March 8, 2002,[46] that featured Black Ops. I learned from the program that these special ops were 100% volunteer. Their missions are classified "even to other members of the military."

If true, that answers a lot of questions I've had about how come the right hand of the military and the bureaucracies don't know what the left hand is doing. I still think they won't talk even if they do know the answers to so many of the questions the POW/MIA families have had through the years.

As the saying goes, there has to be a need-to-know. And of course, the families don't need to know. Right?

Chapter Fifteen

Under The Blanket

"It is our duty to remember."[1]

I mentioned my suspicions about the CIA at the beginning of my chapter on the Reagan years. What did the CIA have to do with the Vietnam War, I asked myself as I became aware that there might be a connection between this clandestine government organization and the Special Forces (Green Berets) of which Jim was a member.

Of course I always understood that the CIA handled government affairs overseas and that the FBI handled our government's internal affairs. But, I had no idea that the CIA had been involved, since its inception, in covert operations in other country's civil wars, or in the prevention of civil wars. Strange how I never read about that in any of our newspapers, or heard about it on the 10 o'clock news.

Even though I understood that Jim, as a Green Beret, would be involved in secret operations for the Army in Vietnam, I didn't know that those operations were securely tied to the CIA and its plans to secretly direct the Vietnam War.

After months and months of investigation, I discovered a lot about the CIA. Some of what I know, I present here as a way to explain many of the curious conclusions I have come to through these past 36 years.

In 1946, President Harry Truman signed the CIA into being with an executive order. The CIA followed in the footsteps of the OSS (Office of Strategic Services), which President Truman dissolved six weeks after Hiroshima. Rear Admiral Sidney Souers was the first director of the CIA. The day after President Truman ordered the creation of the CIA, he had a private ceremony where he presented a black cloak and a small black dagger to Rear Admiral Souers, and knighted him as "director of centralized snooping" and "chief of the Gestapo."[2] A joke?

For each administration after that, the CIA's power came from the President. "It was his secret army."[3] And Congress remained ignorant of what turned into cold war activities by the CIA.

Secretary of State Dean Rusk, under both President Kennedy and President Johnson, said he knew nothing of the CIA operations. Neither did the members of the National Security Council, the group responsible by law for approved covert operations. Even during President Nixon's term, the NSC knew of but one out of every seven covert actions taken by the CIA. In the 1960s, there was no constitutional control of the CIA's work.

Even though President Truman created the CIA, ten years after he left office he said that they had become a danger to democracy. "Those fellows in the CIA don't just report on wars and the like, they go out and make up their own, and there's nobody to keep track of what they're up to. . . It's become a government all of its own and all secret. They don't have to account to anybody."[4]

During President Reagan's term in office, William Casey was Chief of the CIA. In order to make his organization as powerful as he could and protect his power, he had to keep Congress "at bay."[5] The huge arms pipeline to Afghanistan in the 1980s became a great success for the CIA. "But it left a legacy of corruption, betrayal and murder."[6]

During this time, the United States Army became a partner with the CIA. The partnership was subversive. Lying became the order of the day. Arrogance grew as a result and so did deceit.[7] Was that the proper way an army should be conducted in a democracy? I don't think so.

At the entrance of the former CIA headquarters in Langley, Virginia, was the quote, "Ye shall know the Truth, and the Truth shall make you free." How could the spirit of this biblical saying become so distorted and ignored?

It seems that William Casey "tampered with intelligence reports and slanted them to suit White House thinking."[8] Also, it seems that the CIA began its own clandestine war in Vietnam six years before the United States got involved in a war with Hanoi.[9] Laos became a small CIA kingdom in the late 1950s. Lt. Col. Al Shinkle, U.S. Air Force, spent nine years as a professional intelligence officer. He testified, before the House Subcommittee on Asian and Pacific Affairs, in 1978 that "The CIA does not understand military intelligence in time of combat. Every war the CIA had a finger in, from Bay of Pigs to Laos, they lost. . . we can't be all under one cap called CIA."[10]

As a part of their Vietnam operations, the CIA created the ARVN (Army of the Republic of Vietnam) Special Forces troops, an elite unit of commando operations against guerrillas, and they trained the Montagnards from the Central Highlands of Vietnam, who worked with the Army's Special Forces.

The CIA had a radio station called Foreign Broadcasting Information Service, and an airline they called Air America. The original airline was called CAT but when the CIA bought it in 1950, they renamed it. "Air America flew supplies, food and personnel to anti-communist troops in Southeast Asia, including the CIA's 'secret war' in Laos." During the fall of Saigon, Air America helicopters evacuated Americans and South Vietnamese.[11]

The CIA developed a special program called Phoenix, to capture or kill the Vietcong, and they established Counter Terror Teams, the CIA's assassination squads.[12]

Was the Vietnam war a military engagement, or was the Vietnam War a CIA covert engagement with the military as pawns? I wonder!

NOTE: The commander of the Special Forces was never a General even though he controlled the equivalent of two infantry divisions at the peak of the war (from mid-1967 to mid-1968), or 42,000 local mercenaries, and 2,650 American officers and other enlisted specialists.[13]

The money to run the CIA during the Vietnam War came from the black budget, a secret treasury used by the President, Secretary of Defense and the Director of the CIA.[14] The black budget was created to hide their secret wars. "Most of the money to run the CIA always has been hidden in the Pentagon's ledgers."[15] Black seems to be a common word used in connection with the CIA, e.g. Special Forces black ops (operations).

A lawsuit was filed against the CIA in 1998. The Presidents Bush, Clinton and Bush have failed to declassify and release all the documents, which are still denied to the public. President Clinton announced on Veteran's Day in 1993 that the declassification had been completed.[16] It wasn't. In fact, the DOD, CIA and the State Department didn't even notify their organizations to look for all the documents, so those departments only declassified what they had on hand.[17] One reason was that President Clinton did not issue an Executive Order. The National Security Council issued a presidential decision directive instead.

Why are these documents of such importance? The CIA says these POW/MIA documents still involve national security issues. Five hundred and seventy-four records are being held for this reason.

In 2000, the Senate 2001 Defense Authorization Bill S.2549 was passed. This bill allows the DIA to keep covert operation files classified for at least another ten years. That means the DIA will be the only "person" to decide which are covert operation files.

My guess is that all of the information about covert POW/MIA operations will be withheld forever.

This is a blow to all POW/MIA families. Most of this information that affects these families should have been released under the Freedom of Information Act.

After forty years, the CIA still holds the reins on information about what happened to many of our Vietnam War POW/MIAs. Why? Will we ever know?

"The CIA's way is silence," Jeff Stein writes in A Murder in Wartime.[18] A story is told, in Kiss The Boys Goodbye, about Theodore Shackley, the guy in charge of the CIA's secret war in Laos.[19] It seems that Shackley was in line to become director of the CIA. However, when Captain Red McDaniel, U.S. Navy Retired, questioned Shackley right after he retired, Red was disturbed by Shackley's responses. Red happens to have been "one of the most tortured Americans in the history of war--and had never broken." Shackley said to Red, "Aren't you afraid to see me?" Puzzled, Red asked Shackley his view on the men captured in Laos during his secret war. "Shackley denied knowing anything about POWs and refused to talk about the war he'd run in Laos."[20] I don't remember Shackley ever getting the job of CIA Director.

In 1989, Monika Jensen-Stevenson received the following statement in a note from the U. S. Congressional Committee in Washington D.C. "The following information is being handwritten because we are no longer using our computers for this investigation, for security reasons."[21]

Everything is always so secret when it comes to the Vietnam War that it's a wonder the powers-that-be don't bump into themselves coming and going while hiding their information.

In Kiss The Boys Goodbye, Monika Jensen-Stevenson quotes Lt. Col. Al Shinkle, U.S. Air Force as saying, ". . .The CIA does not understand military intelligence in time of combat. As an American citizen, I feel if my country's going to stay strong. . . we can't be all under one cap called CIA--They do not understand."[22]

According to Tim Weiner, in Blank Check - The Pentagon's Black Budget, "The Secrecy and power they (CIA) possessed was a heady brew. It was also a recipe for moral rot."[23]

Chapter Sixteen

Hanging Out To Dry

"If any question why we died, tell them, because our fathers lied."
Rudyard Kipling

There is a secret our government has kept all of these years that is diabolical and a disgrace. The secret is called the POW/MIA Returnee Program.

These men were given new identities similar to the FBI's witness protection program.[1] I understand that some of the returnees were CIA Black Ops spies, and none of their names will ever appear on any published list. They are simply sent to other parts of the world to do spy work under yet another identity.

Some of the families of these men were told that their loved ones were in this program and they could expect to never see them again. At least they were alive. But those family members were also threatened if they ever spoke about this publicly. The other families were told nothing, so they live in limbo, as I do.[2]

Could Jim have been one of those Black Ops whose identity was changed? Was I one of those wives who was not told, or was my imagination running away with me? Whether or not Jim's been part of this program, there has been ample evidence--both circumstancial and real--that a sizable number of POW/MIAs have been returned to this country through this unorthodox program.

When CIA agent Russell Leard was called to testify before the Senate Select Committee on POW/MIAs, he denied everything about the Secret Returnee Program. He also contradicted himself several times, I've been told.

It makes me shake my head in wonderment. Or should I be more truthful, and say that it makes me disgusted and ashamed that our government has been involved in these kinds of secret programs.

Among other things, this program is a violation of these men's civil rights as citizens of the United States.

Brigadier General Thomas E. Lacy, USAF (ret.), testified before the Senate Select Committee Hearings on POW/MIA Affairs, April 2, 1992, on the secret returnee program. He talked about some MIAs who were brought back to this country and channeled through the Veteran's Administration.

With his experience of being involved in the POW issue while in Vietnam, he was able to make this statement in his sworn testimony.

"There was 591 returned in Operation Homecoming. In my experience, in my estimate, based on general things going on, I would say there was 10 to 1 that was left, versus coming back. So in the vicinity of 5,000 to 6,000, maybe more, that was left in Vietnam after the Paris Peace Accords and Operation Homecoming."

Brigadier General Lacy, with the approval of President Reagan, returned to Laos in 1984 to follow up on leads he had of where there might be more POWs. He found a barbed wire enclosed camp with bamboo cages, leg irons, foot manacles, and guard towers, but it was empty.

On his trip to Hanoi, January 1989, the General had an audience with Le Duc Tho to ask if there were any live American POWs. Le Duc Tho's answer was no.

Brigadier General Lacy then said, "If I could show you where some POWs are, would you free them."

"Yes," was Le Duc Tho's answer.

Later, the General went to two prison camp locations. At the second one, northwest of Hanoi, he found Col. Dean Andrew Pogreba, USAF, and three of the five Special Forces men alive who'd been sent to get Col. Pogreba out some six weeks after he'd been shot down in 1965.

The General had known of the U.S. involvement in dropping food and supplies to those men for at least two years while the men tried to make their way to the American lines.[3]

In reading this part of his testimony, never once did the Senate Select Committee members ask why those men were not brought out.

Another person mentioned in the General's testimony, was Major Tommy Gist, USAF, missing since May 18, 1968. Their paths crossed in the summer of 1989 when both were patients at the Veterans Hospital in Oklahoma City. Major Gist was still on the MIA list at that time, which the General knew. Although the General told Major Gist's wife, Sara, about this, she was unable to locate her missing husband. It would appear that the Major is one of the many men the government has placed in the Secret Returnee Program.[4]

Contrast this with the following quote from The Retired Officer Magazine February 1998 article, "The Journey Home."

"Retired Air Force Col. Ronald Bliss remembers the day of his release and a final opportunity to send a signal of defiance to his former captors. 'We had not marched in over six or seven years, but we marched and they came unglued. They wanted us to come out with our heads down, but we came out with our heads up. We looked pretty damn good.'"[5]

These men were lucky. Their government allowed them to live as they had before, when they were brought home from Vietnam.

"His brain has not only been washed, but dry cleaned."
Manchurian Candidate[6]

In this country, where we are led to believe that our government is good, that our government would never hide anything from us, that our government's relations with other countries are always honorable, therein lies an undercurrent of doubt. In some circles, doubt has been growing since the Vietnam War. Albeit slow, too many questions have arisen in the past forty years for us to ignore the possibility that, at times, our government has not been lily white when it came to handling such things as POW/MIAs from the World War II, Korean, Vietnam, and Persian Gulf wars. Nor has the government, under nine presidents, been truthful and forthright in providing information to POW/MIA families--information that they deserved to know, and had the right to know.

Deeply involved in this matter of deception is the CIA, an organization that should be concerned with the protection of this country from evil forces in the world. But what do their covert operations really include? There is evidence that the CIA has been involved in operations that have been detrimental to the men in our armed forces and their families. How could this be possible? Let's take a look.

"The CIA is in business of manipulating the belief systems of entire nations. I doubt that they're above working in their own backyard if it suits them. The most important thing about secret programs is that they prevent not only the bad guys but also the good guys from finding out what's going on. This system gives the holder of the secrets enormous power."[7]

This secret program is a disgrace. Families are lied to time and time again. Military-intelligence officials threaten many. How can we know if our POWs are still in Vietnam, hoping to be found and returned before they are too old and gray, or Vietnam becomes their deathbed? How can we truly ever know if our MIAs are not missing or not dead at all, but were brainwashed and retrained, and living somewhere in the world under a new identity, maybe nearby?

"The notion of the United States running a secret program for the return of POWs from Vietnam and paying what amounts to and is ransom money for these men, is hard to believe. The whole idea of running it secretly simply to avoid the atmosphere of another Iran hostage situation makes the concept even harder to accept. To think that the White House could be successfully blackmailed by the Vietnamese makes this concept completely ludicrous. First of all, why do this secretly? Secondly, is the government capable of keeping something this big secret. And last, how do you keep returned American POWs living in the United States from seeking loved ones and talking to the media?[8]

"Some families believe their loved ones are dead because they have no information to the contrary. Still others who are declared dead have headstones above empty graves in a military cemetery somewhere. There is no proof of life or death in either case.

"You keep it secret by running it from the top of the White House, as was done during the Iran Contra operation. You keep the returned POWs silent by instructing them that if they don't keep quiet, the other POWs waiting to come back won't get their chance and may die in captivity. You remind the stay behinds, deserters and collaborators who are returned as well, that they can be tried and imprisoned as traitors if they talk. You neutralize leaks to the media by flooding Beltway journalists with qualified spokespeople skillfully armed with counter-propaganda. But most of all, you debunk and discredit anyone who comes close to telling the truth about what would have to be perceived as America's largest conspiracy and cover-up operation in history."[9]

> "Oh, what tangled webs we weave when first we practice to deceive."[10]
>
> Sir Walter Scott

MKULTRA is the code name for the CIA mind control program. It is one of the "most disturbing instances of intelligence community abuse on record", according to Jon Elliston of ParaScope, Inc. The program was authorized by CIA Director Allen Dulles in April 1953 upon becoming concerned about rumors of communist brainwashing of POWs during the Korean War. However, through the years, the MKULTRA program became notorious for conducting inhumane tests, financed by the CIA.[11]

One CIA auditor wrote five years later, "Precautions must be taken not only to protect operations from exposure to enemy forces but also to conceal these activities from the American public in general. The knowledge that the agency is engaging in unethical and illicit activities would have serious repercussions in political and diplomatic circles."[12]

The program not only included LSD experiments on people, but other kinds of experiments relating to mind control (parapsychological phenomena): hypnosis, photokinesis, precognition, telepathy, and remote viewing.[13] The studies weren't just for scientific purposes. The CIA spent millions of dollars on dozens of methods to influence and control the mind. Some of their objectives were to "render the indication of hypnosis easier or otherwise enhance its usefulness" and "produce amnesia for events preceding and during their (mind-altering substances) use."[14]

Coincidentally, the movie, Manchurian Candidate, starring Frank Sinatra, Janet Leigh, Laurence Harvey and Angela Lansbury, dealt with the brainwashing of Korean POWs. The soldiers were convinced by mind control methods described above, to participate in a shocking communist plot. Similarities between the film and the Kennedy assassinations kept this 1962 film out of distribution for over twenty years. Why? What was so secretive about mind control operations that the government/CIA did not want the public to know about it, even if the information was just a movie?

What man would allow himself to be brainwashed to the point that he no longer knows his true identity--can't remember his name, his parents, his wife, his children? What could possibly cause a person to become embroiled in such a scheme? And why?

Let me be blunt. Could James Birchim be one of those CIA Black Ops? Could he be spying for the CIA at this moment, with no recollection of his former life?

Could he be like that character portrayed in the 2002 movie, The Bourne Identity, starring Matt Damon? The story revolved around our government's experimental mind control program that created rogue warriors to be used against the enemy. The warriors, whose pasts were erased from their memories, were trained to carry out missions without questioning purpose, danger or outcome. How ironic it is that the story, The Bourne Identity, published years ago as a novel, is so fitting today.

* * *

No one has ever found Jim's body. And we have a marble memorial headstone with no casket at the Presidio at San Francisco that says:

In Memory of
James Douglas Birchim
California
Captain
5th SP Forces Group
Vietnam
July 16 1946
May 10 1971
DSC PH
MIA

After all, Jim was in the Special Forces and what better man to snatch out of the jungle when he was lost off a helicopter (we're told), than a Green Beret who had extensive training for espionage and clandestine operations, plus other drastic measures war demanded (legal or illegal) that he had been taught. Denial by our government that our Army's Special Forces ever operated in Laos or Cambodia, is a prime example of how many Green Berets were caught in what international law deemed illegal.

How better can I end this chapter than to quote Admiral James B. Stockdale, USN (Ret.), Medal of Honor recipient and senior naval officer in a North Vietnam POW camp.

"One's integrity can give a person something to rely on when perspective seems to blur, when rules and principles seem to waver, and when faced with a hard choice of right and wrong. A clear conscious is one's only protection."

Letters from Jim

What would be better to introduce my pictures of Jim than to include some excerpts of his letters to me from Vietnam in 1968.

Besides mentioning the men he was working with and what he was doing, Jim would often tell me about the countryside near where he was stationed. For example, in his 27 September letter, he wrote, "I am finally back in Kontum. This place is so much better than Danang; actually it's in the 'mountain' in a manner of speaking and there's always a good smell in the air. The temperature is mild, where that of Danang is hot or raining."

In that letter he continued by writing, "Came from Danang--went north to Hue--then down to Kontum on a C130. Traveled on a "BLACK BIRD"--A CIA airplane, as we always do going from one place to another via air. Black Bird is a black painted plane camouflaged brown (dark) with no markings. . . I got orders for my Combat Infantryman Badge for the ambush. . . I wish you could see Kontum and the Montagnard people. Both are very fine."

On 30 September, Jim wrote about how he "was punishing those AWOL soldiers that didn't make it back for Sunday formation. . . "This morning ran with my Montagnard platoon. . . Put sandbag in rucksack and took off. Did many pushups."

Even though Jim's life was 100% wrapped up in the war, he did have time to write me about finding a "beautiful cerambycid beetle" he had found "on the ground outside our building this morning."

He added, "There's much to do this afternoon. We'll clear weeds in our wire. The grass is so high in the barbed wire that it's hard to see the wire. This area is beautiful. I guess that it's the Central Highlands. The villages are small; Kontum is about the size of Bishop or Fallon. Of course, that's where the similarity stops."

"Well, things here are uneventful. Right now our reconnaissance team is on standby for Bright Light," he wrote on 20 October. That means that if a team is on a target, gets into trouble, or someone is killed, we move . . . I've been initiated now to C&C. I was on a real honest-to-goodness classified recon mission. Wow! Someday I'll tell you about it. I'm in fairly good shape right now. I'll send photos when I get a chance. . . About the Montagnard people, the more I work with them the more I love them. They are good people. I can't say the same for Vietnamese."

Later in the letter he said, "On the operation I humped the hills. Hell, you wouldn't believe the slope of those hills--45 degrees at least. And we were moving, girl. The damnedest terrain in the world. As well as the slope. It was

261

wet clay and the vines and bamboo was so thick that it wasn't possible to move more than 1 or 1 ½ kilometers in a morning. In addition, the mosquitoes were so thick, I still can't believe it. When we stopped, especially (overnight) in bamboo, I had a cloud of mosquitoes and always leeches.

"NVA soldiers passed within 30-50 feet of our positions. We saw app. 130 NVA soldiers, but they didn't see us until the last day; even then we were extremely lucky.

"It was very interesting.

"Sometimes I think maybe I'll stay in the Army. But I know I shouldn't. I'm gradually losing my mind. Nothing really worries me now, so far. Of course, I haven't been in a real tight situation yet."

Jim's letters continued to come from Kontum. On 4 October he remarked about the scenery again. "In the evening, when the sun sets, the whole plateau is at rest and from our camp I can look out and see green forest, meadows and a high mountain range. It is truly beautiful."

One of the most detailed letters I got from Jim was dated 24 October.

"Well, today I went to Dak To, the launch site for our recon missions in areas Prairie Fire and Daniel Boone. Since our team went off Bright Light standby today, they were allowed to go on a pass. Consequently, I was able to go to Dak To. Actually, I went to Dak To with a team going on a mission to a Prairie Fire target, which is a hot target area.

"Two teams were launched--one into H9, and the other, S3. I went with the team going to S3. It turned out that the team on choppers into H9 was shot out of both LZ's, so only S3 was successfully launched. H9 is one of the most notorious of our target areas. Teams never stay down there for any length of time. Just too many NVA soldiers down there.

"I went to S3 for the ride (not on the mission) actually because I wanted some photos of an operation and a good friend, SSG Joe Walker, was the team leader and his team, RT California, was the one I was on when we hit E-50, a Daniel Boone target.

"Nothing really happened on the ride, but I would like to tell you how the whole operation is conducted. I'm duty officer (tonight) and rather than do nothing, I'll explain the procedure to you because you may be interested. If you're not, no sweat.

"First, the recon team leader, or one-zero, goes to operations--S3, and receives the mission. That is to say, he goes to S3 and reads the message that came down from CCN, Danang, which states the mission--what is to be accomplished. Perhaps the mission will be road reconnaissance and prisoner snatch. OK. He then reads the 'target folder,' after action reports of other teams that have reconned the area in the past.

"Next after insuring that he knows exactly what must be done on the ground, the one-zero goes to the Prairie Fire or Daniel Boone Launch office, which ever applies to his particular target area, and receives a briefing about launch procedures, times and special instructions. He picks up his map there and Signal Operation Instructions, frequencies, call signs, code words.

"He goes next to the key members of his team--which usually consists of two or three Americans and 8-10 indigenous personnel.

"The next step is to get rations from S4 for app. 5-8 days and gather all indigenous team member's rucksacks and pack the meals in them--and then not let them out of sight because, like children, the Montagnards or Vietnamese or Chinese members of the RT will eat the food out of their sacks. When I say indigenous, I mean people native to the country. Of course, along with the chow in the rucksacks must be much equipment, also, and the one-zero will inspect the equipment to make sure that it's all there and serviceable.

"Then, if time permits, there should be a little training on immediate action drills for ambush.

"The team is lifted, at the appropriate time, by Huey chopper into Dak To, or to the target area.

"Now, choppers aren't like any other type of aircraft. They're cold and windy and always seem like they will rattle to pieces. But a chopper ride is interesting because you can look out and see the beautiful rolling hills of Vietnam's Central Highlands. Often, the ride will take you over some Montagnard villages. . .easily distinguished from Vietnamese villages because of two things. 1 – they're isolated location in the hills, not on the lowlands, 2 – their buildings all have a bachelor building like the one I just drew.

"Well, anyway, two choppers, maybe one will carry the team and there will be two escort ships. In addition, there will be Cobras. Cobras are built for one thing-- terrific firepower. There is no room for any more than the pilot and co-pilot.

"When the LZ--landing zone--for the choppers is reached, if there is no excessive ground fire, the team bugs off, moves out of the birds and rapidly off then into the relative security of the forest. If there is excessive firepower from the ground, they say the choppers were "shot off the LZ" and the team goes to a second LZ.

"As soon as the team gets to the ground, moves into the forest and sets up security, radio contact is made and from then on, regular radius contacts are made at scheduled intervals during the day, for every day the team is on the ground. The radio is one of the most important pieces of equipment a team carries, needless to say.

"When the team makes contact with an enemy force, contact must be broken immediately, or, due to the small size of the patrol, it will be in danger. The team can break contact by fire or by humping it, or both.

"Finally, after accomplishing the mission, or because of serious injury to several team members, the team will return.

"Well, that's the breakdown on a C&C Long Range Recon Patrol"

The last letter I received from Jim was dated 5 November, Nha Trang.

"Well, I guess that our next President is now elected--as yet we don't know who it is. I voted for H.H. Humphrey. Maybe he has the courage and leadership to be able to make some bold decisions. We haven't had many leaders in our government. The Kennedys are an exception. I don't think that H.H. Humphrey will be much different than Johnson, though, but we'll see tonight. Maybe Nixon will be elected and end the war. . . It (the war) doesn't make much sense."

You were right, Jim. You were so, so right!

Barbara & Jim Birchim
1965

LT Chavez & LT Birchim
Recondo School
Nha Trang, RVN - July 1968

Two Very Good Friends
Ksor-Mathquay & Nay-Phin

Jim's Friend, Nay-Phin, & Unknown Interpreter

CPT James Douglas Birchim
U.S. Army 5th Special Forces Group
Missing since 15 November 1968
Last seen in the general area of Attopeu, Laos
Height: 167 cm. - Weight: 74 kg.
Hair Line: Parted on right side with receding
hair line
Hair Color: Light Brown
Skin Color: White
Eye Color: Blue
Shape of Face: Oval with a prominent chin
Nose: Pinched
Shoulders: Straight
Show Size: 7

ร.อ. เจมส์ เบอร์ชิม

สังกัดหน่วยรบพิเศษ   สหรัฐอเมริก

หายไปในสงครามเวียดนาม ตั้งแต่ 15 พย. 2511 พบครั้งสุดท้าย
ในพื้นที่เมือง อัตตะปือ   สปปล.

• สูง 167 ซม   • น้ำหนัก 74 กก.
• แสกผมด้านขวา   ศรีษะ ด้านง่ามก่อ • ผมสีน้ำตาล
• ผิวขาว   • ตาสีฟ้า • ใบหน้ารูปไข่ ตาเป็นร่องกลางเลตม
• จมูกโด่ง   • ไหล่ตรง • สวมรองเท้า เบอร์ 2

267

Have you seen this man? He is 5 feet 6 inches tall and probably weighs about 130 pounds. His name is James Birchim and his family thinks he may be in the Dak To – Dak Sut – Kontum area. We haven't heard anything about him since 1968. Please help us find him. If you have any information, please write to:

I.G.W.P., P.O. Box 27343, San Diego, CA 92128 U.S.A. Thank you.

BẠN ĐÃ GẶP NGƯỜI NÀY CHƯA? CAO 1.6, NẶNG 55 KÝ, TÊN LÀ JAMES BIRCHIM, MẤT TÍCH TẠI VÙNG DAKTO – DAKSUT, TỈNH KONTUM, MẤT LIÊN LẠC TỪ NĂM 1968. NẾU BIẾT TIN, XIN BẠN VUI LÒNG LIÊN LẠC VỀ: ĐA TẠ

TÌM THÂN-NHÂN

CPT James D. Birchim
U.S. Army Special Forces
M.I.A. 15 November 1968

Acknowledging your thirty years
of continuing service and your heroism
and act of bravery which won you
the Distinguished Service Cross and Purple Heart

You answered the call,
You followed the orders,
And you continue to hold your post,
And you wait.

And we wait.
On another side of the world.
We hope you hear our prayers.
You will never be forgotten
By your family.

Unidentified Son Tay Raiders

Photo taken off TV screen.
Picture of Jim Birchim?
(back left)

BALLAD OF THE GREEN BERETS

Fighting soldiers from the sky
Fearless men who jump and die
Men who mean just what they say
The brave men of the Green Beret

CHORUS:
Silver wings upon their chest
These are men, America's best
One hundred men will test today
But only three win the Green Beret

Trained to live off nature's land
Trained in combat, hand-to-hand
Men who fight by night and day
Courage peak from the Green Berets

CHORUS:
Back home a young wife waits
Her Green Beret has met his fate
He has died for those oppressed
Leaving her his last request

"Put silver wings on my son's chest
Make him one of America's best
He'll be a man they'll test one day
Have him win the Green Beret."

Words and Music by Sgt. Barry Sadler and Robin Moore
(#21 song of 1960-1969 rock era, #1 for 5 weeks in 1966)

PART VII

Facts and Nothing But Facts

Chapter Seventeen

Families United

"Your perseverance toward achieving the fullest
possible accounting has been a beacon for all."[1]

Officially known as the National League of Families of American Prisoners
and Missing in Southeast Asia, this quasi-governmental advocacy group has
been in business since 1969. At the beginning, it was a "family support" group
that was started by a POW wife in California with an informal newsletter. It
was incorporated in Washington D.C in 1970, and is a "major, if sotto voce,
player in the government game."[2]

This 4,000-member organization is commonly referred to as The League.
The League's sole purpose or goals include the release of all prisoners, the
fullest possible accounting of the missing (discovery and identification of
all remains possible), and the repatriation of the remains of those who died
serving our nation in Southeast Asia.

The League is financed by contributions from family members, concerned
citizens, and veterans groups. It is also eligible for United Way/Combined
Federal Campaign funds.

The Bylaws state: voting members must be those who are "any wife,
parent, child, sibling, grandparent, grandchild, aunt, uncle, niece, nephew,
returned American Prisoner of War from Southeast Asia, and spouses of all
those (just mentioned), of any American who is now or has been listed as
captured, or missing or otherwise unaccounted for from the Vietnam War."

One of the first activities of the The League occured when POW/MIA
family members flooded the North Vietnamese delegation in Paris with
inquiries about the American prisoners and missing men.

The League has accomplished many things through the years. In the late
1970s, The League, along with Congress, put pressure on the DIA office to
process "live sighting" reports.[3]

There has been compelling evidence, documented by The League, that
many "crash sites and known battlefield graves" have been excavated and the
remains stored with either the "Vietnam government or in private hands."[4]

Bohica, a book written by Scott Barnes, was published in 1987. It is "A
True Account Of One Man's Battle To Expose The Most Heinous Cover-Up
Of The Vietnam Saga!" or so the cover says. I mention the book here, because

The League took an active part in investigating Barnes' allegations, and as a result, printed a Research Paper in 1988 entitled, "Bohica: The Facts Behind the Fantasies of the Author, Scott Barnes."[5]

Barnes says he was a former Green Beret, a Drug Enforcement agent, a CIA agent, and a military intelligence agent (secret agent) for our government. The inside book jacket states that he was "asked by the Intelligence Support Activity, a top-secret U.S. Government organization, to participate in a mission to investigate reports of live American prisoners of war in Laos."[6]

Several members of our government called him a liar, in so many words, despite his "testimony before a Senate committee and federal courts, psychological evaluations, repeated polygraph tests, and a near fatal dose of truth serum."[7]

Why? Because he claims he found overwhelming evidence of "Caucasian prisoners speaking American dialogue in Laos." He claims he was ordered to "liquidate the merchandise."[8] Barnes was determined to tell the truth about Operation Grand Eagle through his book Bohica and every other means he could find.

However, The League determined, through their investigation of his allegations, that Barnes was making "serious charges of conspiracy and cover up by the Reagan Administration (implicating) prominent officials and individuals in the private sector. Despite five official investigations into such charges, all of which concluded there was no basis, claims of conspiracy and cover up continue to surface periodically, potentially jeopardizing the POW/MIA issue and ongoing responsible progress."[9]

After all these years, since Bohica was published, there is still controversy about Scott Barnes and the truth. Could he be telling the truth about a cover up by our government? I leave that up to you to answer.

As the years rolled by, The League took more stances on POW/MIA issues. For example, The League made known that Hanoi had identified only two of more than twenty sets of remains recovered between January and August 1993 as Americans. In 1992, only six sets of remains were identified as Americans.[10]

Even though President Reagan declared the POW/MIA issue to be "the highest national priority," that did not mean that members of the bureaucracy would follow the proclamation. The League found itself in the middle of a concerted effort by the National Security Council to ignore the issue in 1980. The NSC sent a memo to Zbigniew Brzezinski during President Carter's administration, stating, "Once again the National League of Families seeks to meet you. They have nothing new to say. So I recommend turning down this request. However, a letter from you is important to indicate that you take recent refugee reports of sightings of live Americans 'seriously.' This is simply good politics: DIA and State are playing this game, and you should not be the whistle blower. The idea is to say that the President is determined to pursue any lead concerning possible live MIAs."[11]

There it is. In writing.

The whole thing is a matter of politics. Why am I surprised?

In 1993, The League made an announcement that "As long as Vietnam continues to benefit financially and politically from field investigations, Hanoi has little motivation to unilaterally repatriate (POW/MIA) remains now being held."

When Reagan took office, The League "helped bring the prisoner of war issue back to a central position in U.S. foreign policy toward Southeast Asia."[12]

From the May 4, 1999, League newsletter, comes the following statement. "The League is again sending a delegation to Vietnam, Laos and Cambodia . . . in an effort to reinforce the families' views on the status of efforts to account for America's POW/MIAs."

During The League's annual meeting, June 1999, in Washington D.C., they presented a paper titled, "Vietnam's Ability to Account for Missing Americans." In there, the following was stated.[13]

"One way of viewing what the U.S. knows and what Vietnam can do is by looking at what Vietnam has not, but could have done. At the end of the war, U.S. intelligence and other data confirm that over 200 unaccounted for Americans were last known alive or reported alive and in close proximity to capture. . . In over 100 of these cases, joint field investigations have reportedly been sufficient to confirm death. If true, remains of these Americans logically should be the most readily available for return since they were in captivity or on the ground in direct proximity to Vietnamese forces. Yet, Vietnam has accounted for very few of these Americans."

In addition, the 1999 report stated, "After two years of no results from the Vietnamese in 1979-80, during a September 1982 ABC 'Nightline' program, the late Vietnamese Foreign Minister Nguyen Co Thach flatly denied that Vietnam was holding any U.S. remains. . . Yet, in 1983, Vietnam returned eight remains with clear evidence of storage. Negotiations for a two-year plan in 1985 brought the largest number of remains obtained to that point; nearly all showed evidence of storage. In 1987, negotiations resulted in the largest number of remains returned during one year--over 60 in 1988--approximately half of which were returned at one time. Nearly all were virtually complete skeletons that showed clear evidence of storage. . ."

After the delegation of League members visited Thailand, Vietnam, Laos, and Cambodia in early May 1999, a report of their trip was presented at the annual meeting in June. Their comments on Cambodia included the fact that

74 Americans were still missing and unaccounted for in that country. They found the Cambodian officials cooperative and anxious to assist in every way with U.S. requests. Mr. Chey Saphon, Royal Cambodian Government historian, said he was more than willing to help with the task of locating records and information. He recognized the difficulty ahead because of the passage of time. One League delegate commented, "Each time an old man dies, a library burns."

One of the results of this meeting was that The League representatives felt there was no longer a reason that U.S. personnel shouldn't visit Cambodia whenever they needed POW/MIA information.

With a watchful eye, The League will closely monitor Lao-U.S. discussions on this issue. As for Vietnam, the Socialist Republic of Vietnam said they would continue to urge Vietnam citizens "to turn over American service member's remains."

In October 2000, 1,993 Americans were still missing and unaccounted for from the Vietnam War. By February 2001, the number was reduced to 1,987 Americans still missing, prisoner or otherwise unaccounted for in Southeast Asia.

According to a League newsletter dated February 8, 2000, one of the most often asked questions is "Why should the U.S. government still expend assets and resources to locate Vietnam War POWs and account for MIAs?" Their answer was, among other comments, "The principle involved is fundamental; it is the right thing to do! Would anyone be willing to volunteer for service in the Military unless certain that if captured or missing, your country would do its very best to return you--alive or dead--to your family and your nation, regardless of the outcome of the war? The answer is that our service personnel must have such confidence. That is a major reason why the National League of POW/MIA Families has such strong support from the military community, both active duty and retired."

The U.S. National Security Council met with a member of the Vietnamese Politburo in 1985 to discuss in private the plan for returning live prisoners and remains. "But the minister indicated that live prisoners were not on the table for discussion. Rather, as discussed through the third party, the subject was hundreds of remains."[14]

In a letter that Ann Mills Griffiths, Executive Director of The League, wrote to me in 2000, she said, "We are determined to continue our fight for implementation of U.S. Government commitments and those made by the governments of Vietnam, Laos and Cambodia to the League and U.S. officials."

Ann Mills Griffiths received a letter from candidate George W. Bush in June 2000, in which he stated his position on the POW/MIA issue. "On the campaign trail, I have spoken with veterans and their families, as well as with loved ones of missing servicemen and civilians. I understand the need for the fullest possible accounting of those who served in American military conflicts, and believe such an accounting must be a high priority for our nation. This is a duty we owe to those who served, a debt we owe their families, and a demonstration to those who serve now and in the future that they will not be abandoned."

It is unfortunate that so many people have criticized The League. In Colonel Milard A. Peck's memorandum of resignation as Chief of the Special Office for Prisoners of War and Missing in Action, he stated that the director of the League is "adamantly opposed to any initiative to actually get to the heart of . . . and interferes in or actively sabotages POW/MIA analyses or investigations. She insists on rewriting or editing all significant documents produced by the Office . . ."[15]

She has access to top secret, code word messages but it seems she is not cleared to read them. Colonel Peck writes that The League's director also receives DIA intelligence well ahead of the analysts. She "routinely impedes real progress and insidiously 'muddles up' the issue. One wonders who she really is and where she came from."[16]

In Colonel Peck's concluding statements, he says, "I am convinced that the Director of this organization is much more than meets the eye. As the principal actor in the grand show, she is in the perfect position to clamor for 'progress,' while really intentionally impeding the effort . . . otherwise it is inconceivable that so many bureaucrats in the 'system' would instantaneously do her bidding and humor her every whim."[17]

In December of 2000, I finally received an answer to the questions I posed at the 1998 League meeting to then head of JTF-FA, Brigadier General Tucker.

He was new to that position and said that he was going to be pushing the Vietnamese for all the information they had. I challenged him to go to Vietnam and ask the Vietnemese for the POW files that were on display in the Hanoi War Museum. I told him the Vietnam Veterans of America had been going to Vietnam for the past two years asking for these files without success. Each time they were given a "shuck and jive" story about why the Vietnamese couldn't find the key to unlock the case.

I said, "How could the Vietnamese stand before us and say with a straight face that they were forthright in giving all information regarding POWs to us when tourists could see the stack of files for themselves in the museum? How could the United States swallow the Vietnamese answer when we know that sitting right before us might be answers to many of the questions about our missing men. It seems to me that this would be an easy assignment for you since there's no question about the location of these files. No digging has to be done, no manpower is involved, no money needs to change hands, especially when the Vietnamese say they're being open and honest in turning over everything they have concerning our POW/MIAs."

Brigadier General Tucker responded by saying he wanted me to get with his Aide-de-Camp to give him the exact location of the files.

Knowing this was a stall tactic on the part of the government, I wasn't going to let this go.

I remained standing before the "august" panel and said, "The woman who saw these files is sitting in this room," and then I asked Sara to please stand up. As she stood, I asked Vernon Valenzuela from the Vietnam Veterans of America to stand. He had been on previous trips to Vietnam asking for the files.

I could tell Brigadier General Tucker and the panel members were becoming uncomfortable with my insistance. Now, he asked Sara and Vernon to get together with his Aide-de-Camp and me.

I thought getting this answer would be an easy way to show the Family members his determination to get a full accounting of our POW/MIAs. This didn't happen.

It wasn't until September 2000, while I was at SOAR (Special Operations Association Reunion), that I was able to query a representative from DPMO about what resulted from my challenge to the General. Three months later, I received a letter from Army Casualty stating they had received an answer to my query from DPMO. This is what the letter said:

". . . a U.S. official was at the museum in Hanoi when Mrs. Birchim's friend requested to see the blue vinyl folders inside the case. The display folders were samples of those the U.S. frequently passed to the Vietnamese during the 1970s and 1980s. The blue vinyl folders were used by the U.S. to display and highlight sample cases where we felt the Vietnemese should be able to provide information. Each folder contained a Joint Casualty Resolution Center, prepared case summary of the incident, in both in English and Vietnemese, as well as descriptive information on the individual. Also included was the photo of the missing man as well as a map depicting the loss location. Various folders were prepared and passed by presidential, congressional, League of Families and other delegations meeting with the Vietnamese in Hanoi and elsewhere. Over a period of almost two decades, hundreds and hundreds of these folders were passed to Vietnamese officials."

A representative from both DIA and DPMO was sitting next to Brigadier General Tucker when I posed my question in 1998. If the information in the letter I received in 2000 was true, then they could have responded to my challenge right there on the spot. So, I'm not buying it!

"There was no political will to act on the families complaints. This country didn't want to hear the word Vietnam. . .It was not the fashionable thing to do."[18]

Ann Mills Griffiths

Chapter Eighteen

A Cry For Help

"To the living we owe respect, but
to the dead we owe only the truth."
Voltaire

One of the greatest advocates for truth in the POW/MIA issue is Vietnam Veteran Senator Bob Smith, R-NH. He spent years trying to get to the bottom of the government's refusal to disclose secret/classified information about what happened to the American prisoners and the missing Americans in the Vietnam War.

The POW issue was personal for Senator Smith. His father became missing after a civilian crash in the U.S., which could be part of his reason for pursuing the POW/MIA scandal.

Senator Smith became involved with the issue in the House, and then in the Senate. He often worked alone as a legislator on this major interest of his. The news media did little to nothing in bringing attention to his attempts to solve the POW/MIA mess. He also had political problems, because many of those responsible for the hiding of information and the non-interest in resolving the POW/MIA situation were high ranking in his political party. Sometimes it seemed POW/MIA relatives and activists were about the only people interested in Senator Smith's crusade.

In 1991, Senator Smith proposed that the Senate create a Select Committee to investigate the issue. "Such a committee would respect no political sacred cows, employ a large staff and subpoena power to answer the most sensitive questions about the history of U.S. POWs from World War II to Vietnam."[1]

Nothing much happened with Senate Resolution 82, until the picture of the three missing men in Vietnam appeared in newspapers. The publicity brought about a renewed interest in the general public. The first hearings were set for November 1991.

It wasn't until September 10, 1992, when the DIA decided for the first time to check on the sources who had provided information about POWs in Hanoi. This was the direct result of Senator Smith's questioning on August 4, 1992, during the Senate Select Committee hearing.

In the Senator's opening statement, he presented reports about 14 Americans believed still alive in Vietnam. He was harsh in his criticism of the POW evidence that the DIA had dismissed in the past. He ended his remarks with "our staff investigators have informed me, after spending hundreds of hours reviewing the files, that nothing has changed in the last five years since these secret critical reports were written."[2]

A delegation of five members of the Senate Select Committee traveled to Hanoi for a three-day visit in 1992. Senators John F. Kerry, Bob Smith, Hank Brown, Charles Grassley and Charles Robb embarked on a fact-finding mission in which they hoped the meetings with Vietnamese officials would be more than ceremonial. They hoped to get some concessions, cooperation, and openness from the Vietnamese as to the POW/MIA issue. Unfortunate, but true to past U.S. experiences in negotiations, all they got were vague promises and the consistent reply that there were no American POWs either living freely in Vietnam, or held prisoner.[3]

Again in 1993, Senator Smith went to Vietnam, this time with Robert Garwood. As Vice Chairman of the Senate Select Committee on POW/MIA Affairs, the Senator wanted to verify Garwood's testimony during his debriefings by the DIA and his subsequent court martial for collaboration. Senator Smith had absolute faith in Garwood's statements.[4]

Upon his return, USA Today reported on 7/12/93 that ". . . after pressing for more cooperation in resolving 2,253 MIA cases from the Vietnam War, Smith said he became convinced some U.S. missing are still alive and accused the Pentagon of 'sloppy' investigative work."[5]

On the same day, the L.A. Times staff reporter in Bangkok, Thailand, Charles P. Wallace, wrote that Smith may have been the first to benefit from a new U.S. Vietnamese relationship "because he received unprecedented access to locations and people."

Further, the article quoted Smith as saying, "We're not doing the job right. . . either we don't have good intelligence capability or they're just doing a sloppy job. I think it's the latter. . . (sloppiness) is very pervasive."

He stated that, "'sensitive satellite imagery' as recently as 1992 indicated that Americans were still being held against their will in Vietnam, a charge that Vietnam vehemently denies and that foreign diplomats in Hanoi view as incredible."

On June 29, 1993, Senator Smith sent Attorney General Janet Reno a letter regarding three criminal violations that he had discovered. He asked her to refer his concerns to the Secretary of Defense and/or the Director of the Information Security Oversight Office for appropriate civil or administrative actions. The violations concerned the undermining of President Clinton's commitment to open all POW/MIA files and to pursue the accounting of MIAs. The following came directly from his letter to Janet Reno.

He charged that there were/was: (quote)

1.)   Several specific incidents of false testimony and statements made to United States Senators or received by the Senate Select Committee on POW/MIA Affairs during its investigation last year. (Cases on file in my office.)

2.)   A potential mail fraud and false personation violation in January, 1993 concerning my Senate office which was possibly committed by an active duty service member with the possible knowledge of and cooperation from the Defense Intelligence Agency POW/MIA Office.

3.)   Potential violations by certain personnel of The Department of State and the Department of Defense of provisions of Executive Order 12356 in relation to the classification of an archival document from the former Soviet Union officially turned over to the United States by Russia on April 8, 1993, and the handling of the disclosure of said document to Congress and the Socialist Republic of Vietnam on April 12, 1993.

I believe the above-mentioned potential federal and criminal violations involve the following 10 persons currently and formerly employed by the United States Government. (The 10 names were listed along with their positions.)

Finally, I am enclosing a report of an investigation recently conducted by the Inspector General for the Commander in Chief, U.S. Pacific Command. The investigation concerned the shredding of POW/MIA reports in March 1993 at the U.S. Embassy in Bangkok, Thailand, under the direction of General Thomas Needham, Commander of Joint Task Force (Full Accounting), U.S. Pacific Command.

End of quote.

I have to ask myself if I've heard or read anything since 1993 as a result of Senator Bob Smith's letter to Janet Reno. What do you think?

At the 30ᵗʰ annual meeting of The League in June 1999, Bob Smith, at that time a presidential candidate, had these words to say. "Simply put, there has not been full disclosure by Hanoi about unaccounted for American POWs and MIAs. The facts speak for themselves. We have not had access to relevant POW information from the Communist Party Central Committee-- including Politburo, Military Affairs Committee, and Secretariat level records from the war. Why can't we see the records of the internal briefings to North Vietnam's leadership during the war about how many POWs they had really captured? If they're not hiding anything, and they've told the truth all these years, about how many POWs they really held, then why can't we see those documents? We also have not had access to prison records where some of your loved ones were known to have been held, and even suspected to have been held, during the war. We have not had full access to Vietnamese wartime reporting on American POWs captured along the Ho Chi Minh Trail in Laos, and at other locations in Laos, such as Lima Site 85, and Sam Neua Province where several U.S. personnel remain unaccounted for. And we have not had a convincing and complete response from the Vietnamese Government about the documents uncovered in the Russian archives in 1993 that indicated Hanoi held more U.S. POWs than they repatriated in 1973."[6]

> "Something very real happened to each of those brave men, and our country will not be at peace with itself until we are morally certain we have done all we could to find out what."[7]

> "Anything less than the truth dishonors all those who sacrificed their freedom and their lives."[8]

Documents abound with testimonies about our government's handling of the Vietnam POW/MIA situation.

For example, in the Conservative Review 1993 article entitled, "Missing American POWs: What Happened? Part II", author Joe Douglass Jr. stated that, "Without serious question, the current search efforts are inherently designed to fail. No 'cooperation' efforts, which constitute the essence--if not entirety--of the U.S. search efforts in Russia, Southeast Asia, and Korea, are likely to obtain confirmation, especially because it is equally clear that the U.S. officials in charge of the search do not want to find anything."[9]

As a footnote, the author tells us how deplorable he considers this sad but true situation. He writes that officials, including U.S. intelligence and the State Department, have lied through the years as well as falsified records and misrepresented information.

This is something that I have been reading and talking about for a long time. Whenever I ran across a statement like Douglass', I always felt better--not because I agreed with this awful truth, but because someone else was putting this truth into print. I was not the only person having these thoughts.

HOUSE INTERNATIONAL RELATIONS COMMITTEE

On November 4, 1999, Michael D. Benge testified before the House International Relations Committee.[10] He said, "While serving as a civilian Economic Development Officer in the Central Highlands of South Viet Nam, I was captured by the North Vietnamese during the Tet Offensive on January 28, 1968. I was held in numerous camps in South Viet Nam, Cambodia, Laos and North Viet Nam. I was a POW for over five years, and spent 27 months in solitary confinement, one year in a 'black box,' and one year in a cage in Cambodia. . .

"I was not tortured by the Cubans, nor was I part of the 'Cuban Program'. There were 19 American POWs that I know of who were tortured by the Cubans in Hanoi during the Vietnam War. . .the torture took place in a POW camp called the Zoo, and the Vietnamese camp commander was a man they called the 'Lump'. . . I decided to research the 'Cuban Program' after repeated claims by the Administration, Senators John McCain and John Kerry, Ambassador Pete Peterson, and members of the Department of Defense that the Vietnamese Government was 'cooperating fully' in resolving the POW/MIA issue. This is far from the truth."

Michael D. Benge's testimony runs for seven pages ending with these words. "As you can see from my document, the Cubans were heavily involved in the Vietnam War. They were in charge of building and maintaining a good portion of the Ho Chi Minh Trail. . .

"We are not seeking revenge. . .we are only seeking an honest accounting for the POW/MIAs. We, like every American should only seek honest answers from our government and its representatives, and competent investigations as to the fate of the POW/MIAs so that their families might find closure to their long suffering grief.

Ignorance? Arrogance? Disinterest? Lack of caring? Incompetence? Obfuscation? I rest my case."

The Cuban's involvement with the Vietnamese against the U.S. in the Vietnam War must be one of our government's best-kept secrets. Benge should have added the word Deceit? to his list of questions above, don't you think?

MINNESOTA STATE SENATE VETERANS AFFAIRS COMMITTEE

Tracy E. Usry, Special Investigator, Senate Foreign Relations Committee – Minority Staff, testified before the Minnesota State Senate Veterans Affairs Committee on February, 8, 1991. Usry was responsible for the "conduct of the legislative inquiry concerning the Prisoner of War/Missing In Action (POW/MIA) issue, initiated by the Honorable Jesse Helms, Senior Senator from North Carolina as well as the Honorable Charles Grassley, Senior Senator from Iowa."

In his 11 page report, Usry stated, "In essence, DOD has been able to construct a rationale to discredit officially nearly every live-sighting report. . .the staff found instances where the Defense Department merely excluded from its analysis certain details of a valid sighting, such as a source's statement about the number of POWs sighted, their physical condition, a description of the camp or cave held in, whether they were shackled, or, whether they were gesturing for food. By excluding such corroborating details, these details would not be known to anyone reading just a summary of the report or DOD's analysis of a report."

That's one way to avoid looking for POWs or MIAs, for sure. The Defense Department should have been labeled DOTD or Department of "Tricky Dicks."

SELECT COMMITTEE ON POW/MIA AFFAIRS

The Veterans of Foreign Wars of the United States testified before the Select Committee on POW/MIA Affairs, United States Senate on November 6, 1991. Robert E. Wallace explained to the committee that the VFW's past yearly pleas had gone unheeded. He stated that their members were not satisfied with the lack of effort on the government's part, in both action and results. He said, "Further, the government continues to shroud its effort in what we believe to be an unnecessary veil of secrecy."[11]

On the same day, J. Thomas Birch, Jr., Chairman of the National Vietnam Veterans Coalition testified. He informed the Senate that since our country has had paid spies and informers for over 200 years, why should we stop now. Paying a spy isn't cheap, but it's worth it to find out about our POW/MIAs in Vietnam, Laos or Cambodia.[12]

Birch mentioned how rigid our country's criteria were in looking at proof of the existence of POW/MIAs. He gave an example of how our government would not find the criteria met if an American escaped from a prison and told of others still there. That is why so many DIA investigations have gone nowhere.[13]

Bill Duker, of the Vietnam Veterans of American POW/MIA Committee, testified that day and among his comments were, "It seems that those designated governmental agencies assigned to investigate crash sites, interview witnesses, review archives, etc. have succeeded in increasing the number of remains returned. We believe these same agencies have failed to expend the same amount of effort investigating the reports of live sightings."

He asked the Senate Committee why our government continues to not achieve its most important goal--to bring live Americans home. "Is this failure due to a 'conspiracy' or a 'cover up' as many feel?"[14]

One of those testifying on November 6th was Joseph E. Andry, past Commander of the DAV (Disabled American Veterans). Andry lost an eye and a leg in the Vietnam War. He told the Senate Committee members that "if a man or woman is good enough to put on the uniform of this country and willing to make the sacrifices necessary to defend this country, then this country's government should do whatever it takes to bring those warriors, or their remains, home. To do anything less would be a moral tragedy and go against the grain of everything this nation stands for."[15]

On December 13, 1968, Major Morgan Jefferson Donahue, USAF, became an MIA in Laos. His brother, Dr. Jeffery C. Donahue gave the opening statement to the committee. He began by saying, "Very simply, the POWs in Laos were abandoned through the mundane and mendacious conduct of international diplomacy. Laos was the ultimate secret war, funded and operated by the CIA and its Thai mercenary army. The Indochina War tore this country apart. In the rush to disengage from it, Messrs. Kissinger and Nixon swept the POWs off the board as if they never existed. They did exist, and they exist today. Until they are brought home, this country will not be whole."

In an October 29, 1991, addendum to Donahue's remarks, is this quote. ". . . POW/MIA intelligence still is classified for the Korean War and World War II. As long as the Government classifies such data, charges of a conspiracy and cover-up will stick; it is just not possible to understand why such data is classified unless the Government is trying to hide the truth about live POWs. 'National security' is an excuse which simply does not hold water after so many years."[16]

Ted Sampley, Publisher of U.S. Veteran News and Report, was another speaker at the November 7, 1991, Senate Select Committee on POW/MIA Affairs. He began his testimony with the statement that both President Nixon's and President Bush's administrations carried on a program of dis-information, discrediting, domestic spying, and misinformation about the POWs and the MIAs. He even went so far as to accuse both administrations of ridiculing veterans, civilian groups, and individuals who believed that the U.S. was not doing enough to find answers to the questions about our missing men.

One story he told the committee caught my attention. It seems that in October of 1988, a plan was developed to try to persuade officials in Laos, Cambodia, and Vietnam to defect with at least one American POW. Money was the carrot.

Jim Copp, a Vietnam veteran and Donna Long, a free-lance journalist and POW activist, joined Ted Sampley and three others who rented boats in Thailand in which to put messages. They had stamped both U.S. and foreign bills with messages of rewards for information about POWs/MIAs. The messages were put in waterproof plastic bags so they would float.

The group hoped these messages would reach Laos. However, on their own, Jim and Donna went into a number of Lao villages to distribute the money. It so happened that they met a Lao government official in one of the villages who arrested them and placed them in jail.

"Jim and Donna were blind-folded, guns were placed at their heads, and their lives were threatened. They were tortured by being kept in solitary confinement and refused sufficient quantities of food. They were at one time physically assaulted and there was at least one attempted sexual assault on Donna during their captivity. Jim lost almost 30 pounds in the 41 days they were held and was seriously ill when finally released."[17]

As I look back on the whole incident when Sam, Bill, Roni and I were detained in Hanoi in 1990, and I almost ended up in prison for three to twelve years, I realize how fortunate we all were not to be imprisoned and treated like Jim Copp and Donna Long had been.

Nigel Cawthorne, author of The Bamboo Cage, was also one of those who testified at that 1991 Senate Committee meeting. He mentioned that his book had not been published in the United States, and that it was difficult to get a hold of in this country.

The Bamboo Cage was published in London.

Kiss The Boys Goodbye, by Monica Jensen-Stevenson and William Stevenson, was published in Canada. Maybe the U.S. publishers were afraid to take a chance on these books, finding displeasure among those in the White House and in the administration. That would wreck their bottom line. I can't help but wonder.

Nigel Cawthorne told the Senate Committee that more than thirty publishers in the United States told him the American public did not want to know the truth about what happened to our POW/MIAs in the Vietnam War.[18]

Of course, that's changed now with Lt. Cdr. Scott Speicher's highly publicised KIA to MIA status change, and the War of Terrorism.

His testimony was a summary of his book. He listed a number of facts that he had received from the Department of Defense's own documents. Among those were:

1) There were more U.S. prisoners taken than anyone ever admitted.
2) Airmen who were shot down were kept in camps around Hanoi and Haiphong if they didn't have strategic information.
3) Injured men were thought to have been taken to China.
4) Prisoners with special knowledge or skills were sent to Russia.
5) Those who were captured on the Ho Chi Minh Trail or similar areas, were forced into slave labor.
6) If the Americans were made to work in Vietnamese strategic projects, they could never be returned because of what they knew.
7) Some of the American prisoners were held by the Pathet Lao. The DOD papers said that these men were never returned, even though

the Lao had promised to do so when the U.S. bombing of Laos stopped.

8) The NSA knew that some of the prisoner hostages were going to be used as "bargaining chips" against the reparations the U.S. had long discussed.

9) An attempt to pay ransom was made on February 1, 1973, five days after the Paris Peace Accords. President Nixon promised to pay $3.25 billion in reparations.

10) Those men returned in Operation Homecoming spoke of being brutally tortured and treated in many inhumane ways. When Congress heard about that, they banned all reparations to Vietnam, Cambodia and Laos, despite objections from the Administration. Congress did not know about President Nixon's secret agreement with Pham Van Dong.

11) Not one penny has ever been paid in reparation.

12) In 1973, Vietnamese Communists made a policy not to return all of their prisoners. Laos followed suit.

13) Since 1973, American prisoners have smuggled letters out of Vietnam. Pictures, aircraft identifiers, zip codes, service numbers, even names have been reported. Hundreds of refugees from Vietnam, Cambodia and Laos have spoken of seeing both white and black captives as they were moved from camp to camp to prevent escape or detection.

Cawthorne ended his testimony with the following statement:
"The case is just overwhelming. I am a writer, not a politician or a diplomat. I have written down the simple truth as I have found it. I have tried to present the evidence to the American people, so that they could make up their own mind. That, I understood, was the American way. There are Americans still alive in captivity in Southeast Asia. It is beyond doubt. What America does about it is up to you."[19]

The Chief Investigator, Senate Foreign Relations Committee, Tracy Usry, spoke at the November 1991 Senate Committee meeting. He found that access to information was denied him at almost every turn. After listing the many ways he and his committee were hindered in their investigation, he stated that unscientific methods were used to identify the returned bodies. The Central Identification Laboratory-Hawaii had lied to previous Congressional committees, and that there had been a premature closure of the U.S. Army Criminal Investigation Command. This resulted in the DOD saving face for the allegations would have been embarrassing.[20]

289

Patricia Ann O'Grady, Ph.D, daughter of a missing Air Force pilot lost in Laos, testified on November 6, 1991, that she was finally told her father had been captured alive. "This information could have been obtained many years ago," she said. "After twenty-four years, I can tell you where his actual captors live today."

The information about her father was released accidentally, however. "Despite contradictory testimony, I can chronicle extensive dishonesty and concealment and document that every claim made by General Tighe and Colonel Peck is absolutely true!"[21] One of her concluding points was that the charade still went on. "Fingerprints and dental records disappear, journalists are attacked, legitimate pictures are discredited."

In his written testimony, Robert A. Apodaca, Captain, USAF, and son of another missing Air Force pilot, asked, ". . . if the POW/MIA issue has the highest national priority, why are hundreds of remains still in Vietnam today, why are agencies allowed to not follow through on reports, why can't we find the fingerprint records for almost 25% of those missing, and why can't we find the identity of three people in a picture?"[22]

Lt. Colonel Jack E. Bailey, USAF, (ret.), testified that he had devoted his time, since retiring, trying to discover information about POWs left behind by the U.S. Government ". . . in their haste to disengage 'with honor' from the war in southeast Asia they were unwilling or unable to win." He concluded, but could not prove, that because of treasonous acts by a U.S. embassy representative in Thailand, American prisoners of war died.[23]

Another daughter of a POW, Shelby Robertson Quast, wrote an eight-page testimony for the hearings. Among other things, when she requested to see her father's file, she was told that the policy of the DIA's special office for POW Affairs prohibited her from seeing it.[24]

For twenty-two and a half years, Gladys Stevens Fleckenstein searched, traveled to Paris, Geneva, and Laos, made speeches, attended flag raisings, and everything she could think of to try to find her son, Lt. Cdr. Larry Stevens, and to keep the public aware of the fact that there were still live POWs in Southeast Asia.

Her quest was over when she saw a picture of her son, along with two other prisoners, that had been brought out by a "special source." Two forensic experts identified her son in that picture. However, the FBI claimed that they had no fingerprints for the three men in the photograph. She then discovered that his birth certificate was missing from the Los Angeles Hall of Records where certificates of her other two sons could be found. Hospital and DMV records for her son, Larry, were also missing.

Gladys Fleckenstein asked, as so many before her in the hearings, "Why should reports of incidents that occurred twenty to twenty-five years ago remain classified? Is it a 'national security' matter or is live POW information being classified in order to cover up DIA's ineptitude?" She concluded that she had "fought the fight all these years, when our government should have brought my son, and all live POWs home, and as full as possible accounting of those who perished. Last, they flew me out over the Ho Chi Min Trail, Laos, and I left my heart and my son in that lonely and foreign land."[25]

Hamilton Gayden, Tennessee Circuit Court Judge, and author of a novel about an American POW also testified on November 6th. It was through his contact, with an American-Laotian, that the picture of Lt. Cdr. Larry Stevens, Col. John Leighton Robertson, and Maj. Albro L. Lundy, Jr. reached the United States.

Gayden testified that he had "accumulated considerable evidence: photographs; finger, thumb and hand prints; human hair including 'root hair'; signatures; written messages; live witnesses; some of the evidence has been discarded by us as false, other evidence will require scientific testing, i.e., DNA hair analysis and comparison; thumb and finger print comparison and interviews of live witnesses; and we may even be able to provide a live video of American POWs. We have already delivered considerable evidence to the Foreign Relations Committee, although we admittedly have no clue as to whether that evidence is secure. We believe our evidence to be 90% accurate."

According to Gayden, ". . . Vietnamese Ambassador to the United Nations, Nguyen Can, who said to a group of us who met with him in the fall of 1989 at the Vietnamese Mission in New York, to paraphrase: We will never be able to account for Americans because your government won't let us."[26]

When Johanna Lundy saw the picture of the three prisoners in Vietnam, she immediately identified her husband, Albro, as one of them. That's what Albro L. Lundy III testified about his mother's identification of his father. He said that the day after the photo of the three men was leaked to the press, not by the family members, the Pentagon held a press conference to say that the photo was a hoax.

Lundy said, "The government has had this photo in its possession since June 1990. . . The photo was not sent to the FBI for analysis until July 1991." At that time, the U.N. Ambassador from Vietnam told Johanna Lundy "that the Vietnamese did not negotiate with the United States regarding POWs held in Laos and that the U.S. must negotiate directly with the Pathet Lao. To this day, not one living American POW has returned from Laos."

The Lundy family has let it be known that the U.S. government has shown a total lack of good faith in following up on leads regarding POWs. They have been lied to, Col. Lundy's file has been tampered with, live sightings and fingerprints have been ignored, and his photograph discredited. "They have in fact deliberately obfuscated the truth. . . It's time to stop the ludicrous charade that has been perpetrated by the Department of Defense."[27]

In Lt. Col. (ret.) Norman M. Turner's testimony, he stated that he found it "absolutely incredible that the government of the United States for which Cheney speaks can make such an about face concerning the 'highest national priority' after a single week of non-investigation in Thailand." He continued with "On a larger scale there seems to be a prevalent presumption in the hearts and minds of our government leaders that unless some individual can present solid, uncontroverted proof of the existence of a POW, the POW doesn't exist. That constitutes a presumption of death which is patent nonsense."[28]

Terrell A. "Terry" Minarcin, also testified. He was a Vietnamese linguist and cryptolinguist, assigned to NSA along with Jerry Mooney from 1967 to 1984. In addition, he was a ground-based voice intercept operator/processing specialist, a technical reporter, an analyst, an intelligence reporter, an airborne voice intercept operator and an airborne instructor. He provided direct SIGINT support to "special operations" including rescue attempts. All of these jobs gave him various forms of information about American POWs--those held in the Hanoi area, in "special" camps, those sent to the Soviet Union, those held in 'New Economic Areas," and those captured after the cease fire in 1973.

He decided to step forward to testify, not for glory, but to let the committee know that he knew, "without a single shred of doubt, that American POWs were left behind in Southeast Asia. . . A terrible wrong" has been perpetrated, he said.

During those years, Minarcin found that all of the American POWs were divided into three categories by the Vietnamese--political/economic exploitation, military exploitation, and general knowledge exploitation. Most of the prisoners fell into the first category. The second group of prisoners were held in order to learn all the Vietnamese could about weapons, communications, and infiltration methods, to name a few.

The third category consisted of men who had expertise, in such areas as electrical engineering, who could be forced by their captors into using their knowledge for military as well as non-military uses.

Among the things that Minarcin learned during those years was the location of Vietnamese interrogation centers other than Hanoi, Soviet run interrogation centers, and "special" camps. One of the systems he worked on dealt with the Ho Chi Minh Trail. "Occasionally, I saw references to American POWs being transported back to North Vietnam," Minarcin testified.

"The last incident I was involved with is the location contained in the 'message' found in the photograph purporting to show Colonels Lundy and Robertson and Commander Stevens. While the location could be viewed as highly speculative, when taken in concert with the six eyewitness' reports (as already presented by the Robertson family), the location is probably valid."

As a part of Minarcin's report, were 37 pages of maps, articles, and information (Appendices A-Q), to prove the points he made in his testimony.

> "The last question that needs to be answered is how to get back our POWs. I believe the best way is to be direct. No matter how distasteful it might be to some, a promise was made to provide aid to the countries of Indo-China. Why not just pay it and be done with it? I am not advocating relations with Indo-China. Nor am I advocating any resumption of trade. All I am saying is that America must live up to its word in that area of the world. If it works and we get all of my comrades home, then fine, well and good. There are still other options if it doesn't work. As the richest nation in the world, $4.25 billion dollars would not hurt at all. It is an option that does have a high percentage chance of succeeding."[29]

The DIA maintained an MIA office in Bangkok known as Stony Beach. Col. John Cole, had been U.S. Army Chief of the Defense Intelligence Agency's Stony Beach Team since 1990. The team was formed in 1987 to "collect and report intelligence required to assist in the resolution of the POW/MIA issue." Colonel Cole testified that "We are fully aware of our sacred trust". . . to the American people and "most importantly, the families of those still unaccounted for. . ."[30]

According to the testimony of Ann Mills Griffiths, Executive Director of the National League of Families of American Prisoners and Missing in Southeast Asia, "The vast majority of the POW/MIA families are realistic; we don't expect miracles. We expect seriousness by our own government, executive and legislative branches, rather than spontaneous reaction to the squeaky wheel or the latest editorial."

Griffiths stressed that the families were not interested in comments from "unnamed 'senior officials,' which dismiss facts and principle in the perceived interest of political or economic advantage."[31]

General John W. Vessey, Presidential Emissary to Hanoi for POW/MIA Matters, also testified at the Senate Committee hearings. He explained that his job was to "shed light" on whether there were live Americans still held by the Vietnamese government, as well as find and return the remains of those who had been killed or died in Southeast Asia.

His nine-page report listed all the various agreements the Vietnamese government had made with his office. General Vessey said he felt he had all of the necessary agreements to be able to obtain the recoverable remains, account for the missing and discover what remained of the live American prisoner issue.[32]

Even Bui Tin, a former Senior Colonel in the Vietnamese Peoples Army, spoke before the committee. He had been expelled from the Vietnamese Communist Party, and had taken political asylum in France. He urged both his former country and the United States, to "put aside our own interests to work for the interest of our two peoples. . . I want to end my statement by calling upon those in Vietnam, if they are honest, to cooperate on this issue. They should open the door widely and welcome any delegations to enter Vietnam to search for the truth."[33]

Senator Bob Smith, New Hampshire, Vice Chairman, Senate Select Committee on POW/MIA Affairs, addressed the session.

"We ought to be ashamed of ourselves," he said. Among the five areas he touched on was the fact that there had been 1500 first-hand live sighting reports with no apparent follow up; that families had been on a "roller coaster ride" because of the "dribble" of information from Vietnam; that there seemed to be a connection between the Soviets and American POW/MIAs; and that nothing had happened to free the Americans captured by the Pathet Lao.

Senator Smith elaborated on each of his points in great detail. His summary included, "It is now 1991, and we still have made little to no progress in Laos regarding an accounting of these men. The boat people poured out of Laos by the hundreds in the late 1970's telling us the men were still there, but we discounted the information. To this day, we are receiving information on alleged POWs still in Laos. . . We never even proposed regular meetings with the Lao on this issue until ten years after the war."[34]

> "I went to Vietnam prepared to fight, prepared to be wounded, prepared to be captured, and even prepared to die. . . but I was not prepared to be abandoned."[35]
> Captain Red McDaniel
> Former Vietnam POW

In his opening statement, Senator Smith quoted Robert Garwood, who escaped from Vietnam in 1979. According to Senator Smith, Garwood told him, ". . . with tears in his eyes: 'I am an American who does not want to go to his deathbed without doing everything possible to convince people who can do something about it that there are live Americans held in captivity in Vietnam long after 1973. My life has been turned upside down because of my providing this information, but I am doing this to make sure my conscience is clear on this issue. What I am suffering now is nothing compared to what those Americans must still be going through in Vietnam . . . I am not the last American to leave Vietnam.'"[36]

Bill Bell also testified to the Senate. He said, "I realize my opinion. . .will not be a popular one, but after having considered the information carefully and being under oath, I felt compelled to answer affirmatively to the question posed to me."

The question? Was there hard evidence that any of the 2,200 listed POW/MIAs had been left behind by the U.S.?

His answer? "Yes."[37]

I can tell you, that was not the right answer--not the answer the Senate wanted to hear. I'd like to add here that because Bill Bell's debriefing was at such a high level, the Senate was not allowed to read it, so there was no follow-up to his testimony.

Last, but not least, was the testimony of Secretary of Defense, Dick Cheney. He said, "The governments of Indochina have consistently denied holding any Americans. We do not, and never will, accept their denials as the last word."

Secretary Cheney discussed "discrepancy cases," which General Vessey had presented to the Vietnamese in 1987-1988. These 119 cases were individuals listed as POWs but were not returned at Operation Homecoming in 1973. They were also those men who were "last known alive" on the "ground or were in communication with friendly forces and in imminent danger of capture." He considered those members of the military as "most likely to still be alive."

In conclusion, he said, "The answers to the questions about Americans unaccounted for do not lie in the files of the Defense Department. The answers must come from the governments of Indochina."[38]

That's an interesting statement, but. . .

* * *

All of this took place in 1991. It reads as if the Senate Select Committee on POW/MIA Affairs had just taken place this year.

Time stopped. It could still be 1991 and, although some remains have been returned, the mind-set of our government has remained the same. Families and loved ones, including Jim's family, my children, and me continue to try to find answers.

Our American servicemen are still prisoners in Southeast Asia, China, Russia, or God knows where. . . or they have died and are buried God knows where.

Under these circumstances, there can be no closure for us--or for our country!

Chapter Nineteen

Last But Not Least

"No institution is deserving of blind loyalty."[1]
Col. Tom C. McKenney
U.S. Marine Corps

One of the most unbelievable stories to come out of the Vietnam War is that of Robert Garwood. In fact, it was such an important story for the American public to know, that Monika Jensen-Stevenson wrote a book about it--Spite House, The Last Secret of the War in Vietnam.

Robert Garwood, a Marine Private, was just ten days short of the end of his tour when he became a prisoner of the Vietcong. He then spent 14 years as a prisoner before he escaped and found his way back to the United States.[2]

According to Patty Hopper, TFO, Garwood made his escape by "slipping a note to a Finnish diplomat in Hanoi who presented the note to the U.S. government. With hard certifiable proof in hand, the U.S. government was forced to secure Bobby's release."

A number of things are unusual about this story. First, when he was captured, he was on a mission for the Marine Corps. But, when he returned home, the same Marine Corps immediately court-martialed him, and convicted him of collaborating with the enemy.

At the same time Garwood was held a prisoner, Col. Tom McKenney was assigned the job of organizing teams of snipers with one of their assignments being to eliminate traitors. According to Col. McKenney, Garwood was one of the names on his list to assassinate. As the book tells, Garwood became an obsession of McKenney's. In return, Garwood's struggle became not only survival as a prisoner, but as a hunted man doomed to die at the hands of his countrymen.[3]

McKenney had an unshakable trust in his government, and its intelligence system. He believed what he thought were hard facts of Garwood's traitorous behavior when he was presented with them.[4] This even included believing that the emasculation of the Special Forces should be carried out. A Vietnamese double agent was assassinated in 1969, providing some politicians in Washington D.C., who thought the war was immoral, the fuel for undermining the Green Berets and the CIA's role in the war.[5]

McKenny began to realize that his own government had "manipulated the situation to seriously undermine, if not destroy, Special Forces, the most effective fighting force it had in this war."[6]

Garwood was not guilty, but it took McKenny 20 years before he finally learned the truth. He believed Garwood's guilt because he was told so.[7] He said, "I was naïve enough to think that one's own side observed a moral boundary and that common decency prevented us from crossing it. I knew about Soviet 'black' propaganda that harmed their own people but never for a second imagined we might have programs for deceiving our own side in ways that sacrificed Americans."[8]

Monika Jensen-Stevenson wrote in Spite House that on November 11, 1991, at the Crystal City Hilton in Washington D.C., she was sitting at the speaker's table at the Annual Meeting of the Vietnam Veterans Coalition. She became aware of a person waiting to speak with her. He did not speak at first, only took both of her hands in his. Then "He began to weep silently. The silence stretched on and on. Finally he said, 'I am Col. Tom C. McKenney. You must know how to reach Bobby Garwood. I directed an official mission to assassinate him behind enemy lines, because I believed what they told me. Would you tell him I will crawl on my hands and knees to beg his forgiveness?"[9]

McKenny said Garwood was innocent of all charges brought against him in his court martial. He had been done a tremendous wrong. "Garwood was one of those mud Marines who had gone face to face with the enemy, for fourteen years, armed with nothing but his own ingenuity and integrity. He was. . .the only American who had beaten their system. . .(he) had remained a good Marine in a way only real jarheads could understand. Even in the most constricted and dehumanizing circumstances, he had gone out and 'whipped butt,' without getting caught. . .(the way he spread) muddy clay all over his body and (crawled) through the gate right past the guard post to the kitchen and back--was classic leatherneck. The same was true of the times he had stolen food and medicine for the other POWs and managed to turn on the Voice of America for only 15 to 30 seconds at a time with guards just around the corner. . .They did their best to break him, but they did not succeed."[10]

His captors even played a statement by National Security Advisor Henry Kissinger, over the camp loudspeaker, that there were no American prisoners left behind. Garwood decided that the tape of Kissinger speaking was a trick. He knew there were others like him still held as prisoners in Vietnam.

"Garwood returned to sanity by religiously following the rules laid down by Ike, now dead for almost eight years. He remembered telling himself, 'Garwood, get the hell out of Vietnam anyway you can because none of the bigwigs of the world care. . .Taking that attitude, I followed Ike's advice again--to avoid confrontations, conserve energy, and learn all I could in order to make my way to Hanoi and perhaps find. . .neutral foreign diplomats. It had to be done without hurting my country or fellow Americans. I was alone anyway, and the war was over. I didn't exist."[11]

Bobby Garwood's story is long and complicated but something Americans should be made aware of, even today. I believe that the government sees his greatest crime as his ability to survive, and to find a way to escape from Vietnam.

For years, family members have tried to prove to the government that men were left behind by using the government's own intelligence. The response has been pretty universal. "If we had proof that any American prisoner was left behind, we'd go over there and bring them home." Bobby Garwood is proof that the government's statement is not true and that the government has closed its eyes and refused to act.

The Vietnamese denied holding Americans, the U.S. denied leaving Americans behind, yet somehow an American named Robert Garwood found a way out of Vietnam. . .in 1979, long after the war ended.

What more can I say?

One of Garwood's stories, told in The Men We Left Behind, was that the guards often told him about some of the Americans who were not being cooperative. He remembered eleven or so of their first names. But the 12th name he remembered caught my attention.

Garwood said that the guards asked him about an American named Jim who had blond hair and blue eyes. This Jim could not speak Vietnamese, and he couldn't stand the fish sauce, known as that country's famous dish. The guards told Garwood that this Jim was from "the village of California."[12]

My heart took a leap! Could it be Jim Birchim?

In 1991, Lt. Col. Bui Tin, former member of the North Vietnamese Army, testified before the Senate Select Committee on POW/MIA Affairs. He said, "'I categorically state' that there are 'not any MIAs or POWs alive in Vietnam today. As for Laos and Cambodia, I do not know the situation as well as in Vietnam.'"

Lt. Col. Tin defected while on an official trip for Vietnam to Paris the year before. "'There is only the single case of (Marine Pvt.) Robert Garwood, who lived freely in South Vietnam and Hanoi and returned to the United States' in 1979, Tin said. Tin also denied that Hanoi has retained the remains of Americans who died in combat or captivity."[13]

Can you believe that? What I find interesting is that Lt. Col. Tin went to such great lengths to discredit Garwood in this manner. Afterall, Garwood is still living proof that the Vietnamese lied for years about American POWs remaining alive in Vietnam.

Later, Senator John Kerry, D-MA, reported that Lt. Col. Tin's information was important as far as certain documents were concerned.

Lt. Col. Tin also testified that no Americans were sent to Russia, but the Russians had interrogated them in Vietnam. Senator John McCain, R-AZ, said he had not been aware of "the Soviets questioning POWs, although he knew Cuban intelligence officers had."

Not only did Lt. Col. Tin confirm that he had bought into the U.S. government's story about Robert Garwood, but he bought into his former country's story that no Americans, dead or alive, remained in Vietnam.

So, what good was his testimony, except to make the liars in our government nod their heads and say, "See, I told you so."

According to The Men We Left Behind, "When Garwood left Vietnam in 1979, Colonel Thai of the CucQuan Phap, Vietnam's Department of Military Justice, warned him not to expose the dirty little secret between Vietnam and the United States."

A "dirty little secret"? Yes. It seems that the U.S. and Vietnam had an agreement to keep "parts of the POW issue unresolved."[14]

Unresolved?

For once I am speechless!

Chapter Twenty

Psychic Warriors

"What is the greatest experience you can have? It is the hour of the great contempt. The hour in which your happiness, too, arouses your disgust, and even your reasons and virtue."[1]

Friedrich Nietzsche

In late 2000, the TV series JAG featured an hour show based on Stargate, the U.S. governments (CIA) top-secret, psychic espionage program.

This program recruits individuals to be psychic spies. "For nearly two decades, the United States military intelligence community delved into the dark world of psychic espionage, recruiting a team of psychic spies to serve as 'remote viewers,' individuals who used their paranormal gifts to transcend time and space and uncover the highly guarded military secrets of other nations."[2]

The JAG show told the story about a naval remote viewer and his psychic operations. Although most naval personnel considered the remote viewer to be crazy, in the end he was acquitted of his Stargate psychic leanings.

I'm astonished at the stories and the other JAG episodes that are now coming out like this, and the other JAG episodes I've mentioned in the book. I wonder where the TV producers get their story ideas? They are all so right-on with things once thought to be fiction, but are now known as fact. The history of our government's long involvement in such programs is still not well known among the general public.

STARGATE

The real story of the Stargate program reads like the long-running TV program, "The X-files."

A set of wooden buildings at Fort Belvoir housed a group of soldiers and Defense Department employees (later moved to Fort Meade). In these buildings an espionage program took place, which turned a hand picked group of soldiers into spies, threatening their imagination and spirituality. This well-kept Stargate secret (originally called Sun Streak), was considered by some of the DIAs at the time as evil and satanic.

The few men chosen for this program were required to give up their families and their beliefs, and submit to the paranormal hell of Stargate. The result was the men developed the ability to perform psychic espionage work.

One of the targets that the remote viewers were involved in was searching for Marine Lt. Col. Higgins, a hostage in Lebanon who was later murdered by his captors. Another was providing "descriptions, phonetic spellings of names, and sketches of houses and meeting places for the terrorists" who caused the destruction of Pan Am Airline's Flight 103 over Lockerbie, Scotland.

Remote viewers were used to find certain ships carrying illegal narcotics during the War on Drugs. Psychic espionage work by remote viewers also included the "choking smoke of Desert Storm, even further back in time to Hiroshima and the darkest days of Nazi Germany."[3]

PSYCHIC WARRIOR

David Morehouse, former Army remote viewer in the Stargate program, tells us in his book, Psychic Warrior, about one assignment he had during the planning of Desert Storm.

"My target lay east of the area of operations, along the coast and inland. I'd been given a map, really just an outline sketch of the eastern border of Iraq, all of Kuwait, and the northeastern borders of Saudi Arabia. My mission was to advance to the encrypted coordinates and examine the surrounding terrain for anything of significance - - in other words, to drop in and see if anything needed attention. . . I might even run into some scud missile units that had so far escaped detection."[4]

All of this roaming through the ether took place in "viewing rooms" where the military-trained remote viewers traveled to whereever their assignment took them. Some of the remote viewers were plagued with nightmares. For most, their lives as the DIA's secret weapon resembled a bad dream. Some had spiritual experiences.

And who was responsible for Stargate? The CIA. "The CIA is in the business of manipulating the belief systems of entire nations. . . The most important thing about secret programs is that they prevent not only the bad guys but also the good guys from finding out what's going on. This system gives the holder of the secrets enormous power."[5]

REMOTE VIEWING THEN AND NOW

It is the opinion of many that remote viewing is still alive and well in the U.S. Even though the CIA tried a dis-information program in 1995, it is the belief of David Morehouse that remote viewing is definitely "all the rage in intelligence. I believe that the CIA is heavily involved in this insidious technique."[6]

The first time our country got wind of this form of control was in 1950 when the Miami News published an article entitled, "Brain Washing Tactics." Of course, at that time, no one knew that these U.S. tactics were created by the CIA, and fed to "an operative who worked under the cover of a journalist."[7] Many suspected that brain washing was communist oriented.

At the time, an electrosleep machine was in use at a Richmond, Virginia, hospital for mentally disturbed patients. It was agreed that this technique could be used for interrogation of POWs or "those of interest to this Agency[8] (CIA)." Autosuggestion was the technique they saw as being useful in indoctrinating certain individuals, as well as an advanced form of hypnotic therapy to "ensure new ideas remained locked in the subconscious"[9] of a person.

These therapies, similar to communist methods, included de-patterning, experimental drugs, psychic driving, isolation, continuous sleep, electroshock, LSD, and other brainwashing techniques.

All of these experiments conducted by the CIA were unethical, as well as violations of the standards governing research in our country.

Unfortunately, the experiments were conducted on persons who did not volunteer, and each was injured by the methods used on them. They were not all subjects from mental hospitals.[10]

As Richard Helms, Director of the CIA in 1968, said at an Allen Dulles Christmas party, "We can spy, not by just looking up their assholes, but by peering down on their heads." It seems that President Nixon had made it clear to Helms that he wanted better results from the CIA's intelligence gathering operations in Vietnam.[11]

The result of this type of mind control experiments makes my imagination work overtime. I wonder how many of our own men in Vietnam were declared MIA when they were really treated to mind control methods by the CIA in order to erase the memory of their former lives. In that way, they could become espionage/terrorist puppets under total control by the CIA.

It seems to me that members of the Green Berets would be prime targets for these methods of espionage. This is stuff made from science fiction and fantasies. But, it could also be a reality. I really believe that.

PSYCHICS SHAKE AND TURN WHITE

I decided I needed a different kind of help at one point when I became very frustrated with the lack of information I was getting from the "powers that be." I had gone to several reputable psychics over the years, and not one of them said that Jim had died in Vietnam. The problem with psychics was they didn't tell me whether they saw Jim as alive or as a part of the spirit world they entered. They weren't definitive. I never told them ahead of time that my husband was an MIA. Sometimes I'd give them a letter in its envelope to hold that Jim wrote from Vietnam.

Once, a woman psychic, Samara, turned white and began to shake. She said, "This is too dangerous. I can't. . .I can't deal with this. . .and you shouldn't either." She refused to see me again.

I saw Kay, another psychic who, after a number of sessions, became very anxious because what she saw was too disturbing to her. We taped the sessions, and she made me promise not to allow anyone to hear the tapes. She said, "There is this shroud over it. There is a lot of evil out there, and if it gets out that I'm telling you this, I'm in danger." She kept saying, "I don't understand what I'm seeing here."

I kept asking her to describe what she saw.

"All I see is this brilliant white sand."

"Well, do you see it on an island? Is the sand surrounded by lots of water?"

"No, there's no water. This is in the middle of a big piece of land, like a continent."

What she described sounded like White Sands, New Mexico. Then she went on to say that this person, Jim, and some other guys were working, and they were being used for their knowledge, and they were working underground. "They're not allowed to talk, they don't go out to stores. There're no malls. There's nothing." She went on and on for about two hours. The psychic was a wreck at the end.

In 1991, I decided to talk to the psychic whom Sara spoke with on a daily basis at that time. The psychic told me some things about Jim that seemed quite believable, like Jim was planted in the situation at that time. She stressed that he had no idea what he was getting himself into, and that he was pushed into whatever it was. He had no way to get out of it, and he was not free to come home. The psychic mentioned something about how Jim was a black belt, or black belt was the name of the project he was involved in.

She also said that a three-letter word was connected with his project, so I presumed that it was CIA or DIA, or some such government alphabet soup. In looking at his picture, the psychic said he had become rough and forceful, not like he used to be. If he was truly alive, then that made sense to me. He couldn't have spent between 1968 and 1991, working for the CIA overtly or covertly, and not become tough.

Not only did this psychic tell me about Jim, she scared me when she began talking about the fact that I was an open target. She said that the CIA had a job for Jim and they wanted him to keep that job. If I got too close to the answers I sought, which I seemed to be doing, then it was likely "they" would have to get rid of me rather than him. And then she said this was all connected to a red-haired man.

Well, I have to tell you, the mention of a red-haired man really shook me up. When I told the psychic that I already knew about the red-haired man, James Gregory, she became very nervous. She talked about the fact that "they" were watching me, and no matter how many friends or support systems I had around me, "they" could get to me.

I tried hard to keep everything in prospective after that phone call, and not go overboard with all the danger stuff. But, I have to admit, when I got home from visiting Sara, and after the phone call to the psychic, I began to think that being by myself in the quiet of my home was scary. I knew, deep inside, "they" could get to me whenever "they" wished, and do anything "they" wanted to.

This is reality, not paranoia, or my overactive imagination speaking. The government intends to keep this issue contained, no matter what.

At that point, I had some long talks with God. I knew that God didn't give us the answers we sometimes wanted to hear, but I needed to know what to do next. Samara had stressed that I was going to loose everything if I didn't stop digging into the POW/MIA issue. I tried hard to listen for God's message to me. What would it be?

X-FILES?

As I read Psychic Warrior, I realized that these specially trained men--remote viewers--were different from what we think of as psychics. And they are different from spiritualists or those with ESP. The idea that a person sitting in a dark room in Fort Meade could be trained to mentally travel to a specific location when given the coordinates by the person controlling the session, boggled my mind.

Morehouse had been aware, as a child, that he had some kind of extra sensory perception ability. But, he didn't know how to use it. It came and went, to his dismay. He was an Airborne Ranger Company Commander, a special operations infantryman and highly decorated. While in the service, he heard about remote viewers. Then, he found himself involved in the Stargate Program, and his life changed forever.

One of the first things I remember reading about Morehouse's experiences, as a remote viewer, was that he had always wanted to know what happened to his buddy whose plane had disappeared. Being in the government's top-secret Stargate Program helped him to go there, psychically. Amazing!

TWO LETTERS

A letter written by Tom Condon, "Lower Flag On Myth Of POW-MIAs" and published in the Hartford Courant on 12 November, 1998, was answered by Cdr. Chip Beck, USNR (ret.), of Arlington, VA one day later. Cdr. Beck offered a counter view of the subject, and in doing so, wrote the editor, "I am a veteran of several wars ranging from Indochina to Desert Storm. Before I retired in 1996, I was a POW Special Investigator for the U.S. Joint Commission on POW/MIAs."

But first, here are some excerpts from Tom Condon's letter to the Hartford Courant's editor.

"Congress last year required that selected federal agencies fly the POW-MIA flag with Old Glory on six holidays, including Veteran's Day. So, Wednesday, the black flag with the silhouette of a prisoner was hanging sullenly in the morning rain over post offices and office buildings, as well as many town halls and Legion halls.

What is the point? . . . Richard M. Nixon was elected in 1968 claiming to have a secret plan to end the Vietnam War. He was lying, we now know. His plan was to keep fighting, to avoid the disgrace of losing a war. But, the Trickster had a problem. The country was tired of the war, peace negotiations had begun and there was no emotional support for the fighting, Franklin said. (H. Bruce Franklin, Rutgers University Press, 1992, "MIA or Mythmaking in America.")

With help from a little-known businessman named Ross Perot, Nixon came up with the POW/MIA issue, with the flag, the family groups, the bracelets. It was brilliant, in its perverse way. It fired up enough emotional support to keep the war going another few years, and get hundreds of thousands more people killed. . . . Hollywood sensed the potential of the POW idea, and turned out the Rambo and Chuck Norris films. Perhaps, Franklin speculates, we couldn't deal with defeat, so we redefined the war with U.S. pilots as victims. Perhaps the movies massaged the national spirit by replaying the war so we could win.

The POW question has now been investigated by three congressional committees, by the National Defense University, by the departments of state and defense. Each case has been exhaustively checked out. There are no living POWs, they all concluded. . . . To keep the myth alive, as true believers do, is a disservice to the families. How can they close the book when they're told of a faint chance their loved one is alive? . . . We learned much about ourselves in Vietnam, at such cost, yet, Franklin warns, we're on the verge of forgetting

306

it. All we remember are the movies. As a first strike back to reality, strike the flags."

When Cdr. Beck responded to Tom Condon's letter to the editor, he said he hoped they would print his counterview. And they did. Excerpts from his letter follow.

"I am a Desert Storm, veteran. Long before that battle, I served in Vietnam, Laos, and Cambodia, from 1969 until the fall of Indochina in April 1975. I also experienced Cold War conflicts in a dozen countries. Throughout, I was involved in special operations, including 23 years as a CIA clandestine service officer. After I retired from the CIA, but before I retired from the Navy, I spent from 1995-1996 as a POW Special Investigator for the U.S.-Russia Joint Commission on POW/MIAs. . . . I cannot say, based on the hard evidence, that any American POWs are still alive in Indochina, North Korea, China, or Russia. Neither can I say all are dead. Two Japanese WWII POWs, well in their 80s, and three Korean POWs, have turned up alive in the past 3 years.

But that's not even the point. What does matter, is that an estimated 9000 'Unrepatriated POWs' were alive at the end of various wars, not just Vietnam, and were not allowed by their captors or circumstances to return home.

This is why the POW/MIA Flag still flies.

Many of these men survived years, even decades after the wars were over, only to die in the Soviet Gulag camps, and possibly prisons in China, North Korea, and North Vietnam. The fact that they might all be dead does not mean that the truth about their immense sacrifices and untold heroism should not see the light of day.

My research as an intelligence officer, and the investigations of other professional investigators and historians, indicates that approximately 9000 American POWs were illegally detained or taken into the USSR over a period of 57 years (1918-1975). Moscow never accounted for any of these secret detainees. . . In the 1930s, American citizens ranging from leftist sympathizers to American intelligence agents were kidnapped in Moscow and imprisoned "incommunicado." One of these agents escaped in 1941, after 5 years in Siberian camps, and walked 4000 miles to safety--in India. It took him a year. I've debriefed the only known survivor who escaped with him.

At the end of WWII, the Soviets secretly incarcerated, until they died, 7000 American GIs that they obtained from German Stalags. . . . U.S. Army documents from 1945 admit that the missing 7000 POWs were placed in the 'MIA column' of accounting (joining the total 78,000 missing from that war) so 'the numbers would balance.'

During the Cold War, 134 American pilots and airmen were shot down over the USSR, some killed, some captured. Because the U.S. did not admit to violating Soviet airspace, Moscow did not need to account for these men. . . . In the Korean War, an estimated 2000 POWs were transferred to Siberia via Manchuria. A Hungarian military officer reported seeing 200 of these American POWs as late as 1964, working on a road-building project. Another 200 POWs were transported directly to Moscow from Korea, via Prague and East Berlin, where they were subjected to a series of psychological, biochemical warfare, medical, and nuclear experiments.

As for the unrepatriated POWs, alive or dead in Indochina, it matters that the truth about what happened to these men comes out. I know two men personally who were captured and held after Saigon fell. One was Jim Lewis, who was released nine months later and died in Beirut. The other was Tucker Gouglemann, who died in late 1976 in NVA prisons. His remains were eventually returned, and forensics verified he was tortured and killed.

Somewhere in the neighborhood of 200 American POWs were reportedly executed around the same time that Gouglemann was killed. There are indications that another 20 survived at least until 1979, just before Bobby Garwood came out.

Having spent more time than most in Indochina, I too am skeptical of most of the live-sighting reports. However, as a former clandestine service officer, I also know that Indochina is an excellent place to cover-up what really happened to the unrepatriated POWs, and it is this information--the fate of our men--that we need to determine.

We have not been told the truth about American's unrepatriated POWs, not in the Indochina War, nor the wars preceding it. As I testified twice before Congressional committees, this lapse in full disclosure extends to components in both the U.S. and Russian governments.

I found boxes of unclassified documents that were being improperly hidden from the public and families within the DOD's own POW/MIA Office. Defectors from the Soviet military and intelligence professions have reported that U.S. POWs were taken into the USSR. These transfers of Americans remain classified secrets in Russia today. . . The only myth about the POWs is that we've been told the truth. Until that myth is exposed for the lie it is, keep the POW/MIA flag flying right up underneath Old Glory. It's meant to keep us honest."

PART VIII

Peek-A-Boo

Chapter Twenty-One

The Media Attacks

"How can anyone be missing? A person can't be missing.
God would know where he is."
                    Sybil Stockdale
                    "Return with Honor" KPBS

Throughout the years, I have had the good fortune of being interviewed for radio, TV, and newspapers. And I have also given speeches from time to time. I've always felt that the more I could do to keep the discussion of POW/MIAs before the public, the better.

As you've read in earlier chapters, I was part of the group that went to Paris in December 1969, to seek information about MIAs from North Vietnamese diplomats. Fifty-seven wives and 95 children took the trip. My daughter Kimberly was twenty months old then, and David my son was nine months old so they weren't able to go as the minimum age for the trip was seven. I spent my twenty-third birthday on the plane feeling very alone, sad, and wondering what I was supposed to do now. Would my life ever be normal again?

Both the San Francisco Chronicle and the San Francisco Examiner interviewed me at the airport when I arrived home. I told them, "You become somewhat deadened. Inside you feel, but it doesn't show on the outside, because people are watching. Maybe each one of us finds strength in our own problems." I remember saying that the trip was exhausting, but "full of hope."

For about five years after that I remained active in the MIA movement. But, because I was busy raising my two children and trying to live a normal life, it was not until 1989 when I realized that I needed to take an active part again to help Jim's family, other POW/MIA families and my own family find some answers. Each of us needed closure to the awful realization that we did not have the truth about what happened to our loved ones lost in Vietnam.

In Chapter Four, I wrote about my 1989 three-week trip to Indochina through an Australian travel agency. I was seeking information about Jim from Vietnamese villagers and anyone I could find there who might have a clue about what had happened on that fateful day in 1968. As a result, I was interviewed a number of times during that year.

On May 19, 1989, the Channel 10 news show in San Diego covered the "Run for the Wall," a cross-country drive to Washington D.C. by Vietnam vets and non-vet motorcyclists. "Forget the War, Remember the Warrior" was their battle cry. A caravan of 50,000 strong arrived in our nation's capitol in time for Memorial Day.

On that show, a Vietnam Vet, named Bill Evans, said, "We want our POW/MIAs back. It's been a long time. We need an answer. I hope to bring home the prisoners of war that we feel are still being held in Southeast Asia and awaken America, and therefore by their awakened being, they'll awaken their Congressmen, their Senators, their President, their elected officials."

The announcer introduced me by saying, "She has hope."

I said, "Remember that there are people still alive over in Vietnam. It's hard to imagine after 20 years that, that can happen but we've got live sightings. They're there."

Channel 8, in San Diego, interviewed me on August 7, 1989. The show started with my pointing to a map of Vietnam. I said, "These areas here are honey combed with POW camps. And so the odds of me getting into here, say next February when I go, are probably real slim."

The announcer then said, "Barbara Birchim knows there are American prisoners being held in Vietnam and Laos. She was in those countries in February of this year. Now, with maps and plans in hand, she's getting ready to go back . . . back to find out what she can about her husband, Jim Birchim, a member of the Army's Special Forces, who disappeared in 1968 on a recon mission into Laos. Though it's doubtful from the information she's gathered, that her husband survived, Barbara is convinced that live Americans are being held."

I continued. "And our government knows where they are."

Announcer: "She says the U.S. government knows there are American POWs in Asia. She said that for years the policy at the time was to ignore it though the secret has never been well kept."

"There are Americans there," I said. "There are wives that I talked to this weekend who have solid, solid evidence that their husbands are walking around in prisons."

Announcer: "During her recent visit to Laos, Cambodia and Vietnam, Barbara Birchim says she repeatedly asked villagers if they knew of Americans alive in the jungles and forests. More often than not, the people would panic or change the subject."

Me: "If there were any Americans, they would have said that there weren't any there. There isn't anybody. I don't know what you're talking about. For the villagers to be that scared, they have to be there."

Announcer: "More importantly, she says others have actually seen American prisoners of war, including members of a Goodwill group in Vietnam, recently. They were being escorted into an area to see what was described as a typical prisoner re-education camp for Vietnamese."

Me: "And, as they're coming in, here were 20 American POWs that were walking back into caves. (Pause) I know there are Americans there."

Announcer: "So, in February, Barbara Birchim will go back to Southeast Asia even though she's found no evidence that her husband survived the war, she says there's plenty of evidence that others did and that's more than enough for her to keep on looking."

Me: "That's why I keep on with this...is to help the ones who are alive."

Announcer: "Barbara Birchim is certainly not alone in her conviction that American POWs still survive in Southeast Asia. There are many others convinced that a lot of evidence has been ignored and that prisoners are being held as collateral for America's broken billion dollar promise."

Channel 10, San Diego, interviewed Bill, Sam, Roni, and me on March 8, 1990 after we returned from our Vietnam trip that year, delivering badly needed medical supplies.

Me: "It's obvious that they're there. I mean, just the reaction of the people tells you that."

Announcer: "But physical proof? No, because the government restricted their movements, but the trip did help in the healing process and help lay some demons to rest."

Bill: "They'll never go away. They're just as. . . probably as vivid today as they were back then, but it helps to deal a little bit more with them."

Roni: "I may have waited 20 years to find out my brother's helicopter just crashed, or that the V.C. killed him on the spot. I mean, you know, I'll never know, but it helps me to be physically there, and see the area and have some sense of what it was like."

Sam: "I say that any veteran who served there, a trip like this, it would do a world of good. Even if you think you're well inside already, it's going to make you understand these people."

Bob Sioss, Channel 8, also interviewed us. He had told me that anytime I did anything or got anything new and smashing, to give him a call. So, I called him and we did more taping. He had tried to get Channel 8 to send him to Vietnam to get some stories, for he had been there before. But they wouldn't do it. Bob left the station over some hard feelings, and that was one of them.

This just points out one reason why Monica Jensen-Stevenson couldn't get her book published in the United States after she was given a $50,000 advance. The publisher backed out. It's hard sometimes to imagine that the government can control something like that, but they do. They can get to anybody.

On the "Inside San Diego" television program, July 31, 1990, Laura Buxton interviewed Barbara Lowerison whose brother, Charles Scharf, was declared MIA on October 1, 1965. She also interviewed me. She told the viewing audience that the two of us had some "dramatic stories" to tell. She asked me to tell the story of Jim's disappearance.

I said, "The government hasn't given me any information that would lead me to think that he's alive. I went for a long time on gut feelings as to whether or not I felt he survived that incident, which I do, and it wasn't until recently that I started getting information that possibly he was still alive."

Laura: "Is that the information that led you to take two trips to Vietnam on your own?"

Me: "No, actually I got the information after the second trip."

Laura: "And what did you find? You had some harrowing experiences in Vietnam."

Me: "Well, my first trip was made because I had made a promise to Jim that when our children were old enough to be self-sufficient, that I would go and see this country. After that trip, it was very obvious that there were Americans still alive over there by the response that I got for asking just, 'Could I please speak to the Americans that chose to stay behind?' And, the Vietnamese becoming so anxious that they would break into a cold sweat or just turn around and leave. They couldn't answer that question. I knew that they were still there and that's why I pursued a second trip. This year I went back carrying about 500 pounds of medical supplies with me and was hoping to get back into the Central Highlands which I was told the first year I could do. This year I wasn't told that I couldn't get there until I arrived in Saigon. And later on, when we got up to Hue, I talked to a Swedish man and a Frenchman who had had no problems traveling up to the Central Highlands and had in fact seen Americans."

Laura: "And you came awfully close to getting yourself arrested."

Me: "Yes, I did. I was leaving leaflets that told of a reward that if any Vietnamese were to bring out any American prisoner of war, that they would receive a reward . . .money. . .and the Vietnamese found some of these leaflets and I was interrogated for four hours in Hanoi and was told that I could be imprisoned for 3-12 years."

Laura: "All of this leads to one thing. . .if there's the slightest possibility that either Charles or Jim could be alive."

Just three months later, on October 11, I was interviewed again on "Inside San Diego." This time, Barbara Lowerison and I were joined by retired U.S. Army Col. Earl Hopper. . .who served in World War II, Korea and Vietnam.

His oldest son was an Air Force pilot lost over North Vietnam and listed as an MIA. The interview took place just after Marion Shelton's death.

Announcer: "The suicide of Marion Shelton last week has cast a shadow over the entire movement. Why has there been so little accounting of so many Americans?"

After an introduction, the announcer asked me, "What do you think happened in Marion's life that caused this terrible turn?"

Me: "Well, the whole issue was so long, so frustrating, was so difficult to deal with that you have really no real concept of what it does to you emotionally and psychologically. It was just too much. She had worked for years to try to bring the truth to the surface, to educate the community as to what was really going on, to get word about her husband's fate and to follow that."

Hopper: ". . .certainly the indications are there that point to a cover-up. . .and there is no doubt that there are certain elements, like Barbara (Lowerison) said, within the government, those nameless, faceless bureaucrats, you cannot put your finger to them, that do not want those men to come home, because if men started coming out today, there'd be political chaos in Washington . . .because there are six (sic) administrations involved since the Paris Peace agreement was signed, since the POWs came home. Nixon, Ford, Carter, Reagan, and now Bush. And if POWs start coming out after 20 years in captivity, then there's going to be a lot of people that's going to have to answer."

Announcer: "But, wouldn't whatever administration brought them home be labeled a hero and really be given a. . ."

Hopper: "But you're presuming that the government's going to bring some men home. I'm taking the assumption that they're not going to be brought home by government efforts. I believe that if men come out, they're going to come out by means other than what the government is involved in, because I don't see the government progressing any place. They keep giving us all the rhetoric - - 'This is the highest national priority' - - we had it for eight years under the Reagan Administration and yet in the Reagan Administration, 125 men were declared dead and now, if that's the highest priority and he's declaring them dead, then I'm sorry."

Later in the TV interview, the announcer said, "You were among those groups who went there. . .to Vietnam, and Laos and Cambodia in a real search for your husband and I find it interesting that when you went you took something with you to try to help identify what your husband may look like today."

Me: "I had an artist do an aging photo on my husband at various degrees and I made up a flyer and had it translated into Vietnamese and took it with me and left it in various places with the Red Cross there and some officials. And it was very obvious on both my trips that Americans were there. I was denied access into areas where other travelers were able to get into with ease, who actually saw Americans and so, I mean, all their attempts to make it look as if there are no Americans being held against their will only reinforced that they were."

Announcer: "So, the feeling is, that if they are there, they're being held against their will."

Me: "Right. But, there are some who have chosen to stay. I need to make that clear. People who have had families and chose to stay behind, but the Vietnamese government will deny that those folks are there, too. But, I rode on the plane next to one, so I knew."

Announcer: "Really?"

Me: "Yeah."

Announcer: "Why would they not make themselves known to their families and relatives at home that they'd chosen to stay there. That's a tough step. But, it's easier than letting us at home spend 20 years of not knowing."

Back to some of the newspaper articles:

On Saturday, September 16, 1989, the San Diego Union ran a story and picture of me speaking at the National POW/MIA Awareness Day ceremonies in Old Town San Diego. The article quoted me as saying, "I am 42 now. It hit me this year that half my life I have been waiting for an answer. . . Today we are trying to bring together an awareness that there are many people still alive there (Vietnam)."

Father Charles Shelton Jr., son of missing Air Force Col. Charles E. Shelton, gave the invocation at the ceremony. He said afterward, "Let them know they will never be forgotten. They will never be abandoned."[1]

The San Diego Tribune also covered the ceremony on September 18. In that paper, the staff writer wrote, under the headline, "The war still isn't over for wife of Vietnam MIA."

"Now she plans another trip to explore Kontum, an area of Vietnam where she has been told there are Americans living in caves. 'The most I could ever hope for is that one of these people up in the caves might have heard where they buried him (Jim), or that he survived the fall and was buried later behind a hut.'

"Birchim's quest has taken on added urgency because her 20-year old son, David, has enrolled in ROTC at the University of Florida. She feels she must resolve the issue of his father's disappearance before her son embarks on his own military career."[2]

A year later, Veronica Shanely, Bill Evans, Sam Van Alstyne, and I were ready to embark on our trip to Vietnam to deliver medical supplies, seek information about Roni's brother and my Jim, and to give some closure for Bill and Sam who had fought there.

On January 18, 1990, the Beach & Bay Press (San Diego area) carried an article about our planned trip. I had appeared on a Channel 8 program in August telling about my 1989 trip. Bill and Sam were watching the show and contacted me. The article talked about this along with the fact that Roni was a medical social worker and a friend of mine, and that we were members of the National League of Families. She was quoted in the paper as saying, "My reasons for going are two-fold, really. I want to get a feel for the land where my brother was lost. Because Vietnam is a third-world country and its medical needs are so great, that's the precipitating factor for going."

Bill said in the article, "I want to go back to see what I destroyed. This whole thing is part of a healing process." Both he and Sam "were LLRPs (Long-Range Reconnaissance Patrols) during their active duty, and both have become actively involved in the P.B. (Pacific Beach) POW/MIA Awareness Committee."

Sam had lived and worked with two native tribes in Vietnam. "He worked with the Montagnards in the Central Highlands, not far from where Birchim's husband was based. Among her missing husband's effects, forwarded to her by the military, was a thick brass band wrapped about with metal wire. (It was really masking tape). She took it to Van Alstyne and asked him what he thought it could be. He removed the wrappings (tape) and four thin brass bracelets were exposed. Sam had been given just such a bracelet by the Bahnar tribe of the Montagnards and his had been lost. 'It brought tears to my eyes when I realized that Barbara's husband had probably had as significant a relationship to that tribe as I had. They are a hard people to get close to, but once you're accepted, it's like you're family to them. The bracelets aren't shared casually,' he said."[3]

After we returned from that 1990 trip to Vietnam, the Times Advocate (San Diego) featured my story, picture and a close-up of Jim's MIA bracelet on the front page of the April 6 paper. A colored sketch of what one artist thought Jim might look like after thirty years also appeared in the article. "I had to do it (go to Vietnam). I made a promise to Jim," the article quoted me as saying. "But the trip proved 'rather nerve-racking all the way through.' The Vietnamese tailed her, bugged her hotel room, and eventually threatened to put her in jail. . . The stated purpose of their 16-day trip was to deliver 500 pounds of donated medical supplies to Vietnamese doctors, but Birchim hoped to use the equipment as 'leverage to get information' about her husband's whereabouts."

I found it very interesting that the paper picked up one of my concerns that most people were not willing to consider. The reporter wrote, "What about her husband's military file, which she said suddenly changed two years ago from 'active deceased' to 'retired deceased'? Does it mean the military brought him back to the States with a new identity and told him to keep quiet so as not to jeopardize the lives of other MIAs?

"Or does it mean someone is fraudulently drawing retirement benefits in her husband's name. Or was it, as the military told her, a mistake, a glitch?"[4]

On Memorial Day, 1990, the Los Angeles Times ran quite an extensive article about paying tribute to those loved ones lost in war. Among the many stories featured was mine. My picture was captioned, "When Jim first turned up missing, I made a promise to him and myself that I would go to Vietnam when the kids were old enough to be self-efficient." The article said, "Barbara Birchim doesn't quite believe her husband is alive, but she isn't sure he's dead, either. . . She is critical of the U.S. government for what she views as inaction and with withholding of information."[5]

I was given a huge spread in the San Diego Sunday Times Advocate on September 15, 1991. A picture of my hand holding a picture of Jim, plus Jim's MIA bracelet on my arm, appeared resting on the map of Vietnam. And a picture of me and the sketches of what Jim might look like after 30 years, appeared with three columns of information inside the "Life in the 90s" column.

I was quoted as saying, "During the war, the government told us repetitively, 'Do not go to the press . . .Be quiet. The quieter you are, the better off our men will be. . .The only way we can get any information is to try to get through the back door. . .like through Senators, or returned military who don't have as much to lose. And some stuff from Laos, Vietnam and Cambodia is from sources there. . .It's totally frustrating. I guess what's hard at this point is that I'm disappointed in our government. We all know they're lying. They might as well say, you're right. We left them behind. Instead they say, 'they're all dead.'"[6]

A few days before that interview, Ronald W. Powell, staff writer for The San Diego Union-Tribune, wrote an article entitled, "MIA Organize to Press for Action." Among those he interviewed were both Roni and me. Of Roni he wrote, "The Shanley family has also knocked on the government's door in vain. Army Sgt. Michael H. Shanley Jr. was aboard a helicopter that went down over Vietnam on Dec. 2, 1969. His sister, Roni, and mother, Veronica, have made at least a dozen trips to Washington D.C. to glean word about Michael's whereabouts.

"Veronica Shanley said she always hoped Michael would come home before she or her husband died. Michael Shanley Sr. died in 1986.

"'Each day I keep asking God if I'm foolish to hang on to this,' Veronica Shanley said. 'He keeps telling me to keep going.'"[7]

I gave a talk to the San Diego POW/MIA Public Awareness meeting in May of 1992. Sam Van Alstyne was chairman at the time. In a report of that meeting, they wrote, "Barbara became curious during the 70s after encountering the status changes and confusion within the Department of Defense itself over certain cases. Jim was one of those. Over the years she has become very involved and outspoken on the POW/MIA issue. Since Jim operated in Laos and our government denied combat operations of this nature, it should not be a surprise that Barbara had her suspicions aroused."

On April 30, 2000, Channel 7 in San Diego covered the ceremony in Balboa Park acknowledging the 25th anniversary of the fall of Saigon. They interviewed several of us San Diegans who were well known as family members of POW/MIAs. At that time, the TV announcer stated that there were still 2028 men missing, 19 of them from San Diego County.

Barbara Lowerison, sister of Charles Scharf, told the viewers, "The war is not over for the families. War will never be over until we have our live POWs returned to us."

In my interview, I said, "It's about remembering the men that were left behind and those that continue to serve. These men (POW/MIAs) are still continuing to serve their country. They could be anywhere in the world and they could be across the border from Vietnam."

"In Quest to Locate Her MIA Husband, Local Woman Finds Her Way"--a headline in the San Diego Union-Tribune, May 25, 2001. Reporter Shay K. McKinley wrote, "It's been more than 30 years since Barbara Birchim last saw her husband, but her quest to discover what happened to him lives on each day."

The article went on to describe how I collect medicines and medical supplies for doctors and hospitals in other parts of the world.

"Birchim discovered that U.S. physicians are required to throw away a lot of good, usable medicines because of federal regulations. 'The volume of throwaway medicines is humungous. I could collect a ton of medicines from doctors every week. . .' Birchim has helped thousands of people in need of heart medication, antibiotics, vitamins and more."[8]

During the regional military briefings given by DPMO at the Family Member Update meeting held in San Diego on January 12, 2002, I was interviewed by staff writer, Michael Stetz, of the San Diego Union Tribune. On page B3, of the January 13 issue, the article stated that I don't "trust the government." (I think the government) "has been aggressive in searching for remains, but not so in trying to find those who might still be alive.

It's frustrating to deal with the ever-changing military bureaucracy. The newcomers (to the bureaucracy) have scant knowledge of these cases."

On one hand, it seems that I have been interviewed a lot. Yet, if the press and TV news really got behind this POW/MIA issue, I feel that it would almost force our government to act because the public would be outraged. As it is, we get these teasers and bits of new information, and then the whole issue dies away until the next time something is leaked.

Chapter Twenty-Two

Lies and More Lies

"We're in a hell of a mess"[1]
Robert McNamara

In 1993, Robert C. McFarlane gave the following address to the 24th Annual Meeting of the National League of Families.[2] McFarlane was a former National Security Advisor during the Nixon years in the White House, working under Dr. Henry Kissinger. He became a negotiating aide during the discussions with the Vietnamese on accepting 100 million dollars instead of 3.25 billion, which was what they wanted in exchange for the American POWs.[3] Excerpts from MacFarlane's remarks follow.

"The Last Battle"
by Robert C. McFarlane

"Today, your government is going through the final stages of a process - – begun roughly 18 months ago – - that before the end of this year will lead to the normalization of relations with Vietnam. If you were to ask the administration if that were true, the response would be, "No, the President has stated that we will not normalize relations with Vietnam without the fullest possible accounting of our POWs and MIAs." That would be a lie. For the evidence is clear. Look at what has happened.

- Two weeks ago the President decided to remove U.S. opposition to Vietnam's access to IMF, World Bank and other development bank loans, thus giving up one of the leading instruments of influence over Vietnamese policy toward providing a full accounting for your loved ones. It's not the first time. Less that two years ago, our government unilaterally agreed to go ahead on Phase I concessions of the "roadmap" before there was performance on the Vietnamese side.

- As we gather this evening, with full knowledge of your meeting dates, a high level mission was sent to Hanoi, thus foreclosing League representation by Ann on the trip --a historical given--and also taking away from Washington many in the policy community who ought to be here responding to your concerns. This delegation of 22 people--far too many for serious negotiations-- includes government officials who have had no role historically in shaping U.S. government POW/MIA policy. What signal does that send to the Vietnamese? It also includes for the first time representatives from respected veteran's groups, an apparent attempt to divide what has been for 20 years a close brotherhood of concerned citizens who support the families on this issue.

- Here in Washington, the Interagency Group, the linchpin of accountability to you which throughout the 80s kept everyone within the government honest and speaking with one voice--has been moribund for almost two years.

- In the field, solid experts with language skills and long histories and relationships with Vietnamese and Lao counterparts are being pulled back. In their places we find replacements, apparently more concerned with closing cases without justification than with a full accounting, and more given to praising Vietnamese "activities" than with getting concrete results. So far this year, only (sic) of our missing has been accounted for. A handful more in the past two years contrasts with over ten times as many in President Reagan's second term.

It doesn't take great vision to see what is happening. The decision on the IMF has led to this high level visit from which some ephemeral "breakthrough" will be announced. The "breakthrough" will be used to justify lifting of the trade embargo in the next few months, and ultimately to full normalization. Why is this happening? It doesn't take uncommon intellect to see that some things have worked and some have not. Firmness, without unilateral concessions, but with strict reciprocity worked; preemptive surrender has not. Why not keep on "keepin' on"? I'll give you my opinion. . . For 20 years, scores of essentially well-meaning people have called for our putting Vietnam behind us. Most of them emphasize the need to heal. (Have you ever wondered why healers usually focus on someone else's grief?) Surely healing is needed. God knows that everyone in this room longs to be healed. But real healing from our Vietnam experience will require much more than rhetoric to make it so. Real healing can only proceed from a deeper understanding by our government of the deep and shattering wound called Vietnam. Clearly the most vivid, irreversible, lasting part of this national wound, is represented by those lost in battle. That's why you are here. But I believe that in your hearts you are here for another reason as well. And in that reason you represent every American, not just the families of the POWs and Missing. The persistent wound--the lasting damage of Vietnam--is our ability to trust our government. And that won't go away until our government starts being honest with us again--on this subject and so many others.

Think back if you will to 1965. Our president led us into war--I commanded one of the first units in March 1965--portraying ambiguous events in a far off Gulf as ultimately threatening our vital interests. That was a lie. Before long our military commander, reflecting knowledge as primitive as that of the president told us that with just 50,000 more troops we'd be home by Christmas. That too was a lie. Later another president and high White House officials countenanced the falsification of military reports to the Congress. We secretly bombed a sovereign country, killing hundreds if not thousands of innocents. That was a lie. And all the while, American men and women died, were lost, taken prisoner and disappeared without resolution. Back home, lives were shattered. But not for nothing. Through the sacrifice of 55,000 dead and those still not accounted for we stemmed the tide, we bought precious time for the ASEAN countries, many of whom are represented here tonight. Through the heroism of these three and a half million American patriots we contributed in a very concrete way to victory in the Cold War and to all that that victory will mean to future generations. It came at a terrible price.

For along with these personal losses also went our trust in our government--that essential presumption of honesty, the glue that has held our country together since the birth of freedom here so long ago. Lying--persistent, unremorseful, deliberate lying--has carved a wound so deep in our body politic that it may never heal. And that, Mr. President, not the memories of military loss--and surely not the families--is what must be put behind us. Our government must stop lying to us.

Here's what you might say (to President Clinton).

You could say that you know--because DIA has told you, Mr. President--that Vietnam could easily provide a full accounting today for hundreds of our loved ones. You could say that because they know that we know, to ignore this truth only damages us. You could say that consequently you will henceforth authorize no loans or extend any assistance except in strict compliance with the terms of the "roadmap" presented to Vietnam over two years ago and that this policy will persist until Vietnam provides the fullest possible accounting for our loved ones. You could put in place an interagency system to carry out this policy such as proved effective in the past. You can put experienced professionals back in the field with the mandate to say nothing publicly until concrete results are achieved.

Or you could do none of these things. Because you may disagree. That is your privilege; that is your burden. Clearly normalization and all the business that would go with it would benefit Americans and would benefit Vietnamese. And over time, real healing might occur. The National League of Families would be saddened by such a decision. But I believe in my heart that if you came here tomorrow and told them the truth--that you are committed to the fullest possible accounting and that you believe that the way to achieve that is to reconcile with Vietnam, that as anguished, doubting and broken-hearted as they might be, you would get the support of the America people and of this League. But you cannot have it both ways; you cannot lie. You must not. For to do so is to assure that the shroud of Vietnam--this 30 year lie by our government to its people will plague you and us and this great country forever more. This is a precious moment in our history Mr. President. Please. . . don't let it pass."

* * *

"A liar is not believed even though he tells the truth."
Chinese Fortune Cookie – received 2002

* * *

And More Lies
On September 20, 1991, The Shirley Show, a TV talk show in Canada, was taped. The subject? Canadians missing in action--are they trapped and forgotten in POW camps in Vietnam? The show aired on the CTV Television Network on October 3, 1991. The audience was made up of POW/MIA families, and CVVT members and associates.[4]

Monika Jensen-Stevenson and William Stevenson, co-authors of Kiss The Boys Goodbye, were program guests, as was Fred Gaffen, author of Unknown Warriors. So were Dan and Betty Borah, parents of Navy pilot Dan Jr., POW. They had recently obtained photos of their son in captivity, which they had with them. Fred Gaffen, spokesperson for the National League of Families was also a guest, as was Cynthia Colby whose brother Lance Cpl. Peter Kmetyk, USMC, is listed as KIA/BNR, and is on the Wall as an American. Sue Devoe, whose brother Douglas was KIA, also joined the group of guests.

According to a printed report issued by The Shirley Show, "We thought the CIA was jinxing the show when they (CTV) lost all power. . . numerous calls were received after the show, the vast majority slamming the position of the National League of Families and Fred Gaffen."

Curious statements, I must say, since this was in Canada, not the United States.

It seems Fred Gaffen, introduced as an expert on Canadian Vietnam Veterans, said on the show that from everything he knew and read, there was no evidence to convince him that there were live POWs/MIAs in Southeast Asia. He must not have been of the kind of thinking found in Kiss The Boys Goodbye.

The host, Shirley, opened the show with, "The Vietnam War was never Canada's war except maybe it was. As many as 30,000 Canadians felt so strongly about that war that they left their homes and families and went to the United States to enlist. Some of those Canadians never came home from Vietnam. Some died. Some went missing in action just like the Americans they fought along side. The families of those Americans speak passionately about their determination to bring home the young men who they still say may be alive and rotting away in prisoner of war camps in Southeast Asia. For Canadians who served in Vietnam, and who may be in those same POW camps, have all been but ignored by the media and abandoned by the American government for whom they fought."

That is pretty damning!

One of the people interviewed was Vicki Briscall, engaged to Warrant Officer Ian MacIntosh, U.S. Army. Vicki said Ian had been on a search-and-destroy mission as an observer on a helicopter, along with the pilot. She was told that they were raked by enemy fire. The helicopter crashed into a tree and then fell to the ground. The pilot said, "I looked at Ian, and he looked dead. So I left him." But afterwards the rescue team found no body. The helicopter was there, and all the pieces, but no body.

Vicki said she didn't believe that Ian was dead. She feared that he had been living in any of a hundred different prison camps.

"I wrote to the government once asking for more information. And they told me, rather curtly, I was only a fiance. I wasn't family. I wasn't supposed to know anything. It was of no interest to me and I should just get on with my life."

When Shirley asked Vicki why Ian went to war for the United States, she said, "Ian had two reasons. Number one was that he was a very big kid, and he thought this was just the most wonderful adventure. He was a paratrooper in Great Britain. He was going to be in a helicopter in the army. He was going to have just such a wonderful time. And he was going to tell most fascinating stories all his life in this village Falkirk in Scotland where presumably I was supposed to live, too. But the other part was he hated communism. He hated it with a passion. And he felt it should be fought wherever it is. And he thought really that we Canadians were a bit complacent. We thought that the United States would look after us."

When Susan Devoe was interviewed, she discussed her MIA brother, Douglas. Her family was told that he died aboard a hospital ship after being hit on the head by a tree, and contracting cerebral malaria. But Susan didn't believe the information. Unfortunately, her father, who was supposed to identify his son's body, decided at the last minute that he didn't want to see it, so he took the undertaker's word that the body was Douglas, even though the undertaker had never seen Douglas before.

"And there are things in the death certificate that are very strange," Susan said. The height and weight was wrong, so was the eye and hair color as well as the complexion. Her brother had two scars, but the body had none. "It makes you wonder. Like in my case, my brother's body was never brought back. It never came back."

Shirley said, "Why would they lie to you?"

"Because he could have been in Laos. He was near the DMZ. No dog tags. Nothing came back that was personalized. . . My brother (the body that was supposed to be my brother) didn't have a military funeral. They claimed they didn't really have time to arrange it. So he just sort of got dumped in the ground as far as the military was concerned. They didn't bother. Which I have always been disgusted about. You know, he deserved that."

I'd like to add that the body of whoever was buried deserved a decent military funeral, even though he wasn't Susan's brother.

When Dan Borah was interviewed, he said, "It's terrible to say but from all of the facts we get and we are told, they are just flat not telling us the truth. They go out of their way not to prove that you might be right. They go out of their way to just say, 'It's not the truth.' So they're disproving everything we're trying to prove."

He continued: "There is no doubt in my mind that there is just as liable to be Canadians there as there are Americans. And we know that there are Americans. So without knowing (for sure), there are probably Canadians there as well, as far as I'm concerned."

Both William Stevenson and his wife Monika Jensen-Stevenson were interviewed during that show. The authors of Kiss The Boys Goodbye spoke of things that I had never heard of before. For example, William Stevenson responded, when asked about the Canadian government's role in the POW/MIA cover-up:

"The Canadian government was approached some years back in Bejing by the Chinese government with an offer of 180 Americans. And the idea was that they would be reintroduced into the States via Canada. The Canadian government decided it would be too embarrassing because having checked with Washington, the answer they got was that they would just as soon not know about this. The answer was influenced by the fact that at that time there was such a strong sense of anger with communism in Asia. Nobody wanted to be dealing with the communists, in the United States that is. . .the External Affairs Minister in Canada, in effect took his orders from Washington."

When Shirley asked Monika why the American government would lie, she said, " Well, there are a good number of reasons. But I'll tell you the main reason probably is that for many, many years, even past the war, the United States government fought a secret war in that part of the world. Laos is the best example. No prisoner came back from Laos. And we fought at least 14 years of a war there and longer. At the time we were negotiating with the Vietnamese the Laotian Communist leader said, 'We have your prisoners.' This is on the record. It's in all the newspaper articles of the time. 'We have your prisoners. But you must negotiate with us if you want them back.' Did we negotiate with the Laotians? We did not. Not one prisoner came back. That's one reason."

Shirley said that she believed Kiss The Boys Goodbye "could never have been published in the United States. . . Tell me why."

William and Monika had first gone to Bantam, William's publisher of his previous books. An agreement was struck--

"And then strange things began to happen. And then finally Bantam broke the contract. We had to sue them. It was settled out of court in our favor. But it taught us that all the warnings that we had been getting were in fact credible. We had been told repeatedly that you'll never get this published. Already another book had suffered the attentions of the intelligence. A book went out of control, which concerned the Iran/Contra scandal. And the technique there was to threaten libel action."

Shirley said, "Some of the strange things that you're talking about is I think that you claim that you had your gas line tampered with and it could have blown you and Monika and your baby sky high. That you got anonymous threatening phone calls. There were very serious things that were going on in your life, yet you never stopped writing this book."

Monika agreed. Then William said. ". . .there was direct interference from the covert operations department of the Pentagon. There were letters written before Bantam decided to cancel our book. . . Once a Canadian publisher had decided to go ahead it was all clear. We then found a partner in New York who was willing to publish the book. Even then, at the very last minute, a team of lawyers interrogated Monika who had to fly back from Southeast Asia to face them. And a great deal of the material had to be taken out of our book. But it has appeared since in another book (Spite House, The Last Secret of the War in Vietnam) published in England, quite independently."

Many accusations were made during those interviews on The Shirley Show. They included conspiracy, cover-up, and the fact that it would have been too politically embarrassing to bring the POWs back.

On October 20, 1991, William Stevenson wrote in his column, "Shirley Show outdoes U.S. competitors."[5] He ended his article with, "The Shirley Show has shown initiative by tackling serious subjects in an early time slot because it doesn't under-rate the intelligence of viewers. As a result, proportionately, it draws bigger audiences than the sometimes bubble-headed talk shows to the south (United States).

"In this instance, as The Washington Times observed, 'not only the defense establishment but also our elected officials (are condemned) for failing to protect the lives of American (and Canadian) servicemen who never came home, but may still be alive. To this day live sightings flow into the DIA, which, where POWs and MIAs are concerned, seems more like a black hole than an intelligence agency'. . ."

FIELD INVESTIGATION REPORT

I had hounded my casualty officer for the answers to some of my unanswered questions, with no hope of ever getting a response. But, to my surprise, I received a letter forwarded to me from Dale E. Hayes, JTF-FA, in April 1993. Of course it had been sanitized, but the letter assured me that "In no instance has substantive material been removed."

The unclassified document referred to the NOK (Next Of Kin or me) of REFNO 1322 (or Jim Birchim). First the paper said that NOK had requested answers to her questions on 3 Mar 93. That was impossible--a lie. I was in Somalia on that date.

The next item addressed was--"NOK questioned the status assigned to Captain Birchim's case and the date that status was assigned. JTF-FA records indicate the Army determined Captain Birchim's official status to be dead. Body not recovered (Status Code 'N') as of 10 May 1971. The 'date status assigned' on the REFNO 1322 biographic/site report will be updated to read 10 May 1971."

The report had said date of death was November 15, 1968, so at least they were admitting an error. But there was no mention of where that date had come from or who wrote it down--by mistake? Surprise! Surprise!

Thirdly, when I was in Kontum, I saw the Bright Light Report. It was written in English. The Minister for POW/MIA Affairs in that province said that all of the reports were in English so he couldn't read them.

I had questioned whether the data about the site where Jim's team was extracted had ever been given to the Vietnamese so they could look for bodies or signs of the incident. The report read, "Vietnamese investigators have access to virtually the same data via the Vietnamese version of the Bright Light data base supplied and updated by JTF-FA computer specialists."

That's nice! But if it's in English, what good does it do? Was that a lie to pacify a NOK? Maybe the JTF-FA had been lied to as well.

MILITARY ID CARD

It may seem that this does not belong here, but my problems with ID cards certainly involved a lot of lies.

When Jim's status was changed to KIA, with no notification of a Board of Inquiry convening, and with no new information about his case, my military ID card was changed to USA/AD Dec (US Army active duty deceased).

I lost all of my benefits when I remarried in 1971, including my ID card. But when I was divorced in 1982, I changed my name back to Birchim, since Jim's and my children were still carrying that name. I was issued a new ID card with the same status except my medical benefits were under CHAMP VA, and I started receiving widow's benefits.

In 1989, I went to Miramar Naval Air Station to renew my ID card. Jim's status on my card was changed to USA/RET Dec (US Army retired deceased). And my medical benefits were reinstated to CHAMPUS, as of 1979. When I challenged the change, I was told, "that is what's in the computer."

"But," I said. "There is some mistake. I didn't notice that CHAMPUS had been reinstated until I signed the card and it was laminated. We need to correct this. I should not be receiving medical benefits under them, and he was active duty deceased, not retired."

The clerk repeated, "No mistake. It says right here, retired deceased."

The September date on my card didn't link to Jim's change in status from MIA to KIA or anything else in his history.

"I d-d-don't know, m'am," the clerk, all of 19 years old, stuttered. "That's what the computer says."

In my booming voice, I said, "Okay, let me see. So, you found my MIA husband, you retired him, and didn't invite me to his retirement party. And then you killed him off again. Is that right?"

The poor clerk was dumbfounded, as were the others in the room. Since he would not change my card, I took it from him, and as I turned to leave, I noticed a man standing to the side, shaking his head. I said to him, "It doesn't matter. I've been going through this kind of stuff for the last 20 years."

I spent over three years going to my casualty officer, and going as high as the Secretary of State, trying to find the answers to why there were changes on my ID card.

"Well, all that information is generated out of the finance center," Lt. Col. Zorn, who worked in the office of the Secretary of State told me when I contacted him at first. He had no explanation for my medical reinstatement except human error. I was not about to let this slide by.

I said, "You might want to look because maybe someone has taken Jim's Social Security number, and is drawing retirement pay." I was trying to give him something to act upon, something that could give me a plausible answer to what was going on.

His answer? "Well, let me check on that."

To me, my questions seemed simple. Who made the changes and why?

After waiting for days and days, he got back to me only to tell me, "No, that's the way it is."

In the meantime, I got the direct telephone number of DEERS, physically located in Colorado, which is the mother brain for all military service people. I called them and pretended I was a social worker in a hospital and I was verifying an ID card. They verified that the category was correct as shown on the card--retired deceased.

When I said there was a discrepancy in the designation, the woman on the other end of the line said the paperwork would have to be processed elsewhere.

So, now I'm back in Washington D.C. and I'm being told, "Oh, Barbara, it's just a clerk typist error. You know. . .garbage in, garbage out. Somebody just stroked a few bad keys."

"Look," I said. "You have been telling me since 1968 that Jim Birchim is dead. . .active duty deceased. No one should be revamping his file to read otherwise."

When I got a stupid look in response, I continued. "Okay, let's play the only two possible scenarios. Someone tried to spell somebody else's name and got too close to Birchim. So Birchim comes up on the computer screen. None of Jim's information would match the other name, so they wouldn't process it. The only other way to pull up Jim's record would be by his Social Security or military number."

When Jim first joined the military, the guys were given a military number. Then, the identification of everyone in the military was changed to Social Security numbers. If someone stroked a wrong number in another's record, and that error matched Jim's number, then he wouldn't have gotten their client's information, anyway.

"How can you explain this?" I said.

"Just go back and have someone redo your ID card, Barbara," I was told. I was becoming quite a thorn in everyone's side at this point. "You're not listening to me. I have tried that and no one will issue me a new card because that's what Jim's status is in the computer."

Someone knew something that shouldn't have been known, and that information found its way along the information line to the finance department. Was someone trying to tell me that Jim was alive and retired, therefore granting me health benefits under CHAMPUS?

Even when I asked my U.S. Representative, the Honorable Duncan Hunter, to help me get an answer to this dilemma, he couldn't get any different information than what I had already received.

Here's a summary of what happened.

August 10, 1989 – Under the freedom of information Act, I sent out requests to the FBI, CIA and DIA for information on my husband.

August 24, 1989 – I received a letter from the CIA that they had no file on Jim.

September 15, 1989 – I received a form from the FBI saying they were searching their files for information.

September 26, 1989 – Another form letter arrived from the FBI stating they were still looking.

October 30, 1989 – The FBI sent another letter stating they were forwarding my request to another government agency.

November 15, 1989 – I received a postcard from the Office of the Secretary of Defense saying they had received my FOIA request.

January 22, 1990 – I called the phone number on the postcard and spoke with Lt. Col. Zorn. He said he had my file and was waiting for information to come from two places, one was Finance. He said he would get back to me in a few days.

March 9, 1990 – I called Lt. Col. Zorn again. He said the information had been declassified, but it really wasn't anything. I asked for a copy, which I finally received. When I mentioned my ID card problem, he referred me to Dept. Chief of Staff for Army Personnel. I spoke with Col. Fitch who said he had no idea why there was a change in my ID card. He suggested I get in touch with my Casualty Officer. I already had. He informed me that he had to notify my Casualty Officer of our conversation. I thought that was fine.

April 16, 1990 – I received a cover letter and copies of DIA documents from my Casualty Officer. Some of the documents were missing. And a FOIA request is supposed to be answered in 10 working days. It had now been five months.

In putting together the chronology for this episode, so I could contact someone else who might be able to help me, I wrote, "What is going on here? Please note that my ID card problem and the release of information from Lt. Col. Zorn both reference Finance. Why does Finance keep coming into the picture? It has been brought to my attention that anyone with a security clearance has a file in the FBI. Jim was with Special Forces and I know that he had a Secret, if not a Top Secret clearance. So why is the FBI denying the existence of a file? And if this file was sent to OSD, then they would have more than a one liner on Jim, wouldn't they? I've asked my Casualty Officer if there is anything still 'classified' on Jim and he says 'no.'

330

"This is not the only strange thing that has gone on with his file. If you could review the files in each of the various departments, maybe you can get a logical explanation for why I'm getting the run-around."

Well, it took me four years to get a corrected ID card and now when I get the card renewed, the medical benefit section has been corrected and Jim's status has been changed to active duty deceased.

But. . .on the form I have to sign, there is date of February 13, 1919 as Jim's birth date--yes, 1919--which doesn't relate to Jim, even the February 13 date.

If 1919 should be 1991, then what happened on February 13 to change Jim's status?

Now, I was telling everyone that the date does not refer to Jim. "That's not my husband," I kept saying. "The date is wrong. You're trying to tell me that someone fought in the Vietnam War who was alive in 1919?"

The answer I get each time I renew the ID card is, "If you don't sign this document, you don't get an ID card."

When I renewed my ID card on August 8, 2001, the computer printout from DEERS went a step further. Jim's real birth date is 16 July 1946. The government changed his MIA status to KIA/BNR on 10 May 1971. The computer printout from DEERS now has Jim's birth date as 10 May 1946. This seems to me to be proof that Jim's new identity was born on the day and month he was declared dead, and the year of his actual birth.

The other odd thing about the form I saw in 2001 was it showed we were married on 30 Sept 1979. My heart leaped when I saw that. Was there a message for me in that date? Or could it be that Jim had remarried in 1979 under another name?

So, each time I have to sign these documents, they are full of major errors and major changes, and with major unanswered questions to get my ID card.

Isn't that incredible?

I could go on forever with Lies and More Lies, but I feel that the whole POW/MIA issue could fit under this title.

Chapter Twenty-Three

Who's Watching Whom?

"Let us have faith that right makes might, and in this faith,
let us, to the end, dare to do our duty as we understand it."
Abraham Lincoln

In the long run, my trips to Vietnam and Thailand turned out to be quite benign. I mean, I did not ruffle any U.S. government feathers regarding MIAs or Jim's whereabouts. At least I didn't think I had.

I did get to Kontum. Yet, in the years since then, my sadness in not being able to get a straight answer as to what happened to Jim, became clouded with yet another strange situation.

I have read a good deal about the CIA, and have watched many conspiracy/intrigue shows on TV and at the movies. Enough, that is, to think that writers have great imaginations when it comes to espionage and spy stories. Like most of us, I've always figured the kind of threats, surveillance, and snooping dramatized in CIA/FBI stories was more dramatic than real.

However, in 1990, I began to suspect otherwise. Either that or I was beginning to go crazy.

THINGS BEGIN TO HAPPEN

After Marion Shelton's funeral on October 4, 1990, Sam, his wife Margo Van Alstyne, Bill, Ronie, and I drove to a small seafood place for an early dinner. When we arrived, we were the only ones there. We were seated in the back at a big table so we could spread out some things I'd brought to show the four of them.

The table was crowded with letters and papers as we ordered our food, and talked about POW and MIA stuff. All of a sudden, I got a feeling that I was being stared at. The hairs began to stand up on my neck, to quote a cliché. Then, I saw a man sitting in a booth very close to us. He was looking at me, like staring. Each time I glanced his way, he was still staring at me. He looked somewhat familiar, but I had just done a number of presentations at veteran's groups, so I thought he might have been in one of the audiences.

After a while, the staring got to me, to the point of giving me cold chills. So I leaned over to Margo, who was sitting next to me, and I said, "That guy over there, with the white beard, kind of looks like Hemingway. Do you know him?" I kept my head down so he wouldn't think I was talking about him. "Is he one of the vets who's been attending any of our functions?"

Margo glanced at him, and in a casual voice, she said, "No, that's the guy who not only stayed in the van across the street from my kitchen window, but also followed me to each of my work assignments the whole time you guys were in Vietnam."

I said, "What?"

"Oh, I guess I didn't get around to telling you about that. I told Sam, though, when he got home."

"What is this all about?"

"Well, as soon as you guys left for Vietnam, this white van parked across the street. It never moved. Every so often, men would get out of it and go back in."

I couldn't believe what I was hearing.

"I used to watch them come and go, and they watched me come and go. It became a joke after a while. And one time I felt like going over there and offering them coffee and donuts."

I leaned closer to her as she continued her story.

"I did wave to them every morning as I went to work, and I'd say, 'Bye...see you later.' They stayed there until you guys got back and then they moved."

"Holy shit!" came out of my mouth without my thinking.

"Yep, Barbara, that's one of the guys who would get in and out of the white van."

Without another word, I gathered all the letters and papers spread out on the table, and said, "I've got to get out of here. I'm going to leave first, and you guys kind of hang around for a while to see what happens. Okay?"

Later, each of them, Roni, Bill, Sam, and Margo, called me to make sure I got home okay. I found out that the man with the white beard from the white van watched them as they walked out of the restaurant so he hadn't followed me.

We figured that all of our phones had been tapped during the six-month period when we were planning our trip. I was certainly naïve about such things, then.

PARANOIA?

Becoming aware of the threats to me, and my friends, began to snowball. The more I learned, the worse it got. I don't want to say I was paranoid, because it wasn't that. But, I must say, my feelings appeared as paranoia to a lot of people.

I kept saying, over and over, throughout the years, "Thank God most of these things happened to me when I had witnesses." Otherwise, I would probably be locked away in a padded cell long before now. I could just hear people saying, "Poor lost soul!"

From the time of Marion's death on, I think "they" shifted the surveillance team from her to me. I had no idea I was being followed. But, it wasn't long after that, that one Sunday morning, about 5 a.m., I heard someone in the house. I walked out on the 2nd floor landing of my townhouse, bent over the stairwell and said, "If there's anybody down there, you better get the hell out because the police are coming."

At that moment, I heard a thump, thump, thump, the front door close, and the dead bolt flip over. Whoever "he" was or "they" were, they were gone.

I got on the phone, called 911, and spoke to a dispatcher. I was told that if the intruders were gone, the police wouldn't have to come. There was no problem, any longer. I couldn't believe it. That was my beginning of a wonderful relationship with the police department.

Even then, I thought the person(s) in my home were probably robbers, though I could find nothing missing. I assumed at the time that it had nothing to do with MIA business.

I think, as I look back on the incident, "they" were putting bugs in my house. Maybe "they" thought no one was home that early morning.

Anyway, as it proved to be true later, my kitchen and living room areas were indeed bugged. I'm not sure whether "they" bugged my bedroom at a later date, but "they" probably did.

It was Monday after the intrusion that I went to the grocery store as soon as I got home from work. I had barbecued Sunday night, and I was going to barbecue again. I was only gone about 45 minutes. After I put the groceries away, I went out to the back porch to start the barbecue.

I unlocked the sliding glass door, and walked over to the gas grill. I was stunned. The gas was on. Now, I know I had turned the gas off the night before, because I checked it the last thing before I went upstairs to bed.

Someone had gotten inside our gated community and turned the gas on, no doubt while I was at the grocery store. It could have blown up if it had been on very long or all night and day.

I remembered reading Monika Jenson-Stevenson's book, Kiss The Boys Goodbye, where she describes how she came home one day and found the gas logs in her fireplace turned on. She could smell the gas. No one had been home to turn the gas on. No one, but "they" would want to scare her into not writing her book.

She wrote that the incident was her awakening to the fact that many POW/MIA families had told about similar bizarre things happening to them. She knew now that the stories were not just tall-tales.

And David Morehouse writes, in Psychic Warrior, that his phone was tapped once he decided to break all rules and write his book about remote viewers. He was harassed through the mail, too. At least that didn't happen to me.

Sonja Anderson, a Hanford Nuclear Reservation employee in 1991, blew the whistle to congressional staffers about unsafe conditions at Hanford. Her phone was bugged. She could hear beeps and clicks. She had hang-ups late at night and two different answering machines became inoperable by someone tampering with them from the outside.

Sonja's daughter kept finding notes on her car saying she was being watched, and two of Sonja's friends heard noises on their phones.[1]

It was Wednesday of the week I found the gas turned on, that the next episode happened. My daughter had graduated from college, and I had the photo of her receiving her diploma sitting on a small table by my front door so I could take it to the frame shop.

When I went downstairs that morning, the picture was gone. What was going on? I walked around the house, talking out loud to the walls.

"Whoever took my daughter's photo, if you think you've seen a madwoman, then you ain't seen nothin' yet. I'm going to the White House and we'll do lunch, dinner, whatever it takes, and I'll get this resolved. You better pay attention, because I'm not kidding."

This was the time when I was contacting people and gathering information, after having gone to Vietnam in 1989 and 1990.

I went outside to my next-door neighbor's. I was livid.

The way my home is setup, it sits in a back corner of the townhouse with three other units overlooking my front door. That means only three doorways form my alcove.

The lady who lived in one of the units had a bedroom window that overlooked my front door. She sat in front of that window every day while she did typing for her husband's business. Her name is Angel.

So, I knocked on Angel's front door and told her I had a question. I said, "Have you seen any strange gardeners around here? I mean, I'm having some real weird things happen, and I thought maybe there were some new people on the block or strangers you've noticed lately."

She kind of thought about that and said, "No, except all the people who keep going in and out of your house."

I about died. "What are you talking about?"

"Well," she said, "for the last three months or so, people have come to your front door and just walked right in. I don't know who they were."

We talked for a while. She finally described them. She said that they were men, but not the same ones all the time. They were always nicely dressed, clean. Some of them wore jeans and sports shirts, others slacks.

"Why are you asking me this?" Angel said.

So, I told her what had been happening.

"Barbara, I had no idea." She didn't know that my husband was MIA. I didn't talk about that to most people.

"Well, the men always went right up to the front door and walked right in," she said. "One man had red hair and a red beard." She thought they were my friends.

Upon hearing that, I asked her if she would mind coming over to my house so I could show her a picture. I thought I knew who that redhaired man could be.

I had some newsreel footage of a lot of veterans in one shot. As soon as she saw that one shot, she said, "That's the guy."

I thanked her and when she left, I called Sam. I told him I had a favor to ask.

"Sure, what is it?"

"I need you to get the license plate number off of the redhead's motorcycle and his van. I want to see who owns them. See if this guy is really who he says he is."

"Sure, no problem," Sam said.

There was a group of Harley riders, many of them Vietnam vets, in the San Diego area, who rode together, often for fund raising purposes and to call attention to POW/MIAs. I don't think anyone ever doubted when a rider said he'd been in Nam, so no one ever checked anyone's story.

I had met the redheaded man. That's how I knew his name. And I thought he was kind of different. He sort of didn't fit, sort of an odd squirrel.

At this point I needed to call in a marker from a friend. I asked her to run the plates through the DMV. It took about a week before the answer came back. The DMV screen had flashed a code referring the viewer to "government use."

Five days went by. That night I came home from work to find my daughter's photo had been returned, only it sat on the bedroom nightstand on the side of the bed where I slept, instead of on the table downstairs by the front door.

Again, I walked around the house, talking to the walls in a loud voice. I thanked "them" for returning the picture. I thanked "them" for not marking or smudging the photo. I thanked "them" for locking the door after "themselves" so no riffraff could come in when I was away at work. I could just see "them" smiling as "they" sat in "their" unidentifiable van somewhere nearby, listening to my every word.

"You can help yourself to anything in the refrigerator, you know," I said. "If there's something in particular you'd like to eat while you're here, I'll leave a pen and paper on the counter so you can jot down Heinekens or anything else you'd like. Actually, I have a great idea. Why don't we carpool since you're obviously following me. You know, save a little gas. I know where I'm going. You don't."

Well, I thought that was pretty funny. But, in the meantime, I had scared the hell out of my neighbor. I said to Angel, "When you see someone coming into my house, call the police immediately."

Someone suggested that I give Angel a camera so she could take a picture of each person who wandered in and out while I was gone.

And then there was Byron who lived in the upstairs townhouse. He sublet his front bedroom to a man who seemed to not be who he said he was. There were so many things about him that didn't fit.

What I mean by that is he was supposed to have come to San Diego to start a carpet cleaning business. He had a big van with a carpet cleaning advertisement on the sides, but the windows were dark. He told Byron he was going to work a certain number of days a week in San Diego to try to setup his business, and then he would go back to Phoenix on the weekends.

Well, the van never moved from its parking spot at the townhouse. I understand that the only time he moved the van was when I was out of town.

Meg, one of my neighbors, happened to see the man outside my front door several times so she said to him, "You know, my carpets are filthy. Would you come and do mine, too?" She gave him her name and number, but he never contacted her. She bumped into him several months later, and asked him why he had never called her.

He said, "Oh, well, I didn't know how to get a hold of you."

Imagine that! She only lived next door.

At one point, when I knew I'd had an intrusion, I decided to have my locks changed. I had given my key to Meg to pick up my mail whenever I was gone. The next time I asked her to pick up my mail, she was going to be gone for a few days so she gave my key to Byron, and asked him to please pick up my mail while she was out of town.

The locksmith came in the afternoon while I was at home, and changed the locks on my house and garage doors. With my new keys in hand, I went to the post office. About 45 minutes later, I returned home and tried to open my garage door with the genie. I could hear the motor, but the door wasn't opening. I got out of my car and walked up to the garage door. The slide bolt on the outside of my garage door, which had been painted over several times through the years in the open position, was now pushed over to the closed position.

There was no way for anyone to slide that bolt closed, unless the person banged on the bolt pretty hard with a hammer to force it closed.

I guess "they" wanted me to know that "they" were watching. The man who rented the upstairs bedroom from Byron with the window that looked down on my front door, knew when the locksmith had come and gone. That man had been a busy bee! He set a record by making his presence known in 45 minutes, even though he didn't appear to get into my house.

My curiosity was peaked, so I decided to call a private investigator I knew in another state. I asked him if he could run the license plate number that belonged to the carpet cleaning van.

He discovered that the van was owned by a church supposedly located in a strip mall. Of course, neither the carpet cleaning service nor the church was located there. Just another piece of information to give validity to my suspicions.

TO CATCH A SPY

Everyone was giving me helpful hints on "How to Catch Your Local Spy."

And that was the beginning of almost ten years of "their" intrusions into my home.

Every time I did something regarding POW/MIA stuff, "they" would make another visit. One time I went to the National League of Families meeting. The Senate Select Committee had put out their interim report with lots of copies for us to take to our TV stations and newspapers. I took an armload home from Washington D.C., and decided to make the rounds.

I was working, so I had to distribute the report during my lunch hour and after work. At the first TV station I went to, I jumped out of my car, locked the doors, and went in to greet the receptionist. By this time I had names and contacts of all these TV stations, so I put a note on the report cover. I wrote, "Dear Bob Sioss, Channel 8. Here's some fuel for the fire. Let me know if you want any more info."

I went right back to my car, maybe gone all of five minutes, if that long. I couldn't get my car door open. Something was wrong with it. That was a pain in the butt, because I was wearing a suit and heels, and I had to climb over the console of my Honda to get to the driver's seat.

I repeated the same routine for three or four more stations that afternoon. Climbing over the console twice per stop got easier each time, believe it or not.

The next morning, I decided that I needed to get the dumb door fixed. I zipped over to my car repair place. I was told it was not a ten-minute job. They had to take the door panel off, so I got a rental car.

When my lunch hour rolled around, I jumped into the rental to make my rounds of more TV stations and newspapers. When I returned to the car after my first stop, the door didn't work. Just like my Honda.

"What the hell is going on?" I yelled. This was too bizarre to even contemplate. Maybe I was going through a bizarre "Karma" phase.

When I returned the car, I told the rental people, "You've got problems with that driver's door. The key doesn't open it once you lock it."

When I picked up my own car, I asked the mechanic if he found out what was wrong with the door.

He said, "Oh, there was a screw kind of thing that popped off from the lever. It pulls the handle up when you turn the key to unlock the door."

"How would that happen?"

"Well, it would be pretty darn hard for the screw to come loose unless you were jimmying the door. I suppose you could do it if you slammed the door all the time."

Now, granted that was a coupe and it was a big door, but I'm not a slammer. The nuns at Catholic school taught me well. They'd make us go in and out of the classroom as many times as it took to close the door softly enough so no one could hear it.

Then a light went on in my head. By George, "they" didn't want me delivering those Senate Select Committee reports.

Well, that ticked me off.

I called my friends and said, "Guess what 'they're' doing now?" That night I got a call from Barbara Lowerison, who said that Insider Magazine, which is like a magazine TV show, wanted the two of us to be on their Sunday morning show, but they wanted to tape ahead of time. She said it was really short notice, but could I come down to the station the next morning at 7:00.

Now mind you, this call was at 7:00 p.m. after I got home from work. "That's cutting it pretty close, since I have an 8:00 o'clock meeting tomorrow morning, but alright, I'll do it," I said.

The next morning, when I went into my locked garage, my car was ticking. I looked around to try to find out where the ticking was coming from. I finally decided it was under the hood.

Could it be a bomb?

Or, was the motor for the flip-up headlights making this noise? It looked like the cover over the lights had closed, so it seemed unlikely that the motor would be running.

I stood there for a few moments mulling over the possibilities of what would happen if I missed my appointment, or if I turned the key and the car blew up, or if the car caught on fire and burned down not only my townhouse but the one above the garage.

The whole thing was beyond being ridiculous. I had had it. I could back out of the garage and take my chances or call the bomb squad. I chose to try to start the car.

I went to the driver's door to open it but it wouldn't budge. And I could tell that it wasn't locked.

Then I went to the other side to open the passenger's door with my key. As I opened the door, I noticed that the overhead light went on and the digital clock was running. I thought my battery would be dead if that headlight motor had been on all night.

I had to get to that TV interview, so I got in the car, said a few Hail Mary's and turned the key. Everything worked fine. After the interview, I went to the repair shop and told the repairman that not only was something wrong with my door again, but the car was ticking.

"That's bizarre," he said. There was that word again. He got his mechanics to work on it while I waited. They found a little grommet wedged in the headlight, and it was not allowing the headlight to completely close. The motor for the headlights kept recycling, causing the noise.

"Oddly enough, there's a grommet missing from your door again," he said. "This time it's gone, and that's what caused your door to not work. It's the same grommet I put there when you were in a few days ago."

"Do you suppose that's the one that was stuck in my headlight?" I said.

"Ah-h-h. . ." he said.

"Let me ask you this," I said. "If that had been going on all night long, would I have been able to start my car?"

"No," he said. "Your battery would have been dead."

Not to scare him any more than I already had, I said to myself, "So, 'they' came early in the morning this time, like five o'clock."

My mechanic's face went white.

I had the feeling that whoever these men were "they" were the same ones who watched my friend Marion. My guess was that since Marion was so active in the POW/MIA situation, the men watching her were double agents. I'm sure that since I was actually going to Vietnam, "they" had put me at the top of "their" list to scare. "They" wanted to make me stop talking and writing and being involved.

Marion went to Vietnam in the 70s, but she went with some kind of diplomatic group. She wasn't there to go to Hanoi or Saigon or to look at crash sites.

I went to Vietnam to talk to the people. I was too active in wanting information, and I was too naïve to know how dangerous it could be. I just went. I was unpredictable as far as "they" were concerned, I'm sure.

I think that around 70% of the soldiers lost in Vietnam were 18 years old. Most of them weren't married, yet, so there were few wives to ask questions. Their parents were from the World War II era, and they believed whatever the government representatives told them. They had no need to push and bang and scream and yell about their sons who were labeled POWs or MIAs, and didn't come home. They also didn't have the physical stamina to withstand a trip to Vietnam to search for their sons, if they wanted to.

Then there was me, out there, stomping around making noises and asking questions.

PHONE TAPPING

I heard from my friend Sara that "they" had tapped her phone. She tested it every once in a while by hanging up, then picking the phone back up to make another call. She could tell that the listener hadn't disconnected yet.

When this began to happen to me, sometimes I would say in the phone, "Okay, guys, I'm going to call my mother, so you can hang up now."

I kept getting the best suggestions from people I told about my tapped phone. For example, I would say, "This is for everyone, so get your hearing aids on good and solid because I'm going to dial now."

At one time or another, I thought about having my house swept for bugs, but I would never be able to leave the house if I did that, because as soon as I went to the store, they would re-bug it.

At one point, I called the telephone company to complain that I thought there was a tap on my phone. The woman I spoke with was very nice. She said they could come to check my house, but my phone could be tapped between the house and the pole. And, she said the equipment was so sophisticated now that they could sit on the freeway and point a machine in the direction of my house to pick up everything being said. I gave up that idea.

It became evident that I needed to find a safe way to talk with my friends, mainly Sara. I needed an ally. So, Sara and I worked out a code system and went out of our areas to use pay phones. If I called and asked about how her plants were, or whether her night jasmine was blooming, she would know she had to get to a particular pay phone, and wait for me to call her from my pay phone. That took some research because not all pay phones can receive incoming calls. We gave each other 30 minutes to get to our phone locations.

Sometimes we needed to send each other information in hard copy, so we set up P.O. boxes that we rented with fictitious names.

This whole thing became quite nerve racking. I was always afraid that I would forget phone numbers or names. I figured out a way to record all this information so "they" couldn't know what I was doing if "they" read my address book or other papers.

Sara became the one person I could talk with who understood what I was going through, the hurt and sadness I felt, and the frustration and anger I experienced. Sara was a great listener, and a good shoulder to cry on. She had experienced the same emotions I had, though she was ahead of me as far as the emotions that went along with her husband being missing.

When I first met Sara, I didn't feel that Jim could be alive. I just knew that the information I got from the government was the most screwed up story I'd ever heard. They were keeping information from me, and there was no reason for that, as far as I could see.

As yet, I didn't have the heart connection that Jim was still alive. I couldn't figure out the nightmares that had started my whole adventure of looking for Jim after so many years. What did it mean when he stood at the foot of my bed and yelled, "Come now or it will be too late."

Sara and I became a support system for each other. And we both needed that. Desperately!

But I digress. I think the reason "they" (who ever "they" are) were playing tricks to scare me into not talking--to keep me from going public with what I knew--to keep me from going back to Vietnam.

I was glad to have witnesses to the peculiar things that were happening to me, like the gas barbecue that had been turned on, and the noises I heard from time to time in my house. And, Sam's wife being watched by someone in the white van sitting across from their house the entire time we were in Vietnam, was the coup de grace.

"Their" continuing to threaten me, and to enter my home, led me to believe that there was a cover up of some kind going on, for sure. "They" wouldn't have bothered with me if I were just a ranting, raving lunatic. I feel that "they" compounded "their" problem by doing those things to me since I didn't fall for "their" antics. That was "their" mistake. Had no one witnessed the stupid tricks, I would have probably been committed to a psych ward, early on. The witnesses were my saving grace.

As it turned out, while we were in Vietnam, Sam's wife could make local calls, but when she tried to make a long distance call to a friend one time, her phone didn't work. I guess "they" decided she would try to call us in Vietnam, and "they" weren't going to let her do that without "their" knowing about it. By the same token, when we tried to call her to let her know when our plane was arriving, her line was dead. We hadn't called her before that, so "they" didn't get to hear a single thing from her phone.

* * *

Before I went to Albuquerque in August of 1991, to visit Sara and meet with Terry who wanted to go to Vietnam with me, I had a strange daydream, sort of like a twilight dream that you have as you're going to sleep. I was eating with Sara in one of my favorite restaurants, and a man with a white beard sat at a table not far from us.

On that first Sunday with Sara, we went to the restaurant I just mentioned, and who should walk in but a man with a white beard, much like the one who stared at me the year before when Sam, Margo, Roni, Bill, and I were together in a restaurant after Marion's death.

The man left after a while, but then another white haired, white bearded man came in and sat near us. By this time I was really spooked. To this day, I am very conscious of men with white beards who appear out of nowhere and get too close to me.

Only four days later, back home in San Diego, I returned from having dinner with Roni, and found that someone had been on the back porch.

I had made an appointment that morning to talk with a reporter from the Times Advocate, and she was going to talk with Task Force Omega members that next Sunday for her article. Before she came to the house, I put Rosie, my pet rabbit, on the back porch and let her go. In fact, the reporter and I talked about Rosie as she played at our feet.

When I came back later that day, I found Rosie in her cage with the cage door locked, and one of the porch chairs moved from the side of the wall so I would notice someone had been there.

The only thing I could figure was that "they" were warning me not to talk with the press. I hadn't made an appointment with the reporter over my own phone. I decided "they" were watching me, and heard me buzz the reporter in through the main gate when she called for the interview.

I decided I had two choices. I could either keep my trap shut and keep my sanity, my rabbit, and my family intact, or do what I felt I had to do for the good of all those other people caught up in POW/MIA issues. I chose the latter.

A week later, I ran into my nextdoor neighbor, and he said he had closed my garage door the other day. He had found it wide open. I thanked him very much, and then began to wonder--in living there for more than six years, I had never left my garage door open. I found it hard to believe that I would have done it now. Maybe it was possible. Maybe somebody else had done it.

When I got back from the Laguna Sawdust Festival a few days later, I came into the living room prepared to see the newspaper I'd left on the floor because I hadn't finished reading it. And I was prepared to see Charles, my teddy bear, on the chair with his hat on, kind of looking at the TV set.

However, the light was right for me to notice something was hanging from Charles' hat in front of his face. I picked off a 14-inch, curly blonde hair from Charles' hat.

No one had been in my house for months except for Rosie and me, and we both had short hair, and I'm not a blonde. Besides, I took Charles' hat on and off twice a day because he slept with me.

The only conclusion I could come to was that someone had been in the house again. That was a pretty subtle thing to have done if someone was trying to scare me because the odds of my seeing that would be almost nill. I doubt the hair had been left on purpose. And I don't think Charles left the house while I was gone, and met some dolly with long blonde hair.

The next morning, I found my car door unlocked when I was at work. I'll never know whether I left it unlocked (quite unlikely), or if someone unlocked it for me.

* * *

The redheaded man I mentioned earlier, left town at last. I found out that James Gregory gave his computer and all his POW items that he was always selling, like T-shirts and bracelets, to members of another organization called Task Force Omega members. No one told me why he left, but my thought was that he had become too visible in the community so "they" had him bow out.

With that thought, I became quite frightened for "they" would be putting a new operative in the redhead's place. Again I would not know whom I was up against. That made me rather nervous.

At the same time, I remembered that James Gregory's personal friend was Storm, a woman with long, curly frosted blonde hair. Could it be Storm who would take his place? Was it Storm whose hair got caught on Charles' hat?

In addition to everything that went on during August and September of 1991, I discovered that someone was tampering with my mail. So, I set up a test. I addressed an envelope and put it in the basket above my mailbox one morning. When I came home at noon for lunch, the letter was not in the basket. The basket facing the other side of the complex was full of letters waiting for the mailman to pick up. I opened my mailbox and I had no mail.

When I got home that night, I had mail. It appears that somebody took my letter prior to the mailman coming. I'm sure, whoever that person was, "he" was disappointed for my dummy letter only had newspaper articles in it.

Just another little form of harassment.

* * *

Early in October, I went to Seaport Village with Bob and Carol Atkinson, friends who were visiting me. I had told them about my problems with intruders, and I thought I knew who one of them was. This was before James Gregory left town. He was in a booth displaying military memorialbilia and information about the POW/MIA issue.

Bob had worked with the DEA and was quite knowledgeable about surveillance techniques. He told me he would like to check James Gregory out. We stopped at Seaport Village so that Bob could see Gregory.

Carol and I walked through the booths while Bob lagged behind, and watched what was going on around us. Bob said that James Gregory was watching me, and later Bob warned me to be careful.

When I got home, my upstairs phone was dead, but the downstairs phone worked just fine. I fiddled with the connection and checked the switch on the bottom of the phone. I even checked fuses to see if they might have something to do with the phone working. Nothing! I had trouble falling asleep that night.

I got up the next morning to find the fuse that controlled my outside porch lights, and the plug in my bathroom had been thrown.

Then, when I got home from work that night, the phone was still dead, so I pulled the phone cord all the way from under my nightstand. The cord had been cut--a nice clean cut. It didn't look like chew marks Rosie might have made.

I left to buy a new cord for the phone so I could use it that night. I have no idea what caused the fuses to be tripped. I decided it wasn't worth worrying about.

THE PLOT THICKENS

In January of 1992, I still had my Christmas decorations up, and had entertained guests one evening. Before I went to bed, I unplugged all the Christmas lights and as I headed upstairs to my room, I looked back at the darkened living room. When I got up the next morning, the lights were turned on, shining from each piece of my Christmas village.

On the first of February, I spoke at a candlelight ceremony at Old Town San Diego for the Vietnam Veterans Association. During the dinner at the Guadalajara Grill, I sat next to Tom Offill, a member of the local chapter of Task Force Omega. He just happened to mention that he had called me during January, and spoke to a man who answered the phone. I tried to convince him that it was impossible. No man had been at my house during that time. Tom said the man was gruff and short with him. Had I had a surprise visitor?

During the middle of February, I began to have strange feelings when I was in my house. I couldn't put my finger on it, but I couldn't sleep. I had weird dreams, enough to scare me. Then, one day when I came home, there was a message on my answering machine saying that 72 Green Beret POWs had been collected in Laos, the Central Highlands, and they were being brought to the Saigon area of Vietnam to await being turned over to the U.S. government.

Just as I began to feel better in my house, having decided my fright was based on the pending release of the POWs, I started to get obscene phone calls on my answering machine--night after night.

On March 2nd, the obscene caller used my name both times he called. Getting a little brazen, I thought. The following night, I found out that the 72 POWs coming out of Laos was a hoax. So sad!

STRANGE MEN IN STRANGE PLACES

Before I left to visit Sara one time, I asked Meg, who lived in the same building that I did, "Would you bunny-sit for me?"

"Oh, sure," she said. "I'll bring in your mail, too. No problem." This happened before the Byron incident I've mentioned earlier in this chapter.

"Well, if you see anybody going in or out of my townhouse, or if you see anything strange going on around my townhouse, call the police."

"Why would you say that?" Meg said.

"Well, I've had some intrusions. My husband is an MIA, and I've had people coming in and out. Angel saw several of them."

Meg's eyes got as big as saucers. She said, "About three or four months ago, I came out of my apartment to get the paper off my porch, and looked straight across at your bedroom. There was a man sitting in the window."

My upstairs bedroom is right across from her balcony front door. If a man was sitting there, it meant he was working with my computer that sat on a desk beneath the window.

"It was kind of strange," Meg said. "He had a turban on his head."

I thought that Meg had lost all sense of reality. I said, "Really?"

"Yes, but he was sitting at a table up there, flipping through papers, and when he looked up and made eye contact with me, he closed the venetian blinds."

I was thinking, if a man is going to be sneaky, he's not going to wear a brilliant red jacket or a turban on his head. I mean, that was too far out.

About a year after that, I happened to go to a small grocery store on the other side of Highway 15 in Rancho Bernardo, and who's in the grocery store but a man with a white turban. How interesting! I've seen men walking up the street wearing turbans on several occasions since then. So, as farfetched as it sounds, Meg wasn't out of her mind.

"No," she said to my question of whether she might have dreamed the visit by a turbaned man.

Her daughter was living with her, and she had a little Sheltie dog. She would let the dog out at night to run a little bit. One time, after letting the dog out about 11:30 at night, she looked up to see a man, dressed in a black trench coat, walking toward her. She decided she should put the dog on his leash, so she called her dog to come to her. When she turned around to look back at my condo, the man was standing in my doorway.

"He looked real mad," she said. "I guess he didn't want me to see him at your door. Then he walked right past me. I tried to nod and say good evening, but he headed straight for the parking lot."

I told her I would leave my porch light on from then on. I think that was the last time Meg's daughter saw that man.

When I returned home from my 1998 trip to Thailand, I found a urine mess in the downstairs bathroom. Before I cleaned it up, I asked both Meg and Byron to come over. I wanted their opinion. Both were disgusted with what they saw, and agreed that it was urine. No one was to have been in my house while I was gone.

In July, I got back from visiting Sara and found some of my clothes hanging out of my locked suitcase as I took it off the carousel at the airport. And a week after that, I could smell cigar smoke in the computer room in my house.

In October 2000, "they" were still around. A friend and I went sightseeing in the San Diego area one day. When we returned, my garage door was open. We both remembered my closing the door before we left. Another day, while my friend was there, one of my outside chair covers was missing and the footstool had been moved. When I spoke with another of my neighbors, he said he found the cover on the ground behind his unit. There's no way it could have gotten there by itself. Once again I had a witness to verify some of these strange things that went on in and around my house.

347

The months of July, August, and September of 2001 also brought reminders that I was still being watched. In July, I discovered one day that the inside panel in the back of the car was completely off. I had left the car locked in the airport parking area when I visited my daughter. The panel wasn't hanging loose when I reached in to take my suitcase out, but it was when I returned home.

In August, the cover on my chair that sits on the porch, was off and on the ground by my wall. The cover is difficult to remove from the chair. The wind can't just blow it off.

And, one morning in September, I opened my locked garage door to find a Molly Maids flyer on my windshield. I would certainly have noticed it there when I drove my car into the garage the night before.

The fact that I felt I was going crazy at the beginning of the scare campaign was soon dispelled when I realized that others witnessed the same things with me. Whew! Such a relief. Whoever "they" were, "they" weren't scaring me, and "they" weren't winning. I was no longer naïve.

CAN PHOTOS LIE?

When I was getting ready to go on my 1992 trip to Vietnam, I decided I wanted to take a full-length picture of Jim with me. I wanted to make some flyers of the picture to hand out when I was there.

I couldn't find the picture. Since time was getting short, I called Washington D.C. to ask for a copy of this photo, which I had sent them for their files in 1968.

The clerk I spoke to told me they would pull the file and send me a copy. About three days later, I received a call from Lt. Col. Jim Cole. He said, "Well, we don't have a picture of Jim."

"I don't get it," I said. "What are you saying?"

He said, "I know there was a picture here, because there is a page that describes the picture, but the photograph is gone."

"Oh, yeah, right! And what do we chalk that up to?"

"Those things just happen," Lt. Col. Cole said. "Don't get your dander up. It's all right, Barbara. I'll query CILHI. They have a copy, and we'll get this taken care of."

About 2 weeks after that, I received this 8x10 glossy from CILHI of Jim standing next to a Vietnamese soldier. I said out loud, "Where in God's creation did they get this?" I'd never seen that photo before.

I went to the phone and called Washington D.C. again. I got hold of Lt. Col. Cole and said, "I just got the picture of Jim that someone in your office sent me. Where did you get it?"

"That's the photo you sent us. It came from CILHI. It's a duplicate."

"No, it isn't. Guess again."

"Well, Barbara, that's the one you sent."

"No I didn't. The photo I sent you only had Jim in it. I've never seen this before."

To this day, and every once in a while when I'm at a National League of Families meeting, I'll ask someone to help me find out where that picture came from. I've done that to every single survivor's assistance officer I've had in the Casualty Branch. Everyone says it came from CILHI. Then I say to them, "Find out where or how CILHI got the picture."

I mean, photos don't just come out of the blue and get sent to CILHI. There has to be a reason. There has to be a name and address of who sent it. Why don't they seem to know that? What does that mean?

I've told everyone I've questioned that the picture looks strange. He never wore his beret in that sloppy manner. At first I thought maybe he was trying to send me a message. Not that he was imprisoned, because he's wearing a sidearm. But, maybe that he was doing something he didn't want to. I've even had people look closely at his insignia. I thought that maybe the insignia was put on backwards. That would mean something was wrong.

Plus, he had lost weight from the other pictures I had of him in Vietnam. This picture had to have been taken after he was declared MIA.

No one will ever answer me. Not to this day.

ENTITIES, OR WERE THEY?

An interesting phenomenon was taking place during this time. I realized that as I got close to my front door, each night after work, I had a sick feeling in my stomach. I would take a deep breath and try to ignore the feeling so I could prepare myself for what I might find inside--the unknown.

I went through a mental checklist each time:

Did "they" come today?

What did they move this time?

Did they take something else?

Did they turn on the gas somewhere else in my

house, like the gas pipe in the fireplace?

I would put the key in the door, and hope there wasn't a bomb ready to go off when I opened the door. And then, once inside, I'd start talking to the walls again.

Rick Farley, Ph.D., my psychologist and confidant, who was retired military and who worked with returned POWs and their families, said to me one time, "Think of all the intrusions you've had with no help for resolution and no way to stop them."

That was so true. I had been to the police station three times. The first time I went, two policemen sat behind a big desk just inside the door of the police substation. All I could see were their heads. Being quite short, I could hardly reach the top of the desk. I said, "I know this is going to sound crazy, but I'm having a problem. I'm an MIA wife, and these people keep coming in and out of my house. I know they're doing that because my neighbors have seen them."

One of the policemen brought his hands up on the counter and said, "I don't think you're crazy."

I noticed that he wore a POW bracelet on his wrist. The bracelet happened to have the name of Marian Shelton's husband.

"I know exactly what you're saying," the policeman said. "But I'm sorry, there's nothing we can do. If it's Federal Agents, we can't prosecute them. If you take pictures of them with security cameras, surveillance stuff, you'll have proof. But, in a court of law, it will only prove that those men were there. The problem will go right back to the government people to handle, not us."

My heart sank.

"My suggestion to you is to be very vocal about what's happening and to stay very visible. The more open you are about what's going on, the less likelihood there will be of their doing away with you."

That was reassuring!

There were many nights that I'd wake up and have a feeling that someone was in my room. My hearing became very acute.

I was well aware that "they" could do me in, so more than once saying, "If you chose to do me in, my request is that you do it quick and painless. You don't need to make me suffer."

Once I even had Frederick, the remote viewer, come to my house after I had told him several times I had these strange feelings.

Before Frederick even got to the door, he could feel something threatening. That was a confirmation for me that I wasn't just imagining things. He said, "There are two things going on here. Your husband has been here. I see him here, the non-threatening one."

He could never fully identify the threatening one(s) who visited me. He said my computer room was where they were. "There's a man here. There's another man, too. Did a man ever live here?"

I said, "Yeah, my son did."

"It's not your son. It's someone else."

It wasn't too much later that I found out about the East Indian with a turban, who had been sitting at my computer in that room.

"There is an entity that is choosing to stay here and bother you and watch you, and that's what all this is about," Frederick said. So, he did some things while he was in the computer room that I didn't quite understand, and he was able to get rid of the entity.

DUTY OFFICER'S LOG

In 1996, I requested copies of some more documents I had found in Jim's file. At that time, they were new to the file and new to me. Included in the batch were copies of a duty officer's log in which notations had been made about me. I don't have the year, but I do have the month and day of each entry. I think it was about 1970.

"May 28 – An Army PW wife made a statement – no notice – am due to send note to Army c/s on this."

- CDR S feels ADM Z will not talk w/GEN W after knowing the real facts. He has compared Army notification with that of Navy's – both the same.

- CDR S asked to be informed of what wife is really like. . . Anti-war G."

Wow! Anti-war? That was the farthest thing from the truth. I never protested the war. Period! Maybe that's one reason why "they" kept such close tabs on me all those years.

The other document I got a copy of at that time was a 3 January 1969 memo from the Asst. Adjutant General, US Army, Vietnam, Proceedings by the Board of Officers, San Francisco. They had requested that Jim's status be changed to KHA (Killed Hostile Action) from MHA (Missing Hostile Action) less than four months after Jim disappeared. This is the only document where I've seen these terms used. The request was denied. The handwritten notation on the memo said that, "although the report is indicative of death, it is not reasonably conclusive evidence of death. Continue as MHA."

As you'll read elsewhere in the book, Jim was changed to KIA in 1971 without additional information. Why?

As for other records about me, I now have a copy of a 23 page confidential report from Bangkok in 1989, unclassified in 1992. On page 5, the chance meeting in Hue that I had with Bill Bell and his team is described in detail. After describing the hotel, restaurant, nightclub, and the people in Bell's group, the reporter wrote:

"While at the hotel meeting with Ky, the team was approached by Mrs. Barbara Birchim, the wife of 1Lt James D. Birchim (Refno 1322). Mrs. Birchim said she was in country as part of an Australian tour group and asked for assistance in gaining SRV approval for her to visit Kontum where her husband was lost. The team chief commended her for her spirit and referred to Mr. Ky since he was a member of the Province People's Committee. Mr. Ky said he would arrange for her to meet with the Foreign Affairs Office the following day. The team did not see her again, and the outcome of her efforts is unknown."

It should come as no surprise that "they" were keeping tabs on me from the time I stepped foot on Vietnam soil. But, being naïve may have been just as well, for I could have been frightened and if so, I might not have gone to Vietnam in 1990, or on the other two trips after that.

I'm glad I plodded ahead in my innocence, for I wouldn't trade those trips for anything.

THE JUGGLING ACT

After I left the letter to Jim at the Vietnam Wall in 1998, I felt I didn't need to go through my mental checklist anymore as I approached my door. Nothing ever happened to my car again after I returned from leaving my letter at the Wall in Washington D.C. I never found anything moved or removed from my house, either. No more leaking gas and no more men looking out of my computer room window.

Not long ago, I was talking with Sister Joan, one of the nuns attached to the Catholic Church I belong to. We were having lunch one day when I mentioned that I was interested in maybe going to Ecuador or Mexico to help as a nurse. I said that I'd have to take a refresher course in conversational Spanish and was wondering if she knew of one.

Sister Joan said, "Barbara, I know just the person you need to talk to. I was called to a home to be with a woman whose husband had just died and in the course of our conversation, she said she couldn't decide whether she should go back to work or not. Then, when I asked if that would be a problem, out of her mouth came, 'No, that's okay. I'll just go back to working for the CIA.'"

Weeks later, I met with the woman to ask her about tutoring me in Spanish. Without my saying a word, she mentioned she was going to have to fly to Washington D.C. for three weeks and then she was going into Columbia, South America. She said, "Yeah, I do that with the CIA, you know."

My point here is that many of those who work for the CIA are unassuming. Sometimes "they" take ordinary people right off the street, so to speak. I always thought that those in The Company were all cloak and dagger. If I ran across one, he would have CIA blasted across his forehead and on his clothing. Then I heard about the Mrs. Pollifax mystery books, about a little old lady who works for the CIA and travels anywhere in the world that the CIA sends her to handle covert actions for them.

Anything is possible when it comes to people working for the CIA.

* * *

EUREKA!

In May of 1994, I decided to put the POW/MIA issue away again. I accepted an assignment with a traveling nurse registry that offered me a position in Eureka, California. It's a beautiful coastal town in the northern part of the state. The area is green with huge trees, blue sky and a wonderful relaxed atmosphere. With all of the intrusions that I'd been experiencing in San Diego, I looked forward to the peace and quiet of this new location.

For the first time in my nursing career, I'd be doing the home care visits instead of selling the services to hospitals and doctors. I looked forward to the challenge of being in the field and getting back to bedside nursing.

The only reason I mention this part of my life is to show that "they" had followed me.

Within a few days of my settling into my apartment, "they" left their mark. The nursing service had arranged for me to stay in an apartment that was the top half of a two-story Victorian house. The owners, who were in their later years, lived on the first floor.

About three days after I moved in, I came home to find the toilet paper gone and all of my cosmetics moved from one end of the cabinet to the other. I stood there in amazement and shook my head in exasperation.

Why did "they" bother to follow me about 1,000 miles to this place? What did "they" think I was going to do?" What did I know that "they" were so worried about my telling someone? If Jim died in 1968. . .?

It saddened me to know that I wasn't going to be able to get away from the POW/MIA issue even for a little while.

Two could play this game, though.

Since I was being harassed anyway, I decided to do some TV interviews, so I called the TV stations and got some airtime.

Some told me I had a lot of tenacity to do that. To me, it was self-preservation. As long as I was quite visible, I felt I would not be harmed.

AS IT TURNED OUT

The continuing anger I felt, in regard to the unfairness of this whole issue, was keeping me focused on pressing for answers rather than giving in to my fears surrounding the threats and intrusions. I learned how to listen to not only words but also to my feelings. Balancing and sorting out all the incoming information and misinformation became a juggling act for me to find the truth.

Through all those years that "they" conducted fear tactics, I somehow managed to hang on to my sanity. . . with the help of my friends, my neighbors and my God.

Chapter Twenty-Four

How Close Can You Get?

"For we were there. We saw the faces. We watched them
die. We knew the pain and felt the pride. Dear God, we
know how hard we tried. We can't forget."
                    From "Vietnam Memorials" Ceremony

My frustration level at trying to find a humanitarian group to link with
had escalated to an all-time high by 1997. In the previous few years, I'd kept my
eyes and ears open for a project that suited my interest and requirements.

The large NGOs (Non-Governmental Organizations) wanted a
commitment of at least 1-3 years in a foreign post, and I didn't want to be
away from home that long. I was willing to be self-funded, so I offered to
procure medical supplies and bring them with me. I'd even stay on site but
for only up to 5-6 months at a time. My idea was that on my return home,
I'd acquire more needed supplies and get ready to return to the same site the
following year.

I began to realize that I just might have to start my own project when I
was unable to find an NGO willing to take me.

The first question became what country would I consider working in?
I knew that I didn't want to work anywhere in a war zone. That eliminated
quite a few countries. I decided to make a list of possible places. Of all those
on the list, there was something in my gut that kept drawing me to Northeast
Thailand as a possible place to start a medical outreach program for women
and children coming across the border from Laos and Cambodia.

I started researching health issues for that area, and collecting medical
donations from physicians and clinics.

This trip was going to be a real adventure!

By the time I was ready to leave, I had acquired names of contacts in
Thailand, Cambodia and India. My plan was to visit these sites, help out
with their existing projects, and decide if one of them fit my interests or if my
project could be linked with an existing one.

I also planned to bring along the names and phone numbers for my
contacts in Vietnam and the foreign news media, just in case.

Two weeks before I left, I received a call from my friend, Frederick
Jackson. There was a sense of urgency in his voice when he said, "I need to
see you."

We met, and without my saying a word to him about what I planned to do and where I was going, he proceeded to tell me that it was important that I be in Northeast Thailand by the next month.

"There'll be a two-week window of opportunity to have a chance meeting with Jim." Since Frederick had never been to that part of the world, he was surprised at what he had viewed, and that's why he'd called me. Then, he described the area where this chance meeting would happen.

I was completely taken back as Frederick described the exact area I was being drawn to as the first choice for my health project.

Could it really be true that I would have a meeting with Jim? Was my intuition once again telling me that Northeast Thailand was where I needed to be? Was it Jim's presence (psyche?) in Northeast Thailand that had been drawing me to that area before Frederick saw this in a remote viewing?

There had to be something to my being driven to that part of the world, and now Frederick confirmed my feelings from a whole different angle. This was too much to write off as coincidental!

Lots of questions flooded my head as Frederick continued to describe what he saw.

"How would I know where to go in Northeast Thailand?" I said. "That's a big area. Would someone take me to see Jim?" My questions came faster than I could verbalize.

"You already know someone living there," Frederick said at last. "This person lives in Thailand, and all you need to do is call him."

"Should I ask him where to meet Jim?"

"No."

"Should I ask if he knows of any humanitarian projects in that area?"

"Yes. That will set your chance meeting in motion."

"Will someone contact me and take me to Jim? How will I know if that person is trustworthy? I mean, if he shows up at my hotel at 2:00 a.m. and tells me I have to go with him, now, how do I know if he's not from the wrong side and will do me in?"

Frederick said, "It's not going to happen like that. You're going to be in a remote area on a dirt road. There's a big, fast moving body of water very close to that road. You're going to be walking on this road, and Jim will be there, too."

I soaked up every word Frederick said. My adrenaline was running at a new high. Who did I know who lived in Thailand? I searched my brain for the name of my contact while Frederick continued to talk.

I asked again, "Are you sure I know this person?"

"Yes, it'll come to you."

Could all this be true? Was God giving me a chance to end this quest? Was I hearing Him months ago when I was first drawn to Northeast Thailand? After all, I'd never been there before so it wasn't like I was going back to a known place.

A couple of hours after our meeting, the name of my contact came to me.

* * *

A fact-finding trip where one is physically carrying hundreds of pounds of donated medical supplies is not easy. Now, with this added dimension of my possibly meeting Jim, thrown into the equation, the intensity of the trip for me magnified.

My attention to detail had taken a giant shift. If I only had a few moments with Jim, what would I most want out of that meeting? How do I encapsulate 30 years? Did Jim even know he had a son named David? And, I certainly wanted to know what had happened to Jim starting with November 1968.

Despite all these questions, what I wanted to know more than anything was whether Jim was free to make his own decisions. I had heard long ago that one of the ways the enemy might have been able to keep their prisoners under control after the war, was to allow them to have families thereby creating less need to escape on the detainee's part. This, plus the fact that by the time those men realized their country had no intention of rescuing them, the men may have surrendered to the enemy's wishes and given up their fight to escape.

So, I was prepared to hear that Jim had another wife and family.

Then, it came to me. My daughter, Kim, had been married in April 1997, and I had photos of her and my son, David, plus all of Jim's family. I selected about two dozen to put into a soft plastic case and listed the people on the back of each photo. Then, I wrote Jim a letter just in case our meeting was so short that I couldn't do or say anything except hand him the packet. I knew I would have to keep the packet with me at all times during my travels.

* * *

July 7, 1997, had come and it was time for me to close up the house and fly to Bangkok. I flew from San Diego to Los Angeles to Taipei and on to Bangkok for a total of 16 flying hours.

The whole time my mind was churning over what might happen during the next three weeks. It still seemed incredible that I would make one call to the only person I knew in Thailand whom I'd met once a few years ago and then for a brief 20 minutes.

And this person was going to set the whole ball rolling?

I'm not sure that what I was feeling could be labeled. This segment of my three-month trip would have been enough by itself, but I had made too many plans and contacts for me to chuck the humanitarian part of my journey.

I had to stay well, pace myself, and keep a clear head. So, after leaving San Diego at noon on July 7, I finally crawled into my bed in the hotel in Bangkok at 0030 hours on July 9.

Since I'd done this long haul several times before, I knew that it was important for me to have a couple of days to get my biological clock tuned to the new time. I also needed to read some of the local papers to get a feel for any "hot spots" that I might have been planning to visit.

One gets a very different perspective on international affairs once one leaves the U.S. Trouble had just started erupting in Cambodia in a vicious way. Airports had been closed in the past 24 hours, and tourists were caught in the middle of a political struggle between the exiled King's sons, Hun Sen and Norodom Ranariddh, over who would be Cambodia's leader.

I had made three different contacts regarding projects before I left the States, but Cambodia went to pot as soon as I arrived in Bangkok, and all travel there was closed.

After several calls to my contact's house in Thailand, I discovered he was stuck in the Cambodiana Hotel in Phnom Penh and couldn't get out.

This part of my trip was not getting off on a good foot. My two-week window of opportunity Frederick had seen would start in a couple of days. I did not have time for an insurrection.

I left my name and phone number with my contact's house-boy who said he'd pass my message along to his boss when he called from Cambodia.

The attempts to connect us were torturous. Each time the house-boy called me, he relayed the message that my contact would call me at a certain time. I'd wait. Nothing would happen. Then he'd tell me to wait for a call during another time slot. It took 36 hours for the miracle to take place.

The phone connection was broken three times, but I finally was able to explain to my contact who I was, and to ask him whether or not he knew of a humanitarian group that worked with women and children's health issues in Thailand.

He remembered meeting me and, without hesitation, he gave me the name of someone he was sure could help me. The name was Sister Marie.

I thanked my contact, hung up and sat on the bed, shaking so hard the springs rattled.

Step One had been completed.

I took a deep breath, tried to center my thoughts, and then dialed the number he'd given me. To my great surprise, Sister Marie answered the phone.

She spoke English. I was elated!

I introduced myself, and told her how I'd gotten her name and phone number, and what I was looking for regarding my humanitarian project. Sister invited me to visit her at the convent where she lived in Sakon Nakhon, which is located in Northeast Thailand, exactly where I was being drawn.

She wanted to show me around the clinic, run by the Sisters, and said we could talk about a joint humanitarian project at that time. All I needed was to let her know when I would arrive, and she'd meet the flight.

Step two was falling into place easier than I had imagined.

I spent the next few days watching the news about Cambodia, getting airline tickets, checking out cyber cafes for internet connections, and networking with people for contacts or ideas they might have for health projects. Also, I had to get the next leg of my trip settled before I visited Sister Marie.

I was certainly not going to Cambodia as I had planned because it was such a political "hot bed." I only had a 3-week visa for Thailand, so I decided to change my plans and go to Vietnam to deliver my medical supplies to some of my old contacts there.

I booked a round-trip flight to Vietnam that would leave in three-weeks, and headed to the Vietnamese Embassy to get my papers started. Now, I was really glad I had brought all the names of my former Vietnam contacts with their phone numbers. Once again, my intuition had steered me right.

I was surprised to meet two ladies, during my stop for dinner, who worked with Mother Teresa in Calcutta. I was glad to have met the ladies because I had already planned to work with Mother Teresa later in my trip. They would make two more good contacts if I needed them. What a small world this is!

Before I left San Diego, I asked a friend of mine if she would be my contact person for disseminating information to my other friends and my family. She was happy to be a part of my project on the home front.

The hotel where I stayed in Bangkok had a fax machine, so I wrote a letter with the changes in my itinerary. I needed to keep people at home informed of where I would be, even if it was only the name of a city. At least they'd have a starting place to look for me if I disappeared.

The Pratunam Park Hotel, where I stayed, was brand new and had just opened in a good section of Bangkok. There were only a few guests in this multi-story building, and it was a good deal at $35 per night, including breakfast. The hotel was within easy walking distance of everything I'd need, except embassies.

The staff was very nice so I asked them if I could store some things there while I visited Sister Marie. They were happy to help me. For them, it meant a return customer.

This was the start of three months of my comings-and-goings at this hotel. They even held my U.S. mail between my stays. It became my home.

On July 15, at 1600 hours, I arrived in Sakon Nakhon, Thailand, the beginning of my "window of opportunity."

I was surprised to find the airport bigger and newer than the one in San Diego, and it had lots of parking.

Sister Marie met me at the airport, along with a young girl named Ning, who drove the car. We headed for the convent/orphanage/eye clinic where I was to stay.

I had a private room in the guest quarters on the 2nd floor of the orphanage--simple, clean, with an overhead fan, and next to the bathroom with its bucket type shower.

Sister E. ran the orphanage. During the days I was there, I would go to the market with the Sisters, staring all the while at everyone's face just in case I might find Jim in the crowd.

In return for her hospitality, I agreed to edit one of Sister Marie's school papers that she had written in English. I also taught English to some of the other nuns.

I wasn't sure whether I should mention that Jim was an MIA, and that I had hoped to meet him on a road somewhere near by.

At 6:00 a.m. the next day, I attended mass, ate breakfast, and then got ready to take a walk when Sister E. asked me if I'd like to go for a ride. We would be gone all day. Of course, I said I would. This fit right in with my hope that I would meet Jim that day. It was his birthday, and I was on pins and needles in anticipation. What a great birthday present this would be if we finally found each other!

Sister E. spoke only a few words of English so our ride together was quiet.

We stopped lots of times at various schools and houses as we drove through the remote areas. At one time, we turned off the two lane black top road onto a dirt road, parallel to a good-sized river.

My senses reacted to the setting, almost identical to what Frederick had described. I stared at each person, house, and sign of life that might lead me to Jim.

The Sister had business in the small village we came to on the dirt road so when she stopped the car, I got out to walk around, ever vigilant for my "chance meeting." I was afraid to blink for fear I'd miss something.

Then, it dawned on me that what was happening was truly amazing. I was in a foreign country, in a remote area, traveling with a Catholic Sister who didn't speak English. On top of that, no one in my family or any of my friends knew where I was. And I was trying to make myself available for this "chance meeting" with Jim.

Unbelievable!

I felt like Jim was watching me all day. As I scanned one hut after another, one window to the next, my gut told me I was in the right place. As I walked around one of the villages, a particular empty building kept drawing me. I didn't have the nerve to go into the place alone. What was holding me back? After all that, I can't believe I didn't go in that building. Instead, I kept saying to myself, "Come out. I want to see you. I'm here."

Sister finished her business, and we left that small village, arriving back at the convent after dark. I put my vigilance to bed as I collapsed with only the hum of the ceiling fan and nature's nocturnal noises to lull me to sleep.

The next day, we drove to more villages where Sister E. distributed food, tablets, and pencils to the children. We ended up at Mukdahan, which is on the Mekong River across from Savannakhet. This day I found the "big water" that I thought Frederick was seeing in his remote viewing.

During the trip, I saw two men in the marketplace who were anglo, but neither of them looked like Jim. I became exhausted looking at everyone I passed by.

I didn't want to be too hopeful, but the setting was just like what I was supposed to find, and I felt so close to Jim. I hadn't felt that connected to him in such a long time.

Even though the following day was filled with things to do, I continued to search faces. Strange how when your senses are overloaded, your concept of time is distorted.

I had been at the convent for four days when Sister Marie took me to a friend's house. He was a Colonel in the Thai Border Patrol, responsible for controlling the border between Thailand, Laos, and Cambodia. He and his wife asked me to stay the night, and then go with him on his rounds of jungle outposts the next day. I found myself becoming deeper and deeper ensconced in my "undercover role," further and further away from my family knowing where I was.

I was quite reluctant to accept the Colonel's invitation, but Sister Marie told me they were lovely people and it would be all right. During dinner at the Colonel's house we exchanged a lot of basic information.

As it turned out, I stayed with them and enjoyed making new friends. It was delightful to have the experience of living with a Thai family, and being exposed to their culture. I even enjoyed their air conditioning since the convent only had fans, and the weather was quite hot and humid. What a treat!

At the same time, I kept asking myself if I could trust the Colonel. I wondered if I should tell him about Jim? Was I being set up? To test him, I gave him a little bit of information and watched his reaction. Right away he knew the term Green Berets, and started to talk about their connection with the CIA. I prayed for God to watch over me more than usual.

I was on the road with the Colonel by 7:20 that next morning. We stopped at six jungle outposts. We had lunch at the Champa resturant, overlooking the Mekong River, with officers from the Chiang Mai region. The Colonel happened to mention Jim to the other boarder patrol officers. One man turned to me and said, "I think you are still looking for your husband."

I didn't know how to answer that. I didn't want them to think I was using the Colonel, or that I had plans to strike out on my own and cause a political stir in order to get attention for the MIAs. As an old OSS friend of mine told me once, I needed to be "quiet as the monkey goes" for fear of divulging too much information.

So, I answered by saying I hoped one day that I would have the full story about what happened to my husband. The man watched me for what seemed an eternity before rejoining in conversation with the rest of the Thai officers.

Afterwards, we stopped at Nakhon Phanom's market place overlooking the Mekong River and Muag Khammouan. The mountain range was gorgeous, very rugged with a misty fog that hung in the valleys, giving an eerie quality to the forests.

Once again, I felt drained from looking for Jim's face everywhere we went. I knew I was in the right place, but there were so many areas where he could have been hiding.

A week later, Sister E. asked me to go to Nakhon Phanom with her. I had another opportunity to be in the area where I felt such a strong presence of Jim.

On July 31st, I got ready to go to Bangkok so I could catch a flight to Vietnam. My mood was not good. I was confused as to why I hadn't had my meeting with Jim since Frederick had always been so accurate. I still felt I had been in the right place. Had I abandoned Jim again?

Sister Marie needed to go to Bangkok, too, so her brother drove us to the airport, which took all day. During the drive I decided to ask her how she first met my Thailand contact, the man who told me to call her.

She said he had been looking for a translator and got her name. She asked me how I knew him, and then began to ask me pointed questions about my family. I took a deep breath and decided I didn't have much to lose. After all,

I hadn't had my meeting with Jim. If she chose to not have me back to work on the humanitarian project because Jim was an MIA, then all I would lose would be a good contact in Thailand.

My reluctance in not telling Sister about Jim before was because I didn't know what her political affiliation was. I also didn't want her to think the only reason I was staying with her was to look for Jim.

I pulled out Jim's picture. She went white! As she stared at him, she said, "I think I've seen this man."

"Alive?" I said.

"Yes, I've seen him a couple of times, and we've talked. He said he was Australian, but I know he is American. His accent was definitely American. I went to school in the U.S. for three years, so I know the difference. Would you like me to take you to see him?"

"Yes! Very much." Again, my heart was racing and my head spinning. "When I get back from Vietnam, could we go there?" I said.

"Sure. We'll go see if we can find him when you return."

I wished I didn't have to go to Vietnam, but my Thailand visa was expiring so I had to leave. I figured, what's a week if Jim's been living there all that time.

When I returned to Thailand and the convent, Sister Marie told me she was leaving, and wouldn't be back until after I was gone.

I had a hard time with that. I had tried to be patient while I was in Vietnam because I knew Sister was going to take me to see the man she thought might be Jim. But now that hope had gone "down the drain."

I was devastated, to say the least. I knew I'd be back in Thailand after working in Calcutta, so I'd have one more chance for Sister to take me to see this man.

Once again my Thailand visa was running out, so it was time for me to go to Calcutta to work with Mother Teresa. She was expecting me in September, and I needed to get my visa for that country. So, it was back to the Pratunan Park Hotel in Bangkok to get the paperwork started.

As it turned out, I arrived in Calcutta just hours after Mother Teresa died. I went to her funeral and worked only a short time with her Sisters since the volume of volunteers had increased to a point that I wasn't needed.

I discovered, on my return to Bangkok, that the rains were causing a flood. It was impossible for me to get back to the northeast section of the country to meet the man Sister thought might be Jim. I resigned myself to the fact that I'd have to come back next year.

My disappointment was unbearable. At that time, I didn't know why my meeting with Jim was doomed not to occur from the beginning.

"Only the dead have seen the end of war."
Plato

As I traveled back to the States from my long, arduous search for a health care project and a "chance meeting" with Jim, I couldn't help but ask myself a lot of questions.

The one that topped my list was why hadn't I seen Jim? Then I realized that maybe we had passed each other, and I just didn't recognize him. After all, one's appearance does change in 30 years.

I gave that a lot of thought and came to the conclusion that I'd know him, even behind the wrinkles. So, feeling better about that, my first call when I got home was to my remote viewer to see what had happened.

With a heavy heart, Frederick told me he had called Sara within hours of my departure to see if she knew how to reach me. He knew my meeting with Jim was off because of the turmoil in Cambodia. He had seen that when we met before I left for Cambodia, but he was concentrating his efforts on Jim and not on what was going on in the periphery of the remote viewing.

He asked her if she could contact me, but she had no way to do that because I had already left for Northeast Thailand.

Since remote viewers see things in a linear way, with only some peripheral ability, Frederick had to stay focused on the main event straight ahead in his vision, which was Jim on the dirt road.

I believe Jim had been there or had just left. The feelings I had toward one of the buildings, in that village where Sister and I had stopped, were too strong for Jim not to have been there. He could have even been watching me from one of the other buildings. Who knows!

* * *

For the next six months, I collected medical supplies and thought a lot about what I'd do if Sister did take me to Jim.

What would my government do if I tried to bring him out? Would they label him a traitor just like they did Robert Garwood?

Would they kill Jim and me rather than have this come to the attention of the U.S. public?

Would Jim even want to come back to the States?

So many questions and so many variables to consider. Nursing school never offered a course in how to deal with this.

PROFILES IN COURAGE

In March 1998, I flew to Albuquerque to visit Sara. She was in charge of a ceremony she called Profiles in Courage, an award program for Vietnam Veterans who had done some outstanding civic service during the year.

I agreed to help her. My job was to pin boutonnieres on the vets who received the awards. To my surprise, two of the recipients were Green Berets. Of course, I mentioned that my husband was one of them. As a result of our conversation, they made Sara and me members of their Special Forces Chapter 56.

I discovered that they were going to hold a Special Forces Convention in Albuquerque later that year, a week after the National League of Families annual meeting in Washington D.C. So, Sara and I decided to attend both meetings.

While I was at Sara's, she suggested I watch a tape she'd made of a program on the History Channel. She said it was about the Special Forces and SOG.

I decided to watch the tape while Sara was busy with paperwork. About two-thirds of the way through the video, a picture of Jim flashed on the TV screen.

I screamed!

Sara came running. "What's going on?" she said.

"Back it up. Back it up. Jim's face was on the screen." I was almost hysterical.

* * *

By the time the Special Forces Convention rolled around, I had prepared some photos of Jim to take to Albuquerque, including the one I got off the History Channel. I thought I might be able to post them on a bulletin board there, in case someone recognized Jim's picture.

As it happened, several men came forward and said they knew Jim and had worked with him. This led to some interesting conversations.

Sara had promised the vets that she and I would put on a candlelight memorial ceremony during their Special Forces Convention. Nothing was setup when we got there that night, so the minutes before "show time" were harried getting everything in place. As we took our seats in the front row of the audience, only a hand-full of people were seated in the ballroom. Sara and I weren't surprised. We certainly understood why folks, who were there to connect with old buddies and have a good time, wouldn't want to be reminded of those who gave their lives.

The lights dimmed, the color guard started into the room. We put our hands over our hearts and turned to face the American flag as it was carried toward the front where we were standing. My God, the room was packed. People were even lined up along the back wall. How did they get in so fast?

Our ceremony included reading some poems written by family members, and our explanation of the significance of what we had placed on the Missing Man table--the lemon, the salt on the plate, the single red rose and the wine glass inverted on a white tablecloth.

We called out each state and territory in remembrance of those who were killed and missing. Buglers played and the chaplain gave an invocation. The ceremony was an awesome experience!

Later, a man came up to me with tears in his eyes. He kept saying, "I'm so sorry. I'm so sorry. I thought your husband was returned."

It turned out that he had worn Jim's bracelet and because he thought Jim was back, alive, the man had taken it off. He seemed to feel that the only thing that kept Jim from returning was the fact that he had taken Jim's bracelet off.

"It's okay," I kept saying.

After he left, I noticed another man watching me from the sidelines. He walked forward and said, "You probably don't remember me. My name is Jerry Estenson."

I don't get choked up too often any more, but I have to tell you, I lost it when I heard his name. Jerry Estenson was Jim's last commander at the Presidio, and the man who brought me the telegram about Jim's disappearance.

I stood there crying and crying, my mascara running down my cheeks, while through my sobs, I tried to explain to Jerry that I usually didn't react that way and how happy I was to see him.

I had a lot of information that Jerry didn't have about Jim, and I offered to share it with him if he was interested. We arranged to meet the next day.

As I spread out the pictures, notes, maps, and other documents, Jerry just shook his head and kept saying, "I can't believe that Jim got into Black Ops."

I had no idea what Black Ops was, but I had a feeling that it was real scummy stuff.

Then, I showed Jerry the picture of Jim from the History Channel that I placed alongside our wedding picture.

"Oh, my God!" Jerry said.

* * *

Several other men came up to me during that Special Forces convention in Albuquerque and told me they knew some guys who were going to attend the September Special Operations Association Reunion (SOAR) in Las Vegas. They said they might be able to identify the men in the picture.

Since I needed a sponsor to attend, they said they'd do the honors. So I went.

At this point, I was showing Jim's pictures everywhere I went. It seemed that one of the men I was being referred to, from Texas, didn't come to the SOG reunion. Some thought he might be able to identify the four men in the History Channel picture, so I was told to call him and was given his phone number.

I like face-to-face discussions rather than telephone conversations, but I called him anyway. The guy remembered the photograph and knew each of the four men. He gave me their names, phone numbers and addresses. He knew none of them as Jim Birchim.

I gathered up my courage, and called the man who I felt was Jim in the picture. He was not. His voice was different. I asked him if he would be willing to look at the picture if I sent it to him. Which I did.

He responded by saying that he was not the man in the picture. The Texas man was mistaken. Then he looked through his records, and found that he had the names and addresses of everyone but the particular man I was interested in.

Another blind alley!

* * *

I must tell you that for years I met with Frederick, who I mention in my 1997 trip chapter, thinking he was a psychic. It wasn't until the photo of Jim appeared on the History Channel in 1998 that I became aware Frederick was a remote viewer. This was the first time Frederick used the term, remote viewer, during our meetings. I always thought what he told me was because he had psychic powers. I had read Morehouse's book by then, and now had a better idea of what Frederick's capabilities were. I met with him when I had burning questions only he could help me with, so that was why I showed Jim's picture from the History Channel to him. I felt this was one way to verify the photo. I was desperate to know if that was Jim or I was crazy!

I spread out several of my wedding pictures, a picture of Jim he had sent me from Vietnam, and the History Channel picture from the video.

Frederick said they were all the same man.

"Who is that?" I said as I pointed to the man I thought was Jim.

"You know who he is," he said without hesitation. He pointed to the History Channel photo. "That's your husband," he said.

"Okay, but I'm being told he's someone else. That his name is not Jim Birchim."

"Yes," Frederick said. "And if you contact any of those men in the picture, they'll tell you he's not Jim Birchim. And they'll do so with a straight face because they don't know him as Jim Birchim. He has a different name."

Here is what Frederick also told me.

1. Jim does not remember that he was a Birchim.
2. The trauma he sustained while he was a prisoner in Vietnam for a short time is the reason for his loss of memory.
3. He was possibly a prisoner for two years.
4. His lack of memory has been enhanced by chemical, or whatever, supplied by our government.
5. Frederick said he could just hear them saying to Jim, "You've been missing for awhile and we're glad to have you back. We still need you to do counter insurgent work for us since you know where some of these prison camps are."
6. He said that Jim was alive, was in the States, and was working under another identity.
7. The problem now was that there were only two people left who knew who Jim was.

My thoughts ran rampant. If he walked out of the jungle with amnesia from a head trauma, the government officials could have easily told him his name was John Doe and he wasn't married. "They" could have convinced him with other personal information, too, that "they" confirmed by changing and sanitizing papers.

He could have been told he was an only child and his parents died while he was in captivity. If so, then Jim probably volunteered since he had no reason to return to the States--no parents, no wife, no children, no nothing.

Frederick warned me that if I pushed for a face to face with Jim, I would start a snowball rolling in a direction I wouldn't like. The government would kill him because it would be too much of an embarrassment for "them" to have him out in public as Jim Birchim.

Frederick informed me that Jim was doing contract work for the government in Southeast Asia, and that's why at one point in time, I was in the right place at the right time.

* * *

I was convinced that, no matter what anyone else told me, I had a picture of Jim working with a Special Forces team headed for North Vietnam in 1970, two years after he was declared MIA in November 1968, and six months before he was designated KIA/BNR on May 10, 1971.

RETURN TO THAILAND

Once again, I found myself schlepping bags of supplies to the airport for a flight to Bangkok this time on April 14, 1998.

According to the weather bureau, that date would be a good time to go to Thailand. The rainy season wouldn't hit until the end of May, so I wouldn't have the same problems with travel that I did the year before.

It was good to get back to see the Sisters and the children in the convent compound. I took some teaching aids with me for the Sisters to use in their schools, and some educational toys for the children. The children had very few toys so my gifts were a big treat for them. It was amazing how the language barrier disappeared between us.

Sister Marie and I decided on which day to take our trip to find the man in question. It was nerve wracking, waiting for the time to come, but I filled my days with projects to do. I helped out in the clinic and taught English to the girls studying to become Sisters.

One day, we had a visitor from Australia, who had worked with Sister many years before. He had just come from Cambodia after delivering medical supplies to a hospital near Angkor Wat. He decided to stay overnight.

That evening, he and I had a long talk. He told of being in Attopeu, Laos, not long before and that interested me. I asked if he'd seen any Americans. I was thinking of going there, I said.

Something told me that if that guy wasn't CIA, he sure was working with a close cousin of the CIA. He advised me, in strong terms, not to go because it was difficult to get around. The roads were in bad shape.

That made me wonder why he had gone there. And then I discovered he had stayed with Sister more than 20 years before, for about a year.

Why did he show up now? When I was there? Why didn't he want me to go to Attopeu? Interesting!

During my stay in that area, I was introduced to a lot of people. It amazed me how many knew the acronym, POW. I had people tell me an American had approached them, a CIA type, asking about POWs, and/or asking whether they had knowledge of any POWs. Some of the people were asked to go across the border to see if they could bring back information about American men being held against their will. I guess some of them did that and they passed on the information they got to the officials.

The question they all asked me was why don't Americans want their men back? That was very difficult for me to explain to them.

The day came! Sister and I made our way to the area where she had last seen the man she thought might be Jim. We stopped at a bakery and she went in. When she returned, she said the baker had seen the man two days before, and gave her directions to the man's house.

Sister and I found the house, and she said she'd go to the door first to ask him some questions. She'd try to get him to come outside so I could see him.

As I waited, my heart pounded so hard, it was deafening.

Out the man walked.

It was not Jim.

The man asked me the name of the friend I was looking for. I assumed Jim would not be using Birchim as a last name, so I played dumb and said I couldn't remember. I gave him Jim's first name, and said I'd heard that he might be working in that area.

When the man asked me what Jim did, I was baffled as to how to answer. I had a trump card I didn't want to play, but it seemed I had no choice. I told him Jim had a background in science and mentioned his specialty.

The man grinned, then asked how tall Jim was. When I told him, he said it sounded just like his friend who also had a degree in that same specialty. Then he gave Sister directions to his friend's house.

I should mention that the area we were in was right along the Mekong River, just as Frederick had seen in his remote viewing the year before.

With the directions the man gave Sister, I doubted we'd find the place. But, after driving along dirt roads with no signposts, Sister found the house. She told me to stay in the car with the other Sisters who had joined us on the ride. I waited, in deep thought, while the Sisters in the back seat chatted in Thai.

From a distance, I saw Sister coming towards us with a man at her side. His height was right, but I knew in an instant it wasn't Jim.

We introduced ourselves and I listened as he said he'd worked for Air America during the Vietnam War. He asked if I'd ever heard of Air America.

"Oh, yes," I said. Yes, indeed. Another CIA connection, I told myself.

He told us he had been upset with the U.S. after he'd returned home from the war. He finished his education and decided to live in Thailand. Even though he'd lived there for 20 years, he didn't speak the language. That seemed too bizarre!

When he asked me about the man I was looking for, I gave him the same answer I gave his friend earlier. Then came a shocker.

This man knew a man who Jim used to work with in the science field prior to joining the Army. I about dropped my teeth! What were the odds of that happening? Could this world really be that small?

Sister and I chatted all the way back to the convent. What struck me were the repeated references made to the CIA by both the Americans and the Thai people. It seemed that that area had, or at least did have in the past, an abundance of people working for the CIA, even after the war. I had high-ranking Catholic priests, well known Buddhist monks, and Thai military say CIA personnel had approached them. Every one of them was asked about the whereabouts of American POWs.

ANOTHER LOST BATTLE

Although I didn't find Jim, it became apparent that Thailand held answers to some of the questions about our POWs. Whether or not I could unlock any of those questions, only time would tell. My quest for the ultimate answer was again a lost battle.

However, my quest had taken me to a beautiful place in the world. I found the culture to be rich in tradition. The people welcome strangers and invite them into their homes. I found a place where I could easily live, so it wouldn't surprise me if Jim were there.

YOU'RE WONDERING

As you've probably noticed, I haven't used the names of the people who are in this part of my story. I have some concerns that there might be repercussions, and I don't want these people to be in any danger.

Chapter Twenty-Five

Interest Escalates

"Never doubt that a small group of thoughtful, committed citizens can change the world, indeed it is the only thing that ever has."

Margaret Mead

I am both amazed and pleased with the resurgence of interest in the Vietnam War since the 21st century began. Amazed because I have spent so many years involved in trying to learn about that war and what happened to Jim-- pleased because it appears that we POW/MIA families are getting much closer to finding out the answers to our questions.

Throughout this book I have written about TV shows, and quoted books and newspaper articles that are about the war. My file gets thicker and thicker with every day, now. I can't begin to quote everything I have saved in the past two or so years. But, there are a few I would like to share for I believe they have a special message.

GREEN BERETS - THE SYMBOL OF EXCELLENCE

On March 24, 2001, the History Channel ran a program entitled, "The Complete History of the Green Berets." Even though I have discussed the Green Berets elsewhere in this book, I would like to repeat some of the things in that documentary that I made note of.

Col. Aaron Bank, considered the Father of the Special Forces, passed away April 1, 2004. He was a great leader, very brave, and intelligent. He organized the group, while fighting in the Korean War. The group was called the OSS during World War II. The OSS was engaged in guerilla warfare, sabotage, and liberation. The members of the OSS had to complete grueling Army training--"no more highly selected than the Green Berets."

To become a Green Beret, the men in the Vietnam War went through strenuous training including:

land navigation
air and sea operations
U.S. and foreign weapons
POW survival (known as SERE)
languages

medical
highly skilled and developed communications
infiltration by air
construction of buildings and bridges
cross culture operations
intelligence
free fall school
water infiltration
humanitarian assistance
foreign internal defense
nation building/training/advisory role
water/jungle/desert/urban survival
tropics/cold weather training
the ability to live day-by-day behind enemy lines

Each A-team (12 men) has mastered all of the above areas. Several of the training areas were added after the Vietnam War.

Col. Arthur D. "Bull" Simons, the epitome of the Green Berets during the Vietnam War, and Master Sergeant Dick Meadows, who held the record for snatching 13 POWs from behind enemy lines, are but two of the outstanding Green Berets who fought so gallantly in the Vietnam War.

It was Col. "Bull" Simons who led the famous raid on the Son Tay Prison, 23 miles west of Hanoi in 1970.

THE MONTAGNARDS

"The Complete History of the Green Berets" would not be complete without mentioning the Montagnards. These people from the Vietnam Mountains came from 31 tribes and had their own language. They have no love for the Vietnamese.

The Montagnards were a most important part of the Green Beret teams. They were exemplary, loyal, dedicated, hard working, and trusted companions. In return, the Special Forces teams trained and taught the Montagnards what they needed to know to fight against the North Vietnamese, and the Viet Cong, as well as fed, clothed, and cared for them as brothers.

SPECIAL FORCES - THE ARMY OF THE FUTURE

The documentary mentioned that urban combat has now become a very dangerous element for the Green Berets. It has become the leading element in the problems they encounter around the world. "They make Rambo look like a punk." The Green Berets are not a bunch of steely-eyed killers. They are in business to "Liberate the Oppressed" wherever that might be. They are the finest class of soldier anywhere--a breed apart, quiet, professional. One person in the documentary commented, "If the Special Forces knew what was going to happen at the Alamo, they would have gone."

These aggressive soldiers have become the world's finest military teachers. For years they have helped build a strong U.S. military presence in the world including their presence today in Afghanistan and Iraq.

Whereas, the average age for a soldier in the American Army today is 19 years, the average age for the Special Forces' (Green Beret) soldier today is 31.

There are two Green Beret arm patches. The one worn on their sleeve is in the shape of an arrowhead with a light blue background. In the center is a gold sword with three lightning bolts running through it. The insignia patch is oval with a sword in the middle and two arrows crossing under it. The words "De Oppresso Libre" appear at the bottom of the insignia.

The Special Forces members are the most highly decorated among American soldiers.

Many Green Berets are among the 58,191 names etched on The Vietnam Wall Memorial in Washington D.C. So is the saying, "Freedom is not free."

After I saw this documentary, I remembered that in 1968, every single SOG recon man in Vietnam was wounded at least once. This unit had the highest loss ratio of any other unit in the country.

* * *

Another History Channel program in 2001, was about Vietnam, entitled, "Television War/Helicopter War." According to this documentary, the Vietnam War will be remembered for many things--"it was very personal."

Today, we seem to accept that the United States lost the war. As stated in the program, it lasted until April 30, 1975, but we did not lose it on the field, "we lost Vietnam in Washington D.C." an interviewee said.

I was moved by one helicopter pilot, who in tears, said, "Going to help was the highest priority." I wonder if he could have been one of the two pilots who flew in where Jim and his team were cutoff? I just can't help but wonder about those kinds of things. Whether he was, or not, I thank him for all of us in America. He rescued our ground troops. How many lives did he save? Even one would have been worth our praising him.

One subject discussed during this documentary was the people who ignored the vets when they returned home. Some still feel all the pain, and carry the guilt for their having survived. If Jim had made it through the war, and had come home to us, would he have experienced that same dismissal for what he went through? How those in our country could have felt that way is beyond me, but then, that's another subject for another time.

THE BOOK OF HONOR

In June 2001, Ted Gup, author of The Book of Honor about the CIA, was interviewed by Barbara Simpson on her KSFO talk radio show (San Francisco). He said, among the many things he wrote in his book, the CIA lies and patronizes families of deceased CIA members. Their unspoken motto is, "We're not going to tell you what happened." They seem to have the presumption that the American public does not have a right to know. It is a way to avoid accountability and responsibility.

When I heard that, I understood better why those of us, who had husbands/brothers/sons in the Special Forces, have been kept in the dark about a lot of things that should have been made available to us with the Freedom of Information Act. Ted Gup said, "Everything is stamped secret (by the CIA) so nothing is secret." Interesting to realize that if everything is secret, then nothing could be considered "non-secret." Hum-m-m!

* * *

PAX TV's "Encounters With The Unexplained" aired a program entitled "Where Are The POWs?" on 1/11/02. The program revealed evidence that live POWs from the Korean and Vietnam Wars still exist. The program's narrator, Jerry Orbach, asked at one point, "Has the evidence always been there for the asking? Is it really possible that the U.S. government, with all its vast resources could miss something so obvious?"

Regarding the American POWs in Korea and Vietnam, Jerry suggested that they had "disappeared into the void of POW/MIA politics." He continued with, "The U.S. government still publicly denies the validity of live POW sightings."

After the program showed more evidence, Jerry said, "But how can the U.S. government discount evidence of these POWs in their own highly classified intelligence documents and how can they discredit eyewitness reports and even communications from the POWs themselves that have been smuggled out of captivity? Is there some compelling evidence, a smoking gun, so to speak, that the government can't or won't face up to?"

At another point in the program, I noted this statement. "Why is it government officials are so quick to brush off evidence of Americans still being held captive by nations with which we were once at war? Unfortunately, as it were, America had more wars to fight. . .Of all the wars in which

American soldiers have fought, none has left so much bitterness and anger on the conscience of the country as did the war in Vietnam. Even while it was in progress, the controversy threatened the nation's stability and today, nearly 30 years later, the specter of loved ones still imprisoned by a ruthless enemy, and abandoned by our own seemingly indifferent government, continues to tear at the fabric of America."

* * *

As I traveled throughout the years, especially during the early ones, I heard people from many countries comment that everyone knew the Vietnamese were holding American prisoners. Travelers like those from Australia, New Zealand, Europe, and many Asian countries couldn't understand why we Americans didn't know what the rest of the world knew.

That is a good question, I would say. How would our government answer that?

"Do the sons and daughters in America ask why didn't my father come home?"[1]

As I wrote this book about my adventures in Vietnam, and about the many years of research I did regarding our country at war in Vietnam, I noticed that not since the early 1990s has there been so much talk about the Vietnam War and its POW/MIAs.

So, I ask you--why? What is it about the early years of the 21st century that makes more and more Americans seek answers to questions a lot of them never had before?

This resurgence of interest in the Vietnam War seems to show up in all kinds of places. On April 29, 2001, the Oakland Tribune (CA) had an article, "Vet's Tooth Only Remains for Burial." The tooth was wrapped in a blanket and fastened to a full-dress Air Force uniform, then buried in a private ceremony in Goleta, California (near Santa Barbara).

In November 1997, the tooth was found at the crash sight of the plane that Lt. Col. Roscoe Henry Fobair had been in. The investigators also found zipper tabs from a flight suit, a 1964 penny, and pieces of a watch.

On April 8 and 9, 2001, newspapers were full of stories about the helicopter that crashed in Vietnam. A JTF-FA team of 7 Americans and 9 Vietnamese died when a Russian MI-17 helicopter slammed into a fog shrouded hillside near Thanh Tranh village in Quang Binh province's Bo Tranh district, 280 miles south of Hanoi. These men were on their way to a possible recovery site to see if it would be worth excavating.

President George W. Bush said, "The families of the service personnel lost in today's tragic accident know better than most the contribution their loved ones made in bringing closure to scores of families across America."

Television has contributed a lot to building interest in Vietnam with documentaries and series episodes.

For example, on March 24, 2001, the History Channel aired a documentary entitled, "The Complete History of the Green Berets." On Memorial Day, May 28, 2001, PBS replayed on their "Talking Back" series, the documentary, "Regret to Inform," that told several women's stories about their loved ones in the Vietnam War.

Again, the History Channel programmed a Vietnam documentary. On June 9, 2001, they ran "Vietnam-- Television War/Helicopter War."

The District, a television series, featured a program entitled "The Secret Return" on their November 10, 2001, show. The plot was about the CIA trying to confiscate a former Vietnam Vet's body so that no one could identify him. One of the CIA guy's lines in the show was, "A little lie serves the greater good." He was trying to convince the D.C. chief of police to give him the body. Who cared who the vet was, anyway?

When things began to get rough and the chief was determined not to let the vet disappear without an acknowledgement of his life and a proper burial, the CIA rep said, "You don't want to open a can of worms. Truth is an illusion. It becomes irrelevant."

Truth is irrelevant? Has that been the policy of our government all these years? Has my seeking the answer to what happened to Jim been a can of worms that no one wanted me to open? Is the truth about my husband, my kids' father, irrelevant?

And then I have to ask--where do statements like that come from in TV show dialogue? Surely those words were not a figment of someone's imagination!

And the list goes on and on. And will probably continue for some time. At least I hope it will continue to bring awareness to more Americans until the POW/MIA disaster ends.

* * *

The "Regret to Inform" documentary was written and directed by Barbara Sonneborn. Her husband, Jeff Gurvitz, was killed February 29, 1968, in the free fire zone of Hoy San in the Quang Nam province in South Vietnam. His remains and dental plates were returned to her in a plastic bag.

"So scared, so young, so far away from home."

Much of this sensitive, moving presentation was filmed in Vietnam as Barbara Sonneborn traveled that country by train. Interspersed throughout were interviews by several women--among them a mother, a wife and a Vietnamese woman. Their stories brought tears to my eyes. Barbara said, "What haunts me is not so much that Jeff died here, but that he had to be a part of this at all."[2]

* * *

When I was in Mogadishu, three different doctors offered to help me get back to Vietnam as they listened to my tales. Now, I was not going around telling everyone that Jim was MIA. But, I guess having a home health nurse working there seemed funny to them when they read my medical credentials.

I thought I would avoid conversations about Vietnam in Baidoa and Mogadishu--you know, sort of have a rest for a while. But it wasn't meant to be.

I must admit that I do not mark the box "widow" on forms. If I did, the problem would be solved. But, I just can't. Even though I don't want to talk about Vietnam and MIAs all the time, I still can't consider myself a widow since I don't know that I am for sure.

To show you how I can't avoid the subject, I went to Germany in 2001. I got on a bus one day and went to the back to find a seat. There were 24 other people with me. However, in front of me that day, were two ladies. When one of them got up to introduce herself, I noticed she was wearing a POW/MIA bracelet.

I couldn't see whose name was on the bracelet, so I asked her about it. She said, "Oh, you probably wouldn't know him. I've been wearing this for years and years. His name is Borah."

I said, "Oh, yeah, I know Borah."

"You do?"

"Yes, I do. My husband is MIA."

I wondered what the odds were of that happening.

I don't wear Jim's bracelet any more. I don't want to be reminded every minute of every day about Jim. It can get to be too depressing.

On the other hand, my friend Sara feels like she can't take hers off. She has had her bracelet on all these years.

We just have two different philosophies about the bracelets.

When I was on one of the Muluku Islands in 1997, I shared a cab from the airport with a couple, and it turned out that he had been with the CIA. I at once said to myself, "Oh, my God! They found me!" How do "they" do that? "They" must be a lot better than I thought. As it turned out, I had dinner that evening with the CIA couple, and we talked a little bit about my issue. It was amazing!

* * *

Some people have said to me, "With the war on terrorism filling everyone's minds right now, why do you think readers will be interested in a book about Vietnam?"

Each time I start to answer this, I discover another book about the Vietnam War being published, or another TV program played, or another movie released, like "We Were Soldiers" starring Mel Gibson, that hit the movie theaters the first week of March 2002.

Because of our war on terrorism, we now have the possibility of a whole new set of POWs and MIAs. The new generation has no concept of the true meaning of these acronyms, much less our government's way of dealing with this issue.

I hope that through reading my story, people will get a better understanding of the ramifications of our soldiers being classified as POWs or MIAs.

* * *

"They came with roses and tears Sunday for another Father's Day At the Wall."[4]

June 17, 2002

I'm not sure how many years it will take for our country's raw feelings to be healed. All I know is that almost forty years has not been enough time. We still hurt. America remains in pain from the unpopular Vietnam War. And now we have the horrific pain we all suffered from September 11, 2001, and the Middle East war we're engaged in to add to our country's pain from the loss of American men and women in Vietnam.

President George H. S. Bush said in 2002, "The rescue effort resulting from the September terror simply shows how far people in our country will go to try to find those who are missing. It has always been true of our military, and I think civilian rescue and recovery efforts show that it is equally true for civilians."[3]

I wonder what our history books will say about the POW/MIA issue?

Chapter Twenty-Six

The Vietnam Wall

"Gone but not forgotten"

After having seen what I thought to be Jim's face on the History Channel show, I decided to take it a step farther, and have his parents view the video without knowing what I thought was on it.

And without any hint from me, his mom and one of his brothers, picked out Jim's picture as it flashed by. The three of us spent the rest of the evening in disbelief, trying to understand what we were seeing, but knowing all the time that it was Jim. We agreed to say nothing about this and to show the video the following night to Jim's father and his sister.

Their reaction was the same. It was the kind of phenomenon that happens when you know your child is hurt or your twin sister is in trouble. There's a connection you feel deep inside that transcends rational thought. It's like an instant heart connection.

As far as I was concerned, I now had proof that Jim was the face on that videotape.

At the Profiles in Courage in 1998, I met Roger Knight, from Special Forces, who was the one who brought me into the Special Forces Chapter in Albuquerque. This connection led me to network with other veteran's organizations. I had made an inroad to get answers in more levels than I had been able to before, especially in Special Forces. As a result, I joined the Special Operations Association, which included individuals from all branches of the military service.

One of the questions I asked was, "Did anyone ever work with a Special Forces person who used an alias?"

"Oh, yes," was the answer in every case.

I was no longer surprised at the possibility that men who worked with him did not know him as Jim Birchim. My pushing this line of questioning got me many different reactions. I was afraid I was beginning to upset some apple carts, so to speak.

After researching the picture, and consulting with Frederick, it became evident to me that I could not push any further for a face-to-face meeting with Jim. I understood now that the government could not let this dirty lie out. The government would go to all lengths, including killing Jim, if necessary.

I was devastated!

For days I walked around in a complete haze. The last thing I would ever want to do was to say something or dig up something that would cause Jim's death. It was clear I couldn't go any further just because of my selfish wants. I would certainly love to see Jim again, but it wouldn't be worth the risk to him. I couldn't be responsible for Jim's demise, not after all that happened in the past 30 years.

At that point I knew I had to write Jim a farewell letter. The time had come when I realized my search was over. For my own sanity, I needed to say goodbye to Jim in writing, and the best place to deliver that letter would be the Vietnam Wall in Washington D.C. on Veterans Day.

Before, I had hope. Now I had no reason for hope. I needed closure.

Writing that letter was very difficult for me. I found that I had never really completed the grieving process. So, now the crying part began.

My tears came at the most bizarre times. And they came and came as I wrote and rewrote that letter.

My mind raced through the major events that took place since 1968. I wondered if maybe "they" would deliver the letter to Jim. Of course, why would "they" if Jim didn't know who he was any more. So many "ifs" floated through my mind.

If I put too much in the letter, "they" might not give it to him. If I put too little, Jim wouldn't know how his family felt about the past 30 years.

I spent months rewriting the letter and reading it outloud. I never got through it without crying. Once I even asked a professional what was going on with me. He told me I had never gone through the grieving process because Jim had never been found.

For the first time, the gut wrenching pain from losing my husband was coming to the surface, and with a power and vengence unknown to me. I felt like my insides were twisting into huge knots, and were then being pulled out of me.

Nevertheless, I continued working on the letter.

Something inside was driving me to read my letter at the Wall, and I hoped I wouldn't make a fool of myself in front of the throngs of people who would be walking and gathering around the Wall that day. I didn't understand this powerful emotion, but that was not the time to stop trusting my gut feelings.

I journeyed to Washington D.C. a few days ahead of Veterans Day that year, and called Joe Sternberg, a good friend of Sara's. He worked for the Vietnam Veteran's Association, and had tickets to hear the President speak at Arlington Cemetery on Veterans Day. He asked if I would like to go with him.

"If you need me to go to the Wall with you afterwards, I will," he said. "If you don't, I'll understand. That's no problem. Anytime you want me to get lost, I'm lost. But I'm here to tell you that I'm your guide and companion for the day, if you want me."

After hearing the President, we walked to the Wall where another ceremony was taking place. We stood there for a long time, waiting for the speakers to finish. Finally, the Park Service allowed the audience to walk past the Wall again. I said, "I've got to do this. . .get it over with."

The grounds were packed. I mean everywhere. I wormed my way up to Jim's panel. Joe came with me. He stepped back a few feet, but within earshot. I was glad he was near. I wanted him to hear the letter, too.

It was hard for me to get started, but after I got through the first few sentences, it was like white noise all around me. I didn't hear anything. I was in my own little world reading the words. My emotions caused me to choke as I attempted to finish the letter. I cleared my throat over and over again, trying not to cry in public, to no avail.

After I finished, I placed the letter at the base of Jim's panel and stepped back.

Joe and I walked away after he gave me a hug.

We returned to the Wall that night for another Veterans Day ceremony. I listened to some of the eulogizing in front of the Women's Memorial before I was drawn back to the Wall.

The crowds had dwindled from that afternoon's crush of humanity. The air was balmy and still. A reverent quietness enveloped the glistening, black marble that is engraved with over 58,000 names. I didn't have that horrendous feeling of sorrow this time. I did notice, though, how the people walked from the beginning down to the end, with a dirge-like cadence, awe struck, and solemn.

The Wall was designed so that it is higher at the apex. One has a feeling of going down into a grave because the Wall gets smaller and smaller as one walks from the apex to either end.

It was 11 p.m. and as I stood to the side of Jim's panel, a man came over and looked at my letter that still lay there. He bent over to read it. It was difficult, because of the dim light, so he pulled out a penlight and read the whole thing.

He started to walk away. I got a strong feeling I needed to speak with him. "Excuse me," I said. "I'm just kind of curious. I'm the one who wrote that letter."

"Oh," he said.

We struck up a conversation. He said, "I walk by the Wall every day."

I got the feeling that maybe he was saying hi to friends he'd lost during the war. His expression was pensive as he scanned the marble panels.

I don't know why I remember that conversation, but he gave his condolences and said, "I'm sorry about your husband. I didn't realize how many were still missing."

A powerful change took place within me at that moment. For me the Wall had not been a peaceful, quiet place. Now, I noticed the Wall had stopped screaming at me.

I was in awe.

The lights on the black marble were still on but the tourists were gone. The quiet had returned.

The Wall and I were at peace, at last.

* * *

While organizing the information for this book, I decided I wanted to include a copy of the letter I left at the Wall. Much to my surprise, my copy of the letter is missing. I've gone through my files, both paper and computer, but I cannot find it.

I contacted the National Park Service and requested a copy of the letter. They are responsible for archiving everything left at the Wall. The letter is not in their archives.

One might suggest that a missing letter would not be so unusual. Anyone could pick up the letter and keep it, or throw it away.

But, a Park Service employee makes rounds every night around midnight, and picks up everything left at the base of the Wall to be archived. The odds that someone else picked up my letter to Jim are slim, since I went back to the Wall at 2300 hours after I left the letter on Veterans Day, and it was still there.

However, I now realize that the "someone else" might have been one of "them," and "they" could have even taken my letter from the archives after it was filed. With "their" power, any record of the letter in the archives could have been erased, leaving no trace for a Park Service employee to find.

So, I don't have the letter to include in this book. However, I do remember some of the things I wrote.

- I wondered if Jim knew about his two wonderful children.
- I asked if he knew about the many trips I made to Southeast Asia looking for answers, and my almost being incarcerated in the infamous Hanoi Hilton.

- I wondered if he knew I was being harassed by the very government he worked for because I was seeking the truth about what was happening to him.
- I ended the letter by saying his family loved him and he would never be forgotten.
- Since I couldn't be responsible for his possible death, I was going to stop being aggressive in my pursuit of the truth.

I do remember the last words I wrote to Jim. "Know that 'they' have not won. You are my hero and will always be in my heart. All my love,
Barbara."

(As far as I know, that was the last time "they" have bothered me.)

THE VIRTUAL WALL

A web site, www.thevirtualwall.org was created by the Vietnam Veterans Memorial Fund. More than 58,226 names appear on the Memorial Virtual Wall. Text entries for about 30,000 soldiers are included, plus over 3000 pictures family members have contributed. Kinko's is the sponsor for The Virtual Wall. Jim Birchim is included.

Chapter Twenty-Seven

An End Without End

"Freedom is the right to question and change the established way
of doing things."
(Address to the International Committee of the Supreme Soviet of
the U.S.S.R., Moscow, September 17, 1990 - - Ronald Reagan)

I can't begin to count the number of times well-meaning people have said
to me, "How did you feel when Jim was lost?" or "How do you feel as an MIA
wife?" or "How do you keep doing this after so many years?"

Let me go back to the beginning--to explain the many kinds of feelings
I've had through the years.

1968

I was pretty numb at the beginning. I believed that the government was
not lying to me. Our country was wrapped up in a war, still, and I was too
young and naïve to question the story about Jim's disappearance. After all, I
was only twenty-one years old, and I had a small daughter and a son yet to be
born. My hands were full just trying to figure out how I was going to survive,
day by day.

As I've mentioned elsewhere in the book, people my parents' age, coming
from the World War II era, believed that the government wouldn't lie to its
citizens. And of course, there was no thought about conspiracy in connection
with that war. I grew up believing what my parents believed. So, when POW/
MIA family members were told during the Vietnam War to be "quiet, we
don't want to rock the boat," that is what most of us did, at first.

I spent many nights wondering "why me?" and wiping away tears in my
eyes when the babies were in bed, asleep. At the same time, there was always
the hope, in my heart, that Jim was going to come home.

I believe it was at the end of January 1969, just a few months after Jim
was declared MIA in November 1968, that I woke up and had the feeling that
Jim was gone. For the previous two months, I'd felt he was with me, but now
the room felt icy cold and void of his presence. Or was it?

For years I remembered that moment when Jim seemed to have left--
was he trying to say good-bye to me? The government was telling me he was
missing, not dead.

This was the start of the push-pull relationship between the government and my emotions. Trusting my gut was something that would take me a long time to perfect.

What the government was telling me was not correct. I began to rely on the fact that the government was not going to give me a final, truthful answer.

I also began to realize that what Jim was trying to tell me was "the Jim I knew" was dead--not the body but his ability to come back to me--ever.

* * *

"You'd Damn Well Care If It Were Someone You Loved"

* * *

MY ANGER PHASE

When I realized Jim was never coming home, that's when I moved into feelings of anger, one of the beginning steps of the death and dying process. My anger was directed two places.

The first was the government.

The other was at Jim.

He didn't have to request a change of assignment but he did, and on purpose, even though he had a young wife, a very young baby, and another on the way. If Jim had stayed at Fort Bragg, he wouldn't be dead or missing.

Jim had chosen war over me. How dare he!

Over the years, I've had to step back from that anger and look at how men, in general, operate and what war and the military does to men. The younger the men, the more control the military has over them. I've come to the conclusion that young men get swept up in the whole military-thing. Plus, men like Jim often have other reasons, too.

For example, Jim felt that because he had more training and was the eldest son, it was his duty to go to Vietnam instead of his brother. The policy of the government was to not send two family members to Vietnam at the same time. When Jim requested a duty station change, that automatically extended his service obligation, but it also meant that he had to go to Vietnam.

I wasn't mad at Jim's family. I was mad at Jim.

I JUST SHAKE MY HEAD

The total senselessness of the whole POW/MIA issue in general, plus the military not making sense, griped me. That's just my personality type. Tell me how it makes sense, and tell me why it has to be done, and I'm okay with it. I may not go along with what is happening, but if I'm told the truth, I can accept the reality of the situation.

That's why I have to ask how officials, returned POWs, or even clear thinking individuals can overlook the obvious fact that there were no prisoners of war returned home either missing a limb or grossly disfigured? No pictures, no news releases by the Vietnamese about their treatment of those men who fell in that category.

Then, I have to ask myself, how can a man like Senator John McCain, having been a prisoner himself, still continue to say that all live POWs were returned home? My only thoughts on why the returning POWs refused to believe that fellow comrades were left behind are that it would not only be unthinkable, but against the code of military conduct. The galvanizing and bonding of relationships between soldiers, especially in the time of war, creates a family bond. So, leaving a family member behind, and still in enemy hands would be too much to bear.

This discovery of leaving our men behind actually dates back to World War I, but did not become public until after the Vietnam War. Our country never seemed to make an active effort to account for missing servicemen during those previous wars. The hard reality is communists have historically held back POWs after every war.

The information about the POW/MIAs from the Vietnam War opened a Pandora's box that the government, I'm sure, didn't want to be responsible for. Now, all of a sudden, the families of U.S. soldiers unaccounted for in Korea were asking questions.

It wasn't that long ago that a South Korean soldier came out of North Korea who said he had just been released from captivity after 40 years. "There're Americans up there still being held," he said.

And so, when people come to me and say our military boys couldn't live that long in the jungle, I feel like saying, "Excuse me. The Vietnamese are living in the jungle. I mean, you take an 18 year old kid who acclimates to a jungle setting eating berries, nuts, beetles, ants, and stuff like that. . .he's going to survive. Because he wants to." The South Korean is a recent example of this. So, is it possible that some of our boys missing from other wars could have survived?

I just shake my head.

NO RHYME OR REASON

If our group of family members had not formed the National League of Families, I daresay the government would have eliminated every man on the POW/MIA list in the Vietnam War.

There appeared to be no rhyme or reason as to why the government was telling such stories, or the lack of stories to the family members. As individuals, families had no clout to fight the bureaucracies, but together as a League, they were able to let their thoughts be known. A strong voice in our government meant help for our POW/MIAs in this war, as well as in future wars. It became harder for the government to sweep things under the rug, so to speak.

For example, members of the National League of Families immediately contacted POW/MIA wives in the Persian Gulf War. Once again, the League will be there as a network to help those families of POWs/MIAs in the 21st Century War on terrorism.

THEN CAME GUILT

Vets from the Vietnam War are not the only ones who have felt guilt about the possibility that some of their comrades were left behind in those jungles and prison camps.

So have we family members. It is a kind of survivor guilt that we've all experienced. Some of us weep, and some of us hit the wall with our fist in anger. But we can't get away from the fact that we are alive--and our loved one from the Vietnam War is not. POW or MIA, it makes no difference--our serviceman is not with us.

Knowing that someone we love might be broken or tortured or slaving in an enemy coal mine or breaking his back working in rice paddies makes it almost impossible to smile or feel happy.

Life goes on. . .and so does the guilt.

As Patty Hopper, Chairman, TFO, wrote in a 2001 memo, "I want my life back and I want closure to the Vietnam War. I want to make sure that this travesty will not happen to my children and grandchildren."

At counseling sessions during those years, I found that feeling abandoned took on many faces. Jim left me for the war--and he didn't come back. Getting a divorce from my second husband was also a form of abandonment--a relationship not working. My counselor told me once, "Your trust of men, saying one thing to you and doing another, becomes less and less each time that happens."

This certainly turned out to be true with each man I've dated over a period of time. In addition, I've never had sparklers or rockets go off the way they did with Jim.

MY ANGER RETURNS

One of my stumbling blocks in life is that I have the need to be fair. The government was not being fair by leaving all those POWs and MIAs behind in Vietnam, Laos, and Cambodia. How could those men be left behind, most of them young boys, when they arrived in Vietnam, only to be condemned to a life in prison--to know we would never come back for them?

That wasn't fair!

And I get angry with that.

The score needs to be set straight!

TO TRUST OR NOT TO TRUST

About 1991, I began to mistrust people. The more I learned the more doubts I had. Was my friend Sara working for the DIA? Was Terry, who I planned to travel back to Vietnam with, really who he said he was? Maybe he was hired to keep an eye on me. That's why he wanted to return to where he had been held prisoner for six years. The things that began happening in my house started not long after I first met Sara. Was that a coincidence or did Sara tell the CIA about my talks with her? Was I trusting my enemy? Maybe I was being setup to return once again to Vietnam only to be swallowed up in a black hole--a prison--never allowed to return to the U.S.

All those thoughts made me sick. What was I to do?

In addition to the turmoil I felt involving my friends, my son David was getting defensive about the POW/MIA issue. He felt that his "mother was getting paranoid," and that worried him. At that time he had an idea that he might want to work for the FBI or the DEA, and my involvement in the POW/MIA issue would ruin that for him. He began to feel that all of the stories I had told him through the years were hogwash, and maybe I was out to hurt him on purpose.

Well, I put a stop to those thoughts. When I got through filling David in on the facts, and all the people who could verify the facts, he calmed down. He said, "If you get any information, hard evidence, that my dad is alive, then I want you to tell me. Otherwise, don't."

I said, "I can do that." And that was the end of that.

Later, in 1991, at one of my appointments with my counselor, Dr. Farley, we touched on the fact that I was having problems with stability in my life. I filled him in on the seven or eight things that were going on at that time to give me problems.

I shared my experience with Dr. Farley about David, my experience at the Wall in July, and my need to put things to rest in my life.

What Dr. Farley said was that, as far as Jim was concerned, I couldn't tell myself someone was dead unless I could see the body. That was why we have funerals and caskets so that people can mentally and emotionally close the door, and begin their mourning.

I had no body. I didn't even have a confirmation as to where Jim dropped from the helicopter. I had nothing except that he didn't come home. This issue would never be over until I had a concrete answer as to what happened to Jim and/or where he was buried.

I said to Dr. Farley, "So basically, I have to carry this around then, right? And I have to carry around the feeling that all these other people (POW/MIA families) are depending on me to fight for them, as well."

His compassionate look said it all.

* * *

By the time I was getting ready to make another trip to Vietnam in February 1992, I was having nightmares again. Three nights in a row I woke up at 5:00. In the dream it was always nighttime. I was in Hailong Bay. Two men broke into my room, raped me, and hung me by the neck in the doorway. Someone coming down the hall scared them off. That's when I awoke each time.

I kept having the feeling that something was wrong-- very wrong--but I couldn't put my finger on it. I called everyone I knew, but they were all fine.

Then I had the feeling that I needed to go somewhere and get help, but I didn't know where. I only had that feeling while I was in my house. I was very scared. One of my friends thought I was "wigging out." About that time, I started getting those obscene phone calls.

Sometimes I wonder how I held on during those terrible months and years.

WIDOW? OR WIFE?

It has been over three decades, and I still don't have a definitive answer to my years of searching for the truth. I strongly feel that Jim did not die in November 1968. Even if Jim is not dead now, I know he is not the same Jim Birchim I once knew.

As Sara said, "Now you've got the picture from the History Channel video tape, and now you think you have Jim's other name. You can have a face to face with him, if you want."

"But I don't need to see him, now," I said.

"I can't believe you're going to stop now when you've worked so hard."

"Sara," I said. "I was told the government might kill Jim if I tried to meet with him. I can't be responsible for his death. I'm really okay with this."

Sara is beginning to come to the same conclusions about her husband. Her situation is very different from mine, but she's coming around to the letting-go stage, too.

Now, when people ask me what my marital status is, I still stumble over what to say. But "wi-wi-widow" just won't come out of my mouth. On the one hand, I believe the Jim Birchim I knew is gone, but on the other hand his body is still alive.

What I am is a wife of an MIA--I am the wife of a Green Beret soldier missing in action from the Vietnam War.

Some people have suggested that my saying I am an MIA wife is because I want to be in the limelight. Others have said I just want to have something to talk about.

"You're crazy."

"You can't let go."

"Get a life!"

I thought about all of those comments, and I tested all of those theories. In order not to be an MIA wife, I would have to erase everything from my memory bank. That would mean I would have to deny that the last 30 plus years didn't happen.

If I denied that my whole adult life happened the way it did, then how am I going to explain all the things I learned?

I learned to travel to foreign countries on my own (except for my first trip to Vietnam in 1989), to over 35 countries like Cambodia, Laos, Vietnam, Thailand, Somalia, Singapore, India, and Bali.

I learned to stand up to dignitaries and Generals and the like, and to talk with them as an equal.

I learned to pursue my beliefs and feelings, to not let people in government "buffalo" me with their bureaucratic gobbledygook.

I learned how to stand up for my principles no matter what the odds.

I learned to believe in myself, and what I know in my heart is important for me to do.

The past 30 years have taught me how to use my nursing skills and humanitarian interests in many different countries. The years have shown me how to walk into areas I would never have thought of before, and to communicate with others in the world despite our language barriers.

This is who I became.

This is who I am.

THE FUTURE

I know that I don't need to participate in everything about POW/MIAs that goes on in the world, anymore. I know I don't need to start crusades or campaigns or organizations in order to stay active in my interests about those men who served our country well, but never were able to get back to their homeland.

I know I need to own up to the fact that family members of POW/MIAs should feel a strong sense of responsibility to be spokespeople and educators for the general public about the continuing POW/MIA issue.

It's like people who were in Auschwitz who won't own up to that fact, yet they carry the tattoo, and wear long sleeves to cover up that they were there.

Why should I wear long sleeves to cover up that I am an MIA wife?

When I bought a new car in 2000, I decided I would support the veterans by choosing an insignia for my license plate. Two insignias really sang to me. One was the POW/MIA insignia, and the other was the Green Beret Special Forces insignia.

For months I tossed it around in my mind.

Once again the comments began to flow.

"Let all this stuff go."

"Relax. Move on."

"It's good you're getting rid of the car involved in all that tampering, and that saw you through the last 12 years."

"Let go, now, of that searching junk."

Yet, I paid attention to my own heart and not others' words.

I choose MIA68 to be placed on a Veterans plate with a Special Forces insignia.

Oddly enough, it was my financial planner who said, "But you're a walking billboard, now. You're going to start the questions all over again. Why are you doing this to yourself?"

"That's who I am," I said.

Strange, but the first person to say anything about my license plates was someone in the National Cemetery when I pulled into the Presidio in San Francisco to prepare for the Tree Planting Ceremony in 2001. One of the gardeners said to me, "Wow, this is really great. Tell me how you got these plates? What do they mean?"

My explanation to him has turned out to be my way of educating people about the POW/MIA issue.

I've made it my policy to continue to give speeches and participate on panels if I feel comfortable about doing so. But, I'm not out there asking for such recognition or opportunities.

I came up with the idea for planting trees at the Presidio because that military cemetery, where Jim's head stone stands, is losing many of its ancient trees, and I couldn't bear to see the land turn into a barren hill overlooking San Francisco Bay. I did not create that beautification plan because I wanted recognition.

I no longer need to go back to Vietnam. I don't feel, heart-wise, that Jim is there. I believe that he has his home here in the United States, but he does still travel to Southeast Asia on Black Ops business. There is no reason for me to try to get to Kontum any longer. It means nothing to me any more.

The man who Jim has become is alive. The Jim Birchim I knew and loved, the father of my children, is gone forever.

* * *

THE EVOLUTION OF MY INTUITION

Over my lifetime, I have come to understand and rename that inner voice that most people label as intuition. I now prefer to think of it as God's phone line.

During those early tumultuous years of dealing with the government, I completely ignored those feelings because I'd rationalize that there was no hold-it-in-your-hand kind of proof to back them up.

My genetic makeup is such that I'm always looking for the reason why something happens. And in the case of the MIA issue, if I could find the "why," then I was sure the government would jump into action.

I really can't remember if there was one specific event that triggered my recognition. Although I had never left my religion, I had strayed away from the formal church. In the 90s, I started going to weekly mass, and learning about the changes that had taken place during my absence.

What I realized was that I never felt that He had left me to walk this journey alone. What I discovered was that although my dialogue with God was the same, I found that being in the presence of others with the same beliefs brought a strength that one can't find on one's own.

Also, during these years, I took two classes about Healing Touch to fulfill my continuing education requirements for my nursing licensure. This opened my eyes even further into the realm of the mind/body connection.

For the first time, people were actually explaining some of the things I was experiencing, but was quick to ignore.

Now I was looking at and listening to those feelings/hunches/intuitions from a totally different viewpoint. I began to act on those feelings without a need for tangible evidence.

To my surprise, my feelings were right about 80% of the time. It's my thought that my intuition is based on a vast amount of information I've absorbed throughout my life. I now understand that the answers through intuition come faster than the information stored in the mind. Although this MIA issue has been a parallel journey in my life, intuition seems to hold the secret for me as to what happened to Jim.

TAPS

"Day is done,
Gone the sun,
From the lakes,
from the hills,
from the sky.
All is well,
Safely rest,
God is nigh."

("The earliest official reference to the mandatory use of 'Taps' at military funeral ceremonies is found in the U.S. Army Infantry Drill Regulations for 1891.")

Postscript One

Perestroika Sunset

by Alan Stang

"And you will suffer with the families at home trying to
pry information out of an unresponsive government."[1]

As we go to print, I would like to draw your attention to a book by
Alan Stang that came out in 1999, Perestroika Sunset: A Daughter's Lifelong
Search for Her MIA Father in Vietnam.[2]

Even though the author wrote his story as a novel, I would like to bring a
number of significant points to your attention that he makes at the beginning
of his book. The reason? Because often novelists fictionalize the truth so it is
easier for readers to swallow. And readers can then assume that the incidents
in the story were the figment of the author's imagination. Not so in this
case!

Here's why I say that. The following quotes relate so closely to my story
that they could have been taken from my life. I hope you believe that I am
not the only MIA wife or daughter or mother who has experienced such an
unbelievable life. Or else, how would Alan Stang imagine all of the things he
put in his novel. They are too much like the truths I have lived, for that not
to be the case.

So, here goes. I hope the following quotes will intrigue you enough to
read Perestroika Sunset.

On page 3, Stang writes, "And international industry had arisen, targeting
the families. More than one had paid serious money for dubious artifacts or
clues, alleged leads, and then had been too embarrassed to prosecute when
the fraud emerged. In Southeast Asia, swindlers with sufficient artistry
to practice in Washington, D.C., wrote profitable scenarios, concocted
expensive 'sighting' and invented 'authentic' meetings and discussions
every bit as dramatic as Stanley's 'Dr. Livingstone, I presume.' They even
conducted lucrative expeditions into Laos to 'investigate' the farces they had
concocted."

On page 9, a man in charge of POW/MIA affairs said to the daughter
about a live sighting, ". . .would you really want me to go to the competent
authorities with rumors? They don't believe anybody's out there. If I give

them something that doesn't check out, they'll toss the whole issue in the garbage. Is that what you want? We need proof on paper."

Stang then wrote, "It was a strong argument. But hundreds, thousands of refugees fleeing Southeast Asia had reported seeing tall, Caucasian prisoners, long after the war. Were they mistaken? Were they all lying to get into the United States? Hadn't some of them passed lie-detector tests? Were all those Caucasians Russian, as the Pentagon had said? If they were Russian, why were they under guard? And why would the guards tell the refugees they were Americans?"

Later, on page 19, dialogue between the daughter and the man in charge of POW/MIA affairs goes like this.

" '. . .the fact that no one else can prove he said it? The lawyers call that hearsay. I've already asked about it. You can't prove he saw your father. You didn't see anything yourself. You're an interested party. All you know is what he told you, and you can't prove he wasn't lying. All I know is what you've said."

'And the letter? In my father's handwriting?'

'Where is the letter, Gay?'

'I gave it to you.'

'You gave me a copy. I need the original. I told you that.'

'But you read the copy.'

'Of course I read it. It proves nothing.'

'It proves my father is alive. It proves others are alive.'

Yes, that's what it says. And everyone wants to believe it. Has it occurred to you that the letter could be a forgery?'"

The man in charge of POW/MIA affairs thinks about what he is telling the MIA's daughter. On page 21, the author writes, "He had been a good soldier. He had been surprised to see that the files he inherited had no category for men who had been sighted. He couldn't enter them in the database. Any report of them was called 'unresolved.' Resolving them meant finding some way to sweep them into the dustbin. . . Each time he did something he knew was a lie, he had felt queasy. But each time he did it, it was easier to do, and now it wasn't a problem any more. It was not as if he were stealing, or giving military secrets to the enemy. . . He couldn't tell her the truth. The truth would make it worse. She would never accept the fact that her father could not come home."

The daughter's friend, whose husband had been labeled POW, had her husband's remains returned after years of waiting for some word about him. He was buried with honors, after which she tossed her POW bracelet in the grave. However, three weeks later, after receiving a phone call from a man who told her the body in the coffin wasn't her husband, she decided to exhume the coffin. She is talking with her friend on page 32.

"'Just as the man said, Mike wasn't in the coffin. Still isn't.'

'Who was?'

'The only thing in the coffin was a small Plexiglas container. There were pieces of something in the container.'

'Pieces of what?'

'A friend of mine runs a lab. I took it to him. I'll call you as soon as I know something. Must run.'"

On page 39, the author writes about "they," just like I have done throughout my book. "They were such charming people, don't you know. There would be nothing to suspect. Showing him the documents in her handbag would be useless. Were she to do so, he would mouth another DOD incantation."

Two pages later, there were the lines, "I know. Halstead was a spook. Probably with the Agency. He was pretending to be an Army Colonel."

The daughter is talking with a man named Dave about the Vietnam War on page 44. The conversation went like this.

"'Dave, what was American policy in Vietnam? What were we fighting about? I've never understood.'

'We went there to lose. That was our policy.'

'No! I can't believe that.'

'If you can't believe it, explain the privileged sanctuaries from which the enemy could attack us with impunity. Explain why we couldn't hit a SAM battery even after it locked on, not until it actually fired. Explain why our aircraft flew sorties with only a few bombs, and why they weren't allowed to divert from Death Valley, which was the reason we lost so many crews. Explain why we had to stay out of North Vietnam. Those are just a few examples.'"

When the daughter's friend got her report back, on page 47, as to what was in her husband's grave, she said, "'. . .there was just enough material in the container to establish beyond any doubt, etc., that what I dug up--pardon me, disinterred--isn't human.'

'What was it. . .?'

'Let's see. The word they use is porcine.'

'My god! A pig? You buried a pig?'

'That's what they said. . . Did you know they declared Mike dead twenty years ago? Wouldn't tell me about it. For years, they played dumb. Now, they say they knew all along. They were protecting his privacy, don't you know. It would be an invasion of his privacy if I found out he was dead. Could anyone really be this stupid by accident?'"

In 1991, Washington, D.C., the daughter is discussing the fate of two POW/MIA wives who were determined to be crazy. On page 50, the author writes:

"'The doctors say she drove herself crazy. Her children told me that. . . please don't do this to yourself! I wouldn't want you to wind up like Helen. Did you know that Peggy Bender has gone crazy, too?'

". . .What had Helen Foster seen? Peggy now was crazy, too. . . Was she, too, 'imagining' things? Should she, too, be put away?"

Further along, on pages 56 and 57, it is determined that Helen saw her POW husband in Peoria.

"'So then, Helen Foster did see her husband in Peoria?'

'We're checking now. We think it could be true.'

'Then why is she locked up?'

'She's in a hospital.'

'All right. She's in a hospital. Why?'

'She would have gone to the media. . . Our orders are that the arrangement be kept discreet. If the media ghouls spill it, the SRV will back out.'

'What about Peggy? Did she see someone, too?'

'We don't know. We're trying to find out.'

'You kidnapped her, too.'

'She's in protective custody.'

'Why don't you just let them (the men) go home?'

'We shall. . .'

'When?'

'When we're sure we have them all. And when we're sure they're ready."

'How could you possibly think they're not ready?'

'. . .none of these men has slept in a bed for many years. None of them has eaten western food. None of them has had a woman. The doctors tell us most of them will be impotent for a while, maybe a long while. All this time, they haven't spoken English. Some of them can't speak it any more. Some of those who can have thick, Vietnamese accents. In many ways, they're really foreigners. They're Vietnamese boat people. Except. . .except they're also six feet tall, and they have American wives and families. Imagine a six foot man--blue eyes, blond hair--a man you last saw on a Norman Rockwell cover, who speaks nothing but Vietnamese; eats nothing but rice, and the insects he can catch; sleeps only on the floor; can't remember for sure who he really is; and can't romance his wife. Some of those wives have been in therapy for years. Some have remarried. Have you ever heard of bends? . . . It happens when a diver surfaces too fast. . . So we're introducing them a little at a time. We keep them in safe houses in communities far from home."

* * *

Does any of this sound familiar? Is it all just fiction? Now that you've read my book, perhaps you can better answer that question than you could have before.

The later half of the twentieth century in the United States will be an interesting one to read about in the history books fifty years from now. I wonder what the historians will say about the Vietnam War POW/MIA issue?

Postscript Two

The Numbers Talk

As of December 2004, POW/MIA Vietnam War statistics have been updated by the Department of Defense (DOD) as follows:

1,406 still missing in Vietnam

55 still missing in Cambodia

377 still missing in Laos

7 still missing in PRC territorial waters

Joint Task Force-Full Accounting (JTF-FA) was renamed Joint POW/MIA Accounting Command (JPAC), in September 2003. JPAC and CILHI are now responsible for joint field operations.

Underwater survey and recovery operations are now being included in the MIA accounting system. As a result, one family's member's suggestion during a League of Families meeting, cadaver dogs are now being used to locate remains in the field.

The search continues for the identity of the man in the History Channel photograph. So far, those men in the photograph who have resembled Jim Birchim have not proved a possible match.

Hopefully, now that I am a member of Special Forces Association (SFA) and Special Operations Association (SOA), I will find someone who can shed light on the mysterious likeness of my husband, Jim Birchim, in that picture.

My thanks go to the members who have shared their experiences and connections. They have been so willing to help me in my quest for the truth.

Postscript Three

Understanding

"Therefore search and see if there is not some place where you may invest your humanity."

Albert Schweitzer

So now I have come full circle.

As I reflect on all of the events over the past 36 years, in regard to getting the answers as to what really happened to Jim Birchim, I'm still left in a quandry.

During the last 14 years I have been given some varifiable evidence of the strong possibility that Jim did survive the November 15, 1968, incident. Collectively, all of the odd bits and pieces that in and of themselves would have been dismissed as not belonging to this case now do fit together with a seeable plausibility. Could I prove it in a court of law? No.

If I were to have written about everything that happened during those years that built my case for thinking the way I do, this book would have filled volumes. To capture the tone inflections and whispers of those confiding in me, from high-ranking officials to the folks in the trenches was impossible to put on paper.

But, no matter how strong my convictions are as to Jim being alive after November 1968, I must admit that on those occasions when I've been emotionally drained from doing battle with the government, I wondered if all this had been a cruel hoax.

That sense of isolation, desperation, betrayal, and anguish is immobilizing.

One moment, all of the work I've done on my search for Jim seems like an eternity. But the copious amount of information I found, along with my intuition, brings me back to my conclusion that Jim is alive.

I'm sure some will come to a different conclusion from reading my book. Remember, these pages do not include every detail of Jim's case.

To those who dismiss the possibility of Jim's survival because they worked in the same arena, and feel they would know if this kind of covert operation was going on, I'd like to say two things:

1. Compartmentalization – the government's way of containing all information

2. Need to Know – the government's giving only the information needed to get a job done

Both are ample reasons why those who think they should know, may not.

In a sense, my long journey to find Jim has prepared me for the next stage in my life.

The reason I wrote this book was to share the first half of my life's quest--its ups and downs, its travails, and its hopes. If the lessons I have learned, both positive and negative, can help those who read my book, then I am satisfied.

Some people may consider this story a fairy tale. But it is not. What I hope people, especially women, will get out of my story is that God gives us only as much as we can handle at any one time. I told myself this over and over again through the years as I searched for my husband.

Sometimes I would wonder what I had done wrong that God would want to see me struggle so. Then, I would realize that with each step I took toward finding Jim, I was getting closer to my goal in a positive way. And however my adventure ended, it would be the right one. It was meant to be.

As I look back on these years, I find a parallel evolution between my growth from a naïve person coming out of my shell--my protective environment--into the real world of lies and deceit that I found as I looked for Jim.

I learned that I was strong enough to ask questions, and that I was not crazy to ask those questions. I was just a mom and a nurse, but I learned more about the whole espionage thing than I ever thought existed, or would have been possible to learn from movies.

For me to have walked into the arena of war/government/secrets/politics/deceit at the age of twenty-two was ridiculous. Yet I was forced to. I learned to address generals and politicians, and say things I would never have said before.

If I had not been an MIA wife, I probably would never have gone overseas by myself. Yet, look at how many times I did that to look for Jim, and also for humanitarian reasons when I went as a nurse to the war zone of Somalia.

Returning each time to the rich culture of the United States, and people complaining about things that were not perfect in their lives, really put me in touch with the difference between a Third World country and America. All the fancy gizmos in the world can't give you friendship or love. I became much more aware of what was really important in life, and that it's not quantity but quality that can make you happy.

I have been given so many tools in the past 36 years, to use for my second life's quest, and I am most thankful for that. I feel like I can really do anything I set my mind to.

I have tried to instill in my children this philosophy.

As for my quest for Jim, I'm not actively pursuing him as I have for so many years. Likewise, I am not walking away or abandoning him. And Jim, if you should happen to read this, know one simple truth. I love you and I'm always here for you.

I'm reminded of a country western song that goes like this--"Life is a dance. You learn as you go. Sometimes you lead, sometimes you follow."

Postscript Four

Living Sentinels

"Standing watch over those who preserved our heritage"

On April 28, 2001, a tree planting ceremony was held at the National Cemetery at the Presidio of San Francisco.

The invitation stated, "in recognition and rededication to those who have given their lives for our nation. We hope that you will unite with the veterans and their families as they remember those who have given the ultimate price for freedom."

The summer before, when I was visiting Jim's headstone at the Presidio, I noticed that the majestic trees, which had stood guard so gallantly over our fallen heroes, were being removed, with no intention of replacement. I decided to do something about it.

I brought the situation to the attention of various veterans groups in the United States, and they responded as I knew they would. My idea turned into the Presidio Tree Project.

I had a bronze-leafed tree designed to be erected at the Presidio. As each person donated money for a live tree, I had a leaf put on the bronze tree inscribed with the name of the deceased veteran in whose memory the donation was made. I worked with the National Cemetery Administration, the Presidio Trust, and the Memorial System Network to ensure that the money donated would result in the trees being planted at the cemetery.

On that afternoon in April, people from all walks of life joined together to honor the memories of our country's fallen who gave their lives for their beliefs. I was surprised and pleased that Brigadier General Madsen, Corps of Engineers, the highest ranking officer in the San Francisco Bay Area, attended.

Col. Roger P. Knight, USA (Ret.), called for the posting of the colors performed by the representatives of the various armed servies. The invocation was given by Cpt. Edward K. Murray, USN, CHC (Ret.).

A letter from United States Senator, Barbara Boxer, and a letter from Ann Mills Griffiths, Executive Director of the National League of Families of American Prisoners of War and Missing in Action in Southeast Asia, were read to those gathered on the Presidio grounds.

On the platform was arranged a row of chairs with a hat placed on each one by the South Bay Recruiting Company, USA. I had asked my friend, Sara, an MIA wife, to read a few words. This is what she said.

"As you reflect on this beautiful and historic setting and as a reminder of why we have gathered together today to honor and remember those servicemen and women who have gone before us, please notice the POW/MIA flag. This flag was designed in 1971 by Mrs. Michael Hoff, an MIA wife and member of the National League of Families, as an ever-present symbol and reminder of the plight of our prisoners of war and missing service members.

"On March 9, 1989, an official. . .(national) flag which flew over the White House in 1988, was installed in the U.S. Capitol Rotunda as a result of legislation passed during the 100th Congress. The. . .POW/MIA flag is the ONLY flag ever displayed in the U.S. Capitol Rotunda where it stands today. Other than "Old Glory", the POW/MIA flag is the ONLY flag ever to fly over the White House having been displayed in this place of honor on National POW/MIA Recognition Day since 1982. Though a League member designed the flag, this flag stands as a visible and powerful symbol of this Nation's concern and commitment to resolve, as fully as possible, the fates of Americans still prisoners or missing and unaccounted for in all wars – thus ending the uncertainty for their families and this Nation.

"John F. Kennedy said, 'A nation reveals itself not only by the men it produces. . .but also by the men it honors, the men it remembers.'

"Today's remembrance ceremony is conducted by the U.S. Honor Guard.

"As the Honor Guard brings in a hat from each of the services, we are visually reminded of those service members who continue to serve in their unaccounted for status. In today's presentation, representing the U.S. Army, we have the actual Green Beret of Capt. James D. Birchim, missing in action in South Vietnam since November 1968. . .and representing the U.S. Air Force, the actual flight cap of Maj. Tommy E. Gist, missing in action over North Vietnam since May 1968. The Coast Guard flight helmet is representative of the one Coast Guard aviator still unaccounted for from the Vietnam War. A cap for the Navy and the Marine MIAs was also placed on the respective chairs. The last hat, which is a baseball cap, represents the civilians who worked along side our military and remain unaccounted for today.

"REMEMBER, all of you who served with them. . .all of you who considered them comrades. . .all who depended on their strength and aid and relied up them for our safety. . .remember them as we do. . .our husbands, fathers, brothers, sons and friends.

"For their joy and their strength, their youth and the moments we shared together. . .surely wherever they are, we are in their thoughts. They have not forsaken us.

"REMEMBER! ALWAYS REMEMBER! THE PRICE OF FREEDOM IS NOT FREE!"

Jerry Estenson, representing the Special Forces Chapter XXII, was one of the two men who arrived at my parent's door to tell me Jim was missing which is why I felt honored that he accepted to be the Master of Ceremonies. He introduced each speaker.

The keynote speaker was Lieutenant General John M. Pickler, Director of the U.S. Army Staff, Pentagon. "We will not rest until they are all in America," he said.

Steve Muro, Director of Memorial System Network, spoke of the Presidio as "a place of peace for those we honor."

James E. Meadows, Executive Director of the Presidio Trust, reminded those gathered there that day, that 450,000 trees had been planted 100 years before, on that hillside overlooking the San Francisco Bay. "Thanks to Barbara Birchim, and everyone who donated money for trees, many of the old, weather beaten ones would now be replaced to live another 100 years, maintaining that beautiful setting."

When Jerry Estenson began to introduce me, he hesitated. With his voice cracking, it took him three attempts to get through what he was tryng to say. He told me later that, "All the should-haves and could-haves came rushing into my consciousness and it seemed like I was swimming against emotions I could not control."

I said a few words about the plaque, and the benediction was given, followed by taps presented by the 91st Division Band, USA. Then we moved from the formal grounds to plant our first tree, as a symbol of those to follow.

Friends of the Urban Forest helped with the planting. Members of Swords-to-Plowshares, a group that helps homeless vets return to the work force, ushered that day.

My involvement with the Presidio Cemetery was really about beautification. The 80 trees to be planted there were to keep that historical setting from being barren one day.

I don't need to continue being involved in that project. The Veterans Administration has now taken over. But, I felt it was important to draw this to the attention of veterans as well as the military, so that is how the tree planting ceremony evolved.

In the April 28, 2001, San Diego Union-Tribune, Brian E. Clark quoted me. "I felt it was important to restore the feeling of strength and vigilance that

408

those old trees conveyed to the cemetery. They are living sentinels standing watch over those who preserved our heritage. To me, it was a matter of honor. . .There are plenty of folks who wanted the cemetery restored to its former beauty. I just had to get the word out."

The article continued with, "The Presidio site became a national cemetery in the 1880s. More than 30,000 veterans and their dependents are buried there, some from as far back as the war with Mexico in the 1840s."

At the June 2001 annual League meeting in Arlington, Virginia, I was part of the agenda for the day. I was proud to report on my Presidio tree-planting project.

I couldn't think of anything more stirring to include in the program for that day of tree planting than a quote from Maj. Michael Davis O'Donnell, from Vietnam, January 1, 1970, who was reported MIA on March 24, 1970.

"If you are able, save for them a place inside of you . . .and save one backward glance when you are leaving for the place they can no longer go. . .be not ashamed to say you loved them, though you may or may not have always. . . Take what they left and what they have taught you with their dying and keep it with your own. . .And in that time when men decide and feel safe to call this war insane, take one moment to embrace those gentle heroes you left behind . . ."

Disclaimer

If you doubted my story when you began to read this book, perhaps you no longer do. What I lived through for 36 years, as I looked for my MIA husband, Jim, is the gospel truth, taken from hundreds of pages in my diaries, journals, trip notes, and Jim's official Army personnel file. Through the years, I have collected books and newspaper articles, official letters, videotapes, and interviews about me, as well as other information, which are where all of my footnotes come from. Not once did I go to the library or the world wide web to gather information for this book, although many people have e-mailed documents to me from time to time with material they thought I would be interested in reading. Every reference and footnote is in the archives I've collected, except for two of the books I quoted--Reaching For Glory, Lyndon Johnson's Secret, written by Michael Beschloss, Simon & Schuster, 2001; and Home To War: A History of the Vietnam Veteran's Movement, written by Gerald Nicosia, Crown Publishers, 1997.

Appendix

1945
Mar. 9—Japanese occupation authorities proclaim independent Vietnam with Emperor Bao Dai as nominal ruler.
Sept. 2—Communist led Vietminh Independence League seizes power under Ho Chi Minh; establish "Democratic Republic of Vietnam."
Sept. 22—French troops return to Vietnam, clash with Communists and anti-French nationalists in Tonkin.

1946
Mar. 6—France recognizes Democratic Rep. of Vietnam as "free state" within Indo-Chinese Federation and French Union.
Dec. 19—Vietminh attack on French troops in north begins eight-year Indo-China War.

1949
Mar. 8—Independent state of Vietnam established with ties to France.
June 14—Bao Dai assumes role as chief of state of Vietnam; nationalists withhold support.
July 19—Laos established as independent state with ties to France.
Nov. 8—Cambodia established as independent state with ties to France.

1950
May 8—U.S. announces military and economic aid to Vietnam, Laos and Cambodia.

1954
May 7—French stronghold at Dien Bien Phu falls.
July 21—Cease-fire signed at Geneva. Partition of Vietnam at 17th parallel into Communist north and anti-Communist south with proviso of free elections in 1956.
Sept. 8—Southeast Asia Defense Treaty (SEATO) established to check Communist expansion.

1955
Oct. 26—Republic of Vietnam established in South Vietnam with Ngo Dinh Diem as president. U.S. promises aid.

1956
April—Last French troops in Vietnam leave. U.S. military advisers train South Vietnamese.
May 8—Free elections to reunify the two Vietnams postponed.

1957
May 29—Crisis in Laos as pro-Communist Pathet Lao forces make bid for power.

1959
April—Increase of Communist underground (Vietcong) activity in South Vietnam, supplied and directed from North Vietnam.

1960
Nov. 11—Unsuccessful military revolt against Diem regime in South Vietnam.

1961
Jan.—North Vietnam and U.S.S.R. aid pro-Communist rebels in Laos.
Mar.—U.S. reacts to threat of Communist takeover in Laos with increased aid and dispatch of troops to Thailand.
July—U.S. steps up aid to South Vietnam; increases role of military advisers.

1962
June 11—Agreement on coalition government in Laos announced.
Oct.—U.S. helicopter units begin air lifts of South Vietnamese troops against Vietcong.

1963
May-Aug—Buddhist demonstrations against Diem government in South Vietnam.
Nov. 2—Diem assassinated in army coup; start of a long series of shaky regimes and coups lasting until 1965.

1964
Aug. 2,4—North Vietnamese patrol boats attack U.S. destroyers in Gulf of Tonkin.
Aug. 5—In reprisal U.S. 7th Fleet makes air strike against North Vietnamese boat bases and oil storage depot.
Aug. 7—Congress passes Gulf of Tonkin Resolution, endorsing all measures to prevent further aggression.
Dec. 31—U.S. forces in Vietnam total 23,000.

1965
Feb. 7—Vietcong attack U.S. installations at Pleiku. President Johnson orders retaliatory raids, beginning the bombing of bases and supply lines in North Vietnam.
Mar. 8—3,500 Marines land at Da Nang as U.S. commits combat troops to support South Vietnamese forces.
June 18—First B-52 raid from Guam.
June 19—Military junta led by Nguyen Cao Ky comes to power in South Vietnam.
June 28—U.S. Army troops in first major operation against Vietcong northeast of Saigon.
July 28—President Johnson orders U.S. forces in South Vietnam increased to 125,000, more if necessary.
Dec. 31—U.S. troops in Vietnam total 181,000.

1966
Jan. 31—U.S. peace offensive fails; bombing of North Vietnam is resumed after 37-day pause.
Feb. 7-8—President Johnson and Ky meet in Hawaii to discuss goals for Vietnam.
June 29—First U.S. bombing raids on strategic targets in Hanoi-Haiphong area.
Oct. 24-25—Manila conference of allied powers fighting in South Vietnam.
Dec. 31—U.S. forces in Vietnam total 389,000.

1967
Mar. 27—New constitution for South Vietnam.
May—Demilitarized Zone swept by U.S. forces.
Sept. 3—Gen. Nguyen Van Thieu and Premier Ky elected president and vice president of South Vietnam.
Dec. 31—U.S. forces in Vietnam nearly 500,000.

1968
Jan. 31—Vietcong launch *Tet* holiday offensive; fierce fighting rages in Saigon and Hue.
Feb. 13—Additional 10,500 U.S. troops ordered to Vietnam to meet increased pressure against Marines at Khe Sanh and to meet Vietcong assaults on South Vietnamese cities.

411

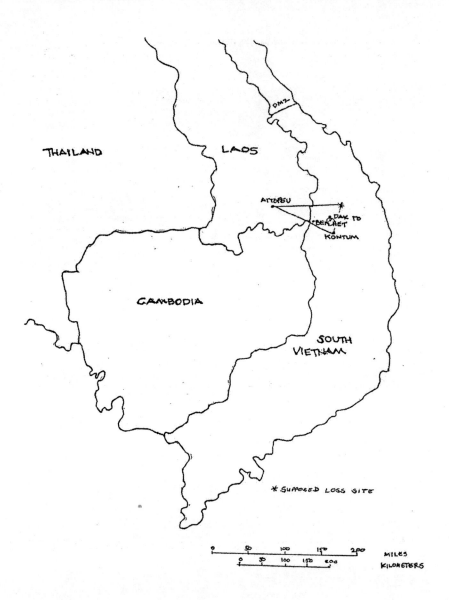

THAILAND

LAOS

DMZ

ATTOPEU   *

     DAK TO
BEN HET
KONTUM

CAMBODIA

SOUTH
VIETNAM

* SUPPOSED LOSS SITE

0   50   100   150   200   MILES
0   50   100   150   200   KILOMETERS

412

CLASS OF SERVICE

This is a fast message unless its deferred character is indicated by the proper symbol.

W. P. MARSHALL
CHAIRMAN OF THE BOARD

WESTERN UNION
TELEGRAM

SYMBOLS

DL = Day Letter
NL = Night Letter
LT = International Letter Telegram

The filing time shown in the date line on domestic telegrams is LOCAL TIME at point of origin. Time of receipt is LOCAL TIME at point of destination

LAC55 SYC110

1968 NOV 21 AM 8 44

SY WA210 XV GOVT PDB 4 EXTRA=FAXWASHINGTON DC 21 1100A EST

=MRS BARBARA L BIRCHIM. DONT DLR BTWN 10PM & 6AM DONT

PHONE CHECK DLY CHGS ABOVE 75 CTS=

19 MERRYDALE RD APT NO 5 SAN RAFAEL CALIF=

THE SECRETARY OF THE ARMY HAS ASKED ME TO EXPRESS HIS

DEEP REGRET THAT YOUR HUSBAND FIRST LIEUTENANT JAMES D.

BIRCHIM HAS BEEN MISSING IN VIETNAM SINCE 15 NOVEMBER

1968. HE WAS LAST SEEN AS MEMBER OF RESCUE TEAM BEING

EXTRACTED FROM AN AREA BY MILITARY AIRCRAFT I WHEN AREA

CAME UNDER HOSTILE FIRE AND HE FELL FROM EXTRACTION DEVICE.

SEARCH IS IN PROGRESS. YOU WILL BE ADVISED PROMPTLY

WHEN FURTHER INFORMATION IS RECEIVED. IN ORDER TO PROTECT

ANY INFORMATION THAT MIGHT BE USED TO YOUR HUSBAND'S

DETRIMENT, YOUR COOPERATION IS REQUESTED IN MAKING

PUBLIC ONLY INFORMATION CONCERING HIS NAME, RANK, SERVICE

NUMBER AND DATE OF BIRTH. THIS CONFIRMS PERSONAL

NOTIFICATION MADE BY REPRESENTATIVE OF THE SECRETARY

OF THE ARMY=

KENNETH G WICKHAM MAJOR GENERAL USA F313 THE

ADJUTANT GENERAL=

WU1201 (R2-65)   THE COMPANY WILL APPRECIATE SUGGESTIONS FROM ITS PATRONS CONCERNING ITS SERVICE

413

WESTERN UNION
W. P. MARSHALL
CHAIRMAN OF THE BOARD

TELEGRAM
R. W. McFALL
PRESIDENT

1968 NOV 27 AM

The filing time shown in the date line on domestic telegrams is LO DONT DLR BTWEEN 10PM & 6 AM=

LA030 SPE146-CTA073 =LS

CT WA042 XV GOVT PD=FAX WASHINGTON DC 27 609A EST=

MRS BARBARA L BIRCHIM, DONT PHONE REPORT DELIVERY

19 MERRYDALE RD APT NO 5 SAN RAFAEL CALIF=

=I REGRET TO INFORM YOU THAT NO ADDITIONAL INFORMATION
CONCRNING YOUR HUSBAND FIRST LIEUTENANT JAMES D BIRCHIM
HAS BEEN OBTAINED. THE SEARCH IS CONTINUING. IN THOSE
INSTANCES WHERE A MEMBER'S FATE IT NOT DEFINITELY
ASCERTAINED THE CIRCUMSTANCES SURROUNDING HIS DISAPPEARANCE
ARE THOROUGHLY INVESTIGATED. OUR REGULATIONS REQUIRE THE
ORGANIZATION COMMANDER TO CONVENE A BOARD OF OFFICERS TO
CONDUCT THE INVESTIGATION WITHIN TEN DAYS AFTER THE
INCIDENT. THE BOARD WILL EXAMINE ALL AVAILABLE EVIDENCE.
INTERROGATE ASSOCIATES AND THOSE WHO CAN CONTRIBUTE
INFORMATION WHICH WILL ASSIST THEM IN ARRIVING AT A
SOUND AND LOGICAL CONCLUSION. THE BOARD MAY RECOMMEND
A CHANGE IN JAMES'S STATUS TO DECEASED SHOULD THE
EVIDENC BE ADEQUATELY CONCLUSIVE TO SUPPORT SUCH A
FINDING. HOWEVER. IN THE ABSENCE OF CONCLUSIVE EVIDENCE
IT IS NORMAL THAT HE BE CONTINUED AS MISSING.
THE REPORT OF THE PROCEEDING OF THIS BOARD OF OFFICERS
SHOULD BE IN MY OFFICE WITHN 60 DAYS. HOWEVER. I WILL
CORRESPOND WITH YOU AGAIN DURING THE MONTH OF JANUARY
1969 AND OF COURSE SHOULD ANY NEW DEVELONMENT OCCUR
I SHALL INFORM YOU IMMEDIATELY=

KENNETH G WICKHAM MAJOR GENERAL USA F-17 THE

ADJUTANT GENERAL

29 November 1968

Dear Mrs. Birchim:

I regret that I must confirm the recent telegram from The Adjutant General in which you were informed that your husband, First Lieutenant James D. Birchim, has been missing in Vietnam since 15 November.

The United States Army and other governmental agencies are making every reasonable effort to secure information concerning your husband and other missing personnel. Extensive and continuous aerial and ground searches are being conducted, and leaflets have been dropped announcing the offer of rewards for the recovery of missing personnel. As soon as any additional information is received, The Adjutant General will pass it on to you without delay.

The Commanding General of Sixth Army has been directed to appoint an officer to assist you in any way possible during this period of anxiety and uncertainty.

With heartfelt sympathy to you,

Sincerely,

W. C. WESTMORELAND
General, United States Army
Chief of Staff

Mrs. James D. Birchim
19 Merrydale Road, Apt. 5
San Rafael, California 94903

DEPARTMENT OF THE ARMY
HEADQUARTERS
5TH SPECIAL FORCES GROUP (AIRBORNE) 1ST SPECIAL FORCES
APO SAN FRANCISCO 96240

AVGB

4 DEC 1968

Mrs. James D. Birchim
19 Merrydale
San Rafael, California 94901

Dear Mrs. Birchim:

It is with profound regret that I must confirm the Department of the
Army report that your husband, First Lieutenant James D. Birchim,
05337358 was missing in action on 15 November 1968. At that time, your
husband's rescue team came under enemy fire while assisting in the
removal of a team from a hostile area. The most thorough search possible
was initiated immediately and as this operation continues, the officers
and men of the 5th Special Forces Group offer our prayers for his safe
return. As First Lieutenant Birchim's comrades in arms, we extend our
sympathy during these days of great stress and anxiety for you.

As soon as further information is developed, it will be forwarded to you.
If we can be of service to you, please do not hesitate to contact us.

Sincerely,

HAROLD R. AARON
Colonel, Infantry
Commanding

416

DEPARTMENT OF THE ARMY
SPECIAL OPERATIONS AUGMENTATION (CCN)
5TH SPECIAL FORCES GROUP (AIRBORNE), 1ST SPECIAL FORCES
Drawer 22, APO San Francisco 96337

4 DEC 1968

Mrs. James D. Birchim
19 Merrydale
San Rafael, California 94901

Dear Mrs. Birchim:

I deeply regret the circumstances under which I write this letter. I realize it is small consolation for your burden of grief during this period; however, I wish to express the condolences of all the officers and men who are members of the organization to which your husband belongs.

Jim was the leader of a rescue team attempting to reach another team that was in trouble in a hostile area on 15 November 1968. The team came under intense enemy fire and while being extracted by helicopter Jim fell from a McGuire rig. A search was launched to locate and recover Jim soon after he became missing. This effort continues and will as long as there is a chance of recovery.

Jim is well trained in the art of survival, evasion and defense and we are confident in his ability to survive the elements. All of us were deeply saddened to learn that he was missing and we offer our sincerest prayers and hopes for his safe recovery.

A board of officers will convene to examine all facts in Jim's case. You will be notified of the results of this board as soon as a determination is made.

Again all of us here in Jim's unit wish to express our deepest concern and sympathy. If I can be of any assistance to you in any way, please do not hesitate to let me know.

Respectfully,

JOHN S. WARREN
LTC, Infantry
Commanding

417

17 May 1971

Dear Mrs. Birchim:

It is with sadness that I write to you at this time of
personal sorrow. The tragic passing of your husband,
Captain James D. Birchim, previously reported missing
in Vietnam, is also a great loss to those who were privileged to serve with him in the United States Army.

I realize how difficult it must be to face the loss of
a loved one and know that words alone offer little consolation. However, I hope you will find some measure of
comfort and gain inner strength in knowing how very important your husband's selfless service was to his country.

The priceless gift of life is the most noble one a soldier can make to protect his loved ones at home and to
safeguard the cherished beliefs for which his Nation stands.
Our strength and security rest on the loyalty and devotion
of American soldiers who today safeguard freedom as did
American soldiers in earlier times of national peril.
You can treasure the thought that for his gift of life
your husband is noble among men who share the blessings
of freedom.

On behalf of all members of the United States Army, I
express heartfelt sympathy to you and your daughter.

Sincerely,

W. C. WESTMORELAND
General, United States Army
Chief of Staff

Mrs. James D. Birchim
39 Knight Drive
San Rafael, California 94901

RONALD REAGAN
GOVERNOR

May 26, 1971

Mrs. Barbara L. Birchim
39 Knight Avenue
San Rafael, California 94901

Dear Mrs. Birchim:

Please accept my deepest sympathy
for the loss of your husband. I
can only pray that his sacrifice--
and yours--will bring the world
closer to peace.

God be with you.

Sincerely,

RONALD REAGAN
Governor

SECRETARY OF THE ARMY
WASHINGTON

June 7, 1971

Dear Mrs. Birchim:

Please accept my deepest sympathy for the
death of your husband, Captain James D. Birchim,
in Vietnam.

We are proud of his military accomplishments
and grateful to him for his contribution to our
Nation's strength. All members of the United
States Army join me in expressing the hope that
the memory of his dedicated service will help
to ease your sorrow.

Sincerely yours,

Stanley R. Resor

Stanley R. Resor

Mrs. James D. Birchim
39 Knight Drive
San Rafael, California 94901

June 16, 1971

Dear Mrs. Birchim:

I have learned with great sadness of the death of
your husband, Captain James D. Birchim. All America
shares your loss, and the deepest sympathies of our
fellow citizens will forever honor your husband's
profound sacrifice.

Mrs. Nixon and I want you to know that you and your
loved ones are in our thoughts and in our hearts.
We pray that the eternal respect your husband has
so tragically earned will sustain and comfort you
in the days ahead.

Sincerely,

Richard Nixon

Mrs. James D. Birchim
39 Knight Drive
San Rafael, California

Missing Gi's Wife

A Brave Woman's Despairing Hope

By Tim Findley

Barbara Birchim, who spent her 23rd birthday Christmas Eve in Paris, was friendly and remarkably calm as she sat in United Air Lines' A l o h a Room at the San Francisco Airport yesterday and said of her husband:

"If intuition means anything, I think he's dead. I can't be sure of that, though, and if there's a 1 per cent chance he is alive, you've got to go on that 1 per cent."

Her husband, Special Forces C a p t a i n James D. Birchim, also 23, has been listed as missing in action in Vietnam since November 15, 1968.

Pert and pretty, Mrs. Birchim h u g g e d her camel's hair coat a b o u t her and talked about her trip to Paris with 57 other wives of Americans either missing or prisoners in North Vietnam.

'HOPEFUL'

"I feel hopeful at least that the (North Vietnamese officials) did see us. The trip was exhausting but (here her voice trailed off) . . . full of hope."

The North Vietnamese, after a brief session with three of the wives (Mrs. Birchim was not one of them, said information on the women's

MRS. JAMES D. BIRCHIM
After Paris trip

husbands would be released gradually.

The B i r c h i m s have two children: K i m b e r e y, 20 m o n t h s, and David, nine months. Mrs. Birchim and the children live with her parents, Mr. and Mrs. E. R. Sherwood, of San Francisco.

POISE

Her poise impressed newsmen at the airport to the extent they asked her how she could be so calm in discussing her husband's possible death.

"Being in the military," she said, "you come to live with death very closely, I guess much the same as a policeman's wife does.

"When he gets his orders, you just don't know if he's coming back."

Mrs. Birchim said now that she's made the trip to try to find out about her husband she's going to "try to lead as normal a life as possible.

'NORMAL THINGS'

"It's time to straighten my ideas a r o u n d to normal things — to think about an a p a r t m e n t, a job, getting back in the world . . ."

But, she explained earnestly, "You become somewhat deadened. Inside you feel, but it doesn't show on the outside, because people are watching.

"Maybe each one of us finds strength in our own problems."

Showing a pretty smile, she said of the 57 women who (with 95 children) made the Paris trip with her, "each one was sort of their own power plant."

Then the smile went away, and she talked of her status: Not a widow, but not quite a wife.

"People don't know what to do with you.

"You're kind of an odd person."

San Francisco Examiner
December 27, 1969

Intuition Tells Her He's Dead

By William O'Brien

"If my intuition plays any part, I feel he is dead," said young and winsome Barbara Birchin, only California wife of a soldier to make a Christmas pilgrimage to Paris seeking information from North Vietnamese diplomas about her missing husband.

"But I don't know," added Mrs. Birchin. "If there was even a one percent chance he is alive — well, you have to go along with that."

Mrs. Birchin is the wife of Green Beret, Special Forces Captain James Douglas Birchin, who has been missing in action since Nov. 15, 1968.

23rd Birthday

Mrs. Birchin celebrated her 23rd birthday aloft above the Atlantic Ocean on the flight which took 58 wives of American servicemen and their 95 children to Paris in the vain hope of convincing the Viet Cong there should be an immediate release of information on captured American soldiers.

Mrs. Birchin's husband also is 23.

She conceded to reporters at San Francisco International Airport yesterday, she was not totally discouraged by the North Vietnamese Christmas declaration they had no ready information on POWs.

She said she was more heartened by the reception of a delegation of three wives of servicemen from her group at the Viet Cong Paris legation.

'Some Hope'

Mrs. Birchin was not in the select group of three but observed there was some hope in the statement the North Vietnamese "would do their best to release all the names" of war prisoners.

Mrs. Birchin indicated her feelings of intuitive doom have been colored by the findings of two Army boards of inquiry into her husband's disappearance in South Vietnam 13 months ago.

From the inquiry boards, she said, it had been determined her husband was one of four Special Forces soldiers "extracted" in darkness from a jungle mission by harnesses slung from helicopters.

Her husband's harness, said Mrs. Birchin, tangled in foliage and he was lifted clinging to another soldier in harness. Gunfire kept the suspended men from being winched aboard the helicopter.

Best information from the soldier to whom Capt. Birchin had been clinging, said the wife, is that the young officer held on for approximately 40 minutes and dropped from an altitude of 2000 feet.

2 Children

Mrs. Birchin notes, however, that the surviving Green Beret was wounded in the shoulder and could have lost track of time and distance, leaving open possibilities the captain dropped from a lower altitude into foliage, survived, and was made a prisoner.

The Birchins are parents of two children, Kimberely, 21 months, and David, 9 months, who the missing husband has never seen.

Her intuition, according to Mrs. Birchin, told her the young captain was alive and well from the day of his disappearance until some point the following January. "But I don't believe he lived past January," she said.

'Normal Life'

Asked to explain, Mrs. Birchin replied that her beliefs are based on the same feelings causing a mother "to listen to a child cry — she can tell when it has been hurt."

Of the anxieties of not knowing, Mrs. Birchin said her immediate future will be an attempt "to lead as normal a life as possible."

Currently, she is living here with her parents, the E. B. Sherwoods. Her husband originally was from Bishop in Southern California.

"The initial shock has worn off," explained Mrs. Birchin. "I am trying to straighten things out. I am trying to find out whether it is time to live by myself in an apartment with my children? Is it time to go out into the world?"

Asked if she would place herself in the same situation again, Mrs. Birchin replied:

"Being in the military, you come to live with death very closely. It is much like being a policeman's wife. The answer is, yes."

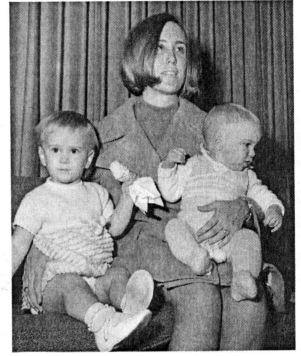

INTUITION TELLS HER HER HUSBAND IS DEAD
Mrs. Barbara Birchin with her daughter Kimberly and son David
—Examiner photo by Walt Lynott

Those who did not return remembered on POW/MIA Day

By Steve LaRue
Staff Writer

Barbara Birchim was 21 when her husband fell from a combat helicopter somewhere between South Vietnam and Laos in November 1968.

"We were both the same age," she said yesterday at ceremonies in Old Town to commemorate National POW/MIA Awareness Day.

"I am 42 now. It hit me this year that half my life I have been waiting for an answer," she said.

Special Forces Capt. James Douglas Birchim and about 2,300 other U.S. service men or women who fought in the Vietnam War are still missing.

Like many relatives, Barbara Birchim feels sure that some service men and women are still alive and held captive in Vietnam, even though almost all have since been officially listed as dead.

"Today we are trying to bring together an awareness that there are many people still alive there," she said as a Marine Corps Color Guard stood at attention nearby.

One of the Marines held the black POW-MIA flag depicting a prisoner encircled by watch towers and barbed wire.

"How many are still alive? We estimate a couple of hundred or so," said James Gregory, spokesman for Over the Wall, an organization dedicated to recovering U.S. Vietnam War POWs.

"The most important thing you can do is to fly the POW/MIA flag under Old Glory," he said.

The Over the Wall group also will hold a candlelight vigil to remember U.S. prisoners of war tonight at 6 p.m. near the cross atop Mount Soledad in La Jolla.

Almost 15 years after the fall of Saigon, now Ho Chi Minh City, the group yesterday also officially opened a permanent POW/MIA Information Booth on Old Town, next to the Vietnam Memorial at the state park's entrance at the foot of San Diego Avenue.

"People have come in with bracelets that they have had from 20 years ago," Gregory said. "They say, 'What happened to this person?'

"Some of them are wearing the bracelets. Some just remember the names. We try to get back to them and let them know. Our primary goal is to get a live American out of Southeast Asia, then to get them all out. One means to do this is to raise public awareness."

About 40 park visitors watched the commemorative ceremonies in Old Town to mark the anniversary yesterday and to open the information center. About the same number glimpsed the ceremony as they strolled through that part of the park.

Some organizers were disappointed at the turnout, although happy that state parks and recreation officials had agreed to make the information center permanent.

Father Charles Shelton Jr., son of missing Air Force Col. Charles E. Shelton, said the invocation at yesterday's ceremony.

"Let them know they will never be forgotten. They will never be abandoned," he said afterward.

The San Diego Union/Diana Rinehart Babb

Barbara Birchim speaks yesterday at ceremonies in Old Town to commemorate National POW/MIA Awareness Day.

TIMES ADVOCATE

25¢ ● FRIDAY, APRIL 6, 1990

KARRIE LIN CARLSON/*Times Advocate*

Barbara Birchim has her husband's MIA bracelet, which marks the day her long wait for news began.

Hanging onto hope

425

Vet's wife seeks answers after 22 years

ROY RIVENBURG/*Times Advocate*

RANCHO BERNARDO — Jim Birchim tried to hang onto a helicopter rope 22 years ago but lost his grip and fell into the jungles of Southeast Asia.

His wife, Barbara, has been hanging onto hope ever since but is ready to loosen her grip after a strange visit to Vietnam last month to look for information about her missing husband.

Barbara Birchim said the trip merely fulfilled a silent promise made long ago. But it also symbolizes the swirl of emotions that continues to haunt the families and friends of MIAs.

Birchim has been living in two worlds — the past and the present — since November 1968 when her 21-year-old Green Beret husband vanished over Laos. Their daughter was just a few months old at the time, and their son was not yet born.

Remarried, then divorced and now living with another man, Birchim still feels the tug of the past and the strain it puts on relationships in the present.

On one side is a grapevine of MIA families spreading hope, rumors and other information from home and abroad. On the other is a desire to get on with life, to put the questions to rest.

"I had to do it (go to Vietnam). I made a promise to Jim," Birchim said.

But the trip proved "rather nerve-racking all the way through," she said. The Vietnamese tailed her, bugged her hotel room, and eventually threatened to put her in jail, she said after returning home to Rancho Bernardo several weeks ago.

Birchim, 43, was joined on the trip by two Vietnam veterans and another woman whose brother is an MIA. The veterans contacted Birchim after seeing her on a television news show discussing her plans to visit the country.

The stated purpose of their 16-day trip was to deliver 500 pounds of donated medical supplies to Vietnamese doctors, but Birchim hoped to use the equip-

Barbara Birchim at her Rancho Bernardo home with some photos and sketches of her husband. Below is one of the sketches.

ment as "leverage to get information" about her husband's whereabouts.

Birchim delivered the supplies, but she wasn't allowed into the area of the country where she thought her husband and other Americans might be. So she and her friends went to Hanoi, where they were caught distributing leaflets offering rewards for information about MIAs, she said.

Birchim and the others were interrogated for several hours and warned that their actions could result in prison terms of three to 12 years, she said.

Please see **HOPE**, A2 ▶

426

'I suddenly remembered [one fellow] when I saw his name [at the Vietnam Memorial]. I visualized his face, his smile, his freckles. . . . He was a real good kid.'

JAY MORALES

DAY: A Time for Memories

Continued from E2

Barbara Birchim doesn't quite believe her husband is alive, but she isn't sure he's dead, either. "I think it's very possible he's wandering around not knowing where he is."

With no solid evidence, the Army in May, 1971, changed James Birchim's status from MIA to "killed in action, body not recovered." In August of that year, she married another Army officer.

The marriage ended in divorce 11 years later. Now 43, she lives in San Diego.

Birchim belongs to the National League of Families of American Prisoners and Missing in Southeast Asia, which seeks information on 2,303 Americans missing or unaccounted for in the region. Independently, she has made two trips to Vietnam, the last in March.

"When Jim first turned up missing, I made a promise to him and myself that I would go to Vietnam when the kids were old enough to be self-sufficient," she said. The responses of villagers there to her questions convinced her that "there are Americans there."

She is critical of the U.S. government for what she views as inaction and the withholding of information. She went to Vietnam, she said, partially because she had to explode the "mystique" of Vietnam. "Now, a lot of the mystery is gone and there's comfort in that."

In the last 18 months, she said, "there have been rumors that there are five to seven Green Berets living in the mountains in the Kontum area [near where Birchim's base camp was] with the Montagnard people." She believes Jim Birchim could be one of them.

She poses the possibility, too, that Americans are being held by "some little militant faction that thinks they're still at war with us."

If he is alive, he is 43 now. Barbara Birchim accepts the possibility that he could be leading another life there. "We've heard stories about men forced to work in the fields, and part of their pay is they give them Vietnamese wives."

But she is adamant that the men and women still in Southeast Asia "have the right to come home" and that their government should be fighting harder for that right.

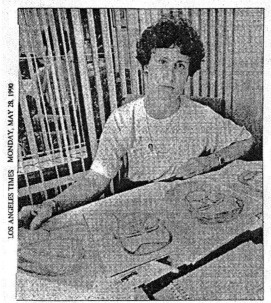

'When Jim first turned up missing, I made a promise to him and myself that I would go to Vietnam when the kids were old enough to be self-sufficient.'

BARBARA BIRCHIM

Barbara Birchim of Rancho Bernardo has been awakened by her lost husband's voice, calling to her, telling her there isn't much time left.

Capt. James Birchim, an Army Special Forces officer, is missing in action somewhere in the central highlands of Laos. Or Cambodia. Or maybe Vietnam.

Ever since their loved ones were declared Missing In Action — some of them more than 20 years ago — San Diego County family members like Barbara Birchim and Sturme Christofferson have toiled without fanfare to bring their men home.

Here is a glimpse of the frustration, the pain and the hope that mark their wait.

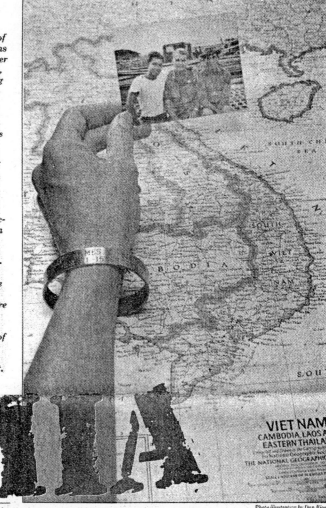

Story by
MARY ENGES-MAAS

Barbara Birchim holds a photo of her husband over a map of Southeast Asia.

Photo illustration by Dan Rice

Another View

Bring home the POWs and MIAs

By RONI SHANLEY

I am a MIA family member. I was in Vietnam last year on a humanitarian and fact-finding mission with the wife of another MIA and two Vietnam veterans. Inexplicably, we were barred from bringing the 500 pounds of donated medical supplies we had collected to certain hospitals and clinics in areas which were on Vietnam's approved tourist list — despite the fact that we had obtained prior approval from the Vietnamese mission at the United Nations.

Was there something they did not want us to see? The Vietnam interior minister was so concerned about what we thought about the POW/MIA issue that he invited us to meet with him in Hanoi. At the end of a very lengthy discussion, he expressed surprise that the U.S. government tells the family members of POWs so little, and said, "At the proper time, you families will have your answers." He did not offer further explanation as to what he meant by that.

The Vietnamese villagers and people in the market places appeared afraid when we asked about Americans living in Vietnam (with no mention of the POW/MIA issue).

We came home with no answers to the whys, but with a stronger belief that the Vietnamese continue to hold some of our men as POWs.

I beg to differ with the assessment of those like Ethel Taylor, former national coordinator of Women's Strike for Peace,

Shanley is a sister of Sgt. 1st Class Michael H. Shanley, who was reported missing in action in Vietnam on Dec. 2, 1969. She serves on the Pacific Beach POW/MIA Committee.

that Vietnam holds no live POWs.

One must go back to the Paris peace accords. It is well documented that the U.S. government knowingly left American POWs behind. For a start, we never negotiated for the 569 men who went down in Laos. What happened to them?

The U.S. team expected approximately 5,000 names on Vietnam's POW list. But they only returned 591 POWs and gave minimal information on a few not returned.

Why is it so hard for those in government working on this issue to acknowledge that we left men behind? Why has the government spent so much time discrediting families, sources and any information on live sightings of POWs? Why does our government tell the press that it has received so many remains back from Hanoi, when some of the remains they have asked families to receive as their loved ones are determined, by second opinion of a forensic anthropologist, not identifiable as their family member and, in some cases, verified as animal bones?

Why is our government now holding trade and diplomatic talks with Vietnam before Vietnam returns our POWs who still remain? Are money and big business more important than our citizens?

I am thankful that the press continues to draw attention to this issue. It seems to me that we need to apply continued pressure on the executive branch of government, especially since President Bush declared, when he took office, that this is a matter of "the highest priority."

I also believe we need to continue to pressure our senators and congressmen to aid in the resolve of this issue. They are in positions of power to take the necessary means to effect change in the

executive branch which can, and hopefully will, mean that we can have our men home.

For the skeptics, I would say that I realize our POWs might all be dead, but one need only to review the significant live sighting reports of the previous two to three years to get a perspective which differs from the government line.

Additionally, I would ask, what about the men who were on Vietnam's list of POWs to be repatriated and who were never returned, without any explanation from the Vietnamese?

What happened to those POWs who were taken in the final days of battle, paraded before the international press, who seemed to be in reasonably good condition, but of whom Vietnam denied any knowledge?

What about the Japanese monk released by Vietnam for humanitarian reasons in January 1989 who reported that five American POWs kept him alive by bringing him bananas from the fields when they were out on forced labor crews?

One needs only to read the Senate Foreign Relations Committee's report issued this May, "An Examination of the U.S. Policy Toward POW/MIAs" to get a glimpse of the travesty committed against our servicemen who were taken as POWs during the Vietnam War.

I submit that it would not take an unreasonable amount of exertion on the part of the U.S. government to bring home those POWs who are still alive.

The Vietnamese government seems desperate for American dollars and trade. The POW issue could be a good leverage tool prior to giving Vietnam trade status. I truly believe they would find a way to save face and respond with appropriate action.

Evidence of missing POWs?: *Senate committee hears evidence that this signal etched in a Laotian rice paddy in 1988 could have been missing POWs' cry for help. Page A-4.*

Possible distress signals in Laos trigger dispute at POW hearing

ASSOCIATED PRESS

WASHINGTON — The letters "USA" and "K" etched into a Laotian rice paddy only four years ago could be distress signals from American POWs, according to Senate testimony yesterday.

A top U.S. intelligence official told a Senate committee that the symbols have not been linked to any unaccounted-for POW. But lawmakers who visited the scene and other officials involved in the POW search process said the letters were almost certainly man-made and meant to be seen from the air.

As in past hearings of the Senate Select Committee on POW-MIA Affairs, the testimony sparked disagreement among panel members and between senators and witnesses over the possibility that American POWs may still be alive in Southeast Asia.

"This may be the only evidence that we find that points to specific men," said Sen. Charles Grassley, R-Iowa.

The committee chairman, Sen. John Kerry, D-Mass., warned against encouraging family members of the missing to believe their loved ones are still alive.

"If we pretend to them that something is a symbol when it's not, we are falsely raising hopes," Kerry said.

Duane Andrews, the assistant defense secretary for communications and intelligence, testified that the Defense Intelligence Agency (DIA), using highly sophisticated and classified photographic techniques, has analyzed several aerial images purporting to show letters, numbers and symbols. The DIA rejected most as shadows cast by trees or overly optimistic interpretations of markings on buildings.

"It's easy to be misled," Andrews said. "Our photo analysts are trained to report what's on the imagery, not what they'd like to be on the imagery."

In two instances, the DIA has concluded that symbols were man-made but has reached no conclusion on what they mean, Andrews said.

■ On Jan. 22, 1988, an aerial image was taken of a rice paddy in northern Laos near the village of Sam Neua as part of a Defense Department POW mission. By the time the photo was analyzed

the following December and follow-up missions flown, the letters had disappeared. But the photos showed a clearly delineated "USA" symbol carved out of the paddy in letters about 12 feet high and 6 feet wide. Below the "USA" letters was another marking that could be the letter "K," a letter used by Air Force pilots to communicate with rescuers.

■ In May and July of 1973, after the signing of the Paris Peace Accords between the United States and North Vietnam, unmanned air reconnaissance craft photographed what appeared to be the numbers "1973" followed by the letters "TH" or "TA." The symbols were etched in the ground or grass in central Laos on the Plane of Jars, a contested area during the civil war between U.S.-supported Royal Laotian forces and communist guerrillas.

"The 'USA' and possible 'K' remain unexplained, despite having tasked every means of information collection available through the intelligence community," Andrews said. He said the "1973" symbol "is unexplained and probably will remain so."

VIỆT NAM RED CROSS   HỘI CHỮ THẬP ĐỎ VIỆT NAM
QUANG NAM—DA NANG PROVINCE   TỈNH QUẢNG NAM - ĐÀ NẴNG

GHI NHẬN
TẤM LÒNG VÀNG

ACKNOWLEDGEMENT THE GOLDEN HEART AWARD

Chúng tôi vô cùng cảm ơn :

We wish to express our sincere appreciation to : BARBARA BIRCHIM

Địa chỉ – Adress : 9620 Chesapeake Drive, Suite 100, San Diego, Cali. 92123

Đã đóng góp vào quỹ cứu trợ NHÂN ĐẠO tỉnh Quảng nam—Đà nẵng

For their contribution to THE HUMANE RELIEF FUND at the Quang nam —

Da nang Province : A Package of Medicine for The "Mother's
Love Health Clinic" in Hoa Quy

ĐÀ NẴNG, ngày 17 tháng 2 năm 1990

Chủ tịch - President

Số : 05 /T LV /CT Đ.

HOÀNG LIÊN

431

HỘI CHỮ THẬP ĐỎ VIỆT NAM
68, phố Bà Triệu, Hà Nội
VIỆT NAM RED CROSS
68. Bà Triệu Street Hanoi
Tel: 6.2315

YÊU CẦU TÌM KIẾM
TRACING FORM

Số:
No:
Ngày:
Date.

Người được tìm kiếm – Person sought

– Họ và tên thường dùng:
Full name JAMES DOUGLAS BIRCHIM

– Ngày, nơi sinh:
Date, place of birth: 16/7/46 CALIFORNIA USA.

Nam/Nữ
Sex M/F MALE

– Họ và tên của bố/mẹ:
Father's name, Maiden Mother's name: JAMES L. BIRCHIM / DORCAS HAYNES

– Hoàn cảnh gia đình:
Marital status: MARRIED

– Quốc tịch:
Nationality: U.S.A.

– Nghề nghiệp:
Occupation SOLDIER

– Ngày biết tin cuối cùng:
Date and nature of the last news: 15/11/68 - LOST BETWEEN DAK TO AND DAK SUT

– Địa chỉ cuối cùng được biết:
Last known address: KONTUM

– Các tin tức liên quan khác:
Additionnal information:

Người yêu cầu – Inquirer

– Họ và tên thường dùng:
Full name: BARBARA LYNN BIRCHIM

– Ngày, tháng, năm sinh và nơi sinh:
Date, Place of birth 24/12/46 CALIFORNIA U.S.A.

Nam/Nữ
Sex M/F FEMALE

– Quan hệ gia đình:
Relationship: WIFE

– Địa chỉ đầy đủ:
Address: P.O. Box 27343
SAN DIEGO, CA 92128
U.S.A.

Ngày   tháng   năm
Date 28/2/90
Chữ ký của người yêu cầu
Enquirer's signature

Barbara L. Birchim

Đề nghị trả lời gửi về 68 phố Bà Triệu, Hà Nội, Việt Nam
All information would be, please, returned to our office
68 Bà Triệu Street Hanoi – Việt Nam

432

GIẤY THÔNG-HÀNH

SAFE-CONDUCT PASS TO BE HONORED BY ALL VIETNAMESE GOVERNMENT AGENCIES AND ALLIED FORCES

이 안전보장패쓰는 월남정부와 모든 연합군에 의해 인정된 것입니다.

รัฐบาลเวียตนามและหน่วยพันธมิตร ยินดีให้เกียรติแก่ผู้ถือบัตรผ่านปลอดภัยนี้.

SAFE-CONDUCT PASS TO BE HONORED BY ALL VIETNAMESE GOVERNMENT AGENCIES AND ALLIED FORCES

MANG TẤM GIẤY
THÔNG HÀNH
nầy về cộng tác
với Chánh Phủ
Quốc Gia các bạn
sẽ được :
- Đón tiếp tử tế
- Bảo đảm an ninh
- Đải ngộ tương xứng

NGUYỄN VĂN THIỆU
Tổng Thống Việt Nam Cộng Hoà

TẤM GIẤY THÔNG HÀNH NẦY CÓ GIÁ TRỊ VỚI TẤT CẢ CƠ - QUAN
QUÂN CHÍNH VIỆT - NAM CỘNG - HÒA VÀ LỰC - LƯƠNG ĐỒNG - MINH.

National Cemetery - San Francisco Presidio

Commerative Medal
For Next Of Kin Of Our Unaccounted For

The Department of Defense Authorization Act of 1984 as public law 98-94 provides for the issuance of commerative medals for families of American personnel missing in Southeast Asia. The Congress finds and declares that as of April 2, 1973

(1) 2494 Americans, military and civilian, are listed as missing or otherwise unaccounted for in Southeast Asia;

(2) Those missing or otherwise unnaccounted for Americans have suffered untold hardship at the hands of a cruel enemy while in the service of their country;

(3) The loyalty, hope, love, and courage of these families provide inspiration to all Americans;

(4) The Congress and the people of the United States are committed to a full accounting for all Americans missing or otherwise unaccounted for in Southeast Asia; and

(5) The service of those missing and otherwise unaccounted for Americans is deserving of special recognition by the Congress and all Americans.

The Speaker of the House of Representatives and the President Pro Tempore of the Senate are authorized jointly tp present, on behalf of the Congress, to those American personnel listed as missing or otherwise unaccounted for in Southeast Asia, to be accepted by next of kin, bronze medals designed by an artist who is an in-theater Vietnam Veteran, in recognition of the distinguished service, heroism, and sacrifice of these personnel. and the committment of the American people to their return.

Barbara Birchim, in background, taking picture.

RUSSELL K OGDEN · RONALD L REED · DOYLE E SALLEE · WILLIAM H SCHAEFE
SPENCER Jr · WYATT S THOMAS · TERRY M WESTERGARD · CHARLES R BOGAR
RANIN Jr · JOSEPH W BUCHANAN · PATRICK J CARROLL · ANTHONY T CULOTT
MES L EPLIN · FREDERICK M GILSINGER Jr · DENNIS G HANSON · JAMES A BOOT
CHARLES T HERSHEY · ROBERT W JASURA · ARTHUR E KEESE · DONALD L KEETER
AYBERRY · THOMAS W MORRIS · STEPHEN M MacCALD   S A NORRIS
L · ROBERT R RADES · JAMES C HATHORNE Jr · DALE F R   C SANTI
RY A TRUELOVE · CHARLES E YOUNG · FRANCIS BALDINO · DAVID A BRA
AM E CARLSON · DONALD H GREINER · LESTER R DAVIS · FRANK L DON
WILLIAM H FABIAN · DAVID   Jr · JOHN E FLETCHER · MASON G
R · RICKY L CORNE   E HATTON · GABRIEL H   HILL
S · WAYNE M HOR   MORRIS · ROBERT T JONES   EDY
PASCHAL Jr · CHARL   MMER · DELMAR SHELLEY · D   SON
OOD · KARL E WEBER   AKI Jr · JAMES D BIRCHI   WN
ER H GARMS · FRANK   STEVEN E JOHNSON   OY SKI
N R MELDAHL · BRENT A   ONARD L THOMPSON   WN
Y W ARMENTROUT · ROBER   Jr · EDDIE C KIMBL   EY
NUEL DE LUNA Jr · JAMES G D   ROBERT R HILL   GE
MER · MARIAN JAMILSKI · MICHAEL D JARRETT · CARL F K   OR
JORGE L NIEVES · WILLIAM H NOLTE · GORDON L PATTERS   OR
HARD A SITO Sr · MICHAEL VILLARREAL · ROBERT C WIECHER   ON
HAR · JAMES M YOUNG · PHILLIP R ANDERSON · JACK A DO   RBY
ONNIE LEE CLARK · RICHARD C CLEVELAND · CHESTER   COX
MAS F CALLAHAN · FRANCIS M FINNERTY · RONALD   OW

W 39

D H GREINER · LESTER R DAVIS · FRANK L DO
D A FIALKO Jr · JOHN E FLETCHER · MASON
NDOLPH E HATTON · GABRIEL HERRADA · JE
VID M MORRIS · ROBERT T JONES Jr · BRUCE
PLUMMER · DELMAR SHELLEY · DONALD A TH
ANCIS C AKI Jr · JAMES D BIRCHIM · WILLIA
GENMILLER · STEVEN E JOHNSON · ROBER J
EDER · LEONARD L THOMPSON · ROBERT TRI
RT F BALSLEY Jr · EDDIE C KIMBLE · WILLIAM
G DESCHENES · ROBERT R HILLIARD · RUSSELL
MICHAEL D JARRETT · CARL F KARST · EDDIE V
M H NOLTE · GORDON L PATTERSON · LEOND
ROBERT C WIECHERT · STANLEY

Bibliography

Anton, Frank. Why Didn't You Get Me Out? A POWs Nightmare In Vietnam. New York: St. Martin's Press, 2000.

Barnes, Scott. Bohica: A True Account Of One Man's Battle To Expose The Most Heinous Cover-up Of The Vietnam Saga!. Canton, Ohio: Bohica Corporation Inc., 1987.

Beschloss, Michael, Reaching For Glory: Lyndon Johnson's Secret, White House Tapes from 1964-1965, New York: Simon & Schuster, 2001.

Cawthorne, Nigel. The Bamboo Cage: The Full Story Of The American Servicemen Still Held Hostage In Southeast Asia. London: Pen & Sword Books Ltd., 1991.

Jensen-Stevenson, Monica. Spite House: The Last Secret Of The War In Vietnam. New York: W.W. Norton & Company, Inc., 1997.

Jensen-Stevenson, Monika and Stevenson, William. Kiss The Boys Goodbye: How The United States Betrayed Its Own P.O.Ws In Vietnam. Toronto, Canada: McCelland & Stewart Inc., 1999.

McConnell, Malcolm, Inside Hanoi's Secret Archives: Solving The MIA Mystery. New York: Simon & Schuster, 1995.

Morehouse, David. Psychic Warrior: What The Government Doesn't Want You To Know. New York: St. Martin's Press, 1996.

Nicosia, Gerald. Home To War: A History of the Vietnam Veteran's Movement. New York: Crown Publishers, 2001.

Plaster, John L. SOG: The Secret Wars Of America's Commandos In Vietnam. New York: Simon & Schuster, 1997.

Sauter, Mark and Sanders, Jim. The Men We Left Behind: The Tragic Fate Of POWs After The Vietnam War. Bethesda, MD, 1993.

Sheehan, Neil. A Bright Shining Lie. New York/Toronto: Randon House Inc., 1988.

Stang, Alan. Perestroika Sunset: A Daughter's Lifelong Search For Her MIA Father in Vietnam. Los Angeles: Patton House, 1999.

Stanton, Shelby L. Green Berets At War. New York: The Ballantine Publishing Group, 1985.

Stein, Jeff. A Murder In Wartime. New York: St. Martin's Press, 1992.

Thomas, Gordon. Journey Into Madness: The True Story of Secret CIA Mind Control And Medical Abuse. New York: Bantam Books, 1990.

Weiner, Tim. Blank Check: The Pentagon's Black Budget. New York: Warner Books, Inc., 1991.

RESOURCES

Department of the Army
TAPC-PER
2461 Eisenhower Avenue
Alexandria, VA 22331-0482
http://www.perscom.army.mil/

Department of State
Office of AmCitizens Services and CM
CA/OCS/ACS/EAP
2201 C Street, NW
Washington, DC 20520

DPMO (Defense POW/MIA Office)
http://www.dtic.mil/dpmo (date information re: POW/MIA accounting)
http://lcweb2.loc.gov/pow/powhome.html
or
http://lcweb.loc.gov (re: efforts made to account for MIAs)

Embassy of Laos
2222 S Street, NW
Washington, DC 20008

Embassy of Vietnam
1233 20th Street, NW, Suite 400
Washington, DC 20036

Headquarters US Marine Corps
Manpower and Reserve Affairs (MRC)
Personal and Family Readiness Division
3280 Russell Road
Quantico, VA 22134-5103
http://www.usmc.mil

National Archives and Records Administration
National Archives at College Park
8601 Adelphi Road
College Park, MD 20740-6001
http://www.nara.gov/nara/nail.html (NARA Locator)

National League of Families of American Prisoners and Missing in Southeast
Asia
1001 Connecticut Avenue, Northwest, Suite 919
Washington, D.C. 20036-5504
202/659-0133 (update live)
www.pow-miafamilies.org

Navy Personnel Command
Bureau of Naval Personnel
Casualty Assistance Branch
(NPC-621P)
5720 Integrity Dr.
Millington, TN 38055-6210
http://p621@persnet.navy.mil

Task Force Omega, Inc.
14043 North 64th Drive
Glendale, AZ 85306-3705
http://www.taskforceomegainc.org

USAF Missing Persons Branch
550 C Street West, Suite 15
Randolph AFB, TX 78150-4716
http://www.afpc.af.mil/

Glossary

Air America – CIA airline during Vietnam War

AFFA – Americans for Freedom Always

ARVN – Army of the Republic of Vietnam (South Vietnamese Army)

ASEAN – Association of Southeast Asian Nations

AWOL – Absent Without Leave

BNR - Body Not Recovered

Black budget – President's secret treasury used to fund any program he, the CIA, and the Secretary of Defense want to keep from the public

Black Ops – Covert operations behind enemy lines

Blackhawk Down – Blackhawk was a helicopter shot down in Mogadishu resulting in 18 American casualties, 1993

BOHICA – Bend Over Here It Comes Again

Bright Light – SOG code name for POW rescue attempts behind enemy lines, later became the name for the form used to summarize the statistics for each POW/MIA in the Vietnam War.

California, RT – name for one of recon teams in CCN, Danang. Joe Walker was One-Zero in fall of 1968.

CAS – Combined Area Studies

CEA – Communications and External Affairs

C&C – Command & Control. Danang field headquarters for SOG's cross-border operations. Also generic for those long range recon patrol operations.

CCC – Command and Control Central, Camp Reno, Danang

CCN – Command and Control North, Camp Villa Rosa, Kontum

CCS – Command and Control South, Camp Torres, Ban Me Thuot

CIA – U.S. Central Intelligence Agency

CIDP – Civilian Irregular Defense Program

CILHI – Central Identification Laboratory, Hawaii

CINCLANT – Commander in Chief Atlantic Command

CINCPAC – Commander-in-Chief Pacific

CSI – Center for Study of Intelligence (CIA)

Daniel Boone – SOG's code name for operations in the Cambodian area. Replaced in 1969 with code name Salem House.

DASD – Deputy Assistant Secretary of Defense

DAV – Disabled Amnerican Veterans

DCO – Deputy Communications Officer

DCS – Deputy Chief of Staff

DEER – Dependent Eligibility Enrollment Record

Delta Force – a unit of today's Special Forces, evolved from Vietnam War

DIA – Defense Intelligence Agency

DIAI – Department of Internal Affairs and Immigration

DMZ – Demilitarized Zone, 17th parallel, the separation between North and South Vietnam.

DNA – Deoxyribonucleic acid, a molecule found in the cells containing the genetic blueprints of life.

DOD – Department of Defense

DOS – Department of State

DOTD – Department of "Tricky Dicks," slang for DOD

DPMO – Defense Prisoner of War/Missing in Action Office, served as the central point for all issues pertaining to the POW/MIA policy matters within the DOD, established in 1993.

DRV – Democratic Republic of North Vietnam

DSC – U.S, Army Distinguished Service Cross, second to the Medal of Honor

DVA – Department of Veteran's Affairs

5ᵗʰ Special Forces Group – Official headquarters in South Vietnam for all Green Berets, except the SOG Green Berets who took their orders from the Pentagon and Saigon.

FAC – Forward Air Control

FOB – Forward Operations Base, a place where Special Forces and mercenary troops were trained and housed in a permanent camp – FOB 2, (Kontum, 66-Nov 68).

FOIA – Freedom of Information Act

H9 – A target destination

Ho Chi Minh Trail – A camouflaged corridor in the jungle in Southeastern Laos, occupied by the NVA after 1959, used for transporting supplies and soldiers during the war in South Vietnam.

IMF – International Money Fund

JCRC – Joint Casualty Resolution Center, began in January 1973 to account for American service members missing from the Vietnam War. JCRC was replaced by JTF-FA in 1992.

JPAC – Joint Prisoner/MIA Accountability Command

JPRC – SOG's cover organization responsible for the Bright Light rescue attempts of American POWs

JTF-FA – Joint Task Force-Full Accounting, DOD agency responsible for conducting field operations to account for Americans missing from the Vietnam War

Khmer Rouge – Faction of Khmer Communist Party, Cambodia, led by Pol Pot

KHA – Killed Hostile Action

KIA – Killed in Action

KIA/BNR – Killed in Action/Body Not Recovered

Live Sightings – Evidence of Americans still held in captivity in Southeast Asia

LLRP – Long-range Reconnaissance Patrol

LKA – Last Known Alive

LPDR – Lao People's Democratic Republic

LPF – Lao Patriotic Front

LSI – Live Sighting Investigation: conducted by members of Stony Beach, assisted by JTF-FA, based on reports of eyewitness accounts of live American POWs in Southeast Asia.

LZ – Landing Zone

MAC – Military Assistance Command

MACV – Military Assistance Command Vietnam

MACVSOG – Military Assistance Command Studies & Observation Group, Saigon: 1/24/64-4/30/72

McGuire Rig (also known as Strings) – Rope-like device dangling from a helicopter, used to rescue SOG recon men where landing was impossible

MIA – Missing in Action

MHA – Missing Hostile Action

MKULTRA – Code name for the CIA mind control program.

Montagnards – Vietnamese hill tribesmen recruited as mercenaries for SOG and other Special Forces units, commonly called "Yards" by the Americans

NARA – National Archives and Records Administration

National League of Families for POW/MIAs in Southeast Asia – The League/ The National League

New Hampshire, R.T. – Reconnaissance Team, Lt. James Birchim, team leader, November 1968

NGO – Non-Government Organizations

NOK –Next of Kin

NSA – National Security Agency, responsible for code breaking and intercepting enemy signals

NSC – National Security Council

NVA – North Vietnamese Army

ONE-ZERO – (1-0) Code name for SOG recon team leader

OSD – Office of the Secretary of Defense

OSS – Office of Strategic Services

Paris Peace Accords – agreement signed by U.S. National Security Adviser Henry Kissinger in Paris on January 27, 1973

Pathet Lao – North Vietnamese backed Laotian forces

PAVN – People's Army of Vietnam

PFOD – Presumptive Finding of Death

PL – Pathlet Lao

PNOK – Primary Next of Kin

POW – Prisoner of War

PRA – Personnel Recovery Accounting

Prairie Fire – SOG's code name for operations in Laos area, replacing code name Shining Brass in 1967

PRC – People's Republic of China

PRG – Provisional Revolutionary Government

PRG (Vietcong) – People's Revolutionary Government

Project Delta – Special Forces recon unit, operated inside South Vietnam

Recon Team – A SOG team usually consisting of 12 men: 2-3 Special Forces men and 9 Montagnards. However, most One-Zeros took only 6-8 men to avoid detection.

Remote Viewer – Psychic spy program developed by U.S. Intelligence community, used to transcend time/space and to uncover the highly guarded military secrets of other nations.

RT – Reconnaissance Team

S3 – Operations or target area, depending on use

Sanitizing – Process of declassifying documents by blacking out sensitive material

SAR – Search and Rescue/Recovery

SCU – Special Commando Unit

SIGINT – Signal Intelligence

Secret Returnee Program – Patterned after the Witness Protection Program for POW/MIAs from Vietnam War

SOA – Special Operations Augmentation

SOG – Studies and Observation Group, the OSS of Southeast Asia, a Vietnam War's covert special warfare unit

SCO – Service Casualty Office

Sheep Dipping – Secret process of removing all connection with the U.S. government and rehiring soldiers as civilian contractors

SRV – Socialist Republic of Vietnam

SSG – Staff Sergeant

Strings (slang for McGuire or STABO rig) – special webbed gear used as an emergency extraction rig for attaching to a rope from a helicopter hovering above treetops

Stony Beach – A DIA team, based in Bangkok, Thailand and Hickam Air Force Base in Hawaii, responsible for conducting live sighting and LKA investigations in Southeast Asia

SWAG – Stupid Wild Ass Guess

TDY – Temporary Duty

USA/AD – U.S. Army Active Duty

USA/RET – U.S. Army Retired

Vermont, R.T. – Reconnaissance Team in Laos that NCO William Copley was a member of, November 1968

Viet Cong (VC) - South Vietnamese communists during the Vietnam War

Vietnam Veterans Memorial – monument in Washington D.S., also known as The Wall, containing the names of all those who died during the Vietnam War

VIVA – Voice in Vital America

VNOSMP – Vietnam Office for Seeking Missing Persons

VVA – Vietnam Veterans of America

Witness Protection Program – devised by our government to use when they changed the identity of returning POW/MIAs from the Vietnam War

Yards – Slang for Montagnard tribesmen

Footnotes

Chapter 2

1. 1985 letter from Col. John R. Oberst, DPMO Administration Casualty File, declassified for PNOK, 1999.
2. 1981 letter to James Birchim from Rear Admiral Jerry O. Tuttle.
3. 1981 letter to Mrs. James Birchim from Rear Admiral Tuttle.
4. CG/USARV LBN RVN report, May 1971.
5. 15 May 1971 letter from J.S. Warren to Casualty Branch, Dept. of Army, Washington, D.C.
6. Report - Copley, William Michael, Staff Sergeant/US Army, MIA 16 November 1968, Laos, loss coordinates: 144000N 1071754E.
7. JCRC-CCD-SD Request for Information from Maj. Gray, Chief, Site Development Branch to Chief, CSI, 8 May 1974.
8. Jensen-Stevenson, Monica, Spite House: The Last Secret Of The War In Vietnam, pp. 192-193.
9. Ibid.
10. Jensen-Stevenson, Spite House, p. 194.
11. Ibid.
12. McConnell, Malcolm, Inside Hanoi's Secret Archives: Solving The MIA Mystery, p. 18.
13. Plaster, John L., SOG: The Secret Wars of America's Commandos in Vietnam, p. 148.
14. Ibid.
15. Plaster, SOG, p. 149.
16. Lunden, Joan, "Behind Closed Doors" TV show, 1/25/01.
17. Stanton, Shelby, Green Berets At War, p. 42.
18. Plaster, SOG, p. 46.
19. Ibid.
20. Ibid.
21. Stanton, p. 43.
22. Sprague, Edmund, as told to, "No Greater Loyalty," Interview with an editor @ Vietnam Magazine, 1991, p. 44.
23. Stein, Jeff, A Murder in Wartime, p. 272.
24. Benge, Mike, "Montagnard Persecution is Vietnam's Dirty Secret," Insight, 7/23/01, pp. 44-45.
25. Stock, Greg, Special Projects Officer, Save The Montagnard People, Inc., "Abandoned Allies, The Montagnard People," 2001, p. 1.
26. Stock, p. 5.

27. Regan, Carl J., "Montagnard Refugees from Vietnam In Cambodia," 7/26/2001, pp. 4-5.
28. Decherd, Chris, Associated Press, "First Group of Vietnamese Hill People Heading to U.S.," reprinted in San Diego Union-Tribune, 6/4/02.

Chapter 3

1. Douglass Jr., Dr. Joseph, "Missing American POWs: What Happened?" Conservative Review, Part I p. 25. An expanded version of an article which appears in the November/December issue of 1993. "The purpose of this is to provide skeptics with additional detailed information." Dr. Douglass is a defense analyst and author.
2. Douglass Jr., p. 31.
3. Ibid.
4. Douglass Jr., Part II p. 12.
5. Douglass Jr., Part II p. 7.
6. Douglass Jr., Part II p. 8.
7. Ibid.
8. Douglass Jr., Part II p. 14.
9. Ibid.
10. Ibid.
11. Ibid.
12. Douglass Jr., Part II p. 15.
13. Douglass Jr., Part II p. 15-16, footnote 10.
14. Martin, Harry W., "Senate Report Reveals POWs from WW II Still Held," Napa Sentinal, 3/17/92, p. 6.
15. Ibid.
16. Brown, John M.G., "U.S. Has Historically Neglected POW/MIAs", reprint in The Sunday Oregonian, Portland, OR, 12/2/90, from Veteran's Outlook, Vol. VII, March 1991, pp. 44-45.
17. McConnell, Malcolm, Inside Hanoi's Secret Archives, p.48.
18. "Hearts and Minds" TV documentary, 1974.
19. Lopez, Greg, "Ex-POW Says He May Not Be The Last," "People" column, Rocky Mt. News, 7/21/91.
20. "Hearts and Minds" TV documentary.
21. "The Ron Reagan Show," television, September 1991.
22. Evans, David, "Were POWs Abandoned? A Debate At A Critical Time," The San Diego Union, 11/7/90, p. B-7.
23. Gilroy, Peter, "The MIA Mystery: One Man's Journey," The San Diego Union, 8/25/91, pp. D1-5.
24. Holland, John R., President, AFFA letter, 2/15/96.

25. "Keeping The Promise," Task Force Omega Newsletter of Southern California, June/July 1999, p. 1.
26. Commentary by Major Mark Smith, retired, Task Force Omega Newsletter, pp. 7-8.
27. Franklin, H. Bruce, "The MIA Myth: Why The White House Created A Fantasy," Section C, Perspective, San Jose Mercury News, pp. 1C, 4C.
28. "Status of the POW/MIA Issue," The National League of Families report, 1/25/99, p. 2.
29. Ibid.
30. U.S. Senate Committee on Foreign Relations Republican Staff, "An Examination of U.S. Policy Toward POW/MIAs," 5/23/91, pp. 8-1 to 2.
31. Ibid.
32. Ibid.
33. Associated Press, "Vets Tooth Only Remains For Burial," The Oakland Tribune, 4/29/01, p. 4.
34. U.S. Senate Committee on Foreign Relatiaons Republican Staff, p. 8-3.
35. U.S. Senate Committee on Foreign Relations Republican Staff, p. 8-4.
36. Epstein, Miles Z. & Donaldson, T. Douglas, "The Men We Left Behind," The American Legion, March 1992, p.33.
37. Cawthorne, Nigel, Prisoners of War, an "Eyewitness Nam" series #13, Great Britain: Orbis Publishing Co., p. 37.
38. Cawthorne, pp. 5, 7, 9, 12, 16, 18, 20, 21, 22, 23, 24, 27, 29, 32, 38, 40, 44, 49, 57, 63.
39. Cawthorne, p. 38.
40. Cawthorne, p. 290.
41. Cawthorne, p. 11. For good information on the subject, pp. 11-30.
42. McConnell, Malcolm, Inside Hanoi's Secret Archives, p.51.
43. McConnell, p. 80.
44. Jensen-Stevenson, Monika and Stevenson, William, Kiss The Boys Goodbye, pp. 1-2.
45. McConnell, p. 81.
46. McConnell, p. 80.
47. Mcconnell, p. 134
48. McConnell, p. 138.
49. Jensen-Stevenson and Stevenson, p. 141.
50. Ibid.
51. Burns, Robert, "Navy Changes Status of Gulf War Pilot," Associated Press, National Alliance of Families, 1/11/01, www.nationalalliance.org.
52. Associated Press, "Gulf War Pilots Status Changed," The San Diego Union-Tribune, 1/11/01.

53. Benge, Mike, "A Vietnamese Evalution of Relations Between Vietnam and the U.S.," National Alliance of Families Bits 'n Pieces, 8/1/98, excerpted from Literary Vanguard Magazine #539, Mat Than, 7/1/98.

Chapter 4

1. McConnell, Malcolm, Inside Hanoi's Secret Archives, p. 389.
2. McConnell, p. 151.
3. McConnell, p. 146.
4. Stanton, Shelby L., Green Berets At War, p. 76.
5. Jensen-Stevenson and Stevenson, Kiss The Boys Goodbye, p. 25.
6. Cawthorne, Nigel, The Bamboo Cage, p. 15.
7. Jensen-Stevenson and Stevenson, p. 175.
8. Jensen-Stevenson and Stevenson, pp. 394, 397.

Chapter 5

1. Galloway, Joseph L., reprint in Rocky Mountain News, 7/24/91, from U.S. News & World Report, (quote from W.T. Sherman to U.S. Grant).
2. Associated Press, "MIAs May Be Alive, Not Captives, Lawmakers Say," 2/20/86.
3. Calla, Gerald, "POW/MIA: POW/MIA Scams Cloud The Issue of Americans Missing in Asia," Soldier of Fortune magazine, November 1991, pp. 46-51.
4. Clark III, W.D., "These Men Have All Been Positively Identified!" 1991.
5. Associated Press, "U.S. Loses Fingerprints of 3 MIAs," Rocky Mt. News, 7/25/91.
6. Bryant, Carleton R., "Forensics Expert Identifies MIA Photos From Laos," The Washington Times, 1991.
7. Bryant, Carleton R., "Truth of 'MIA Photo' Proves Hard To Verify," The Washington Times, 1991.
8. Castaneda, Carol, "Vigil For Vanished," USA Today, 7/22/91.
9. Clark III, W. D.
10. Soto, Natalle, "Boulder Magazine Says MIA Photo May Be Bogus," Rocky Mt. News, 7/21/91.
11. "Live Sighting Reports of U.S. POWs," Task Force Omega of Illinois, Inc., from 11,000 pages of live sighting reports provided by the U.S. Government, unclassified document dated December 1972, source

unknown. Names listed: Mr. Cook, Capt. Coveleski, Mr. Scott, Graoch.

12. "Information passed to 525th Phu Bai for Bright Light Project. . ." inserted in Live Sighting Reports of U.S. POWs, Task Force Omega of Illinois, 4/16/84.
13. Ibid.
14. "Information passed to 525th Phu Bai for Bright Light Project. . ." Task Force Omega of Illinois, List of U.S. Personnel From Photos, 4/11/89.
15. Caldwell, Robt. J., Ed. Opinion Section, "Vietnam POW Reports Must Be Pursued," The San Diego Union, 8/17/86, p. C-7.
16. Ibid.
17. Ibid.
18. Caldwell, pp. C-5, C-7.
19. "Summary of 18 July 1991 Meeting with Gen'l John W. Vessey, Jr. Special Presidential Emissary to Vietnam for Humanitarian Affairs," p.3.
20. O'Shea, Lynn, "Bits n' Pieces," National Alliance of Families, lynnpowmia@prodegy.net, p.1.
21. Castaneda, Carol, "Vigil for Vanished," USA Today, 7/22/91.
22. Spolar, Christine, Chicago Tribune, "Sources: U.S. Pilot May Be Iraq Captive," The Contra Costa Times, 3/12/02, p. A8.
23. Bernasconi, L.H., POW/MIA e-mail, 1/14/01 lhbernasco@aol.com.
24. Simpson, Barbara, "Barbara Simpson Show," KSFO, San Francisco, 3/16/02.
25. Cawthorne, Nigel, The Bamboo Cage, p.292.
26. Connell, Malcolm, p. 246.
27. Connell, Malcolm, p. 137.
28. Connell, Malcolm, p. 136.
29. Anton, Frank, Why Didn't You Get Me Out?: A POW's Nightmare In Vietnam, Title Page.
30. Anton, Frank, p.31.
31. Anton, Frank, pp. 167-168.
32. Anton, Frank, p. 180.
33. Anton, Frank, p. 184.
34. Anton, Frank, p. 179.
35. Anton, Frank, p. 57.
36. Anton, Frank, p. 170.
37. Anton, Frank, p. 230.
38. Anton, Frank, p. 232.
39. Anton, Frank, p. 232.
40. Anton, Frank, p. 215.
41. Anton, Frank, p. 216.

42. Anton, Frank, p. 225.

43. Anton, Frank, p. 217.

44. National League of Families program, 30th Annual Meeting, June 16-19, 1999.

45. U.S. Senate Committee on Foreign Relations, Republican Staff, 5/23/91, p. 8-4.

46. U.S. Senate Committee on Foreign Relations, Republican Staff, p. 8-5.

47. Ibid.

48. Kerwin, Katie, "Professor Seeks to Prove Flier Alive in Vietnam," News Northern Bureau, 1991.

49. Lubarano, Alfred, staff writer, "The Untold Story of Baron 52: Their Flight Was Supposed to be a Secret, Not Their Fate," Part II p. 4, Philadelphia Inquirer, 1/14/98, e-mailed by O'Shea, Lynn M., National Alliance of Families for the Return of America's Missing Servicemen World War II – Korea – Cold War – Vietnam, 1/15/98.

50. "The Mock Burial of MIAs," Congressional Record – Senate, S 14623, 10/5/90.

51. Associated Press, "Man in Recent Photo Identified as Navy Pilot Missing in Asia," The San Diego Union, 11/4/91.

52. Hicks, Lesli, "Finding The Fallen: USAA Members Help in the Search for POW/MIAs," USAA Magazine, May/June 2002, p. 17.

53. Sauter, Mark and Sanders, Jim, The Men We Left Behind, p.26

54. Doney, Norman A., "POW/MIA Report," The Drop, Special Forces Association magazine, Fall 1999, p. 72.

55. Sauter and Sanders, p. 243.

56. Sauter and Sanders, pp. 257-258.

57. Sauter and Sanders, p. 254.

58. Personnel Recovery and Accounting: POW/MIA Accounting, Defense POW/MIA Personnel Office, 6/7/01, p. 37.

59. Barker, Richard, "Transcription of Richard Barker's Statement (From his handwritten notes to me) Confidential, Memo File from POC:bg (attorney), 4/2/86, pp. 1-59.

60. Cawthorne, Nigel, The Bamboo Cage, pp. 208-210.
   NOTE: Glomar Java Sea: oil drilling ship owned by Global Marine Inc. of Houston, hired by Atlantic Richfield under contract with the Chinese government. The Glomar sank in the South China Sea, 10/25/83, when hit by a typhoon. (Rumor: the CIA used the Glomar as a listening post. It didn't sink from a typhoon, but was torpedoed by the Vietnamese as a spy ship.) Thirty-five bodies were found. Twenty-one Americans among 46 others were missing. Reports from many sources said the Glomar survivors were seen in Vietnam and/or were said to be held in Vietnam.

The U.S. Government declared them "missing-unaccounted" for as though they were MIAs.

61. Barker, p. 1.
62. Ibid, pp. 44-45.
63. Ibid, p. 47.
64. Ibid, pp. 51-53.
65. Ibid, p. 57.
66. PAX TV, "Encounters With The Unexplained," 1/11/02.
67. "Trip Report for TDY to Moscow, Drasnoyarsk, and Irkutsk, Russia, 9/26/01, e-mail from Powmiafam, 3/29/02, pp. 2-3.
68. Sauter and Sanders, p. 12.
69. McConnell, pp. 114-118.
70. Ibid, pp. 129-130.
71. Ibid, p. 129.
72. Sauter and Sanders, p. 12.
73. Cawthorne, p. 180.
74. Sauter and Sanders, pp. 373-375.
75. Jensen-Stevenson and Stevenson, pp. 338-339.
76. Scowcroft, Brent, White House National Security Advisor, Bush Administration 1991, helped negotiate the Paris Peace Accord with Kissinger.
77. Sauter and Sanders, p. 374.
78. Sauter and Sanders, p. 380.

Grieving Families

1. Clark, Michael S., Ph.D. candidate, "Findings From the MIA Study Regarding Grief Reactions in the MIA Families," Department of Psychology, Academic Divisions of the New School for Social Research, 65 5th Avenue, New York, NY 10003.
2. Clark, "Pilot Study," p. 2.
3. Ibid.
4. Ibid.
5. Jensen-Stevenson and Stevenson, Kiss The Boys Goodbye, p. 15.
6. Jensen-Stevenson and Stevenson, p. 106.
7. Jensen-Stevenson and Stevenson, p.13.
8. Jensen-Stevenson and Stevenson, p. 5.
9. Epstein, Miles and Donaldson, T. Douglas, "POW/MIAs – The Men We Left Behind," American Legion magazine, March 1992, p. 24.
10. Epstein and Donaldson, p. 28.
11. Epstein and Donaldson, p. 30.

12. Cawthorne, Nigel, The Bamboo Cage, p. 267.
13. Cawthorne, Nigel, p. 276.
14. Cawthorne, Nigel, pp. 264-266.
15. "I Know My Brother's Alive," TIME magazine, 1/13/92, p.16.
16. "Hoping Against Hope: The MIA Mystery," Newsweek magazine, 7/29/91, p. 25.
17. Santoli, Al, Parade section, The San Diego Union-Tribune, pp. front page, 4-6.
18. Roberts, Cokie, "Why MIAs Live On: How It Feels When One of the Family is Missing," The San Diego Union, 9/25/91, p. B-7.
19. Cawthorne, p. 276.
20. "Freedom Now: For Our Abandoned Prisoners of War," Task Force Omega, Inc., Americans Fighting For America.

Chapter 6

1. Scott, Sir Walter (1771-1832), A Treasury of the Familiar, Edited by Ralph L. Woods, New York: The MacMillan Company, 1948.
2. "Capricorn," Mademoiselle magazine, February 1990, p. 202.

"Missing"

1. Commander A. Dodge McFall, USN, was lost at sea in December, 1996 "as his squadron prepared for its second tour off Vietnam. Despite an intensive three-day search, his body and A-4F aircraft were never found." A year before he died, he wrote an article, "Farewell to Spads," which was published in the U.S. Institute Proceedings magazine. Cdr. McFall's daughter, Gardner, wrote an elegy for her father (The Pilot's Daughter, St. Louis: Time Being Books, 1996) which included his poem "Missing." "Missing" was reprinted in Proceedings, August 2000, p. 37.

Chapter 7

1. Stanton, Shelby L., Green Berets At War, pp. 3-5.
2. Stanton, p. 49.
3. Stanton, p. 52.
4. Ibid.
5. Beschloss, Michael, Reaching For Glory: Lyndon Johnson's Secret, based on White House Tapes, 1964-1965, inside of back jacket. (For further reading- - Beschloss, Michael, Taking Charge: The Johnson White House Tapes, 1963-1964, New York: Simon & Schuster, 1997.)

6. Ibid, p. 444.
7. Beschloss, p. 343.
8. Beschloss, p. 348.
9. Beschloss, p. 349.
10. Beschloss, p. 378.
11. Beschloss, p. 384.
12. Beschloss, Appendix.
13. Anton, Frank, Why Didn't You Get Me Out?, p. xi.

Chapter 8

1. Cawthorne, Nigel, The Bamboo Cage, p. 6. (For a good accounting on the subject, read pp. 45-55.)
2. Ibid.
3. McConnell, pp. 47-48.
4. McConnell, pp. 64-65.
5. McConnell, p. 65.
6. Sauter, Mark and Sanders, Jim, The Men We Left Behind, p. 127.
7. Leggett, Honorable Robert L. and Riegle, Honorable Donald W. Jr., "How to Bring the POWs Home Along With the Rest of the Troops," Congressional Record: Proceedings and Debates of the 92nd Congress, First Session, 3/23/71, p. 1.
8. Jensen-Stevenson, Monica and Stevenson, William, Kiss The Boys Goodbye, p. 7.
9. Cawthorne, p. 55.
10. Jensen-Stevenson and Stevenson, pp. 8-9. "Pearls" is the term given to the French captives by the Vietnamese during the first Indo-China War.
11. Blair, Mike, "Fate of POWs Said to Hinge on Paris Talks," SPOTLIGHT, 300 Independence Ave. S.W., Washington, D.C. 2003, either 1992 or 1993.
12. Sauter and Sanders, p. 148.
13. Cawthorne, inside front dust jacket.
14. Burke, James Lee, Bitterroot. New York: Pocket Books, 2001, p. 455.
15. Sauter and Sanders, p. 83.

Chapter 9

1. McConnell, Malcolm, Inside Hanoi's Secret Archives, p. 62.
2. Final Interagency Report of Reagan Administration on POW/MIA Issue in Southeast Asia, 1989, report cover.

3. Final Interagency Report, p. 5.
4. Final Interagency Report, p. 7.
5. Final Interagency Report, pp. 8-9.
6. Final Interagency Report, pp. 15-16.
7. Caldwell, Robert J., "Vietnam POW Reports Must Be Pursued," Opinion Section, The San Diego Union, 8/17/86, p. C-1.
8. Caldwell, pp. C-5 & 7.
9. Caldwell, p. C-7.
10. Final Interagency Report, p. 21.
11. Final Interagency Report, p. 23.
12. Barnes, Scott, Bohica, back cover.
13. U.S. Senate Select Committee on Foreign Relations Report Republican Staff, 5/23/91, pp. 4, 4.b.
14. U.S. Senate Select Committee, p. 2.f.
15. U.S. Senate Select Committee, pp. 3m 3.c.
16. U.S. Senate Select Committee, pp. 4.d, 4.f, 5.b.
17. Martin, Harry V., "Senate Report Reveals POWs From WWII Still Held," 3/17/92, p.6.
18. "Golden Triangle" – where Thailand, Cambodia and Laos meet.
19. Martin, p. 6.
20. Ibid.
21. McConnell, p. 138
22. McConnell, p. 139.
23. Sauter, Mark and Sanders, Jim, The Men We Left Behind, p. 192.
24. Sauter and Sanders, p. 193.
25. Ibid.
26. Sauter and Sanders, p.21.
27. Ibid.
28. Sauter and Sanders, pp. 323-324.
29. Sauter and Sanders, p. 164.
30. Tivan, Edward, "On The Trail of the MIAs," L.A. Times magazine, 10/27/91. P. 10.
31. Sauter and Sanders, pp. 173-174.
32. Sauter and Sanders, p. 216.
33. Barnes, Scott, Bohica, Publisher's Update page, Smith, Robert, "Denying the Truth About Our MIAs," The Washington Times, 7/17/87.
34. Barnes, Publisher's Update page, Williams Jr., Nick B., "U.S. to Discuss MIAs and Some Aid to Hanoi," L.A. Times, 8/4/87.
35. Barnes, Publisher's Update page, Wines, Michael, Times Staff Writer, "Hanoi Agrees to Speed MIA Hunt, Vessey Says," 8/11/87.

36. Barnes, Publisher's Update page, "Vietnam to Resume Talks on Missing U.S. Soldiers," The Bakersfield Californian, 8/4/98.
37. Cawthorne, Nigel, The Bamboo Cage, p. 260.

Chapter 10

1. National League of Families newsletter, 7/10/96, p. 1.
2. Pilcher, Carter, Office of Senator Hank Brown, Senator from Colorado on the Senate Select Committee, Memo, 10/16/91.
3. Caldwell, Robert J., "Did Clinton Trigger a Vietnam Bo9oby Trap?", Sunday Insight section, The San Diego Union-Tribune, 2/6/94, p. G1.
4. Caldwell, p. G5.
5. National League of Families, p. 1.
6. Ibid.
7. National League of Families, pp. 5-6.
8. National League of Families newsletter, 8/7/98, p. 13.
9. Nicosia, Gerald, Home To War: A History of the Vietnam Veteran's Movement, p. 623.
10. National League of Families newsletter, 5/4/99, p. 1.
11. National League of Families newsletter, 4/7/00, p. 7.
12. National League of Families, p. 9.
13. National League of Families, Board of Directors Candidate's Statements, 1999-2001, p. 7.
14. Brunnstron, David, Reuters News Service, reprinted in The San Diego Union-Tribune, 11/9/00.
15. New York Times News Service & Associated Press, Hanoi, Vietnam dateline, reprinted in The San Diego Union-Tribune, 11/18/2000, p. A23.
16. Wright, Robin, Los Angeles Times, reprinted in The Oakland Tribune, 11/19/00, p. NEWS 1.
17. Mydans, Seth, New York Times News Service, reprinted in The San Diego Union-Tribune, 11/20/00, p. A1.
18. National League of Families statement, "Vietnam's Ability to Account for Missing Americans," 6/13/01.
19. Wetterling, J.D., "God, Country Forgiveness," Memorial Day, 2001, (publication unknown), p. B-5. Author wrote a novel based on his Vietnam experiences, www.wetterling@juno.com.
20. Lubarano, Alfred, The Untold Story of Baron 52, 1/11/98 & 1/14/98, Parts 1 and 2.

Chapter 11

1. Ad by Congressman Mac Collins, 3rd District, GA., National League of Families 30th Annual Meeting program, June 16-19, 1999.
2. National League of Families newsletter, 3/20/01, p. 3.
3. Van Deerlin, Lionel, "Rescuing Our Boys in 'Nam," The San Diego Union-Tribune, 9/20/00.
4. Beck, Cdr. Chip, "Bush's Remarks on POW/MIA Day Break New Ground," Editorial OP-ED, 11/17/00. Cdr. Beck is USNR (ret.), Arlington, VA., Beckchip@aol.com.
5. National League of Families newsletter, 3/20/01, p. 3.
6. Ibid.
7. National League of Families, p. 4.
8. Goldsborough, James O., "President Kennedy, American & the Realities of Veitnam," The San Diego Union-Tribune, 1/4/01, p. B7.
9. Ibid.
10. Dean, John, "Hiding Past and Present Presidencies: The Problems With Bush's Executive Order Burying Presidential Records," 11/9/01, reprinted by Patty Hopper, Task Force Omega, 3/30/02, p. 6. John Dean is a FindLaw columnist, former Counsel to President Nixon.

Letters from the Birchim Family

1. Sherman, Steve, former Special Forces, now has his own computer data base for men who served in the Special Forces.
2. Brooks, Lt. Col. Mac, Chief, POW/MIA Affairs, Army Casualty Officer.
3. Warren, Lt. Col. John S., infantry commanding officer. Signed the official "I deeply regret" letter announcing Jim's disappearance, and the letter changing Jim's status from MIA to KIA/BNR.
4. Hoech, Col. Carl, helicopter pilot who picked up Jim.

Chapter 12

1. "One Picture That Cannot Tell a Story," Outlook Section, U.S. News & World Report, 7/29/91, p. 5.
2. McConnell, Malcom, Inside Hanoi, p. 141.

Chapter 13

1. Wetterhahn, Ralph, "One Down In Kamchatka," Retired Officer magazine, January 2001, p. 55.
2. DPMO Accountability Study, 1999, p.7.
3. DPMO Study, p. 8.
4. DPMO Study, p. 4.
5. "POW/MIA Accounting, 1999," Department of Defense, p. 4.
6. "Vietnam's Collection & Repatriation of American Remains," DASD, Defense Prisoner of War & Missing Personnel office, June 1999, p.12.
7. "POW/MIA Accounting," p. 28.
8. "POW/MIA Accounting," p. 10.
9. Wetterhahn, p. 55.
10. "POW/MIA Accounting," p. 37.
11. "POW/MIA Accounting," p. 25.
12. DPMO Study, p. 4.
13. "POW/MIA Accounting," p. 33.
14. "POW/MIA Accounting," p. 29.
15. "POW/MIA Accounting," p. 30.
16. "POW/MIA Accounting," p. 31.
17. "Helicopter Crash Kills All Aboard," Contra Costa Times Sunday edition, 4/8/01, p. A13.
18. Joint Task Force Full Accounting letter to National League of Families, 5/11/99.
19. Joint Task Force, front piece.
20. "Vietnam's Collection & Repatriation," p. 11.
21. "Vietnam's Collection & Repatriation," p. 13.
22. "Vietnam's Collection & Repatriation," p. 20.
23. "Vietnam's Collection & Repatriation," p. 27.
24. "Vietnam's Collection & Repatriation," p. 42.
25. Swift, Earl, "We'll Bring Them Home," Sunday Times Parade magazine, 7/22/01, p. 4.
26. Swift, p. 5.
27. Swift, p. 6.
28. Ibid.
29. Ibid.
30. Ibid.

Chapter 14

1. Manchester, William, "Thoughts on the Business Life," Forbes magazine, 5/28/01, p. 228.
2. Plaster, John L., SOG, p. 23, and Stein, Jeff, A Murder in Wartime, p. 45.
3. Stein, Jeff, p. 45.
4. Sheenan, Neil, p. 364.
5. Stein, p. 45.
6. Sheenan, p. 364.
7. London, Joan, "Behind Closed Doors," television series, 1/25/01.
8. Ibid.
9. Stein, p. 45.
10. Stanton, Shelby, Green Berets At War, p. 304.
11. Ibid.
12. Stanton, pp. 304-305.
13. Stein, p. 71.
14. Jensen-Stevenson, Monika and Stevenson, William, Kiss The Boys Goodbye, p. 147.
15. Jensen-Stevenson and Stevenson, p. 146.
16. Ibid.
17. Ibid.
18. Ibid.
19. Ibid.
20. Jensen-Stevenson, Monika, Spite House, p. 53.
21. "The Warrior Tradition," The History Channel, 1998.
22. Ibid.
23. Ibid.
24. Plaster, John L., SOG, inside dust jacket.
25. Crerar, Col. J.H., U.S. Army (ret.), "Review Essay," MACV SOG: New Books Reveal Vietnam's 'Secret War,' Special Warfare, spring 2000, p. 28.
26. Plaster, p. 20.
27. Crerar, pp. 30-31.
28. Sauter, Mark and Sanders, Jim, The Men We Left Behind, p. 276.
29. Sheehan, Neil, A Bright Shining Lie, p. 379.
30. Plaster, inside front dust jacket.
31. "Review Essay," p. 31.
32. "Review Essay," p. 32.
33. Plaster, inside back dust jacker.
34. "Review Essay," p. 34.
35. "Review Essay," p. 28.
36. "Review Essay," p. 29.

37. Plaster, p. 195.
38. Plaster, back dust jacket.
39. Plaster, p. 193.
40. Plaster, pp. 135-136.
41. Ibid.
42. Ibid.
43. "Review Essay," p. 33.
44. "An Examination of U.S. Policy Toward POW/MIAs" by the U.S. Senate Committee on Foreign Relations Republican Staff, 5/23/91, pp. 7-1 to 7-5.
45. See Chapter 16, footnotes 1 to 4, 8, 9.
46. "JAG," television series, 3/8/02.

Chapter 15

1. Philadelphia Vietnam Veterans Memorial Society, 30th Annual National League of Families Meeting program, June 16-19, 1999.
2. Weiner, Tim, Blank Check, p. 114.
3. Weiner, p. 127.
4. Ibid.
5. Weiner, p. 141.
6. Weiner, p. 142.
7. Stein, Jeff, A Murder In Wartime, p. 399.
8. Jensen-Stevenson, Monika and Stevenson, William, Kiss The Boys Goodbye, p. 11.
9. Jensen-Stevenson and Stevenson, p. 182.
10. Jensen-Stevenson and Stevenson, pp. 187-188.
11. Wagner, Angie, "CIA Honors Heroes of Long-secret Air America," Associated Press, The San Diego Union-Tribune, 6/3/01.
12. Sheehan, Neil, A Bright Shining Lie, pp. 18, 732.
13. Sheehan, p. 557.
14. Weiner, p. 5.
15. Ibid.
16. Hall, Roger, "Suing the CIA on Behalf of Abandoned POWs," American Online, MIA68VN, 6/5/99, pp. 2-3.
17. Civil action: Roger Hall Plaintiff vs. CIA Defendant, #98-1319, on behalf of Abandoned POW/MIAs, 6/11/99.
18. Stein, p. 140.
19. Jensen-Stevenson and Stevenson, pp. 147-148.
20. Jensen-Stevenson and Stevenson, p. 229.
21. Jensen-Stevenson and Stevenson, p. 416.

22. Jensen-Stevenson and Stevenson, p. 188.

23. Weiner, p. 181.

Chapter 16

1. Hendrix, David E., Deposition, U.S. Senate Select Committee on POW/ MIA Affairs, Washington D.C., October 29, 1992, pp. 76, 78.

2. Hendrix, David E., Deposition, pp. 33, 68.

3. Lacy, Ret. Brig. Gen. Thomas E., USAF, Senate Select Committee Hearings on POW/MIA Affairs, April 2, 1992, p. 49.

4. Lacy, Ret. Brig. Gen. Thomas E., pp. 53-90, 102-117, 150-165, 173-182.

5. Shelley Davis, "The Journey Home," The Retired Officer magazine, February 1998, p. 37.

6. Condon, Richard, Manchurian Candidate, Korean War novel about a POW, brainwashed into participating in a shocking communist plot. The movie was released in 1962. "Similarities between the film and Kennedy assassination kept this film out of distribution for over 20 years." (Quote from video tape.) The movie starred Frank Sinatra, Janet Leigh, Laurence Harvey and Angela Lansbury.

7. Morehouse, David, Psychic Warrior, p. 301.

8. Rogers, Glenn, The Secret POW Returnee Program, The California Zephyr, Fall 1994, Volumne 7, Issue 2, p. 1.

9. Ibid.

10. Sir Walter Scott

11. Elliston, Jon, "MKULTRA: CIA Mind/Control," Dossier Editor, ParaScope, Inc., 1996, p.1.

12. Ibid.

13. Elliston, p. 2.

14. Elliston, p. 3.

Chapter 17

1. National League of Families 30th Annual Meeting program, 6/16-19/99.

2. Donohue, Cathryn, "POW/MIA, A Support Group's Turmoil," The Washington Times, 10/13/91.

3. McConnell, Malcolm, Inside Hanoi's Secret Archives, p. 136.

4. McConnell, p. 215.

5. "BOHICA, The Facts Behind Fantasies of the Author Scott Barnes," a research paper published by The National League of Families, 1988.

6. Barnes, Scott, BOHICA, inside jacket.

7. Ibid.
8. Ibid.
9. A research paper, 1988.
10. McConnell, pp. 215, 382.
11. Epstein, Miles Z. and Donaldson, Douglas T., "POW/MIAs: The Men We Left Behind," The American Legion magazine, March 1992, p. 33. The entire 20-page article is worth reading.
12. McConnell, p. 336.
13. "League Delegation to Southeast Asia," paper presented to National League of Families annual meeting, June 1999.
14. Ibid.
15. Peck, Col. Milard A., memorandum of resignation as Chief of the Special Office for Prisoners of War and Missing in Action, 1991, p. 10-3.
16. Peck, p. 10-4.
17. Ibid.
18. Shore, Benjamin, correspondent in Washington, D.C. for Copley News Service and Boston Globe, "U.S. Official Admits Americans Were Abandoned in Vietnam, San Diego Union, 11/7/91.

Chapter 18

1. Sauter, Mark and Sanders Jim, The Men We Left Behind, p. 346.
2. Sauter and Sanders, p. 317.
3. McConnell, Malcolm, Inside Hanoi's Secret Archives, p. 226.
4. Jensen-Stevenson, Monika, Spite House, pp. 350-351.
5. "Vietnam MIAs," USA Today, 7/12/93.
6. Smith, Bob, U.S. Senator, Prepared remarks by Presidential Candidate for 30th Annual National League of Families meeting, 6/18/99.
7. Douglas, Joe Jr., "Missing American POWs: What Happened? Part II," Conservative Review II, 1993, p. 14.
8. Duker, Bill, Vietnam Veteran's of American POW/MIA Committee, testimony before the Senate Select Committee on POW/MIA Affairs, November 1991, p. 3.
9. Ibid.
10. Benge, Michael D., testimony before the House International Relations Committee, 11/4/99, p. 4.
11. Wallace, Robert E., Commander-in-Chief, Veterans of Foreign Wars of the United States, testimony before the Senate Select Committee on POW/MIW Affairs, 11/6/91, p.3.
12. Birch, J. Thomas Jr., National Vietnam Veterans Coalition, testimony before the Senate Select Committee on POW/MIA Affairs, 11/6/91, p. 4.

13. Birch, p. 2.
14. Duker, p.3.
15. Andry, Joseph E., past Commander of the Disabled American Veterans, testimony before the Senate Select Committee on POW/MIA Affairs, 11/6/91, p. 3.
16. Donahue, Dr. Jeffery C. (brother of Major Morgan Jefferson Donahue USAF, MIA in Laos, 12/13/68), testimony before the Senate Select Committee on POW/MIA Affairs, 10/29/91, Addendum to "A POW/MIA Conspiracy and Cover-up? It's in the Policy!" p. 1.
17. Sampley, Ted, publisher of U.S. Veteran News and Report, testimony before the Senate Select Committee on POW/MIA Affairs, pp. 3-4.
18. Cawthorne, Nigel, author of The Bamboo Cage, testimony before the Senate Select Committee on POW/MIA Affairs, 10/31/91, p. 1.
19. Cawthorne, pp. 1-4.
20. Usry, Tracy, Chief Investigator, Senate Foreign Relations Committee, testimony before the Senate Select Committee on POW/MIA Affairs, 11/7/91, p. 1-3.
21. O'Grady, Patricia, Ph.D, daughter of POW in Vietnam, testimony before the Senate Select Committee on POW/MIA Affairs, 11/6/91, p. 1.
22. Apodaca, Robert A., Captain, USAF, testimony before the Senate Select Committee on POW/MIA Affairs, 11/4/91, p. 5.
23. Bailey, Lt. Col. Jack E., USAF (ret.), testimony before the Senate Select Committee on POW/MIA Affairs, 11/7/91, p. 2.
24. Quast, Shelby Robertson, daughter of POW in Vietnam, testimony before the Senate Select Committee on POW/MIA Affairs, 11/4/91, p. 8.
25. Fleckenstein, Gladys Stevens, mother of Lt. Commander Larry Stevens, POW in Vietnam, testimony before the Senate Select Committee, 11/4/91, pp. 2, 5.
26. Gayden, Hamilton, Tennessee Circuit Court Judge, author Of a novel about an American POW, testimony before the Senate Select Committee on POW/MIA Affairs, 11/6/91, pp. 1, 3.
27. Lundy III, Albro L., son of Albro L. Lundy II, POW in Vietnam, testimony before the Senate Select Committee on POW/MIA Affairs, 11/7/91, pp. 5, 7-8.
28. Turner, Lt. Col. (ret.) Norman M., testimony before the Senate Select Committee on POW/MIA Affairs, 11/7/91, p. 8.
29. Mirarcin, Terrell A., Vietnamese linguist and Cryptolinguist, 1967-1984, testimony before the Senate Select Committee on POW/MIA Affairs, 1/22/92, pp. 3, 5-8, 46.

30. Cole, John Cole, U.S. Army Chief of the Defense Intelligence Agency's Stony Beach Team, testimony before the Senate Select Committee on POW/MIA Affairs, 11/6/91, pp. 1-3.
31. Griffiths, Ann Mills, Executive Director of the National League of Families, 11/7/91, p. 7.
32. Vessey, Gen. John W., Presidential Emissary to Hanoi for POW/MIA Matters, testimony before the Senate Select Committee on POW/MIA Affairs, 11/5/91, pp. 1-9.
33. Bui Tin, former Senior Colonel in the Vietnamese Peoples Army, testimony before the Senate Select Committee on POW/MIA Affairs, 11/7/91, p. 4.
34. Smith, Bob, Vice Chairman, Senate Select Committee on POW/MIA Affairs, address before the committee, 11/5/91, pp. 3, 6, 14.
35. Smith, p. 15.
36. Ibid.
37. Sauter, Mark and Sanders, Jim, The Men We Left Behind, p. 22. Also see Bell, Garnett E., Chief U.S. Office of POW/MIA Affairs, Hanoi, testimony before the Senate Select Committee on POW/MIA Affairs, pp. 1-4.
38. Cheney, Dick, Secretary of Defense, testimony before the Senate Select Committee on POW/MIA Affairs, 11/5/91, pp. 3, 11 26.

Chapter 19

1. Jensen-Stevenson, Monika, Spite House, p. 360.
2. Jensen-Stevenson, front dust jacket.
3. Ibid.
4. Jensen-Stevenson, front of dust jacket.
5. Jensen-Stevenson, p. 164.
6. Jensen-Stevenson, p. 196.
7. Jensen-Stevenson, p. 204.
8. Jensen-Stevenson, p. 205.
9. Jensen-Stevenson, back dust jacket.
10. Jensen-Stevenson, p. 359.
11. Jensen-Stevenson, p. 229.
12. Sauter, Mark and Sanders, Jim, The Men We Left Behind, p. 211.
13. Shore, Benjamin, Copley News Service, "Ex-Hanoi Office Denies MIAs Remain," The San Diego Union, 11/9/91, p. A-22.
14. Sauter and Sanders, p. 32.

Chapter 20

1. Morehouse, David, Psychic Warrior, p. xii.
2. Morehouse, back cover.
3. Ibid.
4. Morehouse, pp. 199-200.
5. Morehouse, p. 301.
6. Morehouse, p. 303.
7. Thomas, Gordon, Journey Into Madness, p. 97.
8. Ibid.
9. Ibid.
10. Thomas, pp. 372-373.
11. Thomas, p. 271.

Chapter 21

1. LaRue, Steve, Staff Writer, "Those Who Did Not Return Remembered on POW/MIA Day," San Diego Union, 9/16/89.
2. Brossy, Julie, Staff Writer, "The War Still Isn't Over for Wife of Vietnam MIA," San Diego Tribune, 9/16/89.
3. Nelson, Trish, "Local Members of POW/MIA Committee Journey To Vietnam," Beach Bay Press, 1/18/90, p. 14.
4. Rivenburg, Roy, "Hanging Onto Hope: Vet's wife seeks answers after 22 years," Times Advocate, 4/6/90, p. A-1.
5. "Honor Guards: For Those Touched by War, Memorial Day Is Chance To Remember," Los Angeles Times, 5/28/90, p. E-3.
6. Enges-Maas, Mary, "Life in the 90's," 9/15/91, p. D1, D9.
7. Powell, Ronald W., Staff Writer, "MIA Kin Organize to Press For Action," San Diego Union-Tribune, 8/12/91 p. B-1, B-3.
8. McKinley, Shay K., "On A Mission," San Diego Union Tribune, 5/25/01, pp. 6, 8.

Chapter 22

1. Beschloss, Michael, Reaching for Glory, p. 349. Quote spoken by Robert McNamara, Secretary of Defense, to President Lyndon Johnson at 6:40 p.m., 6/10/65.
2. McFarland, Robert C., remarks to the 24th National League of Families Annual Meeting, 1993, reprinted in the Task Force Omega of Southern California, Inc. newsletter, July 1993, pp. 1-6.
3. Cawthorne, Nigel, The Bamboo Cage, p. 60.

4. The Shirley Show, taped 9/20/91 by MediaReach Inc., Toronto, Canada, aired 10/3/91, transcript pp. i-ii, 1-18.
5. Stevenson, William, "Shirley Show Outdoes U.S. Competitors," newspaper known, probably Canadian, 10/20/91.

Chapter 23

1. "Hanford's Haunted Scientist," Knight-Ridder News Service, Seattle Times, 9/21/91.

Chapter 25

1. Sonneborn, Barbara, wife, writer, director "Regret To Inform," PBS documentary "Talking Back" series, 5/28/01.
2. Ibid.
3. Hicks, Lesli, "Finding The Fallen: USAA Members Help in The Search for POW/MIAs," USAA Magazine, May/June 2002, p. 18.
4. Dart, Bob, Cox News Service, "Children of Vietnam Casualties Try to Stay in Touch," reprinted in Contra Costa Times, 6/17/2002, Front Page.

Chapter 26

1. Wheeler, Linda, "Online 'Virtual Wall' Puts Faces To Names Of Vietnam Casualties," Washington Post, reprinted in Sunday Contra Costa Times, 10/28/01, p. A30.

Chapter 27

1. "POW/MIA," Task Force Omega, Inc., informational publication, cover, 2001.

Postscript: Perestroika Sunset – a novel

1. Hopper Sr., Col. Earl P., U.S. Army (ret.), former chairman, National League of Families, back dust cover.
2. Stang, Alan, Perestroika Sunset, pp. 3, 9, 19, 21, 32, 39, 41, 44, 47, 50, 56, 57.

Index

Smith, Maj. Mark 43, 49, 450
Smith, Senator Bob xiii, 58, 59, 86, 187, 281, 283, 294
Smith, Sgt. 22, 25
SOAR 279, 367. *See* Special Operations Association Reunion
Socialist Republic of Vietnam 165, 277, 283, 446. *See* SRV
SOD 23. *See* Secretary of Defense
SOG 28, 236, 243, 245, 246, 247, 248, 365, 367, 374, 437, 440, 441, 442, 443, 444, 445, 446, 448, 461. *See* Studies and Observation Group
Solzhenitsyn, Alexander 56
Somalia 217, 218, 219, 221, 222, 327, 391, 404
Sonneborn, Barbara 377, 378. *See* "Regret To Inform"
Soviets 38, 39, 40, 64, 101, 102, 105, 171, 294, 300, 307
Special Forces xiv, xv, xvi, 2, 3, 5, 15, 16, 20, 21, 22, 23, 24, 27, 29, 31, 35, 36, 37, 43, 68, 69, 78, 84, 89, 100, 117, 137, 156, 174, 195, 209, 222, 233, 234, 236, 238, 239, 241, 242, 243, 244, 245, 247, 248, 251, 252, 253, 256, 260, 297, 298, 311, 330, 365, 366, 368, 372, 373, 374, 375, 380, 392, 402, 408, 441, 442, 444, 445, 453, 459. *See* Green Berets
Special Forces Group
5th Special Forces Group 20, 22, 239, 245, 442
Special Operations Association Reunion 279, 367
Special Operations Augmentation 245, 446
Spec Ops 78
Speicher, Lt. Cdr. Michael "Scott" 86
SRV 51, 71, 151, 165, 177, 351, 400, 446. *See* Socialist Republic of Vietnam

Stargate Program 305
Sternberg, Joe 381
Stockdale, Adm. James B. 260
Stony Beach 62, 76, 227, 229, 234, 293, 443, 446, 466
strings 444, 446
Studies and Observation Group (SOG) 31, 243, 446

T

"The Book of Honor". *See* Ted Gup
"The Shirley Show" 323, 326, 468
The League 10, 40, 50, 62, 74, 75, 77, 79, 125, 177, 179, 184, 192, 193, 204, 205, 206, 231, 232, 233, 236, 274, 275, 276, 277, 278, 283, 388, 444. *See* National League of Families of Prisoners and Missing in Southeast Asia
The Mortician 52, 99
The Virtual Wall 384
The Wall 12
Tighe Jr., Lt. Gen. Eugene F. 170
Truman, President Harry 251
Tucker, Brig. Gen. Terry 278, 279
Tuttle, Rear Adm. Jerry O. 15, 448

U

U.S. Senate Committee on Foreign Relations 85, 95, 249, 450, 453, 462
Usry, Special Investigator Tracy E. 285
Uyeyama, Terry 75

V

Van Alstyne, Margo 332
Van Alystyne, Sam 122
Van Deerlin, Congressman Lionel 189
VC 25, 31, 239, 446. *See* Viet Cong
Vermont, RT 24, 446
Vessey Jr., Gen. John W. 86, 112, 166, 173, 293, 452
Viet Cong (VC) 18, 52, 78, 84, 93,

156, 197, 239, 373, 446

Printed in the United States
30944LVS00001B/97